NETWORKED MEDIA, NETWORKED RHETORICS

RHETORIC AND DEMOCRATIC DELIBERATION
VOLUME 10

EDITED BY CHERYL GLENN AND J. MICHAEL HOGAN
THE PENNSYLVANIA STATE UNIVERSITY

Editorial Board:

Robert Asen (University of Wisconsin–Madison)
Debra Hawhee (The Pennsylvania State University)
Peter Levine (Tufts University)
Steven J. Mailloux (University of California, Irvine)
Krista Ratcliffe (Marquette University)
Karen Tracy (University of Colorado, Boulder)
Kirt Wilson (The Pennsylvania State University)
David Zarefsky (Northwestern University)

Rhetoric and Democratic Deliberation is a series of groundbreaking monographs and edited volumes focusing on the character and quality of public discourse in politics and culture. It is sponsored by the Center for Democratic Deliberation, an interdisciplinary center for research, teaching, and outreach on issues of rhetoric, civic engagement, and public deliberation.

A complete list of books in this series is located at the back of this volume.

NETWORKED MEDIA, NETWORKED RHETORICS

DAMIEN SMITH PFISTER

The Pennsylvania State University Press | University Park, Pennsylvania

Library of Congress Cataloging-in-Publication Data

Pfister, Damien Smith, 1977– , author.
 Networked media, networked rhetorics : attention and deliberation in the early blogosphere / Damien Smith Pfister.
    pages cm — (Rhetoric and democratic deliberation)
 Summary: "Examines key moments in the early history of the blogosphere to understand how bloggers use digital media technology to engage in public argument. Explores blogging from a rhetorical perspective, asking how the digital medium of communication changes the conditions for persuasion"—Provided by publisher.
 Includes bibliographical references and index.
 ISBN 978-0-271-06460-4 (cloth : alk. paper)
 ISBN 978-0-271-06461-1 (pbk. : alk. paper)
 1. Blogs—Political aspects.
 2. Rhetoric—Political aspects.
 3. Deliberative democracy.
 I. Title. II. Series: Rhetoric and democratic deliberation.

HM851.P49 2014
006.7'52—dc23
2014019338

Copyright © 2014 The Pennsylvania State University
All rights reserved

Printed in the United States of America
Published by The Pennsylvania State University Press,
University Park, PA 16802-1003

The Pennsylvania State University Press is a member of the Association of American University Presses.

It is the policy of The Pennsylvania State University Press to use acid-free paper. Publications on uncoated stock satisfy the minimum requirements of American National Standard for Information Sciences—Permanence of Paper for Printed Library Material, ANSI Z39.48–1992.

For Carly and Darlene

CONTENTS

Acknowledgments ix

1 Three Challenges for Public Deliberation 1
2 Cultural Technologies of Publicity: Rhetorics, Public Spheres, and Digital Communication Networks 18
3 Flooding the Zone After Trent Lott's Toast 51
4 Ambient Intimacy in Salam Pax's *Where Is Raed?* 89
5 Shallow Quotation on *RealClimate* 134
6 The Prospects of Networked Rhetorics 174

Notes 197
Bibliography 247
Index 265

ACKNOWLEDGMENTS

One of the genuine pleasures of writing a book is the opportunity to acknowledge the vast network of influences and support that produced it. Because I take networks seriously, I am thrilled to be able to recognize those who impacted the current project most directly.

My time at the University of Pittsburgh shaped this project in profound ways. Gordon Mitchell deserves an immense amount of credit for suggesting that I write about blogging and, more importantly, for serving as an intellectual role model and interlocutor. His influence—and penchant for metaphor—inflects key parts of this book. John Lyne asked me early on how I was going to make this project have staying power after the heyday of the blogosphere; for that, and for conversations over the years that fundamentally shaped my own rhetorical sensibilities, I am deeply appreciative. Pete Simonson instilled in me an appreciation for the intellectual history of mass media and a pragmatic attitude toward mediation. He is, in the best sense of the word, a real pal. I cite John Poulakos, Barbara Warnick, and Brent Malin within these pages, but their contributions to my thinking about rhetoric and media runs deeper than a line in a bibliography. Other colleagues are owed a hearty thank you as well. I was lucky enough to receive an informal rhetorical education through chats at the Squirrel Cage with Michelle Gibbons, emails about ancient Greek translations with Michele Kennerly, evening walks with Mark Porrovecchio, discussions of cynicism with Michael Vicaro, and ongoing conversations with Lisa Keränen, Ron Von Burg, and Alessandra Beasley Von Burg.

At the University of Nebraska–Lincoln, I've been lucky to have the support of my colleagues Dawn O. Braithwaite, Aaron Duncan, Jody Kellas, Kathy Krone, Karen Lee, Ron Lee, Kristen Lucas, Bill Seiler, and Jordan Soliz. One of the joys of graduate teaching is the ability to present ideas in seminars and watch them evolve through conversation with students. I'm especially indebted to my advisees Scott Church, Jon Carter, Darrel Farmer, Sarah Jones, Adam Knowlton, Jessy Ohl, Rachel Stohr, and Janell Walther, who, along with Josh Ewalt and Getachew Godana, either read early drafts of the manuscript or critically engaged the major ideas in seminar conversation. Jessy Ohl deserves a special commendation for his work in the final stages of manuscript preparation as my research assistant. His substantive feedback on the manuscript, alongside the grunt work, has improved it immeasurably and for that I am eternally grateful. Institutional support in the form of a Maude Hammond Fling Faculty Research Fellowship from the University of Nebraska–Lincoln Research Council supported publication of the book. Under the auspices of an Undergraduate Creative Activities and Research Experience grant from the University of Nebraska–Lincoln, Carrie Adkisson provided helpful editorial assistance in the early stages of the manuscript. Justin Eckstein read a late draft of chapter 3 and provided incisive feedback. Danielle Wiese has the distinction of working her way through the entirety of this manuscript twice—her enthusiastic support of the project at key junctures kept my spirits high. Joan Leach and Valerie Renegar responded to early slices of this project in ways that affirmed my general argument while challenging me to push it further. Stephanie Schulte's pointed criticism of versions of the first two chapters helped me think about the broader audience for a book on networked rhetorics. Gavin Schmidt from *RealClimate* provided useful feedback on a draft of chapter 5.

Parts of chapter 3 were published as "The Logos of the Blogosphere: Flooding the Zone, Invention, and Attention in the Lott Imbroglio" in *Argumentation and Advocacy* 47, no. 4 (2011): 141–67. I am grateful to Dale Hample, the anonymous reviewers, and especially Cate Palczewski for early editorial guidance on this chapter. A small part of chapter 5 was published as "Networked Expertise in an Era of Many-to-Many Communication: On *Wikipedia* and Invention," in *Social Epistemology* 25, no. 3 (2011): 217–31. Johanna Hartelius and Jim Collier provided useful feedback that is reflected in these pages.

My interactions with members of The Pennsylvania State University Press have been nothing short of fantastic. Mike Hogan, Cheryl Glenn, Kendra Boileau, Robert Turchick, Laura Reed-Morrisson, and Patty Mitchell worked hard to provide guidance throughout the publication process. The reviewers of this manuscript provided exactly the push I needed to focus my argument.

I am extremely grateful for administrative staff at the University of Pittsburgh—Peg Chalus, Mary Hamler, Janet Donofrio, and Brandi McClain—and at the University of Nebraska-Lincoln—Betty Jacobs, Cheryl Kruid, Kathy Thorne, and Donelle Moormeier. This bureaucratic nincompoop would have long been lost in the institutional maze were it not for the help of each of these people, who have been far kinder to me than I deserve. You all have made my working life immeasurably richer.

A special thank you to Jacob Woods, who built what is possibly the world's finest porch swing, on which a substantial amount of this book was revised. Accompanying me on that porch swing most of the time were arguably the world's finest pups, Thora and Loki, who made the process of editing not just bearable but enjoyable. Their tail wags are very much appreciated.

My mother, Darlene Smith, has supported me in innumerable ways. Here's one: many years ago, as I contemplated pursuing graduate school, I expressed apprehension about the writing demands that would accompany life as a faculty member. She gently reminded me that writing books was what I had wanted to do since I was a third grader. Though the kinds of books I envisioned writing as an eight-year-old involved more robots and swords, I reminded myself of her observation at various points when the writing of this book got tough. I count myself fortunate that we get to live in the same town, sharing a mutual love of cooking, gardening, dog parking, and much more. I hope that, in some small way, this book helps balance the ledger for what I owe her.

My partner, Carly Woods, happily indulged my wonderings and wanderings during the ten-year incubation of this book. Virtually every idea here, great and small, has been turned over in conversation with her. She is my favorite interlocutor: generously tough, appreciatively critical, and playfully serious. I count myself absurdly fortunate to be building a life with her.

I

THREE CHALLENGES FOR PUBLIC DELIBERATION

A crowd gathers for a public debate on government surveillance programs. As the debate begins, the speakers present basic arguments about the ethics and efficacy of new surveillance technologies. Each delivers carefully crafted witticisms primed to undercut the opponent's arguments. Those clever barbs are, to the chagrin of the audience, the only original part of the debate. Neither advocate advances an argument that transforms the way people understand the controversy. There's no middle ground sought, no concessions made. At times, the debate devolves into outright bickering, especially when the debaters cross-examine each other. The arguments themselves recycle the standard talking points and shopworn arguments of two retrenched, polarized, and predictable sides. The audience leaves with a gloomy sense of the controversy's intractability and the grueling banality of public deliberation.

A city council considers demolishing and rezoning part of an old neighborhood to clear the way for a new shopping development. Affected residents band together and initiate a grassroots letter-writing campaign to influence the city council vote. In letters to city council members and the local newspaper, they explain their fear that corporate monoculture will dominate the rezoning and threaten the historical buildings that give their community character. The editor selects a few of the letters, featuring them alongside letters by citizens who are more supportive of the rezoning plan. A newspaper article reports on the budding controversy, though the reporter's dispassionate tone muffles the dynamic energy of the neighborhood residents. The council members follow the conversation in the local paper, but they decide that the residents' concerns about changing the character of the neighborhood are, in the end, not reasonable. When compared to the city economists' calculations showing the tax revenue accruing from the new development, the residents' objections seem too inchoate—warm and fuzzy feelings pay no bills. The council votes to rezone.

An energy company considers building a nuclear power plant to accommodate soaring electricity demand. As part of a public relations effort, the company organizes a series of community meetings designed to dispel concerns about the safety of nuclear power. Local environmental groups protest outside the meetings to rally public opinion against the energy company's plan. Their tables feature brochures and charts showing how non-nuclear, renewable energy sources would provide safer, cleaner energy and boost job growth in the area. Familiar elements of protest populate the scene: chanting and singing, theatrical skits and puppet theater, fired-up speeches and heated conversations. In covering the protest, a local television news story features a back-and-forth between a representative of the environmental group voicing concern about nuclear energy, followed by a response from the energy company's scientists. The scientists shoot down each of the citizens' arguments, responding to each claim with counter-evidence and a greater command of the technical jargon of energy policy. With so much trained expertise and lived experience, as well as the accoutrements provided by credentials, the scientists appear more credible and knowledgeable than the protesters. The energy company resists the citizens' entreaties and goes nuclear.

These three allegories—plausible composites of familiar democratic activities enacted through a range of media—draw attention to a trio of longstanding challenges for public deliberation. The first example highlights the challenge of *invention*. The well-worn grooves of the controversy interfered with the debaters' invention of novel lines of argument that could otherwise set the audience off on a shared quest for illumination. The debaters simply parroted familiar arguments. The second example underscores the challenge of *emotion*. Concerns expressed by neighborhood residents were dismissed because their "feelings" did not register in the "rational" parameters set by the city council. The intense but ineffable emotions surrounding neighborhood preservation could not compete with the tangible replenishing of the city coffers. The third example suggests the challenge in democratically incorporating *expertise*. The scientists' arguments trumped citizen objections through technical reasoning. No surprise here, as judgments about complex problems by specialists are often privileged.

Though the familiar, the rational, and the specialized help manage the complexity at the heart of contemporary life, making these values paramount stunts democratic deliberation. Were these values sufficient for governance, citizens would be satisfied with variants of Plato's philosopher-kings making decisions on their behalf. Most citizens wisely reject this autocratic model, as human history is a bloody trail of cautions about commonplace, reason-driven, and expert discourses gone awry. But deliberation fares no better when uncritically privileging the inverse: the creative, the emotional, and the nonexpert. Without some familiar arguments, public discourse becomes illegible to audiences. Without a clash of reasonable propositions, demagogues too easily fan base emotions. Without specialized knowledge, deliberation devolves into the exchange of uninformed opinions. Democracy's trick is to balance the creative with the familiar, the emotional with the rational, and the public with the expert. In other words, healthy democratic public cultures temper routinized institutional logics with innovative arguments, blur the distinction between reason and emotion, and stimulate conversation between experts and publics. The three opening allegories can be refigured as enduring questions for public deliberation: How can arguments be creatively invented to advance public debate on controversial issues? How can emotion in public life be usefully integrated into decision making? How can experts and nonexperts jointly deliberate without the domination of technical reasoning?

The persistence of these questions suggests that challenges related to invention, emotion, and expertise are constitutive of democratic public cultures. Negotiating these challenges successfully means that decisions made in democratic cultures receive legitimacy—in other words, citizens accept that judgments are fair and for the public good. Traditionally, citizen participation generates this democratic legitimacy, as their involvement in iterations of communicative performances check institutional preferences for the familiar, rational, and expert. In predominantly face-to-face societies like the Athens of antiquity, where the voice was the primary medium of expression, a culture centered on oratory developed to assess competing opinions. In the more complex societies of the past few centuries, face-to-face contexts were supplemented by the mass media of print, film, radio, and television. The mass media functioned as attention gatekeepers, circulating for public consideration what they endorsed as valuable contributions to the ongoing conversation and, conversely, locking out perspectives perceived to be dragging down the tenor of public debate.

Even as these three opening allegories usefully orient attention to the democratic challenges of invention, emotion, and expertise, they are historical anachronisms. To be sure, all three of these activities—oral public debate, letter writing to newspapers, and marching in the streets to shape television coverage—are part of the contemporary repertoire of democratic practice. But missing from these allegories is an account of how these practices are now embedded in a web of internetworked media: web pages, blogs and microblogs, podcasts, video sharing portals, social networking sites, wikis, and much more. In a maturing, networked public sphere, live public debates spark parallel argumentation on blogs and microblogs. What used to be letters written to newspaper editors are more likely to appear as comments threading off a news story. Social protests are coordinated and publicized through an intermeshed web of blogs and social networking sites. Internetworked media respond to, and further stimulate, fundamental alterations in contemporary public deliberation. Changes already under way in the political economy of the mass media accelerated with the advent of digital mediation. One effect of the diffusion of digital media technologies has been to destabilize the conventional journalistic stimulants of democratic discussion. Another effect has been to produce an exponentially more information-rich media ecology that overwhelms traditional communication filters. Yet another effect is that citizens, experimenting with new communication technologies, have introduced novel rhetorical practices that do not fit squarely into received theories of democratic deliberation. What is now known as the blogosphere is a central part of this broader story.

The Ascent of the Blogosphere

Networked Media, Networked Rhetorics: Attention and Deliberation in the Early Blogosphere explores how internetworked media influence public deliberation in an era of information abundance. Specifically, this book examines how citizens exploited the expressive possibilities of a new media genre—weblogs, or blogs—to craft collective attention patterns. Coming after the first wave of static web pages in the 1990s, but before the widespread diffusion of the more hyperconnected web represented by Facebook, YouTube, and Twitter (founded in 2004, 2005, and 2006, respectively), the early blogosphere represents a formative moment for digitally networked communication and deliberation. Blogging went from a trifling curiosity in the late 1990s to the new normal between 2001 and 2006. As it became more popular, the "communicative intercast" of posts, hyperlinks, trackbacks, and comments among the multitude of blogs began to be referred to as the blogosphere.¹ One reason for the ascendance of the blogosphere is that blogging is a genre supportive of many subgenres.² Many blogs resemble public diaries, spanning a range of topics drawn from everyday life. Other blogs are more thematically driven, hosting conversations on every imaginable topic: electoral races, legislative wrangling, opinion poll tracking, business news, celebrity gossip, music reviews, film criticism, cooking tips, drinking tips, sports insights, traveling tales, and many, many other subjects. Blogs now serve assorted stakeholders in specific discourse communities: lawyers read blogs dissecting Supreme Court decisions, do-it-yourselfers follow blogs detailing home improvement projects, graphic designers flock to blogs that document Photoshop disasters, and, of course, there are blogs that serve citizens' desires to argue about civic affairs. The flexibility of blogs in form and content led to their rapid rise, with tens of millions of active blogs across the world now participating in the communicative hubbub of public life. More significantly, the basic architecture of blogging—a unique, permalinked, and time-stamped post with dedicated, threaded comments—now prevails across internetworked media genres. For example, social networking sites mimic blog architecture by allowing easy publication of posts with comments attached to each status update.³ Even institutional news sites (the "old" broadcast media) now integrate commenting features on individual articles. The blog, departing from the print metaphor that resulted in early web publications being referred to as web *pages*, is one of the first native genres of the internet.

Bloggers are not the only networked intermediaries now influencing public argument and democratic deliberation. The blogosphere interfaces with web pages, wikis, podcasts, video sharing portals, microblogs, social networking sites, and a panoply of other networked genres. This communication network—a network of networks—constitutes a complex ecology that interacts with more traditional broadcast media, such as newspapers, books, radio, film, and television, as they too become networked into a converging, digitized circuit of communication.⁴ Rather than tackling this contemporary web of influence, *Networked Media, Networked Rhetorics* examines early episodes in blogging's history. This kind of documentation is important, given the fast-paced movement of networked public culture. "When it comes to technology," historian of Silicon Valley Leslie Berlin explains, "the focus is always forward, and the notion of pausing and taking a breath and seeing where you came from—there's just not time for it."⁵ Narrating a recent history of the blogosphere details the development of a new media genre but, more importantly, it also chronicles the early emergence of the networked public sphere. By examining how bloggers engage in new modes of public address to shape deliberation, I hope to illuminate how the challenges of invention, emotion, and expertise are negotiated as the mass-mediated public sphere fades in favor of an internetworked public sphere.

Early moments in the history of the blogosphere exert outsized influence in how citizens imagine the democratic potential of new technologies.[6] They become part of the *mythos* of the blogosphere, subtly shaping subsequent citizen participation. *Networked Media, Networked Rhetorics* analyzes three of these archetypal deliberative episodes.

- *The investigative and interpretive work of Glenn Reynolds, Josh Marshall, and Atrios in the wake of Senator Trent Lott's controversial comments about Senator Strom Thurmond.* In December 2002, Trent Lott made what were widely seen as remarks sympathetic to segregation in a birthday toast to Strom Thurmond, the 1948 Dixiecrat candidate for president. Lott's comments roiled several prominent bloggers, who connected dots from the senator's past that portrayed him as an unapologetic advocate for racial discrimination. The institutional media eventually picked up the story, building hydraulic pressure for Lott's eventual resignation as Senate majority leader. Glenn Reynolds characterized his blogging during this episode as "flooding the zone," implying that blogging saturated public discourse by working the controversy from every imaginable angle. The metaphor of flooding the zone signals the inventional capacities of the blogosphere.
- *The narration of life in prewar Iraq by Salam Pax.* In early 2003, before the U.S.-led invasion of Iraq, a cosmopolitan Iraqi citizen going by the "nom de blog" of Salam Pax detailed his experience of living on the precipice of war. The visceral, raw posts published by Salam Pax—who became, in the short history of the blogosphere, the most linked-to blogger ever—gave a highly personal view of the invasion. Salam Pax's blogging produced what another blogger called "ambient intimacy," a constant cycling of affect into public life. The metaphor of ambient intimacy gestures to the recuperated role of emotion in the networked public sphere.
- *The intervention by RealClimate bloggers in public discussions about climate science.* In late 2004, a group of climate scientists formed a blog dedicated to providing scientific context for news stories

about global warming. The scientists refute editorials published by deniers of anthropogenic warming, comment on popular culture artifacts that enter into the climate debate, and translate key scientific developments related to climate change for a public audience. The scientists at *RealClimate* participate in translation, or "shallow quotation," to transfer highly technical scientific claims into public spheres of argumentation. Shallow quotation, best represented by the offset pull quotes that bloggers use when citing other websites, aptly describes how knowledge claims move between expert and public discourse communities.

These three case studies were chosen in part because the broadcast press, which had a bias toward blogs with a civic focus, magnified their centrality through extensive coverage. Structural inequities that preceded networked media are reflected in the limited diversity of participants at the heart of these case studies—a reminder that the networked public sphere is not one free of power.[7] Nonetheless, these three deliberative episodes are disruptive inflection points of the kind that punctuate the history of democratic practice.[8] Often coinciding with the introduction of new communication technologies, these inflection points spark democratic iterations that introduce alternative ways of envisioning and negotiating the challenges of invention, emotion, and expertise.[9]

Some of the early speculation about the implications of blogging for democratic practice was predictably—and ahistorically—breathless. "The revolution will be blogged" sloganized what promised to be the death knell for the broadcast mass media and the birth of a new mode of citizen participation. While situating the intercast of bloggers as a site of deliberation that breaks with tradition is tempting, the term "blogosphere" is etymologically situated in a longer and richer historical trajectory. A key popularizer of "blogosphere" justified the portmanteau by noting, "the root word is *logos*, from the Greek meaning . . . human reasoning about the cosmos."[10] The idea of "sphere" as indicating range or influence comes from the early modern European context, as in "sphere of influence" and "public sphere." The origin of "blogosphere," then, invites a historical-critical theorization of deliberation in internetworked public cultures through comparison to the two prior sociopolitical formations it etymologically references. Ancient Athens and the European bourgeois public sphere are rich historical predecessors, analogues, and foils for understanding contemporary deliberation. These cultural formations, too, faced changes stimulated by the interaction of new information technologies and democratization. In the classical era of Athenian democracy, writing amplified the activities of the agora, where a privileged class of citizens conversed in a space that supported the circulation of news and opinion. Later, at the onset of what became known as the modern age in western Europe, the circulation of print publications supported an even more extended conversation about the issues of the day. The parallels to contemporary times are apparent, given how the new medium of the internet encourages the kind of lateral, argumentative communication usually thought to sustain democratic public life.

However, bloggers' contributions to negotiating the democratic challenges of invention, emotion, and expertise receive decidedly mixed reviews. In terms of invention, blogging is often identified as activating citizens' argumentative energies and unique competencies as they connect with fellow deliberators. But it is also perceived as producing an unmanageable noise-to-signal ratio in public communication, contributing nonsense, invective, and repetition to an already crowded mediasphere. Blogging is also analyzed through the vocabulary of emotion. The ease and personalization of blogging affords an unequivocal reveling in the partial, subjective, contingent self. That blogs are so often personal is one of their most compelling features. But some skeptics see that feature as a bug, as bloggers are often considered too emotional and uncommitted to the standards of rational-critical debate supposedly institutionalized in journalistic norms. Discourses of expertise are also yoked to blogging. Some bloggers are recognized experts in their field, contributing deeply informed running commentary on breaking news. But bloggers are also often seen as dilettantes, shallowly treating issues they barely grasp and mangling complex controversies with ham-handed postings. Almost every criticism of blogging is a criticism lodged throughout history against the art of rhetoric: it is excessive bloviation, emotional venting, and inexpert prying. It is sophistry instead of real knowledge. These uncharitable interpretations of blogging elide the potency of rhetoric in even internetworked public cultures. The promise of rhetoric has always been to satisfactorily, if contingently, manage the challenges surrounding invention, emotion, and expertise at the heart of democratic public life. Thus, one goal of this book is to make the association between rhetoric and blogging more explicit: to use the rhetorical tradition to show how blogging shapes public deliberation and to use blogging to identify features of networked rhetorics.

Networked Rhetorics and Networked Rhetorical Imaginaries

Invention, emotion, and expertise are, not incidentally, keywords of the rhetorical tradition, loosely linked to the classical triumvirate *logos, pathos,* and *ethos. Logos, pathos,* and *ethos* are elementary terms in the rhetorical lexicon, conceived in the classical context as modes of proof that speakers could draw upon to press their case. Rhetoric is a *technê*, a productive craft or art; it is also dynamic, changing with technological innovation and cultural needs. A new communication technology necessarily changes the nature of the *technê*, as entrepreneurial rhetoricians leverage the novel expressive possibilities afforded by a new medium of communication. Similarly, rhetoric's scope and function fluctuate with changing cultural conditions. In some cultures, it is conceived as primarily pertaining to producing oral and civic discourse; in others, it is considered a metahermeneutic for all symbol use.[11] As rhetorical practices change, they create new communication problematics that, in turn, require a recasting of old rhetorical theories and the generation of new ones. For example, citizens are participating in new genres of communication, like blogs and mash-ups, in tandem with more recognizable forms.[12] These changing conditions of mediation merit the development of a "new rhetoric" capable of guiding public advocacy and deliberation in contemporary times.[13] *Networked media* spur *networked rhetorics*.

Networked media is a vastly preferable term to "new media," "digital media," "social media," "participatory media," "multimedia," or "multimodal media." "New media" is terrifically imprecise. What's new about a technology that is now thirty years or older, depending on when the counting begins?[14] The "old" mass media of film, radio, and television, by swapping analog for digital technologies and absorbing networked architectures, further complicate the referent of "new media." "Digital" risks overdetermining the importance of the technology at the expense of appreciating the cultural uses of the medium. The significant part of digital mediation is not the nature of the technology but the kind of networking logics that it enables. "Social media" suggests that media was antisocial before the internet, which, despite the old saw that television breeds passivity, is demonstrably untrue. Media—from the voice to the television and internet—are necessarily at the heart of human sociality.[15] "Participatory media," given the actual numbers of people producing and interacting with content, is more hopeful than descriptive. "Multimedia" smells like the 1990s. "Multimodal media" is suggestive, as it hints at how modes of communication like sound, image, and text converge through digital media technology. However, it implies that prior media systems were in some way unimodal, which is unsupportable given the nexus of word, sound, and image in the oral world. Even print blended word and image.[16] "Networked media," as a truncation of *inter*networked media, reflects a core dynamic at work in new digital technologies with a more optimal balance between richness and precision.

Networked rhetorics, then, indexes a set of communication practices under the conditions of internetworked mediation. My use of the plural "rhetorics" implies a multifaceted phenomenon that stretches beyond the account I provide here about the blogosphere. There have always been rhetorics, not just *a* rhetoric, and understanding the communication dynamics of a new media system requires a recognition of the multiplicity of rhetorical practices and theories that undergird them. As a heuristic, though, "networked rhetorics" provides an alternative to "digital rhetoric" in thinking about how digital media technology and rhetoric can be theorized together.[17] "Digital rhetoric" is an evocative rubric, but a gentle shift in emphasis toward the networked provides another angle of vision to apprehend patterns of contemporary communication. Much as the "digital" in digital media privileges the technology, so does the "digital" in digital rhetoric privilege the media technology, resulting in an intense focus on how digitality reworks delivery.[18] As obviously important as that particular canon of rhetoric is, digitally networked media technologies bear on rhetorical theory in many other ways as well. "Networked rhetorics" focuses attention on communication practices rather than technologies. My colleague Val Renegar once affirmed this contrast to me by noting, "I don't feel digital, but I feel networked." Precisely. The rubric of "networked rhetorics" accounts for that feeling better than "digital rhetorics." It is the elevation of the concept of "networks," rather than the mere digitality of rhetorical practice, that challenges predigital theories of rhetoric and public deliberation.

A fast-developing vocabulary of terms indicates the profusion of networked rhetorics. Part of this lexicon is populated by the names of new genres of communication, like blogs, wikis, and social networking sites; part of it includes hybridized concepts like the "networked public sphere" or "flash mob"; and, as this project demonstrates, part of it is reflected in figurative language that appears in the meta-talk about internetworked communication. A metaphor used to characterize blogging is what initially attuned me to the broader significance of this new genre. Like many people, I first learned of blogging in the wake of Trent Lott's toast to Strom Thurmond. This particular episode connected several of my longstanding interests: innovative communication practices spurred by new media technologies, argumentation about civic controversies, and the career implosion of retrograde Southern politicians. As I followed the controversy, I ran across the term "flood the zone" used by blogger Glenn Reynolds. Without having a definitive sense of what the phrase really meant, I grasped that it captured something vital about the flow of argument in the blogosphere. It hinted at the ability of bloggers to publish quickly, from many disparate perspectives, allowing them to saturate the field of public discourse, commandeer public attention, and thus shape public opinion.

Flooding the zone, alongside the metaphors "ambient intimacy" and "shallow quotation" derived from the two other case studies, is part of the unfolding *networked rhetorical imaginary*. A rhetorical imaginary refers to how a culture imagines the role, function, features, norms, and values of communication. It is the collection of conceptual terms—the grammar—that constitutes the landscape of communication practice in any particular public culture. Rhetorical imaginaries function as implicit interpretive frameworks that citizens draw upon to understand and participate in the conventions of public communication.[19] They are the communicative analogue of social imaginaries. For Charles Taylor, a social imaginary encapsulates "the ways people imagine their social existence, how they fit together with others, how things go on between them and their fellows, the expectations that are normally met, and the deeper normative notions and images that underlie these expectations."[20] In formal and informal cultural performances, individuals are drawn into a complex matrix of imagined relations with other citizens, institutions, ideologies, networks, and objects.[21] If, as Taylor explains, "the social imaginary is that common understanding that makes possible common practices and a widely shared sense of legitimacy," then citizens invariably find themselves embedded in a cultural milieu that is so pervasive it is difficult to imagine an alternative.[22] A social imaginary is often premised on useful fictions: fictional, as how we imagine our relations with each other is not necessarily how they actually are; useful, as these imagined relations nonetheless provide shared understandings that interpellate individuals into communities, however uneven and dysfunctional that process may be.

The emergence of new imaginaries both manages and consolidates broader changes. The modern social imaginary, as a historical phenomenon, shifted public imagination toward new ways of negotiating the political, social, and economic changes accompanying modernity. The concepts of the public sphere, the sovereign rule of the people, and a price-competitive market were alien to earlier generations of Europeans, habituated to believing that dynastic authority channeled divine will, that the people existed to serve the throne, and that barter was the only vehicle of economic exchange. Yet the shifting social imaginary naturalized these new practices of modernity in a way that completed the transition away from premodern arrangements. A social imaginary functions to do just this—to adapt people to changing practices of interrelation.[23] Our senses of self and culture are both funded and constrained by these shared imaginings. While a social imaginary directs attention to the social, every social imaginary is underwritten by a rhetorical imaginary.[24] The "market," "public sphere," and "sovereign people" referred to actual social practices in the early modern era, but were established as keywords in the modern firmament only with the powerful rhetorical act of naming. Naming congeals a practice by orienting our attention to a phenomenon. These rhetorical innovations consolidate practices as meaningful categories of experience, illustrating Robert Asen's observation that "collective imagining may function as a background process or it may be engaged actively" in thematizing nascent conventions.[25]

Social imaginaries and, by extension, rhetorical imaginaries are neither static nor singular. The social imaginaries that constitute cultures are regularly revised as critical inflection points reshape public imagination. The events of September 11, 2001, for example, required U.S. citizens to recognize that the familiar state-to-state conflict that shaped so much of modernity was being supplanted by the rise of networked extremists. These destabilizations of the imaginary also occur with new media technologies because, following Marshall McLuhan, the diffusion of a new medium "alters the pattern of interdependence among people."[26] New media amend, and sometimes alter wholesale, a culture's imaginary by making possible new practices that gradually "come to count as the taken-for-granted shape of things, too obvious to mention."[27] The practices made popular by blogging include instantaneous publication, easy "sampling" and "remixing" of digitally networked discourse fragments, and an inter-threaded commenting system that supports many-to-many communication on a global scale. Bloggers actively interpreted these new practices as they became evident, but as blogging became normalized, these practices receded into the rhetorical imaginary. They simply became part of the culture.[28] Part of the task of *Networked Media, Networked Rhetorics* is to recover these practices by examining early episodes where the potentiality of blogging was made sense of by participants. By connecting how the affordances provided by networked media change practices related to the invention of public argument, the role of emotion in public life, and the exercise of expertise, I aim to theorize a shift in sensibilities as people participate in, make sense of, and enact new modes of thinking, feeling, and being. While none of the changes I document in this book are as dramatic, perhaps, as the concepts of citizen, market, and public sphere, they are fruitfully read as microrevolutions in the networked rhetorical imaginary that perhaps adumbrate broader shifts to come.

Four Principles for Studying the Blogosphere

As a result of broad cultural, economic, political, and technological changes, the modern imaginary is transforming into a networked imaginary. But new forms of imagined relations hardly announce themselves as such. Alterations to imaginaries are in some way unknowable, since they are inherently abstract, accreted from loosely related practices and sedimented in opaque layers of historical time. How, then, might the networked rhetorical imaginary be critically explored? Four principles guide my analysis in *Networked Media, Networked Rhetorics*.

The significance of blogging, and the broader networked public sphere, can be appreciated by toggling between panoramic analysis of broad cultural formations and fine-grained exploration of specific communicative practices. I explore invention, emotion, and expertise in internetworked cultures through the context provided by rhetorical theories emanating from classical Greece, early modern Europe, and the late modern culture of the United States. *Networked Media, Networked Rhetorics* participates in the "zooming and hovering" of what Debra Hawhee and Christa Olson call pan-historiography, "simultaneously posing big-picture questions and fine-grained ones."[29] This approach has an affinity with rhetorical critic Kenneth Burke's method of circumferential analysis. Burke, whose spirit pervades this project, recognized that "one may place the object of one's definition in contexts of varying scope."[30] Expanding or contracting the circumference invariably shapes analysis in heuristically powerful ways. At times, I focus on a single blog post, or a single comment on a blog post, drawing a circumference so tightly around an object of analysis that a reader might reasonably ask, "So what?" At other times, I dramatically expand that circumference, drawing analogies between historical periods to situate blogging in a longer historical trajectory of media technology and rhetorical practice—to which a reader might reasonably object that I am playing too fast and loose with diverse stretches of time.[31] The promise of adjusting circumference is in the potential to strike a balance between appreciating blogging on its own terms and situating blogging in larger patterns of communication and culture. I hope the reader can approach the circumferential movement with charity, looking for how micro- and macroanalysis of blogging both informs our understanding of media, rhetoric, and deliberation *and* stimulates imaginative amendment, extension, and dissension.

Theories of blogging and the networked public sphere must be developed with a pragmatic spirit. Drawing on the rich rhetorical imaginaries of the classical and early modern eras does not imply any kind of progressive evolution that situates the contemporary networked moment as inevitable or ideal. While the internet is certainly introducing substantial changes to human communication and culture, I disavow the utopian strain that plagued much early and popular speculation about internetworked media. Instead, a pragmatist vein grounded in the rhetorical tradition streaks through *Networked Media, Networked Rhetorics.*[32] In this spirit, each case study illustrates how the affordances of networked media stimulate deliberative legitimation processes while simultaneously producing new problematics for public culture. The binary sensibilities inherited from the modern imaginary produce "deliberation traps" that frustrate citizens' participation in public argument by, as each respective case study demonstrates, privileging institutional agenda-setting, conceptualizing reason as distinct from emotion, and lionizing expert opinion at the expense of public engagement. Bloggers' unique rhetorical practices play a role in evading these late modern deliberation traps. Yet while rhetorical activity in the networked public sphere dodges some traps, new ones are being set as the networked sensibilities I detail are co-opted or taken to extremes. The final section of each case study chapter thus examines how flooding the zone has been co-opted by institutions to frustrate democratic deliberation, how ambient intimacy creates a propensity for oversharing, and how shallow quotation can run amok.

Representative anecdotes of blogging contain the emergent lexicon of the networked rhetorical imaginary. In my moment of scholarly curiosity about the

Trent Lott episode and "flooding the zone," I picked up on what Burke calls a "representative anecdote."[33] A representative anecdote is a richly allusive but condensed story or example that, like the rhetorical figure of synecdoche, is a part standing for a whole.[34] Part of the premise of this book is that blogging is a representative anecdote of the networked public sphere: understand blogging (the part), and we understand the networked public sphere (the whole) better. The tradition in rhetorical studies of analyzing "great speeches," such as Martin Luther King Jr.'s "I Have a Dream" or John F. Kennedy's inaugural address, recognizes these moments as representative anecdotes of prevailing attitudes, hidden assumptions, privileged modes of proof, dominant metaphors, and cultural preferences. Although representative anecdotes necessarily reduce the richness of a particular phenomenon to bound the analytical field, effective ones possess scope to range beyond the specific instance. So, while a focus on the blogosphere as a representative anecdote of the networked public sphere does reduce the complexity of the contemporary networked media ecosystem, my concentration on the underlying affordances of networked media provides the necessary scope to be useful in comprehending larger shifts in the networked rhetorical imaginary. The value of the representative anecdote is not merely to provide a detailed case study, but to develop a vocabulary that allows us to understand and adjust to changing times.[35] "When the emphasis of society has changed," Burke states, "new symbols are demanded to formulate new complexities, and the symbols of the past become less appealing."[36]

The three case studies at the heart of this book were chosen precisely because they function as representative anecdotes that organically produced or popularized a novel conceptual term constitutive of the networked rhetorical imaginary. Flooding the zone, ambient intimacy, and shallow quotation signify new sensibilities related to invention, emotion, and expertise. By elevating these native terms as tools to explore communication patterns in the networked public sphere, I adopt an emic stance that seeks to theorize networked rhetorics from the inside out rather than uncritically applying communication templates from other rhetorical imaginaries.[37] In identifying a vocabulary for how people persuade through networked media, I follow a tradition in rhetorical studies of thematizing communication patterns to better understand their functions and critically interrogate their use. The process of naming new rhetorical phenomena, in turn, expands the communicative repertoire citizens may draw from to influence public deliberation.

Metaphors of communicative practice mark cultural sensibilities. Each of the indigenous conceptual phrases emerging from the case studies is a metaphor—unsurprisingly so, for the presence of new practices is often revealed through metaphoric language. The genesis of each of these metaphors is slightly different. Flooding the zone was thematized in the process of blogging about Lott's toast; ambient intimacy was coined as the broader internetworked ecosystem grew; and shallow quotation (a term borrowed from Charles Willard) is my own supplement to translation metaphors that accompanied discussion of *RealClimate*. Metaphors often abbreviate representative anecdotes into a supercharged discourse bundle, drawing attention to similarities and dissimilarities between two things being compared. In Burke's whimsical phrasing, they clarify the "thisness of a that, or the thatness of a this."[38] Because, as George Lakoff and Mark Johnson underline, "new metaphors are capable of creating new understandings and, therefore, new realities," we must take metaphor seriously.[39] Metaphoric criticism, a kind of rhetorical criticism that explains how metaphoric figuration shapes belief, knowledge, and action, involves peeling apart the metaphor, seeing how it came to be, what it signifies, and how it works, as well as who employs it—and to what ends.[40]

The metaphors at the heart of each case study reflect how bloggers implicitly developed strategies that disrupted conventional attention routines and pivoted public focus to pressing issues. Attention is a crucial democratic resource in information-rich, internetworked public cultures that feature media flowing from mouths, mobile devices, computers, tablets, televisions, newspapers, books, radios, films, and even everyday objects. Citizens must concentrate the attention of others lest their public discourse become lost in a datastream of undifferentiated fragments jostling for position. While blogging, like any communicative practice, can distract attention from topics that deserve more discourse, *Networked Media, Networked Rhetorics* examines cases when bloggers successfully marshaled public focus on issues meriting more intensive deliberation. Each case study chapter, then, analyzes these organic metaphors for what they imply about how patterns of networked communication focus attention. To put the networked metaphors of invention, emotion, and expertise in context, I add a wrinkle to metaphoric criticism by turning it on rhetorical theory itself. Rhetorical theory throughout history is dominated by metaphoric language. Thus, in each case study, I trace metaphors used to describe invention, emotion, and expertise at key points in the history of rhetorical theory. This metarhetorical analysis of the metaphors of rhetorical theory highlights a rich and variegated history of theorizing about communication. A metarhetorical analysis gives insight into the varied ways in which a culture envisions or conceptualizes rhetoric itself, which provides context for understanding the changes in rhetorical practices manifested in the contemporary metaphors of flooding the zone, ambient intimacy, and shallow quotation.

The next chapter explores three cultural technologies of publicity: rhetorics, public spheres, and digital communication networks. These cultural technologies coalesce, sustain, structure, and transform attention. I then turn to each of the case studies, in chronological order, beginning with the aftermath of Trent Lott's toast, turning to Salam Pax's pre–Iraq War narration, and concluding with *RealClimate*'s engagement with climate science. In the final chapter, I consider how more contemporary developments in the networked public sphere create the conditions for what I call "hyperpublicity," which I see as potentially undermining the spirit of play that might otherwise support rhetorical experimentation. I also propose a research agenda for networked rhetorics, identifying six loci for the continued development of networked rhetorical theories to inform citizen participation and strengthen the deliberative practices that constitute the networked public sphere.

2

CULTURAL TECHNOLOGIES OF PUBLICITY:
RHETORICS, PUBLIC SPHERES,
AND DIGITAL COMMUNICATION NETWORKS

The contemporary networked world is not the first to sense discontinuities from cultural, technological, political, and economic changes. In their own tumult, the classical and the modern eras can inform contemporary public deliberation. The city-state of Athens circa 350 B.C.E. is of particular interest as a site of democratic gathering: intellectually, it was the heyday of Plato and Aristotle; geographically, it was the birthplace of democracy; culturally, it placed rhetorical performance at the center of social life. Writing was the new media technology, city life introduced new forms of territorial organization, Panhellenic ideals presented alternatives to parochial attitudes, and novel modes of governance were being tested. Despite the political innovations of Athens, the social attitudes of the time winnowed democratic participation down to a relatively small, male, propertied elite. Potentially radical, but deeply flawed: such was the legacy of Athenian democracy as it shaped Western cultures. Preserved in the textual remnants of thinkers like Gorgias, Plato, Aristotle, and Isocrates, debates in Greek antiquity about the nature of reality, the capacity for citizen self-governance, the ethics of persuasion, and the optimal form of justice have influenced democratic gatherings throughout history. For example, the modern era in Europe, beginning in the sixteenth century and consolidating in the seventeenth, drew inspiration from Athenian democratic practice in another period of broad ferment. During this time, the printing press was the new and destabilizing media technology, the formation of the nation-state reorganized political territory, tales of the globe's startling cultural diversity circulated through public culture, and representative democracy aimed to generate transparency and accountability for ever-more-complex governing institutions.

The networked era features a confluence of parallel changes: the diffusion of internetworked media, an erosion of the nation-state's primacy, a dramatic increase in encounters with cultural diversity through the movement of people, products, and ideas, and transnational organizations required to regulate the global economy. Communicative interaction about the challenges of living together now occurs in the *networked public sphere*, an array of interconnected contexts sustained by traditional institutions of the press and newer networked intermediaries. What does this communicative interaction look like in practice? Thomas Pettitt's schematic construction of the "Gutenberg Parenthesis" (see fig. 1) helps answer this question by comparing cultural performances in oral, print, and internetworked cultures.[1] Pettitt argues the performative norms of the Gutenberg era ought to be conceived as an interval, or parenthesis, that interrupts what appear to be the more continuous norms of oral and networked culture. When orality dominated, culture involved re-creating canonical works through live performances. For example, during the Athenian summer festival Panathenaia, a "grand singing procession" wound through the city streets as a collective performance of traditional songs for the specific purpose of giving glory to the gods.[2] Bards were the repositories of collective cultural memory, orally relating tales of past heroes and deeds through song and story. By contrast, the modern period forged a system of culture making that relied on the individually crafted, original, authentic, and stable printed text. The novel, conceived as a process of genius composition, was the apogee of creative production that, with some combination of skill and luck, became a part of the canon of great literature.

Networked media, following the logic of the Gutenberg Parenthesis, afford creative performances with a more striking resemblance to oral than print culture. Much like bards, bloggers freely appropriate and borrow from multiple sources, while adding elements that transform the original artifact. Bloggers recontextualize the story from their own perspectives by appropriating fragments from a wild variety of sources. A blogger's post is often further remixed by other bloggers, creating hyperlinked layers of interpretation in which the original item persists only as a palimpsest. This remixing of discourse fragments, sometimes with little or no regard for citationality, harkens back to oral culture. The medium, though, makes a difference: networked rhetorics are often multimodal instead of just linguistic, are archivable in a way that oral speech is not, and circulate faster and wider than speech.

PRE-PARENTHETICAL	GUTENBERG PARENTHESIS	POST-PARENTHETICAL
re-creative	original	sampling
collective	individual	remixing
con-textual	autonomous	borrowing
unstable	stable	reshaping
traditional	canonical	appropriating
performance	composition	recontextualizing

Fig. 1   Thomas Pettitt's "Gutenberg Parenthesis"

Pettitt's figure of the Gutenberg Parenthesis cues us to culturally, technologically, and historically unique modes of communication that citizens draw upon to make opinions public in a way that stimulates follow-on argument and discussion.[3] These creative norms mapped out by Pettitt align with three intertwined cultural technologies of publicity operating in concert in the networked public sphere. An early cultural technology of publicity—rhetoric—extends a taproot to ancient Greece. Rhetoric's power to shape attention was amplified with a later cultural technology of publicity, the print-supported public sphere, to address democratic challenges in more complex and pluralistic cultures. Digital communication networks are the latest cultural technology of publicity. These networks build on prior technologies of publicity, requiring the attention-shaping power of rhetoric to sort through abundant information and producing new ways of fulfilling the public sphere's democratic function.

Rhetorics as Cultural Technologies of Publicity

The Athenian agora, a marketplace where people went for goods but stayed for conversation, looms large in retrospective understandings of the early Greek rhetorical imaginary. In the agora, people spoke on a wide range of topics, providing an informal site for the speechmaking and dialogue central to Athenian life. It was the heart of the *polis*, "the place where information was most visibly circulated."[4] Although the agora was primarily sustained through orality, the new technology of writing allowed public conversation to be extended across time and space starting around 350 B.C.E. No one mastered the new medium of writing like Isocrates, prompting David Perlmutter to identify him as a proto-blogger for taking advantage of a new technology to disrupt deliberative routines.[5] Part of the Isocratean legacy is a recognition of how the circulation of rhetoric through media more permanent than speech could stimulate judgments with higher degrees of legitimacy while inculcating positive attitudes toward the *polis* and the common good.[6]

The agora's sustaining conceptual power can be located in the spirit of openness and public argument that it represented, especially in contrast to *symposia* and *hetaireia*. A *symposion* was a private drinking party, often hosted to preserve aristocratic social networks and increase political influence.[7] *Symposia* were perceived as antidemocratic because the unsavory whiff of private aristocratic mingling was antithetical to the openness thought to be the basis of the *polis*.[8] The real danger of *symposia* was that they might become *hetaireia*, private clubs that used food and wine to convert social ties into networks of undemocratic political influence. *Hetaireia* had been key units of political power in an earlier, more oligarchic Athens.[9] Around 400 B.C.E., a law was passed that made overthrowing the democracy or forming a *hetaireia* subject to prosecution, the functional equivalence of these two activities apparently not lost on legislators.[10] Given the legacy of these conniving, culinary cabals of earlier Athens, democratic practice became intertwined with publicity rather than secrecy.

The "sharing of words and deeds," as rendered by Hannah Arendt, was the foundation of the *polis* and the heart of the classical rhetorical imaginary.[11] Part of rhetoric's usefulness was in making public the thoughts, needs, and desires of the *demos*. Creating a shared, public, political realm through rhetoric was considered even more important than legislation. Legislators could be called in from abroad, but only citizens could participate in the communicative life of the *polis*. Participation in public life thus required a familiarity with rhetoric. Rhetors needed to know how to invent, arrange, stylize, memorize, and deliver speeches (known as the "canons" of rhetoric). Rhetoricians taught Athenians how to speak effectively so that they could defend themselves in a court trial, make a case in front of the Assembly, or deliver a memorable oration at a festival. Rhetoric was an art of advantage, a way of persuading others of a particular version of the good, the true, and the beautiful. Since speechmaking needed to be "methodized and imparted to the masses," rhetorical treatises emphasized the grammatical nature of speech itself: the primary components of a speech, different types of speeches, varieties of audiences, emotions to appeal to, and key logical forms.[12] The agora provided a forum for civic culture where variant descriptions of the world intersected and transformed each other. Without speech to, in Arendt's formulation, "materialize and memorialize" novel insights about civic affairs, political power in oral cultures lost the ground from which to assert itself.[13] The most fundamental legacy of classical Athens, then, is that democracy is a *communicative* and *shared* affair. Occasions to exercise shared communication were frequent, designed to create conditions for people to go on together in the mutual project of Athens.[14]

A contrasting model of communication, which I will refer to as "informationism," haunts rhetoric's history from Plato to, more recently, cybernetic theories of computing.[15] Plato, the *ur*-informationist, considered rhetoric a *pharmakon*, or drug, that intoxicated the masses instead of enlightening them. For Plato, language is inherently duplicitous, so we would be advised to eschew rhetoric and get down to "the Real," which can be best accounted for with clear, brief, sincere communication based on the rational faculties of measurement. The real was encapsulated in Plato's Theory of the Forms, idealized abstractions like Truth, Justice, and Beauty that could only be grasped (and partially, at that) through philosophical dialectic. Variations on the Platonic critique of rhetoric stretch to the present day, with rhetoric opposed to the knowledge gained from philosophical insight, conflated with shallow speech not backed by deeds, or associated with propaganda—see Hitler, Adolf—and deception. Rhetoric is really rhetrickery.[16] Ironically, the idea of "the Real" as sitting outside of language is quite rhetorically effective, placing rhetoric in a tenuous intellectual and institutional position throughout much of human history.

For informationists in the digital era, "the Real" is pure data, an attitude partially traceable to mid-twentieth-century thinking about communication technology. In the 1960s, Claude Shannon and Warren Weaver defined communication as the transmission of information from sender to receiver, susceptible to noise that polluted the message.[17] This model of communication was enticing for technicians who were, like Shannon and Weaver, working on minimizing undesirable feedback over telephone lines. Their focus on algorithmic processing of messages supercharged the perception that communication is primarily an informational transaction rather than a rhetorical interaction.

Informationism appears ascendant in a world of "Big Data" that promises to improve social systems by improving information flows. Bill Gates, informationist *par excellence*, promises a "plan to fix the world's biggest problems" by "setting clear goals, choosing an approach, measuring results, and then using those measurements to continually refine our approach."[18] Informationism presumes that all systems can be understood as complex aggregates of operationalizable information, that data speak for themselves, and that better decisions would be made if individuals and institutions could just get a more ideal discovery and distribution of information.[19] This kind of "Big Data fundamentalism," as Kate Crawford explains, is "the idea [that] with larger data sets, we get closer to objective truth."[20] Such a fundamentalism is hopelessly naïve. If it were that easy, I submit, the world would face far fewer problems. While information is important, it is not everything. Information may be crucial to informing options for action, but mustering the will to set goals, choosing approaches, settling on measurements, and making sense of the data are all tasks that involve layers of argument and persuasion.

The blogosphere could fit into informationist paradigms, as blogs *do* execute a number of crucial information tasks in contemporary democracies. Bloggers produce information about their political opinions. Bloggers provide information about other citizens, about the government, about corporations, about publics and their problems. They dissect, correct, and add to other sources of information. Blogs can be seen as knowledge management systems that introduce useful ways of organizing, presenting, and managing information flows.[21] However, viewing blogging as merely a mechanism for information exchange obscures the greater significance of this genre of networked communication. Adopting an informationist perspective on blogging cannot help but feed into the prominent critique of blogging as increasing the noise-to-signal ratio in public communication—a criticism that relies on a mathematical metaphor derived from Shannon and Weaver's work about how meaning is made meaningful. But deciphering meaning from a blog post is not exactly like trying to reduce noise on a telephone line. Though the content of internetworked technologies is reducible to digital strings of ones and zeros, the making, circulation, and reception of meaning is far more complex. Information is never just information, and the circulation of raw data by itself cannot rearrange human relationships. Neither, technically, can there be such a thing as raw data. Interpretation always interposes itself between data and publication.[22] Bloggers can write about an event they witnessed, but they can never do so as neutral observers. Once they start using symbols, bloggers—alongside the rest of us—are caught in a web of mixed and shaded meanings, complexities involved in naming and describing, and the dead certainty that audiences will impose their own idiosyncratic reading strategies. In other words, information is never just information, because it is caught in a web of rhetorical meaning. To broaden the purview of communication beyond information shuffleboard is to invite a more sophisticated consideration of power, culture, audience, and ideology.

My critique of informationist conceptions of communication extends Richard Lanham's indictment of what he calls the C-B-S model of communication. The C-B-S model represents what are often taken to be the communicative ideals of Clarity, Brevity, and Sincerity.[23] These three criteria, inspired by a spartan, businesslike, and scientistic approach to language, are often held out as normative ideals to which individual speech acts should aspire. We should be clear, speak plainly, and articulate our ideas with an elegance derived from simplicity. We should be brief and to the point. We should also be sincere, by saying what we mean and meaning what we say. Clarity, brevity, and sincerity are presumed especially important for public communication, which is often marked by obfuscation, long-windedness, and outright deception. These are the communicative norms that informationism spawns: if participants in a controversy would only adhere to telling the truth, simply and clearly, than otherwise intractable issues could be resolved satisfactorily. However, theories of communication that privilege the C-B-S norms tend toward formalism. Herbert Spencer's rhetorical theory of the nineteenth century, for example, aimed to reduce the "friction and inertia" involved in conveying meaning, leading him to muse "whether economy of the recipient's attention is not the secret of effect, alike in the right choice and collocation of words, in the best arrangement of clauses in a sentence, in the proper order of its principal and subordinate propositions, in the judicious use of simile, metaphor, and other figures of speech, and even in the rhythmical sequence of syllables."[24] Persuasion clearly is not just a function of form, and oiling the machinery of language with the right collocation of words hardly eases the frictions inherent in communication. Even the best grammarians still argue. Underwritten by what I. A. Richards refers to as the "Proper Meaning Superstition," the erroneous assumption that every word has one and only one definition, the C-B-S model suffers from a weak theory of meaning.[25]

The criteria of clarity, brevity, and sincerity are especially dubious in hypercomplex cultures. Certainly, some level of clarity is desirable to aid intelligible conversation. However, the idea that words carry one and only one meaning is belied by the fact that many of our most resilient public controversies—like the morality of genetic enhancement or worth of preemptive war—turn on arguments about the very definitions of terms.[26] Moreover, the standards of clarity are radically divergent for different publics. What is clear language to the specialist may well be opaque to the nonspecialist. Even expert-to-expert communication is, owing to specialization, often an exercise in reconciling unfamiliar terminologies. Clarity is an impossible standard, since people bring varying assumptions, histories, and interpretations to any message. Misunderstanding is more the norm of communication than an outlier.[27] And while brevity is often the soul of wit, it is hardly a satisfactory norm when serious issues must be comprehensively explained. A discussion of war, health care, or the national debt is not done justice by competing bumper stickers—or tweets—alone. Democracies need extended iterations of back-and-forth communication to inform decision making. Finally, the sincerity criterion, too, is problematic, for how does one successfully gauge another's intent? Cultural preferences for sincerity beg all sorts of questions about authenticity that are more closely associated with an outmoded, romantic view of the communication process.

In addition to failing as a workable model of communication, the C-B-S model strips away most of what is interesting about communication. There is a richness to communication that is denuded by conceiving it only as a method of information transmission. By contrast, a rhetorical conception of public communication recognizes the vibrancy of symbolic interchange. Kenneth Burke recognized rhetoric as "the use of language as a symbolic means of inducing cooperation in beings that by nature respond to symbols."[28] Sentient creatures employ all sorts of symbolic means to bend each other toward particular beliefs or courses of action: speech, writing, images, yelps, music, poetry, whimpers, television, film, art, podcasts, blogs, and more. Burke situated rhetoric as "the region of the Scramble, of insult and injury, bickering, squabbling, malice and the lie, cloaked malice and the subsidized lie"; yet alongside these "malign inclinations" are "benign elements" grounded in compassion for others.[29] It is this mix of rhetoric's corruptibility and correctability, to borrow a phrase from Thomas Farrell, that makes rhetoric so capable of exploring human interaction, whether in the agora or the blogosphere.[30]

Despite the prevalence of informationism in networked public culture, recent developments in digital media technology set the stage for a rhetorical renaissance. The conditions for rhetoric's resurgence can be ascertained by contrasting the modern, industrial economy with the contemporary, networked economy. Following Richard Lanham's formulation, the industrial age privileged the production of "stuff," material products sold to consumers. Anything that did not pertain to stuff was dismissed as being "fluff." Rhetoric was one of those fluffy things; it was style, not substance.

But the centrality of stuff as the basis of economic value no longer holds as much sway. In the new economy, the fluff used to describe the stuff creates value too—maybe even most of the value. Graphic designers, computer programmers, marketers, middle managers, and most definitely university professors are linked by their primary emphasis on symbolic crafting. In the United States, with a steady decline in the agricultural and manufacturing sectors, the class of symbol crafters is steadily growing. The 1989 film *Say Anything* cinematically marks the crisis of stuff and ascendance of fluff. In that film, Lloyd (capably played by John Cusack) responds to his girlfriend's father's question about what he wants to do with his life by proclaiming, "I don't want to buy anything, sell anything or process anything. I don't want to buy anything sold, bought or processed, sell anything bought, sold or processed or process anything sold, bought or processed as a career."[31] Lloyd does not want to deal with stuff. A (thankfully never made) sequel—*Say Something?*—would surely feature Lloyd firmly settled in a career managing, or perhaps data mining, fluff. Lanham's point is that fluff is not really that fluffy. For example, the new corporate common sense that the brand is more important than the product reflects the importance of fluff. For symbolic fluffers, "'capital' in this new economy [is located] in the literary and artistic imagination, the powers that take the biogrammar we inherit and spin from it new patterns for how to live and to think about how we live."[32] Learning how to craft fluff, as it turns out, is crucially important in managing the complexity of an information-abundant world.

That we do live in a world of information abundance is surely the prevailing commonplace of our internetworked times. This is not exactly a new sentiment, for privileged citizens in every culture after the invention of writing opine that the steady accumulation of texts defies the ability of any one lifetime to engage them all.[33] Throughout most of human history, though, waiting to receive information was akin to standing outside and hoping for a sprinkle. The challenge now is to not get soaked in the downpour. More data are available and accessible than ever before in human history because of how digital media technologies transform publication and preservation.[34] In terms of publication, more people are now able to publish directly to a global, interlinked circuit of communication. A. J. Liebling's aphorism "the freedom of the press is guaranteed only to those who have one" is a stark reminder of the capital-intensive nature of publication before the networked era. While the digital divide still cordons off some citizens from access to publication, learning to set up a blog is much easier than learning to set up a newspaper and requires quite a bit less money. Alongside the swell in personal publication is the ease of digital preservation. The point hardly needs belaboring: a wall of music albums now fits on a flash drive, thousands of movies can be stored on a laptop, and nearly a hundred thousand books can be digitally squeezed onto a tablet device (numbers that will soon be dwarfed as storage media capacities steadily increase).

My own information journey from the early 1990s to the early 2010s is indicative of the abundant datastreams supported by internetworked media. My engagement with media in the 1990s was fairly typical of any middle-class high school and then college student in the United States: a newspaper in the morning, some radio or a compact disc (then the hot new media technology) during the day, television at night, and, when lucky, the obligatory date movie on the weekend. I read a lot of books. Like most high school students back then, I used the medium of my voice an awful lot, often mediated by the landline telephone. Without a doubt, my days were filled with media of some kind or another. My current media ecosystem still involves those steadfasts in some ratio, but is complemented now by a plenitude of internetworked sources. My daily morning routine involves scanning several major news websites, featuring hundreds of fresh stories per day. My email inbox constantly hovers at 100 messages, with more new messages a day than I care to—or can—address. Since 2004, I have sent over 17,000 emails and received 58,000. My RSS feed, which aggregates posts from the blogs I follow, indicates 5,000 unread items, with about 100 posts added per day. The family Netflix queue is permanently stuck at the maximum of 499 movies. The DVR reports a mere 4 percent free space remaining. My music library stores 122 gigabytes of music, and I often listen to a new album every day from one of the many music sites on the web. I can boast that I have beaten several games on the Nintendo Wii, but confess that far more remain only partially completed. My Amazon wish list contains a hundred books, never mind that my shelves are populated with more than a few unread ones. Facebook and Google+ feed me hundreds of status updates per day. YouTube. Twitter. Vine. Reddit. My phone constantly announces text messages. And on and on. Although there are certainly people with much lower levels of attendance to networked media, many *digerati* would look at me as though I were on an information diet!

So what does information abundance mean for contemporary public culture and rhetorical practice? This question, which also haunted early mass communication theorists, is newly salient in the context of networked communication. In the 1940s, Paul Lazarsfeld and Robert Merton wondered if "exposure to this flood of information [from the new mass media of film, radio, and television] may serve to narcotize rather than energize the average reader or listener."[35] This "narcotizing dysfunction" threatened civic engagement, as citizens favored attending to the artifacts of the new electronic media rather than their communities. By the early 1990s, W. Russell Neuman tempered the fears of Lazarsfeld and Merton by claiming that "the accumulated research of the past several decades confirms that the average audience member pays relatively little attention, retains only a small fraction, and is not the slightest bit overloaded by the flow of information or the choices available among the media and messages."[36] People figure out how to sort through piles of information. They must. Neuman intimates that the use of a new medium simply trades off with the use of an old medium, since human attention is essentially a finite resource. The 1950s saw television in the living room partially displace radio listening in the home. More recently, for younger generations, internetworked devices largely supplant watching a dedicated television screen. Can Neuman's claims about attention management for the mass audience translate seamlessly to the networked audience? Or do the more radical increases in information present a heightened challenge for human communication in networked cultures? Consider the following: in 2005, researchers in the new field of interruption science learned that office workers were interrupted every eleven minutes with an urgent email, phone call, or other kind of electronically mediated message. On average, it took workers twenty-five minutes to return to the original task.[37] The numbers from today would surely be more sobering. Interruption is the norm not just in the office, but in everyday life as well. When was the last time that you participated in a conversation without the ring, ding, or beep of a phone call, text message, or other kind of notification emanating from a mobile device? When citizens are plugged into the internetwork, they are likely dealing with "juggler's brain."[38]

Distraction seems built into the foundation of networked media, the hyperlink. Lev Manovich, in his early and influential *The Language of New Media*, goes so far as to advance the claim that the hyperlink is at odds with the practice of rhetoric: "Traditionally, texts encoded human knowledge and memory, instructed, inspired, convinced, and seduced their readers to adopt new ideas, new ways of interpreting the world, new ideologies. In short, the printed word was linked to the art of rhetoric. While it is probably possible to invent a new rhetoric of hypermedia that will use hyperlinking not to distract the reader from the argument (as is often the case today), but rather to further convince her of an argument's validity, the sheer existence and popularity of hyperlinking exemplifies the continuing decline of the field of rhetoric."[39] Manovich concludes that "rather than seducing the user through a careful arrangement of arguments and examples, points and counterpoints, [and] changing rhythms of presentation . . . [new media] bombard the user with all the data at once."[40] For Manovich, the panoply of hyperlinks creates metonymic abundance, fueling jumpy navigation habits that leave web users with no time or motivation to make sense of it all. In making this argument, Manovich follows a long line of critical thought suspicious of how new media technologies undermine conventional rhetorical practices. However, his assessment follows only if one takes a limited view of rhetoric as style without substance, mere ornamentation that seduces through the arrangement of arguments and eloquent turns of phrase invoking rhythm, metaphor, and other rhetorical figures.[41] A thicker conception of rhetoric suggests that hyperlinked environments function as marketplaces (or, to decommodify it slightly, "agoras") of attention through the fusion of what is traditionally binarized as style and substance.[42]

Lanham's refiguration of rhetoric for an era of information abundance adopts this thicker conception:

> Economics, as we all remember from Introduction to Economics, studies the allocation of scarce resources. Normally we would think that the phrase "information economy," which we hear everywhere nowadays, makes some sense. It is no longer the physical stuff that is in short supply, we are told, but information about it. So, we live in an "information economy." But information is not in short supply in the new information economy. We're drowning in it. What we lack is the human attention needed to make sense of it all. It will be easier to find our place in the new regime if we think of it as an economics of attention. Attention is the commodity in short supply.[43]

Lanham situates rhetoric as an economics of attention, because "it tells us how to allocate our central scarce resource, to invite people to attend to what we would like them to attend to."[44] Framing rhetoric in economic terms is not entirely unproblematic, as it coincides with late capitalism's interest in extracting the "productive value of human attention."[45] The old one-liner "I'm so poor, I can't even pay attention" is no joking matter now, as the scramble for attention is a serious matter for capital. Capitalism is catching up with a longstanding assumption of rhetoric: attention undergirds all activity. But attention is not a commodity in the conventional sense, as it expands and contracts with the circulation of messages. Attention is a resource that rhetoric activates. As a consequence, Todd Oakley argues that the "common denominator" of rhetorical theory throughout history is "the practice of one individual or group *directing the attention* of another individual group about a past, present, future, or imagined situation."[46]

This common denominator of attention is part of rhetoric's hidden curriculum. In classical times, Aristotle maintained that one of the audience's fundamental defects was its inattentiveness. Thus the introduction of a speech must be aimed at channeling the audience's attention to the matter at hand.[47] Following the guidance of Aristotle, teachers of public speaking still emphasize the importance of the "attention-getter," a startling fact, moving story, or well-timed joke that draws the audience in to the rest of the speech. Just as important are "attention-sustainers," the rhetorical methods that one uses to vivify language throughout a speech. Speech professor James Winans's early-twentieth-century textbook *Public Speaking* proposes that "many of the problems of public speaking, plainly enough, are related to attention," observing that "we well know how common it is in conversation to talk on about our affairs, our ideas, our stupid adventures, our smart children, calmly ignoring the yawns of our hearers."[48] More recently, Karlyn Kohrs Campbell privileges attention by claiming that "nearly all [rhetorical] strategies catch and hold attention and, in that sense, make ideas more vivid."[49] Burke, too, wonders whether responses to situations crucially involve "*the nature of attention* in the first place."[50] This insight about attention is clearly not lost on the commercial world. Marketers and advertisers continually push the envelope through shock-and-awe visual strategies that become more spectacular each year. This, however, is attention conceived *thinly* as capturing people's senses so as to subject them to a message.

This thin model of attention comports with a traditional (informationist) vision of rhetoric as ornamented speech—mere fluff—that prettifies discourse to get attention, but lacks substance. In this view, rhetorical figures like alliteration, anaphora, and allusion shout "look at me!" but enjoy limited value beyond that initial grab of attention. But attention can be conceived more *thickly*, as a constitutive process. Rhetoric shapes not only *what* that we think about, but *how* we think about it. The decision to use *networked* instead of *digital*, or *rhetorical* imaginary instead of *social* imaginary, is an effort on my part to shape how we attend to the larger concepts of media, rhetoric, and the imaginary. Pettit's Gutenberg Parenthesis is a visual figure that draws attention to similarities and dissimilarities between cultural performances in different eras. The metaphors attached to each case study likewise draw attention to one phenomenon in the terms of another. Rhetoric directs our attention to one way of perception, thinking, and feeling, and not another. Rhetoric shapes *how* we attend to phenomena through the valences, emphases, and weightings involved in signification. To say that attention is constitutive, then, is to recognize that how we perceive the world, how we understand our identities and relationships, how we engage in meaning making, and how we transform conventions all derive from attention processes.[51]

More information demands more tools to focus attention demands more rhetoric—there's a motto for the networked age. With "the utopia of perfect information," Lanham notes (tongue in cheek), comes "the return of stylistic filtration" to make sense of it all.[52] Rhetoric focuses attention through style, converting information into something like prudential knowledge. Wisdom, not just information, is necessary to make good decisions. Given the centrality of attention in the theory of rhetorical communication outlined here, a definitional mash-up is in order. Combining Burke's conception of rhetoric ("the use of language as a symbolic means of inducing cooperation in beings that by nature respond to symbols") with Lanham's observations about rhetoric and attention yields a synthetic understanding of rhetoric as *the use of symbols to focus attention in beings that respond to symbols in order to induce cooperation and facilitate judgment*. Put another way, rhetoric is that expressive art which shapes attention patterns capable of coordinating and transforming interaction. This definition sutures rhetoric's aesthetic and pragmatic sides. Emphasize just the aesthetic dimension, and rhetoric becomes literary and formalist; emphasize only the pragmatic dimension, and it becomes crass. Eloquence should be prized because it expands our repertoire for shaping attention processes, thus opening up new possibilities for interpretation and judgment. When the aesthetic and pragmatic dimensions of rhetoric are working in concert, it becomes an art capable of changing attitudes and controversies.

With this perspective on rhetoric, it is hard to conceive of bloggers as anything but rhetorical, crafting collective attention patterns through symbol use. Bloggers are quite reflexive about the relationship between blogging and attention, half-jokingly cast as "the attention-seeking barking of lonely poodles."[53] While some bloggers engage in the relentless rat race for (thin) attention and the steady trickle of ad revenue that it provides, other bloggers conceptualize their role in guiding public attention more robustly. Rhetoric—and the closely related practices of argumentation and persuasion—is central to how civic bloggers make sense of their own practices.[54] *DailyKos* founder Markos Moulitsas Zúniga explains that the hyperlink usefully transforms traditional techniques of public argumentation: "[w]hen bloggers make an argument, we can add a link to support our premises."[55] The invocation of the word "premise" signals the absorption and circulation of the language of public argument by bloggers. Bloggers commonly deploy terms from rhetorical theory when they compare claims, interrogate premises and inferences, produce or examine evidence, or question the credibility of advocates. Using the language of argumentation more commonly found in college textbooks, bloggers move rhetorical criticism of public address from a rarefied practice of the academy into everyday life.

If Lanham is right that the attention demands of the networked public sphere set the stage for a revaluation of rhetoric, then we need a richer account of how, exactly, new digitally networked intermediaries shape attention patterns through public argument. Classical theories of rhetoric, alone, do not suffice to make sense of contemporary public deliberation. Rhetoric operates in conjunction with two other cultural technologies of publicity, the public sphere and digital communication networks, to establish the enabling conditions of the networked public sphere.

Public Spheres as Cultural Technologies of Publicity

At the onset of the modern age in the fifteenth and sixteenth centuries, a series of cultural, political, economic, and scientific revolutions problematized feudal patterns of interdependence in Europe. The early modern era saw democratic civil society develop as a response to the accountability concerns raised by the nation-state and corporate institutions. It was in this context that Athenian insights into democratic culture were rediscovered and valorized, so much so that the early modern age is often called the neoclassical era. Jürgen Habermas's *Structural Transformation of the Public Sphere* explains how the bourgeois public sphere absorbed the Greek ideological template that valorized public argument.[56] But instead of personal fame as a motivating *telos*, the bourgeois public sphere prized truth as arrived at through consensus. And rather than speech starring as the communicative mode that sustains the common life of the national *polis*, the cultural uses of print promised to keep newly minted democratic institutions in touch with public opinion.

Historically, the genesis of the bourgeois public sphere is a crucial stage in displacing the divine right of royalty and generating a more democratic rhetorical imaginary. The monarchs dominating European history until the Enlightenment engaged in what Habermas refers to as "representative publicity," parading themselves *before* the public rather than *for* the public to secure legitimacy for their decisions.[57] The quote widely attributed to Louis XIV of France, "L'État, c'est moi"—"the state, it is me"—pithily captures the prevailing elision between the king's body and the state.[58] For a subject, the proper relation to the state was genuflection. The bourgeois public sphere offered an alternative to representative publicity by loosely linking public spaces through print publications that fostered discussion and debate about civic affairs. Democratic legitimacy, in the bourgeois rhetorical imaginary, developed through the bottom-up, iterative development of public opinion. Newspapers set the agenda for conversation. The new coffeehouses of England, salons of France, and taverns of Germany were key sites of democratic gathering to discuss printed news, congeal public opinion, and enrich political culture. These discussions were idealized as status-free zones where the quality of contribution was supposedly valued more than the amount of coin in one's purse. From a contemporary vantage point, this presumption of bracketed status is laughable, since, like their predecessors in the Athenian agora, the participants self-selected for gender, ethnicity, and class based on the social norms of the time. But the processes of public reason, debate, and discussion form the basis for what Habermas identifies as the productive kernel at the heart of an otherwise deeply exclusionary and flawed ideology: critical publicity.[59]

The idea of critical publicity manifests two key elements foundational to the modern rhetorical imaginary: first, that arguments about civic affairs ought to be conducted in public rather than in private; and second, that public arguments should be evaluated on their ability to withstand critical scrutiny.[60] The publicity norm carries hints of the Greek fear of *hetaireia*, but in the context of modern institutions like the state and the corporate firm, which use bureaucratic obfuscation to conceal decision-making processes. To form reasoned *public* opinion, as opposed to untested and *privately held* opinions, Habermas argues that the bourgeois practiced what amounted to a new genre of public communication: rational-critical debate. For democracy to work, citizens could not simply assert ill-formed opinions in public discussions. They would need to develop strong reasons and be willing to submit them to the public scrutiny of their peers, who were increasingly well versed in norms and standards of argumentation and evidence. In the self-conception of the bourgeois, this process of rational-critical debate would draw out and correct poor reasoning and thus produce more justifiable and enlightened judgments. The bourgeois elevation of criticism as an evaluative mechanism was surely a better method for guiding governance than the monarchical alternatives of whim or force, yet it evinces early modernity's too-strong faith in the ability of a public's reasoning abilities and perhaps even in the idea of reason itself.

However, the advantage of criticism as a way to sort through arguments is that it is *reflexive*, meaning that the criteria for judging arguments are subject to debate alongside the specifics of any particular issue. Criticism's reflexivity makes public opinion a dynamic, organic creature that accommodates—even hungers for—divergent interpretations. But public opinion can only be used as a democratic barometer if one can measure it, which is what newspapers claimed to do. Initially, editors of print publications literally sat in on the rowdy coffeehouse discussions to get a sense of public opinion. Thus, the press materialized as a mediating layer between the *demos* and the elected, filtering through claims and counterclaims to set the agenda for public debate, process competing arguments, and facilitate good judgments by governing bodies. Newspapers and pamphlets supported sites of democratic gathering outside the penumbra of the state for public opinion to coalesce. It was through this complex and messy process that public opinion became a democratic counterweight to authoritarian modes of decision making.

This relationship among citizens, the press, and democratic institutions is much neater as an imaginary than in practice. As the early modern bourgeois eventually learned, their idealization of rational-critical argumentation norms imperfectly generated the consensus necessary to legitimate decision making. Critics of Habermas invariably make this point: the reality of deliberation in the public sphere rarely, if ever, met the idealization. This is especially true of the bourgeois public sphere. A culture that valorized the status of one's argument rather than the status of one's standing explicitly excluded non-national, non-male, and non-bourgeois participants. A culture that lionized rational-critical debate was quite likely often neither rational nor very critical. A culture that claimed to eschew authority undoubtedly allowed it to creep back in through implicit credibility assessments of fellow citizens. These observations productively puncture the fantasy that the bourgeois public sphere smoothed the way for the seamless translation of public opinion into democratic decision making. But these critical threads miss the point that Habermas obliquely makes, which is that the very idea of these norms expanded the possibilities for democratic participation during the modern age despite the practical difficulties in institutionalizing them.[61] The bourgeois public sphere relied on an imaginary that, while flawed in key respects, transformed attitudes and relations in the modern era. And despite all the problems with critical publicity, some variant of it is inevitable for democratic public deliberation.

If, as Thomas Farrell indicates, "rhetoric is the primary practical instrumentality for generating and sustaining the critical publicity which keeps the promise of a public sphere alive," then public deliberation is intimately involved with attention processes.[62] Craig Calhoun trenchantly posits that public discourse "cannot be about everything all at once. Some structuring of attention, imposed by dominant ideology, hegemonic powers, or social movements, must always exist."[63] Let's add rhetoric to that list of attention structures. To gain traction in public deliberation, rhetorical activity must be compelling enough to focus citizens' deliberative energies. "To get our attention," Arthur Lupia points out, "an utterance made during the course of deliberation must fend off competitors such as a person's preoccupation with certain prior or future events, the simultaneous actions or utterances of others, and even the color of the wallpaper."[64] Distraction (at least from civic affairs) is the natural resting position for citizens with lives to lead. Only with rhetorical action do citizens focus their attention on a particular issue and thus form a public.[65] Ideally, as Habermas argues, "the broad circulation of comprehensible, attention-grabbing messages arouses a sufficiently inclusive participation" to set the machinery of democracy in motion.[66] Yet with the attention challenges created by abundant streams of rhetorical activity characteristic of networked media, accusations of "attention-deficit democracy" are frequent.[67]

Attention is at the heart of public deliberation, defined by James Bohman as "a dialogical process of exchanging reasons for the purpose of resolving problematic situations that cannot be settled without interpersonal coordination and cooperation."[68] Since deliberation is a rhetorical activity, there are several points of contact between Bohman's conceptualization of public deliberation and the remixed Burke-Lanham definition of rhetoric that foregrounds attention.

- "Dialogical process." Deliberation is a process, not a product. While there may very well be a by-product of deliberation (like a decision, a vote, or a record of what was said by whom), deliberation is essentially processual. This process is modeled on conversation among multiple people, either face-to-face or scaled up through broadcast or networked media. A dialogical process assumes that the convergence of multiple perspectives produces a whole greater than the sum of its parts. Dialogical argument expands the horizons of participants as they attend to how other people reason and reflexively evolve their own beliefs. The process of argumentation changes the participants even as they try to change each other.[69]

- "Exchanging reasons." "Reasons" should not be interpreted strictly as falling into the domain of formal logic, with p's and q's organized into neatly structured proofs.[70] Reason can be viewed expansively as justification, which occurs through stories, songs, images, fiction, analogy, metaphor, and a host of other rhetorical means. Interlocutors use reason to expand how fellow citizens attend to an issue. This more rhetorical (as opposed to logical or philosophical) approach to reasoning acknowledges how a range of symbolic forms persuasively affects an audience. This is not to say that all reasons are weighted equally. Reflexivity about the quality of reasoning makes public deliberation dynamic, as participants argue for privileging certain reasons and dismissing others in certain situations. Needless to say, different reasons are persuasive to different audiences, who may react to the same reason differently on different occasions.

- "Resolving problematic situations." Deliberation is not usually called for where people agree. Rather, deliberation is used to resolve controversies in a fashion satisfactory to the parties involved. Controversies contingently close through compromise or, more promisingly, through the transformation of how citizens perceive a problem that creates new avenues for resolution.[71] Addressing and resolving these issues in public venues, as opposed to smoke-filled back rooms, lends greater legitimacy to the decisions made in the collective's name. The consent of the governed is the bedrock of democratic governance, and as more citizens are absorbed into processes of deliberation, the chances that they recognize the results as legitimate are generally increased.

- "Cannot be settled without interpersonal coordination and cooperation." Deliberation is an alternative to the raw exercise of power. While controversies are often seen as intractable and based on incommensurable differences, the fact that deliberation occurs at all presupposes certain commonalities—that differences can be attended to through symbols instead of fists, that all stakeholders should be allowed to voice their opinions, and that good-faith efforts to understand alternative viewpoints are desirable.

Deliberation is no panacea for all public problems; yet, to adapt Winston Churchill's famous quote about democracy, public deliberation is probably the worst form of conflict resolution except all those other forms tried from time to time. Developing a robust democratic public culture requires a combination of formal and informal sites for citizens to come together and compare notes about collective life.[72] These sites of deliberation—public spheres—are communicative arenas where the shape of public life is thematized, problematized, revised, and enacted. The bar, book club, email listserv, backyard barbeque, blogosphere, and coffeehouse thus constitute public spheres whenever citizens turn their attention to affairs that bear on the broader questions of living together.

My fairly permissive view on public spheres as sites of civic argument accounts for the kind of conversation happening rather than the kind of medium it is happening through. Admittedly, anxiety about the state of the public sphere tends to increase whenever new media rearrange patterns of communication and interaction. Habermas's *Structural Transformation* is an exemplar of this genre, featuring mass (communication-audience-culture) as an offending adjective indicative of a culture-consuming rather than culture-debating society. This critique mirrored a widespread fear among elites of the early to mid-twentieth century that mass culture would deaden citizens' critical faculties by appealing to the lowest common denominator.[73] Though Habermas eventually backpedaled on this position (with copious assistance from research in communication, media, and cultural studies), the underlying concern about the deflation of the late modern public sphere is a common refrain.[74] Richard Sennett's *The Fall of Public Man* (1974) and Robert Putnam's *Bowling Alone: The Collapse and Revival of American Community* (2000) similarly advance this declinist view of the late modern public sphere.[75] The declinist narrative goes something like this: citizens of the United States were once filled with a public-oriented spirit characterized by the rich associational contexts that de Tocqueville identified ("America was a nation of joiners"), but are now plagued by atomized, individualistic pursuits like watching television or, more contemporarily, playing on the mobile phone. Sennett inverts the thesis that David Riesman developed in his landmark 1950 book *The Lonely Crowd*. Riesman bemoaned the rise of the outer-directed personality that gauged self-worth from external markers like consumption ("keeping up with the Joneses") and approval of others (evidenced by the popularity of books like Dale Carnegie's *How to Win Friends and Influence People*). Outer-directed personalities supplanted the inner direction of prior generations cultivated through engagement with arts and play. Sennett claims, instead, that citizens were becoming inner-directed to the point of total self-absorption, leaving behind the outer-directedness necessary to maintain a vibrant public. Arendtian echoes reverberate in this hypothesis: without the sharing of word and deeds in public, the preconditions for an effective public sphere dissipate.

Putnam's *Bowling Alone* extends this declinist hypothesis with extensive social science data somewhat overshadowed by the representative anecdote reflected in the title. The public was glued to private television sets instead of heading to the community-building lanes, prompting Putnam to (melodramatically) wonder, in a chapter title, "What Killed Civic Engagement?" For Putnam, the cultural changes initiated by the mass media are telling indicators of the decline of community and social capital. At the beginning of the twentieth century, music aficionados trekked to the town's music or dance hall to listen, as a group, to a program. By the end of the twentieth century, Putnam bemoans the fact that he could rock out (or, as the case may be, waltz out) to his "hi-fi Walkman CD" player whenever and wherever he wanted.[76] There's more in this observation than a lesson in how rapidly media technologies become antiquated. Putnam's hypothesis is that the abundance of personal media produces a fragmented, privatized population interested more in infotainment than civic engagement. We are, in Neil Postman's inimitable phrasing, "amusing ourselves to death," a sentiment captured in cultural critic Kurt Cobain's mumbling of "here we are now / entertain us."[77] Instead of a bustling Main Street or downtown, which, like the agora, drew diverse groups together for a mix of shopping and social interaction, postwar suburbs spurred the development of shopping malls that catered to affluent, usually white, consumers. "[T]he commercializing, privatizing, and segmenting of physical gathering places that has resulted from allowing the unfettered pursuit of profits to dictate a new metropolitan landscape," explains historian Lizabeth Cohen, "has made more precarious the shared public sphere upon which democracy depends."[78] Sennett, Putnam, and to some extent Cohen breathe new life into Habermas's fear that late modern democracies are culture-consuming (or just plain old consuming!) rather than culture-debating societies.

Would the internet, with promises of "virtual community" swirling around in the mid-1990s, counteract the decline in social capital provided by more traditional face-to-face engagement? Perhaps, according to Putnam, but the jury was still out on whether the internet would become "predominantly a means of active, social communication or a means of passive, private entertainment" like television.[79] This binarization (active-passive, social-private) rigs the game too much in favor of the declinist narrative. Blogging, moreover, confounds these simple dichotomies. Is reading a blog passive, because it is receiving information from a screen? Is it active, because it often involves intense cognitive processing of the rhetorical activity of others? Is it public, because it is interactive and involves a community of commenters and bloggers weighing in on an issue? Is it private, because the experience of blog reading is usually done alone? These questions suggest that the pessimistic assessment of the late modern public sphere's status requires reconsideration in light of digitally networked mediation.

Digital Communication Networks as Cultural Technologies of Publicity

The preceding account of the decline of the public sphere is by no means uncontested. Even before the growth of the internet as a medium for public communication, the work of the public was still done through the mass media, social movements, and citizen gatherings on a different scale, in different forms, and with different levels of success than the Athenian agora or bourgeois public sphere claimed. While Putnam's skepticism about the early internet's civic potential was warranted, the rapid growth of blogging—and eventually other, similar forms of networked media—testifies to a vitalization of public deliberation. Indeed, the steady diffusion of blogging from 2000 to 2006 could be interpreted as a manifestation of citizens' desire to fill the void created by the deterioration of public spaces like the much-idealized town hall and Main Street.[80] Though many early bloggers were professional writers, many more were simply opinionated citizens who spent hours and hours blogging without monetary compensation. These bloggers settled for compensation of a decidedly civic type, enjoying the intrinsic goods of conversation and argument, strengthening existing relationships while making new acquaintances, and shaping public conversation on current affairs.[81] That older modes of public congregation, like the bowling league, weakened does not necessarily imply that social networking and public argument disappeared with them. New patterns of communicative interdependence are blossoming in the "networked public sphere," a term that reflects the civic intercast of communication under conditions of digital mediation. Historically, networks are a crucial cultural technology of publicity—the agora and bourgeois public sphere were, if nothing else, communication networks that made rhetoric public. But as Manuel Castells's work on the network society shows, the power of networks is revved up by the diffusion of digital media technology.[82] Castells contends, "as a historical trend, dominant functions and processes in the Information Age are increasingly organized around networks. Networks constitute the new social morphology of our societies, and the diffusion of networking logic substantially modifies the operation and outcomes in processes of production, experience, power, and culture."[83] Digital communication networks now enfold and refigure the prior cultural technologies of publicity of rhetoric and the public sphere.

The "network society" is Castells's term for the changes triggered by the interconnection of a globalizing economy, the development of new information technologies, and the changing norms of public culture.[84] Castells's commitment to avoiding determinism, which I share, requires appreciating how these three interlocking motors of change destabilize modern social arrangements and precipitate new, networked imaginaries. Economically, the post–World War II crisis of industrialism resulted in an erosion of the manufacturing base for many countries, ultimately producing a service economy founded on symbolic dexterity. State and corporate policy decisions, alongside changes in supply and demand, encouraged a global economy to develop as the master network of economic networks. Globalization features layers of industrial firms manufacturing goods in one place, and, through serial subcontracting, delivering and selling them in another. The flows of global capital, and to a much lesser extent labor, incidentally broadened cultural interactions between populations that were heretofore largely cordoned off from one another by national borders. The very idea of a global economic structure requires a global communication system, for companies need a way of sending messages to different parts of the world more efficiently than horseback or train allow. As information technologies evolved from the fax machine to email, so did the possibilities of globalization. At the same time, the rearrangement of the conventional business model from stuff-oriented to fluff-oriented exacted costs from quintessentially modern intermediaries like the newspaper industry. The reading of a physical newspaper, in steady decline for decades, plunged further with the growth of internetworked intermediaries. Why pay for the stuff of a physical newspaper when one can read the fluff for free? Why wade through the digital version of the newspaper, studded with obnoxious advertisements, when one can get the main idea in a series of pull quotes on blogs?[85]

Technologically, the advances in computerized communication networks during the 1970s rival the invention of the alphabet or the printing press. Specifically, the development of the microprocessor in 1971 allowed the miniaturization of computing technology and thus the panoply of devices that constitute the contemporary digitally networked infrastructure. For Bruce Bimber, these technological advances create information-intensive environments with five effects on the circulation of civic knowledge: (1) expanding the number of low-cost channels to distribute information from political organizations; (2) allowing elites and organizations to gain access to low-cost information, creating a greater tailoring of political messages; (3) providing forums for citizens to engage in many-to-many, lateral communication; (4) accelerating the circulation of news in a massively interlinked, global circuit; and (5) archiving information on a scale and with accessibility never before seen.[86] Taken alone, any one of these would be a significant development. Together, these five features underline the dramatically different circulation of communication under conditions of digitally networked mediation.

Alongside economic and technological changes is the rise of cultural pluralism. In the United States, power brokers in government, business, and culture were predominantly privileged white men until the mid-twentieth century. Cultural homogeneity was reinforced pedagogically at disciplinary sites, like schools, with predictable communicative consequences. Rhetorical critic Michael Calvin McGee brilliantly describes this homogenization:

> In the not-too-distant past. . . . [e]ducation was restricted to a scant minority, and as a result the content of an education was so homogeneous that an orator could utter two or three lines in Latin, identified only with the words "as Tully said," in complete confidence that any reader/audience/critic would be able to identify the source of the words—and even recite the next several lines from Cicero's *De Oratore*! Except for everyday conversation, all discourse within a particular language community was produced from the same resources.

Further, all discourse found its influence on the same small class of people who comprised the political nation. And it was the same small class that received the benefits of a homogenized education. There was little cultural diversity, no question that there was in every state a well-defined dominant race, dominant class, dominant gender, dominant history, and dominant ethnicity.[87]

The sacrosanct nature of traditional texts dissipated as public culture became more heterogenous.[88] Cultural pluralism accelerated with the new social movements of the 1960s and '70s that rejected the suffocating sameness of the post-war 1950s. In May 1968, student movements in France decided that they were not satisfied with a future defined by a grey flannel suit and life as an "Organization Man" (part of the student movement critique was that women were structurally prevented from applying for positions of power in public organizations). Instead of surrendering to a lifetime of vertical ladder climbing, citizens involved in this and similar movements fanned out into more horizontally structured affinity groups. Their ability to (temporarily) stop French society drew heightened attention to movements revaluing the norms, styles, and values of historically marginalized groups.

The new social movements, according to Castells, were oriented toward transforming "the value of freedom and individual autonomy vis-à-vis the institutions of society and the power of corporations; the value of cultural diversity and the affirmation of the rights of minorities, ultimately expressed in terms of human rights; and the value of ecological solidarity."[89] These new social movements problematized the grand narratives of modernity captured in ideographs like progress, enlightenment, freedom, and even science. Rather than useful values to motivate human flourishing, these terms were identified as dangerous cultural constructions carrying oppressive baggage. It was in the wake of these movements that artistic and intellectual currents labeled "postmodernism" flourished.[90] Postmodern critique draws attention to the inadequacies of modern imaginaries in providing a normative baseline for how contemporary culture should be organized.[91] Of course, one can't be "post-" forever; at some point, cultural organization takes on affirmative qualities. The network society, or, alternatively, internetworked public culture, is this affirmative description.

The networked media ecology both manages and creates complexity. As Castells acknowledges, networked forms of organization are coexistent with human culture (gossip networks, for instance, historically regulated communities). However, "beyond a certain threshold of size, complexity, and volume of exchange, [networks] become less efficient than vertically organized command and control structures, *under the conditions of pre-electronic communication technology*."[92] To realize efficiency gains, actors in modern societies tended to structure networks into differentiated, vertical, and institutionalized systems of knowledge and organization. These vertical hierarchies formed effective attention structures capable of addressing many of the problems societies faced as they became more complex. For example, legislative bodies are centralized, vertical institutions of deliberation ideally designed to focus attention on problems in the lifeworld and suitable for managing the level of complexity in the modern era. But our contemporary moment is in part defined by a ratcheting up of complexity akin to the increase in complexity from premodern to modern cultures. The shift in complexity isn't from rural to urban living arrangements, as in industrialization, but from local to global scales of interrelationship. The shift isn't from the sporadic, irregular news updates through the mail to the daily punctuation of the newspaper, but from this daily punctuation to a continuous and instantaneous news cycle. These changes reverse the centralization of attention structures through the mass media and institutions that were a defining feature of modern public cultures. Instead, internetworked cultures privilege decentralized attention structures that rely on modes of postpublication filtration to direct publics' attention.

In hypercomplex societies, networked media empower a whole set of new political intermediaries—bloggers, wikipedians, social bookmarkers, and video artists—as participants in and organizers of public argument.[93] Digital communication networks interconnect these new nodes where communication is produced, circulated, and/or received. Each node functions as a potential relay for information, obviating the need for a central node to collect, parse, and distribute. But not all nodes are created equally. Communication networks, contrary to the libertarian fantasy of better living through networked media, are shaped by the social: gender, race, class, religion, sexual orientation, and other identity features shape the centrality of any given node.[94] The importance of a node is also related to the communicative functionality it provides. As Castells explains, "nodes increase their importance for the network by absorbing more relevant information, and processing it more efficiently. The relative importance of a node does not stem from its specific features but from its ability to contribute to the network's goals. . . . When nodes become redundant or useless, networks tend to reconfigure themselves, deleting some nodes, and adding new ones."[95] This generic account of networks fits the blogosphere, where reputations rise and fall based in part on the speed, frequency, and quality of contribution—in other words, based on their ability to process information rhetorically into something meaningful.

Castells's emphasis on nodes underlines the value of digitally networked forms of organization: "their self-expanding processing and communicating capacity in terms of their volume, complexity, and speed; their ability to recombine on the basis of digitization and recurrent communication; [and] their distributing flexibility through interactive, digitized networking."[96] These features—scalability, survivability, and flexibility—are refractable through a blogcentric prism. First, digital networks are scalable, able to serve small publics or global ones. The blogosphere includes subnetworks of differing complexity, from the simple, personal blog aimed at the small world of friends and family to larger, more densely interconnected and global public blogs. Bloggers utilize more or less free storage space and broadband access to handle the volume of their communication, which can be minimal at some times and voluminous at others.[97] Unlike more sclerotic media institutions, bloggers can adapt to changing conditions, easily adapting the frequency, quantity, and style of blog posts as needed.

Second, digital networks are survivable—call it the "DARPA effect." The Department of Defense's Defense Advanced Research Projects Agency (DARPA) is often credited with initiating research on internetworked communication to ensure a survivable communications network following a nuclear attack. As a consequence, the distributed nature of digital communication networks defies conventional regulation. In China, state censors block blogs that are critical of the Communist Party. But there simply are not enough censors to track every blog, never mind all the other genres of networked media, and networked intermediaries can use privacy software to evade their watchers.[98] When the Iranian government cut off access to the internet through broadband lines in the wake of the 2009 election protests, Iranians flocked to networked media, like Twitter, accessible through mobile phones. Although censorship is a serious problem, often with deadly consequences, efforts at state control of the internet are akin to squeezing one end of a long balloon. Censorship of digital communication networks is a prominent demonstration of the drastic mismatch between modern sensibilities and networked logics, as blocking information flows is only temporarily successful in an era of survivable networks.

Finally, digital networks are flexible. The sheer diversity of blogs shows how they meet networked citizens' needs for civic engagement, entertainment, DIY craft advice, and virtually every other topic of interest imaginable. The flexibility of blogs is enhanced through the process of digitization, which aids media convergence. While blogging began as primarily a text-based activity (in this way, early bloggers could be considered "throwback publics" invigorated by a refamiliarization with textuality), it is now a decidedly multimodal communication form, integrating images, audio, and video. This flexibility in terms of rhetorical production is matched by flexibility in linking practices. Bloggers ascend and descend a ladder of influence as linking practices change over time. Some bloggers hit the "A-list" owing to a certain diligence, or a specific area of expertise, or timely contributions, or simply because they are hilarious. Digital networks are flexible enough to prioritize certain nodes over others, depending on the situation.

Castells's account of the network society compellingly names our contemporary moment, directing attention to how the cultural technology of digital communication networks shapes public culture. Neither Castells nor I see the network society as being a total break from the past or an inevitable, totalizing phenomenon. The following four caveats about the network society hypothesis are intended to check the potential cyberutopian impulses, or "web apologetics," latent in considering the implications of this brave new networked world.[99]

Caveat 1: Networked sensibilities are situated between unifying underlying logics and multiplying cultural practices. It would be inaccurate, and potentially dangerous, to assert one unified and totalizing version of internetworked public culture. Just as Dilip Gaonkar observes that there are multiple modernities, so are there culturally specific instantiations of networked public cultures.[100] Yet for all the variety that exists among various cultural formations, there are also striking parallels across them. Modernity introduced challenges associated with industrialization, the secularization of value, and the spread of science as influential cross-cultural phenomena; so, too, must contemporary public cultures accommodate globalization, diversity, and information abundance.[101] These are common challenges with culturally specific variations. If the metaphors constituting the networked rhetorical imaginary derived from each case study of *Networked Media, Networked Rhetorics* are indicative of fundamental changes wrought by networked media, then the insights generated by my analysis of each trope are, with the necessary tweaks and accommodations, portable to other cultural contexts. It is fair to ask, though, how long these culturally distinct variations will persist. If, historically, different imaginaries congealed because of geographic distance, how different can different imaginaries be in a global and communicatively interconnected world?

Caveat 2: Theories of networked public culture do not account for much of the world that remains un-networked by information technology. The digital divide looms as a marker of major inequalities within and between certain nation-states. To some extent, these inequalities were created during the modern era, especially through colonization, and demand serious redress (if it is, indeed, desirable for the entire globe to be internetworked). We should be careful not to paper over the serious access inequities that persist into the twenty-first century. Digitally networked societies profit, in part, based on an ability to offload the nastier parts of modernity, like resource extraction, onto less densely networked—and regulated—countries.[102] But, as the science fiction writer William Gibson famously declared, "the future is already here, it's just not evenly distributed."[103] The general trend is toward cheaper computing devices able to interact with the global internet, and it is difficult to imagine a world where this process stops or reverses—barring an apocalyptic tragedy. Moreover, Castells argues that despite a persistent digital divide, "everybody is affected by the processes that take place in the global networks of this dominant social structure . . . because the core activities that shape and control human life in every corner of the planet are organized in these global networks."[104] Consequently, theorizing public deliberation in intensively digitally networked cultures is a crucial element in understanding the very possibilities for global justice.

Caveat 3: There are significant counter-trends to the internetworking of culture. The most obvious of these counter-trends are fundamentalisms of all stripes. Many fundamentalists are not satisfied with returning society to modern times, for nothing less than a total rollback to premodern value structures will satisfy them. While terrorist networks like al-Qaeda are often pointed to as the prime proponents of premodern fundamentalism, certain strands of evangelical Christianity and orthodox Judaism also represent counter-trends to internetworked public culture. Of course, fundamentalism extends beyond religion. Market fundamentalism, as represented by Milton Friedman and the Chicago School, is similarly under threat, as the conventional logics of capitalism are being revised in an era of networks. Despite their best efforts, a smart wager is that fundamentalists will lose traction in contemporary public life precisely because their antiquarian prescriptions no longer match networked sensibilities. At the same time, the unpredictability of transition, and the flexibility required to live in networked public cultures, may well trigger reactionary spasms of fundamentalist movements. The networking of public culture proceeds in fits and starts, in uneven if somewhat concentric circles, subject to a host of unpredictable social, economic, and political factors. But it is a genie unlikely to be returned to the bottle.

Caveat 4: Networked sensibilities hybridize, rather than supplant, modern sensibilities. It would be an error of the first degree to assume that networked logics can sweep away more than four hundred years of modern history. The basic elements of the modern social imaginary—citizenship, the nation-state, markets, and democracy—are here to stay in some capacity. This is not to say that they will not face significant challenges and need refashioning to be serviceable for contemporary public life. These legacies of modernity must hybridize by incorporating networked sensibilities. The contemporary media ecology shows this hybridization, as the traditional news article published in the morning paper is now coupled with regularly updated blogs authored by the newspaper's journalists and available around the clock on newspaper websites. So, too, must a key inheritance from the modern imaginary hybridize: the public sphere. If the early modern public sphere hybridized the agora's principle of openness and appreciation for rhetorical performance with the new print medium and bourgeois cultural values, then we might well expect the public sphere to rehybridize in the context of networks and the norms of contemporary public culture. The splicing of the network metaphor into the public sphere provides the conditions for a fundamental transformation of a quintessentially modern concept.

The objection might reasonably be raised that retaining the term "public sphere" is a lost, or worthless, cause. Indeed, it is entirely possible—even likely—that another term will ultimately arise to supplant the notion of the public sphere.[105] But in this transitional moment, it is the networking of the old public sphere organs and the ascendance of new deliberative actors into a networked public sphere that is visible. Despite the familiar criticisms of the public sphere—that it is a spatial metaphor for a set of nonspatial practices, that it assumes a monolithic entity, that it privileges those with power—conceptualizing civic communication as functioning in a networked public sphere is preferable to abandoning the term. First, many of the criticisms of the "public sphere" are made possible through a curious translation choice of *Öffentlichkeit*, the German word Habermas uses to describe the bourgeois public sphere. *Öffentlichkeit* is more faithfully translated as "publicness" or "openness," suggesting a *process* of testing ideas in the crucible of public argumentation.[106] The translation of *Öffentlichkeit* into "public sphere" metonymized the spatial dimension of the public square at the expense of the imagined. That metonymy gradually loosened as mass and then networked media delinked communication from spatial co-presence. The concept of the public sphere *should* function as an inclusive metaphor for communication dedicated to the civic as a way to guide collective, democratic opinion formation. Second, the idea of the public sphere is a legacy of modernity so firmly rooted in our intellectual traditions that resisting the term conceptually may well be futile. It is exceptionally resilient as a charismatic marker of deliberative forums.[107] The portmanteau "blogosphere" shows how attractive—and portable—the public sphere is in representing the values of open, public, democratic discussion.[108] Finally, I follow Burke in noting how banishing terms simply conceals their function.[109] Jettisoning the language of the public sphere in the hopes that some new conceptualization of public deliberation would somehow avoid problems associated with the trio of challenges surrounding invention, emotion, and expertise risks a cyberutopianism of the most unsupportable sort. Instead of wiping away this legacy of modernity, refracting our understanding of contemporary public deliberation through the logic of networks offers a more pragmatic way to consider the opportunities and challenges of civic life.

Although the networking of the public sphere is still in its infancy, it bears all the markings of a structural transformation on par with Habermas's articulation of the original structural transformation.[110] In the longer term, this transformation will surely rearrange social categories, relationships, and imaginaries in ways that are barely perceptible now. However, the contours of the networked public sphere are detectable. Yochai Benkler describes the networked public sphere as shifting from a hub-and-spoke model with unidirectional communication flows to a more distributed communication architecture with bidirectional links enabled by the lowering of publication costs.[111] The distributed architecture of the networked public sphere disintermediates traditional actors, like the press, by expanding the number of intermediaries capable of generating publicity. "Attention in the networked environment," Benkler suggests, "is more dependent on being interesting to an engaged group of people than it is in the mass-media environment, where moderate interest to large numbers of weakly engaged viewers is preferable."[112] In addition, many citizens now conceive of their participation in public discourse in qualitatively different ways that encourage argumentation.[113] These citizens engage in an "information-driven structure" rather than an "event-driven structure" like the press, meaning that they parse bits of information as they are circulated rather than waiting for traditional news pegs like press conferences.[114] Although the decentering of traditional intermediaries in favor of a multiplicity of attention gatekeepers risks cacophony, Benkler concludes that "the network seems to be forming an attention backbone" that is more resistant than the modern public sphere to noncommunicative steering media like money.[115] Thus, as the case studies endeavor to show, the networked public sphere maintains some of the democratic functions of the early modern public sphere despite the fact that the imaginary of the seventeenth-century bourgeois no longer prevails.[116]

Conclusion

The networked public sphere ought to be seen as an outgrowth of the agora and the modern public sphere. Rhetoric, the public sphere, and digital communication networks share, as cultural technologies of publicity, a central role in sustaining argument about civic culture. I have attempted to blur the lines between rhetoric, the public sphere, and digital communication networks, arguing that the networked public sphere is a unique hybridization of the three cultural technologies. This is in contrast to Pettitt's conception of the Gutenberg Parenthesis. Pettitt explains that he is "attracted by the way 'parenthesis' suggests development over time: a before, a during and an after, with the implication that the postparenthetical period after and the pre-parenthetical period before may have more in common with each other than either has with the parenthetical phase that came in between: syntactically a parenthesis interrupts a line of thought which resumes when the parenthesis closes."[117] The Gutenberg Parenthesis (as a rhetorical figure) directs our attention to how the communicative patterns of internetworked cultures resemble those of the agora even more then the late modern public sphere.

This is a heuristically powerful claim, but it overstates the synchronicity between classical and networked communication norms, for two reasons. First, one key variable preventing a smooth resumption of pre-parenthetical sensibilities in the postparenthetical era is the evolution of communication media. Rhetorical practice in ancient Greece assumed small, homogenous communities that thrived in face-to-face settings. The conditions of networked media, as the case studies make clear, alter communicative practices. To take a simple example, *ethos* in the Greek context could be established as one lives in community with others, but as globally networked citizens we cannot so easily judge the character of a distant blogger. Second, the communicative norms of broad stretches of historical time cannot be so easily generalized. Conceptualizing preparenthetical norms as discrete entities risks assuming the universality of those norms. But communicative norms are always disputed, even within a particular public culture. The contest between Aristotle and Plato over the status of rhetoric, for example, provides a template for this disputation—one only modestly revised over the past two and a half millennia.

Thus, the key divergence when theorizing communicative norms is not, perhaps, so much between the classical (preparenthetical), modern (inside the parenthesis), and networked (postparenthetical), although there is much heuristic value in conceiving of these as distinct *public cultures* with dominant media that support particular kinds of democratic gatherings and expressive possibilities. Instead, the key difference is between rhetorical and informationist models of communication that are at work in every era. To reinterpret Pettitt, then, postparenthetical networked communication norms share more in common with the *rhetorical* norms of classical Greece than the more *informationist* norms of late modernity. Perhaps, then, a milder rhetorical figure could replace the relative harshness of the parenthesis: the Gutenberg Comma. As a figure, commas offset a phrase, but are integrated more smoothly into the syntactical flow. When used well, commas provide crucial clarification to the broader sentence's meaning. In this way, modernity ought not be theorized as an interruption but as a historically situated cultural formation that is crucial to understanding contemporary communication. The network form does not sweep away late modern informationist communicative norms so much as it provides a robust alternative to those norms by facilitating the reintegration of rhetorical sensibilities regarding invention, emotion, and expertise.

3

FLOODING THE ZONE AFTER TRENT LOTT'S TOAST

Bloggers' use of inventive reasoning to transform public argument puts the *logos* in the blogosphere. For Aristotle, *logos* was a mode of proof that involved finding the right reasoning or argument, which, "by showing or seeming to show something," would move an audience.[1] In the blogosphere, the generation of inventive rhetoric is a visible and dynamic process. The key word here is *generation*: argumentation is a social act that sparks the invention of novel perspectives. When this sense of invention is placed at the heart of *logos*, rhetoric becomes a substantive rather than ornamental art, capable of shaping attention patterns in ways that transform controversies.[2] Trent Lott's infamous December 2002 toast to Strom Thurmond, in which he made comments perceived as sympathetic to segregationist politics, displays some of the blogosphere's specific inventional capacities. I begin with *logos* for a few reasons: chronologically, the Trent Lott toast is widely considered "the founding myth of the blogosphere's journalistic potency"; rhetorically, Aristotle prioritized *logos* as the primary proof, with *ethos* and *pathos* subordinate to it; and pragmatically, it is the most straightforward case of how bloggers affect deliberation through argument.[3]

I begin in a metarhetorical vein, tracing metaphors of invention throughout the history of rhetoric. This metarhetorical investigation identifies a recurring tension in how diverse rhetorical traditions conceptualize invention: invention is considered either as a product of one who *discovers* some external truth *or* as a process through which one *generates* an argument.[4] The discovery model of invention assumes that the truth is out there and that, through some approved rationalist enterprise, a thinker apprehends and transmits it to others. This is the informationist model of invention. The data speak; they just need some finding. The generative model of invention is considerably more pragmatic, assuming truth is made, not found. In this latter model, there is no assumption of a capital-T

Truth "out there" to be found, but arguers, all too occasionally, agree upon what is often referred to colloquially as little-t truths. The generative model of invention assumes that the very process of arguing transforms how the involved parties attend to an issue by revealing unpredictable lines of argument and novel interpretations.[5] These two models of invention are often seen as polarities. Yet neither provides a wholly satisfactory account of invention in deliberation. The discovery model undercuts citizen participation by presuming that "facts" are not transformed through argument from diverse standpoints. The generative model too easily ignores the recalcitrance of the world.[6] A rhetorical perspective on invention cuts across the middle, recognizing *kairotic* moments requiring a blending of discovery and generativity.[7] This is especially so in the context of public *moral* argument that relies on contested or uncertain facts to make value judgments.

Far from being an idiosyncratic preoccupation of rhetorical history, I sketch this tension between discovery and generativity to help explain the clash between the traditional institutional press and the early blogosphere. I then examine the Trent Lott imbroglio, with a particular focus on the deployment of the trope "flood the zone" as a signifier of the inventional prowess of the blogosphere. Next, I broaden my scope to consider the role of invention in the networked public sphere, specifically taking issue with Habermas's critique of digitally networked intermediaries. In the final section of this chapter, I examine how flooding the zone is co-opted by democratically unaccountable institutions to frustrate deliberation.

Invention Between Discovery and Generation

How is it that an inventor—of things or of rhetoric—comes up with an idea? To reduce the inventional process to a series of eurekas is surely too simplistic. This question, while abstract, is a critical one for understanding bloggers' roles in producing rhetoric that influences deliberation. Invention is usually considered a black box, a process that can be hinted at and talked around but not explicitly detailed. John Muckelbauer conjectures that invention "cannot be *explained* representationally (as if it were a theme or an idea). Perhaps it can only be *demonstrated* performatively."[8] Over the course of rhetoric's history, this inexplicability of invention produces highly metaphorical accounts of the inventional process that ping-pong between rhetorical and informationist orientations.

The earliest model of invention in the Greek tradition leans toward the generative end of the inventional spectrum. The Sophists, who preceded Plato, Aristotle, and Isocrates, deployed a model of invention elegant in its simplicity. The fragment known as *dissoi logoi*, the theory of conntervailing or twofold arguments, grounds this model of invention.[9] From this fragment, and what we know about the contentiousness of the Sophists, contrariness or clash appears to be the dominant metaphor of invention in Sophistic thought.[10] By pitting two ideas against each other, a rhetor generates new insights into or transformations of public argument. Hegel's gloss on the Sophists emphasizes that their focus on eloquence was "to show the manifold points of view existing in a thing, and to give force to those which harmonize with what appears to me to be more useful."[11] Embracing the artistry of language invites us to pay attention to a thing in multiple ways, prompting alternative ways of thinking about an issue. This conflictual model reflects the internal dialogue that an inventor of public discourse engages in, since thinking itself is modeled on public debate.[12] Instead of trying to find the *truer* argument, the Sophists judged on the criteria of the *better* argument, as tested by the ability of an argument to withstand public criticism.[13] This Sophistic model of invention is adopted most memorably in the twentieth century by the pragmatist John Dewey: "Conflict is the gadfly of thought. It stirs us to observation and memory. It instigates to invention. It shocks us out of sheeplike passivity, and sets us at noting and contriving."[14] Bloggers, in their own disputatiousness, often follow this Sophistic sense of invention through clashing arguments.

Plato's philosophy reacted to the teachings of the Sophists, whom he considered rhetorically promiscuous and thus amoral. He countered the Sophists' more generative model with one closer to the discovery end of the spectrum, which comported with his peculiar blend of metaphysics and epistemology. As Plato's Socrates tells Phaedrus, reasoning "is a remembering of what our soul once saw as it made its journey with a god, looking down upon what we now assert to be real and gazing upwards at what is Reality itself."[15] It is significant, then, that the Platonic term for truth is *aletheia*, literally unforgetfulness or unconcealing. For Plato, unforgetting the truth is a gradual process achievable only through dialectic. Karen LeFevre analogizes this process to "plants growing from seeds ... invention is the unfolding of the individual's ideas, feelings, personality, patterns, or voice, all of which are seen as existing independently of others."[16] This seed metaphor most accurately mirrors Plato's model of invention.

Like the seed, whose genetic code provides a *telos* that guides growth, the materials needed for invention are already encoded in the soul and will, if necessity demands it, bear fruit. Invention occurs according to an inner plan, regardless of the influence of others. Care for a seed encourages it to flourish and neglect makes it wither; so, too, with the soul. Just as the mixing of good and bad seeds can ruin a crop, the mixing of good and bad souls can ruin a *polis*. This is why Plato argues that introspection is the only route to real knowledge, and why social intercourse undermines the philosophic act. The flip side of this perspective is seeing invention as a social process, where the act of arguing manifests innovative insights, understandings, and judgments.

By identifying invention as the primary value of rhetoric, Aristotle's teachings on rhetoric contrast with Plato's philosophy: "[Rhetoric's] function is not to persuade but to see the available means of persuasion in each case."[17] "To see" translates from *theoresai*, meaning "to be an observer of and to grasp the meaning or utility of." The "available means of persuasion" translates from *to endekhomenon pithanon*, interpreted as "what is inherently and potentially persuasive" in a case. For Walter Ong, the visual metaphor tied to knowledge production for the ancient Greeks gives invention a highly "visual and spatial component: one *looks* for things in order to find them; one *comes* upon them."[18] A rhetor who can observe and grasp the significance of potential objections is more likely to account for them and thus make a stronger case to an audience.

The visual is only one component of Aristotle's larger topographical metaphor for invention. For Aristotle, being able to see the means of persuasion requires a sophisticated understanding of the *topoi*, which renders as "place" or "location," of reasoning. The *topoi*, also referred to as commonplaces, are general or specific argument schemes rhetors use to build an argument toward a certain conclusion. The opposition *topos* is an example of the *topoi*: "to be temperate is a good thing; for to lack self-control is harmful."[19] This sort of commonsense reasoning historically made the *topoi* useful argumentative shortcuts that rhetors were wise to understand. Aristotle recommends, in a topographical spirit, that "any one who intends to frame questions must, first of all, select the ground from which he [sic] should make his attack; secondly, he must frame them and arrange them one by one to himself; thirdly and lastly, he must proceed actually to put them to the other party."[20] "Ground," in the preceding quotation, is sometimes translated as "vantage point," lending weight to the centrality of the topographical metaphor.[21] When building a case, rhetors must find the high ground, for the higher they climb, the better the range of their vision and thus their ability to observe or grasp the available means of persuasion.[22]

Cicero and his fellow Roman rhetorician Quintilian tweaked Aristotle's topological theory of the commonplaces with venatic, or hunting, metaphors. Cicero's masterpiece *De Oratore* recommends "in art, in observation, and in practice alike, it is everything to be familiar with the ground over which you are to chase and track down your quarry."[23] The right argument is out there, but it demands a skilled hunter to detect the trail. Quintilian links this venatic metaphor specifically to the commonplaces:

> Let us now turn to the "places" (*locos*) in the sense of the secret place (*sedes*) where arguments reside, and from which they must be drawn forth. For just as all sorts of produce are not provided by every country, and as you will not succeed in finding a particular bird or beast, if you are ignorant of the localities where it has its usual haunts or birthplace, as even the various kinds of fish flourish in different surroundings, some preferring a smooth and others a rocky bottom, and are found on different shores and in diverse regions (you will for instance never catch a sturgeon or wrasse in Italian waters), so not every kind of argument can be derived from every circumstance.[24]

For Quintilian, commonplace arguments occupy their own ecology, distributed like species of fish across ponds and streams. Knowing where good arguments lie depends on knowledge of the shaded spots where they are likely to be. The venatic metaphor supports the discovery or the generative model of invention, depending on the vision of nature that subtends the metaphor. Either, as William Eamon hypothesizes, nature is a "geometrical cosmos . . . a reality whose essential features could be known by reason," or, as Cicero and Quintilian imply, it is a dense forest full of tracks and traces and signs that need interpreting.[25] So what happened between the time of Cicero and Quintilian, with their more generative sense of hunting for novel arguments, and the late modern, scientific rhetorical imaginaries that advantaged the discovery model? To put it succinctly: Christianity, the printing press, and Peter Ramus.

For much of the world influenced by Christianity, rhetoric became primarily a method of biblical hermeneutics. The rhetorical theory of Augustine of Hippo demonstrates this approach. Augustine began his career as a teacher of rhetoric at the end of the fourth century. Influenced by

Neoplatonist intellectual currents, he moved away from his more classically oriented rhetorical roots, converted to Christianity, and became a priest and theologian. Though the Church was able to take the teacher out of the rhetoric classroom, it could not strip the rhetorical worldview out of the teacher. Augustine tried to reconcile his prior commitments to rhetoric with the absolutist teachings of the Church. "The validity of logical sequences is not a thing devised by men," Augustine proclaims in *On Christian Doctrine*, "but is observed and noted by them that they may be able to learn and teach it; for it exists eternally in the reason of things, and has its origin with God."[26] This is an evolution of the discovery model, with God's Word, as documented in biblical scripture, replacing Plato's Forms. Augustine restricts invention to hermeneutics, identifying *logos* as "of very great service in searching into and unraveling all sorts of questions that come up in Scripture."[27] Invention, rather than being able to generate actionable areas of agreement in the secular realm, was tied instead "to the examination and solution of the ambiguities of Scripture."[28] The truth of the "good news" was to be apprehended by the audience, not developed by the speaker.[29] Invention thus becomes a tool for revelation.

The development of the printing press a millennium later reinforced discovery models of invention. By making available more texts, the printing press made it easier, as the old adage goes, to stand on the shoulders of giants. Although this colloquialism underlines how knowledge production is a generative and social process, print introduced a cultural logic that lionized the individual author by making texts traceable to producers in a way that oral tales were not. This feature of print culture intersected with the developing norms of capitalism and science to consolidate an individualistic interpretation of the creative act, most obviously through the idea of individual intellectual property rights.[30] Intellectual property rights codify in law a perspective on the inventional process as an individualized act of genius rather than a social, collective process of co-construction.[31]

Augustine's theology and the influence of print culture affirmed informationist sensibilities privileging the discovery model of invention. But it was the influence of Peter Ramus, a seventeenth-century French teacher and philosopher, that consolidated the discovery model in systems of modern education. His key move was to reorder the relationship between rhetoric and dialectic: "There are two parts of rhetoric: Style (*elocutio*) and Delivery (*prenuntiatio*); these are of course the only parts, the ones proper to the art.... Rhetoric therefore will keep this particular task, that it takes the matter found and related by Dialectic, and laid out in clear and correct speech by Grammar, and then embellishes it with the splendor of the ornaments of style, and renders it acceptable with the grace of vocal tone and gesture."[32] Ramus assigned invention to logic, consigning rhetoric to the task of making dialectic more palatable to listeners through ornamentation. The reassignment of invention from rhetoric to logic fell prey to the modern conceit that science would furnish the key equipment for a better world. As Scottish rhetorician Hugh Blair argued, "knowledge and science must furnish the materials that form the body and substance of any valuable composition. Rhetoric serves to add the polish."[33] This confluence of Christianity, the printing press, and Peter Ramus partially explains how the discovery model of invention came to dominate Western thinking. This is not, however, to suggest that generative models were not also present in modern times. Vico's early eighteenth-century rhetorical theory offers a pointed if underappreciated counter to the dominant discovery models: "we do not just discover the truth, but make it."[34] Nietzsche, in the late nineteenth century, famously noted that truth was an illusion that deflected attention from how language was a "mobile army of metaphors, metonyms, and anthropomorphisms."[35] More recently, scholars in mid-twentieth-century rhetorical studies attempted to retrieve invention from the clutches of informationism by relying on cosmological metaphors that hint at how the juxtaposition of alternative "worldviews" engenders novel perspectives.[36]

Tracing these two models of invention grounds my assessment of how the norms of networked media depart from the professed norms of traditional journalism. Many practitioners in the traditional press style themselves as reliant on a discovery model of invention, whereas participants in networked media operate more in the middle of discovery and generation. Though I want to be careful not to homogenize journalistic or blogging practice, the contrast can be made in general terms before examining how the specific instance of the Trent Lott case bears out the difference. Traditional broadcast journalism assumes that journalists need a particular kind of training to do journalism. This training involves learning how to trace evidence trails, assemble a cohesive narrative, write for an eighth-grade audience, and double- and triple-check sources (among other practices). The attitude bound up in the discovery model of invention, when taken to extremes, moots the value of citizen participation in public argument. Why get citizens involved when their contributions don't change the underlying facts of a case? This creates a deliberation trap, for journalists without an appreciation of the generative power of invention are likely to default to established sources in positions of power. Although access to these sources can be useful, an over-reliance on official sources, as the Lott case shows, artificially narrows public debate and diminishes the potential contributions emerging from more peripheral communicative actors.

Of course, actual journalistic practice can be seen as incredibly venatic (and thus generative), as journalists hunt for, assemble, and make sense of clues about a story. Though the back stage of journalism is generative, the front stage is styled around tropes of discovery. The professional norms of journalism—contested and dubious, but persistent—are objectivity, impartiality, and neutrality. The journalist ought to "seek truth and report it,"[37] establishing the verifiable facts of the case in concert with an editor specially trained in smoking out mendacity and obfuscation. Journalistic codes and ethics standards institutionalize these journalistic norms. These professional norms inculcate specific attitudes in journalistic practitioners. This is how ideology works: the modern imaginary positioned journalists at the center of the democratic process as arbiters of truth, and many journalists are successfully interpellated by these cultural assumptions.[38] Big-J Journalism is highly incentivized to claim privileged access to the truth; as a practice, it closely aligns with philosophy in its commitment to the discovery of the truth and belief in objective knowledge.[39] Blogging lines up with rhetoric inasmuch as practitioners largely eschew absolute truth claims, embrace partiality and interpretation, and more explicitly try to negotiate competing claims. This difference in orientation is partially related to audience: mass media developed norms of objectivity, impartiality, and neutrality to attract the largest possible audience, but networked media are able to narrowcast to more defined audiences and thus adapt their public discourse accordingly.[40] The blogosphere's more generative mode of invention relies on collaboratively piecing together communicative fragments to weave a polyvocal, even downright dissonant, account. Knowledge claims about controversies are not pronounced by a journalist or editor but gradually developed through an iterative back-and-forth process of public reason-giving through posts and comments. Truths are not discovered; they are made through a process of claim and counterclaim, revision and synthesis, and they only achieve some kind of truth status by becoming consistently useful.[41] While traditional journalism is invested in producing an argumentative *product*, a completed story that authoritatively reflects the day's events, bloggers engage in a *process* of public argument that is constantly evolving through the continuous and iterative publication of distinctive perspectives.[42] During this process, bloggers produce copious amounts of arguments with vastly varying quality, resulting in deep reservoirs of argument drawn upon by citizens in their engagements with each other.

My invocation of reservoir is not incidental, given how, in the words of Ulrich Beck, a "new metaphor of liquidity" carries growing explanatory power for theorists of contemporary public life.[43] Zygmunt Bauman describes contemporary conditions as "liquid modernity"; Arjun Appadurai underlines the importance of "navigating" assorted "cultural flows"; and Manuel Castells famously claims that the network society is structured by a "space of flows."[44] This liquid language permeates networked public cultures. Networked communication is bundled in *datastreams*, it *flows* through nodes and hubs, and it *saturates* our culture. Opinion and information more easily *cascade* in networked environments. One *surfs* the web and *streams* feeds. In 2001, Cass Sunstein's *Republic.com* popularized another liquid metaphor, *argument pools*, that would often be used to interpret the blogosphere's impact on deliberation. An argument pool supplies claims, reasons, and evidence to citizens. A shallow argument pool yields a slanted, superficial conversation, whereas a deep argument pool invites more robust consideration of multiple perspectives. According to Sunstein, citizens deal with information abundance by tailoring their attention economies to like-minded viewpoints that confirm preexisting ideological inclinations, thus producing ever-shallower argument pools from which citizens draw.[45] Networked media become a "driver of homogeneity" rather than, as the broadcast media purport to be, a "driver of opposition."[46] The result? Distributed enclaves of deliberation that foster extremism and foreclose opportunities to discover the common ground necessary to legitimate public deliberation. If public argument is sealed off from scrutiny in wider deliberative arenas, then the potential good that may arise from citizens conversing with each other will not be actualized.

Is there any role for enclaves in public deliberation? Even Sunstein acknowledges that enclaved deliberation occasionally improves the sophistication of reasoning, thus potentially deepening the reservoirs of argument that citizens draw upon in making decisions. The civil rights movement relied on protected sites of discussion to hone arguments before taking them to broader spheres of public deliberation. Robert Branham's exploration of how debating in prison fueled Malcolm X's argumentative prowess is an extreme, but salient, lesson in how enclaves at a remove from the public sphere can usefully fund public deliberation.[47] Enclaves, which can encompass cultural, material, and/or mediated publics, potentially function as rich sites for invention.[48] So, is the blogosphere a network of enclaves that produce shallow argument pools and cultural fragmentation? Or does the blogosphere, at least occasionally, function as a protected site capable of deepening argument pools that shape the broader public debate usefully? I aim to thread the needle between these two questions, arguing that, even with the risks of group polarization, the blogosphere performs a valuable democratic function by expanding the *topoi*, or lines of argument, that shape public deliberation. Bloggers do this, in the terms of another liquid metaphor, by *flooding the zone* with public discourse.

Bloggers Flood the Zone

Senator Strom Thurmond's one-hundredth birthday was celebrated in the Dirksen Senate Office Building on Thursday, December 5, 2002. Thurmond, who ran for president of the United States in 1948 on the Dixiecrat ticket as a stalwart segregationist, was retiring from the Senate after a long career. As Senate majority leader, Trent Lott took the stage to share some prepared comments about Thurmond. The senator from Mississippi soon veered off-script, saying, "I want to say this about my state: When Strom Thurmond ran for president, we voted for him. We're proud of it. And if the rest of the country had followed our lead, we wouldn't have had all these problems over all these years either."[49] These spontaneous comments were met with "an audible gasp and general silence" by the audience.[50] The epideictic occasion sublimated the potential significance of Lott's comments as other speakers effusively praised Thurmond's accomplishments. On Friday, December 6, the major metropolitan newspapers reported on the celebration of Thurmond's birthday, but made no mention of Lott's toast. The major television networks ran a total of one story on the toast, at 4:30 A.M. on December 6.[51] The lack of coverage is somewhat surprising, as the broadcast media tend to jump on stories when they first break in order to scoop the competition.[52] Yet it took almost a week after Lott made his comments for the story to resurface in the institutional press and set off a chain of events culminating in Lott's resignation.

Why did the mass media press not pursue this story with more fervor in the immediate hours and days following Lott's comments? Part of the answer involves the restriction of inventive rhetorical contributions resulting from the political economy of the mass media at the time. In the United States, during the thirty years leading up to 2000, fifty mass media firms had shrunk to just five.⁵³ The centralization of mass-mediated communication channels reduces opportunities for peripheral voices to break through established attention routines and reset the public agenda. This problem of viewpoint diversity is further compounded by the increase in syndicated material and the decrease in investigative journalism and newsroom workforces.⁵⁴ Finally, in the race for thin attention spurred by advertiser dollars, media institutions homogenize and polarize public opinion to dramatize conflict.⁵⁵ *The Daily Show* host Jon Stewart's memorable 2004 appearance on CNN's *Crossfire* articulated the erosion of the mass media press as a site of quality debate in the United States. Stewart called out co-hosts Tucker Carlson and Paul Begala as partisan hacks echoing stagnant talking points in an artificial "debate" format "hurting America."⁵⁶ The *Crossfire* model reflects tendencies across the institutional press: established pundits represent extreme opinions, their well-rehearsed sound bites aim at scoring immediate political gain, and the shades of grey that should color public controversies are glossed over because nuance makes for bad spectacle. The political economy of mass-mediated deliberation thus reduces the *topoi*—the manifold lines of inquiry that potentially populate any controversy—of public argument.

The specifics of the Lott case ground these general observations about the political economy of the mass media. Esther Scott argues that the Lott story failed to receive mass media press attention in the immediate wake of his comments because of the historical ignorance of reporters and editors, the phenomenon of pack journalism, and the absence of televisual conflict.⁵⁷ Veteran *Washington Post* writer Tom Edsall explained that his editors simply failed to recognize the significance of Lott's comments. Edsall notes, "I just think that people now see Strom Thurmond as this doddering old guy . . . and have no knowledge of the central role he played in southern politics."⁵⁸ Edsall's unique knowledge about the significance of Lott's comments, gleaned from authoring two books on race and politics, allowed him to contextualize Lott's comments better than his colleagues.⁵⁹ Pack journalism, the tendency for news reporting to become homogenous within and across organizations, also reduces the range of invention.⁶⁰ Reporter Ed O'Keefe explains pack journalism in the context of Lott's toast: "if something is newsworthy . . . everyone will get it . . . if they didn't all get it, then it couldn't possibly be a newsworthy item."⁶¹ Sometimes consensus immediately congeals around the newsworthiness of a story, converting hegemonic interpretations of relevance into journalistic common sense. The clubbiness of journalists with each other and their official sources often leads to protection rather than investigation. Finally, the absence of an immediate televised response also delayed press coverage. Since the Lott story failed to make the cut the day after Thurmond's birthday, it was quickly considered old news. O'Keefe disclosed that since there was "'no on-camera reaction'" that immediately critiqued Lott's comments for a television audience, the story did not stick.[62] After a few days, reporters simply could not interest their editors in the story. "For the story to move in the press," Edsall explains, "you've got to get a new news peg on it every time."[63] Advertising dollars do not reward old news.

The political economy of the institutional mass media constructs a field, in Pierre Bourdieu's sense of that term, in which actors are organized by power relationships and governed by implicit rules or norms that shape perception and action. The journalistic field shapes news production in a way that produces a narrower ideological debate, increases the dramatization of news, and routinizes certain rules of the game and codes of conduct.[64] Fields with a high degree of internal coherence are resistant to new, inventive perspectives. Though fields tend to create powerful inertia, they are not immune to change. Bourdieu hypothesized that increasing the number of people engaging in journalistic activity would transform the journalistic field and, indeed, the growth of the blogosphere had just that effect.[65] Although bloggers did function much like traditional investigative journalists, the fact that they were largely *outside* the journalistic field gave them a different vantage point from which to assess the newsworthiness of Lott's original comments. During the weeklong dip in news coverage from the institutional mass media, bloggers dug deeper into Lott's past and debated the implications of his seemingly pro-segregationist comments. Three bloggers were instrumental in shaping this conversation in the blogosphere, eventually driving the story back onto the agenda of the mass media press: Atrios on *Eschaton*,[66] Josh Marshall on *Talking Points Memo*, and Glenn Reynolds on *Instapundit*.[67]

Bloggers faced a key rhetorical challenge in identifying what the phrase "all these problems over all these years" referred to in Lott's toast. "These problems" is vague enough to defy an automatic linkage to segregationism, especially for reporters unfamiliar with the complicated nuances of Southern politics. Bloggers used the vast, searchable archives of the internet, alongside the capacity to reproduce and circulate artifacts from the past digitally, to shape perceptions of Lott's toast.[68] At 1:21 P.M. on December 6, the pseudonymous blogger Atrios published the first of many posts on the Lott toast.[69] Atrios wrote, "the problems Lott is referring to are the Civil and Voting Rights Acts," and he updated the same post later with "Lott is also likely referring [to] lots of other horrible things like the *Brown* decision as well."⁷⁰ A second update pulled a snippet from *Slate* contributor Tim Noah, who quoted Thurmond as saying, "there's not enough troops in the army to force the southern people to break down segregation and admit the Nigra race into our theaters, into our swimming pools, into our homes, and into our churches."⁷¹ Basic search functions equipped bloggers like Atrios and Noah to take advantage of the internet's archival properties and reintroduce historical material into public conversation.

Atrios, at 6:02 P.M. the same day, posted two additional pieces of historical evidence that demonstrated "what Senator Lott was proud of in 1948 Mississippi."⁷² He reproduced a Dixiecrat ballot from the 1948 election proclaiming "a vote for Truman . . . means the vicious FEPC—anti-poll tax—anti-lynching and anti-segregation proposals will become the law of the land and our way of life in the South will be gone forever." Atrios then posted a reproduction of part of the Dixiecrat platform: "The negro is a native of tropical climate where fruits and nuts are plentiful and where clothing is not required for protection against the weather. . . . The essentials of society in the jungle are few and do not include the production, transportation and marketing of goods. [Thus] his racial constitution has been fashioned to exclude any idea of voluntary cooperation on his part." The ballot and platform were dramatic visual evidence that connected the problems Lott referred to with racial integration. In public argument, evidence shapes probability statements.⁷³ Was Lott's comment implicitly endorsing segregationism? The Dixiecrat ballot strongly suggests so, thus giving weight to bloggers' accusations of racism. The ability of bloggers to produce and publish evidence like this underlines the increased significance of primary evidence in networked argument practices. A "see for yourself" culture that privileges linking to original evidence replaces the "trust me, I'm a reporter" *ethos* central to the institutional press.⁷⁴

The circulation of the Dixiecrat ballot and platform demonstrates what Alex Halavais speculates is bloggers' unique capacity to identify points of specified ignorance.⁷⁵ Specified ignorance is the Mertonian concept of "the express recognition of what is not yet known but needs to be known in order to lay the foundation for still more knowledge," resonating with Aristotle's articulation of *logos* as laying down certain claims so that other arguments may be built upon them.⁷⁶ Though Merton developed this concept in a scientific context, public controversies demand a similar process in gathering available evidence and making claims that can then support subsequent public argument. In networked terms, Atrios's ability to unearth and interpret—to discover *and* generate meaning—made his node more central in the broader network of deliberating actors.

Josh Marshall, a freelance journalist whose *Talking Points Memo* blog began during the Bush-Gore recount controversy in November 2000, first posted about Lott's toast at 3:20 P.M. on Friday, December 6. He, too, identified Strom Thurmond's presidential campaign against Harry Truman in 1948 as mobilizing segregationist sentiment. Marshall quoted Lott's remarks at Thurmond's birthday celebration before concluding, "just another example of the hubris now reigning among Capitol Hill Republicans" fresh from mid-term victories.[77] The Lott comments were not the only news story at this time. *The Drudge Report* had recently reported that presidential contender John Kerry had paid $150 for a haircut, presumably undercutting his populist appeal. As Marshall observed, "on *Inside Politics* the John Kerry hair story made the cut, not the Trent Lott segregation story."[78] Atrios, too, noted that the John Kerry haircut story made CNN's *Inside Politics* while the Trent Lott story languished.[79] These efforts to draw attention to the distorted agenda-setting of the institutional press are instances of gatewatching.[80] The institutional press is traditionally thought of as a gatekeeper, deciding what stories deserve attention. One key deliberative function of bloggers is to monitor and critique these gatekeeping decisions. If the press is the "fourth estate," then bloggers are part of a "fifth estate" of press critics.[81] By criticizing story topics and frames, bloggers serve a valuable function in arguing about how scarce public attention should be allocated. Since most blogs operate without strong editorial guidance, this unedited media criticism supplements traditional and gatekept avenues of media critique like letters to the editor. Most importantly, the process of critiquing dominant frames, introducing variant frames, and reconciling contrasting frames stimulates the expansion of the lines of argument, and, reflexively, arguments about arguments, in public controversies.

Glenn Reynolds's blogging pushed the Lott story in front of a much wider (and more politically conservative) audience. Reynolds, a University of Tennessee law professor, began blogging at *Instapundit* in August 2001 and was one of the most frequently updated and linked-to sources in the burgeoning network of bloggers. December 6, the same day on which Marshall and Atrios began blogging on Lott, Reynolds posted "Trent Lott deserves the shit he's getting from Atrios and Josh Marshall," interlinking other blogger's posts with his own.[82] Reynolds argued that the contentious comments proved that Lott should not be majority leader, imploring readers to peruse the sample Dixiecrat ballot hosted on Atrios's blog. This process of interlinking and commenting filters public argument, often amplifying the most trenchant observations above the banal. What began as a fairly weak impulse of disapproval in the Lott case eventually propagated through the intercast of weblogs, gaining traction as more bloggers linked to Reynolds, Marshall, and Atrios, which in turn increased the centrality of these particular actors as communicative nodes.

In the twenty days following Lott's comments, Reynolds posted ninety times, with hundreds of links, pull quotes from other blogs or news sites, and snippets from readers' emails. One day, however, stands out as indicative of bloggers' ability to invent and circulate public arguments. In the title of his very first post on December 8, just two days after Lott's toast, Reynolds wrote, "FLOOD THE ZONE!" in all caps, signaling that he was intending to saturate *Instapundit*, and by extension the blogs of those who frequently linked to him, with Lott stories.[83] And saturate he did. He posted ten times that day, from 8 A.M. to almost midnight, exemplifying the shift from the daily punctuation of the analog mass media to the continuous flow of information characteristic of networked media. Reynolds's first post excerpted a snippet from Virginia Postrel's blog expressing general outrage. His second post recapped a story, originally on Geitner Simmons's blog, about how Thurmond, in July 1948, rescinded a routine invitation to William H. Hastie, the governor of the Virgin Islands, when he learned Hastie was not white.[84] His third post explored more of the history of segregationism.[85] A fourth post linked to a group calling for Lott's ouster, with Reynolds concluding, "seems the Blogosphere is way ahead on this one. Where's everybody else?"[86] And on and on Reynolds went, displaying the ability and agility of blogging to aggregate news and opinion by relentlessly posting updates.

The term "flood the zone" reappeared as post titles in subsequent days, indicating the centrality of the trope to Reynolds's self-conception of his rhetorical interventions.[87] Though Josh Marshall did not explicitly adopt the language of flooding the zone, the same strategy was implicit in his blogging, as he "just started hitting it and basically hitting it and hitting it and hitting it."[88] Importantly, the concept of flooding the zone gained traction not just among the blogging elite. Reynolds, soon after the first "flood the zone" post, posted the feedback of a reader who emailed him: "I'm glad that you are 'flooding the zone' with this one," indicating a diffusion of this concept into the public grammar.[89] Flooding the zone *can* be an explicit strategy, as when Reynolds or other bloggers call for more public discourse on an issue. However, an explicitly coordinated campaign to flood the zone is not a precondition for copious amounts of public discourse to be produced by networks of bloggers. The presence of a controversy that ignites public conversation is usually enough for bloggers and other digitally networked intermediaries to saturate the field of public argument from different perspectives.

The genesis of the flooding the zone metaphor highlights bloggers' unique inventional capacities. This particular trope originates in sports strategy as one approach to defeating zone-based defenses. When a team drops into a zone defense, an arrangement where defenders guard an area of the playing field rather than an individual offensive player, an efficient offense sends multiple players toward the zone covered by a single defender. Offensive players overwhelm the solitary defensive player, allowing the playmaker to pick an open target easily. The concept migrated from the sports field to the journalistic field when Howell Raines became the *New York Times* editor.[90] As a reporter for the *Tuscaloosa (AL) News*, Raines absorbed the strategy of flooding the zone from the legendary University of Alabama football coach Paul "Bear" Bryant, who utilized this strategy on the football field. Raines explicitly adopted the flooding the zone philosophy in the coverage of Enron's collapse and the *Columbia* shuttle disaster, assigning hordes of *New York Times* reporters to cover the story from every angle.[91] According to Raines, "you have to concentrate your resources at the point of attack."[92] By flooding the zone, *New York Times* reporters hoped to uncover new evidence and perspectives on major news events, overwhelming their competitors' efforts for viewer attention. However, Raines's approach burned out his reporters.[93] The strategy of flooding the zone for traditional journalistic outlets bumps up against the material limits of reporter time and energy. The blogosphere, in contrast to the journalistic resources at even major news outlets, offers many more eyeballs and fingers capable of sifting, reporting, interpreting, and posting.[94]

Just as rational-critical debate was a key part of the bourgeois rhetorical imaginary, flooding the zone reflects a self-conceptualization of how bloggers participate in public deliberation. When bloggers flood the zone, they unleash a tide of postings that crash into extant argument pools, reshaping the horizontal and vertical contours of public argument.[95] Glenn Reynolds interpreted flooding the zone as meaning "covering a story to the extent that other outlets can't ignore it."[96] According to Reynolds, "blogs are good at picking apart a story from lots of different angles at once, while big media outlets tend to be more similar in their coverage."⁹⁷ Instead of homogeneity of coverage, blogs encourage creative, generative argument from many perspectives. This claim coheres with Sunstein's assessment that enclaves deepen argument pools by multiplying diverse viewpoints. It also comports with the Sophistic sense of clash as an inventional strategy. In the information-rich and digital environment of the internet, bloggers easily collect, parse, post, and reflect on fragments circulating through the institutional media and the blogosphere. Such a process aids invention, as bloggers make sense of the dense layers of evidence and argument surrounding contemporary events. Flooding the zone is particularly useful as a strategy for public argument mediated through the internet, since search engines return results based in part on recency and frequency of links. As a post becomes linked to by other bloggers, search engines, social bookmarking sites, and other aggregators reflexively identify it as capturing public attention, pushing the post to ever-larger audiences by creating a positive feedback loop.

As the blogosphere and other sites of networked public argument matured, this ever-enlarging cycle of attention became colloquially referred to as "buzz." Buzz is consistent with the "blogswarm" metaphor commonly found in scholarly and popular discourse to describe the activities of bloggers. A blogswarm occurs, as Adam Schiffer explains, "when one side of the political spectrum is whipped into a frenzy by a story that it perceives to be worthy of intense, sustained coverage."⁹⁸ Schiffer's conclusion in the Downing Street Memo controversy he analyzes is that internet "buzz was the only apparent bridge between the memo leaks and the eventual American coverage of their substance."⁹⁹ Blogswarms are especially likely when they involve political scandals that energize a partisan body politic.¹⁰⁰ The power of a blogswarm depends on the intensity of digital "humming" that multitudes of bloggers create, and, following the internal logic of the blogswarm metaphor, the institutional press cannot ignore a story if the buzz is loud enough. The buzz metaphor expresses how issues that gather attention in digital environments often mark important topics meriting broadcast press coverage. Yet there is an implicit—and impoverished—theory of attention structuring the blogswarm metaphor. The assumption that a blogswarm shapes the press agenda presumes that mere buzz can move an issue toward the center of the contemporary media ecosystem. This trickle-up theory of press attention assumes that crude attention markers, like number of bloggers posting, number of posts on an issue, length of comment threads, density of interlinkage, and popularity of shared links on social bookmarking sites, automatically shape the broader agenda for public conversation. The ways in which these attention markers shape public deliberation cannot be discounted. But the blogswarm metaphor's focus on the power of buzz elides a more fundamental contribution that bloggers make to public deliberation: the invention of novel arguments.[101] It isn't that bloggers simply pay attention to certain issues, thus directing the focus of the press. It is their ability to (occasionally) invent and develop novel arguments by flooding the zone that is significant. This contrast between blogswarm and flooding the zone addresses D. T. Scott's question about why some controversies that receive attention from the blogosphere fail to result in broader press coverage, resulting in what he calls a blog-flop.[102] At least part of the answer, to accompany the structural and situational features of any controversy, must be the quality and inventiveness of argumentation produced by bloggers.

The intellectual work that Josh Marshall did underlines the importance of invention, not just "buzz," in shaping public deliberation. Marshall's role in (re)discovering, circulating, and interpreting two key artifacts helped shift public opinion on Lott. On December 9, Marshall posted a quote from an interview the *Southern Partisan* magazine conducted with Trent Lott in 1984. In that interview, Lott said, "I think that a lot of the fundamental principles that Jefferson Davis believed in are very important to people across the country, and they apply to the Republican Party."[103] Three days later, Marshall published the full text of the interview on his blog.[104] Lott's Confederate apologetics lent credence to the charge that he was more actively involved in segregationist organizations than his official biography revealed. New questions then surfaced about his cozy relationship to the Council of Conservative Citizens (CCC), a group that evolved from the pro-segregation White Citizens' Councils of the civil rights era.

On December 11, Lott tried to explain his way out of the budding controversy on conservative talk radio host Sean Hannity's program. Hannity asked him what his relationship to the CCC was, and Lott asserted that his only involvement with the group was as a speaker at an open forum they sponsored. On his blog, Marshall reproduced the relevant transcript text of Lott's interview with Hannity, and then responded with two pull quotes that undermined Lott's story.[105] First, he linked to a 1998 *Washington Post* story, sent to him by a reader, that quoted Lott in the CCC newsletter as saying that the group defended "right principles and the right philosophy." Second, he linked to a 1999 *New Republic* story that claimed Lott was actually a dues-paying member of the CCC. Marshall's ability to undermine

Lott's claims with concrete evidence to the contrary prevented Lott's prevarication from shaping the public debate on his comments. As Marshall noted briefly after this original post, "everyone who's sentient and even remotely keeps up on politics has known about this stuff for years—at least since the last Trent Lott–segregation scandal broke back in late 1998. Sad to say, everyone just agreed not to pay attention, not to care."[106] By contrast, actors in the burgeoning networked public sphere *did* pay attention to the Lott issue by connecting the dots of his past more thoroughly and persistently than the institutional press ever had.

The same day Lott appeared on Hannity's show, Josh Marshall broke another story about Lott's role in a tax exemption case involving Bob Jones University from 1983. Marshall reported that Trent Lott filed an *amicus curiae* ("friend of the court") brief on behalf of Bob Jones University, which was suing the Internal Revenue Service for taking away its tax-exempt status because of the university's prohibition on interracial dating.[107] Just two hours after the initial post, Marshall followed with "Is TPM your source or is TPM your source? Here's the Amicus Brief which Trent Lott submitted on behalf of Bob Jones University in 1981."[108] Marshall's blog provided a site for him to publish the primary document in full for readers to download. In the brief, Lott writes that "racial discrimination does not always violate public policy," a remark that would receive prominent attention in newspaper accounts in the coming days.[109] Ironically, given the prevalence of the flood the zone metaphor throughout this controversy, Marshall concludes his post by writing "drip, drip, drip," as though each new piece of evidence were adding to a stream of evidence inexorably leading to Lott's ouster.

The surfacing of the *Southern Partisan* interview and the *amicus* brief tempt deference to the discovery model of invention. After all, was it not the discovery of these documents that turned the tide against Lott? The circulation of the documents was indeed a prerequisite, but the generative, interpretive moves focused public opinion when bloggers framed this evidence as an indictment of Lott's character. The blogging by Atrios in response to these developments shows how bloggers generate new frames through the process of rhetorical criticism. On December 13, this rhetorical sensitivity was on display at *Eschaton* as Atrios unleashed a powerful critique of apologists who claimed that Lott was referring to Thurmond's advocacy of states' rights and limited government: "What I hope comes out of this is the recognition and understanding that when a politician in the south goes on about 'states' rights' they are speaking in code that is well understood by a portion of the electorate—black and white. I don't mean that all supporters of federalism are objectively pro-segregation (Very big of me, no?), just that in certain contexts and from certain people the use of that phrase and related ones is nothing more than a big 'FUCK YOU' to the black population. They get it. And, enough of the whites get it too."[110] The following day, Atrios responded to critics elsewhere in the blogosphere that took issue with this post by acknowledging the rhetoricity of language: "I'm just saying that from certain speakers—and to certain audiences—the phrase [states' rights] is a code phrase."[111] This rhetorical sensibility is absolutely crucial to interpreting the greater web of meaning attached to "states' rights," which was a central struggle for Lott's critics. An ahistorical defense of states' rights lent Lott some philosophical backing for his commendation of Thurmond, whereas a more complex understanding of that term's genealogy linked Lott to an outright defense of segregationist politics.

As these stories roiled the blogosphere from December 9 to December 11, the traditional institutional press began to take notice.[112] At 5 P.M. on December 11, the Associated Press (AP) released a story on Lott's involvement in the Bob Jones University case. AP reporter John Solomon wrote, "the old court papers surfaced on a day when Lott tried to quell criticism."[113] Solomon's passive framing of how the *amicus* brief "surfaced" neatly omitted the role that Josh Marshall and *Talking Points Memo* played in publicizing that particular document. Marshall lambasted the AP later that evening: "One other thing. Next time the AP rips off a story we broke at 11 AM and runs it as their own story at 5 PM maybe they could toss in a little attribution? I know it's their rep and all but do they have to be so slimy[?] Dow Jones Newswires caught wind of the Bob Jones Amicus Brief from the story TPM broke too. But they were classy enough to say we'd broken the story."[114] If the Trent Lott episode constitutes the founding myth of the blogosphere's journalistic potency, then this is probably the first shot fired in what would come to be perceived, at least for a while, as a battle between journalists and bloggers for citizen attention. Solomon's choice to not attribute the story of the *amicus* brief to *Talking Points Memo* suggests the perception of a credibility gap. Even though Marshall broke the story, the practice of citing bloggers was rare and potentially threatening to the status of journalists. Marshall, on the other hand, argued for an expansion of the basic journalistic norm of attribution to encompass stories developed from the blogosphere. Attribution norms are robust in the blogosphere, since the hyperlink and the ease of quoting others' texts are so conducive to recognition.[115]

But journalists, like many professionals, tend to be skeptical of new intermediaries poaching on their traditional turf. To demarcate journalism from blogging and buoy their own centrality and legitimacy, many journalists styled themselves as distinct from and superior to blogger upstarts.[116] Much of this styling revolved around journalists' ability to discover evidence rather than generate interpretations. Blogging was figured as subjective, and journalism was objective. Bloggers were novices; journalists were credentialed. Bloggers may be fact-checkers, but journalists discovered the facts. John Jordan identifies these rhetorics of professionalism as the key axis along which the press, with its complex system of accreditation and presumably careful editorial layers, constructed bloggers as potentially mendacious sources that contributed nothing to public discourse but information overload.[117]

The ways in which this boundary work privileges a discovery model of invention at the expense of a generative one can be demonstrated with two examples. First, the role of mass media journalists is elevated by positioning bloggers as parasites, as in this screed by reporter Kurt Anderson: "For now, bloggers are a second-tier journalistic species. They are remoras. The *Times* and CNN and CBS News are the whales and sharks to which Instapundit, Kausfiles, and Kos attach themselves for their free rides. (Remoras evolved special sucking disks; bloggers have modems.) If the sharks and whales were to go extinct, what would the blogging remoras do? Evolve into actual reporters?"[118] Anderson's position is that, whatever else bloggers may do, the discovery of facts remains the province of large news organizations. As Anderson intimates, many remoras maintain relationships based in commensalism, meaning that they gain something from their hosts, but the hosts gain little. Yet the ways in which journalists benefitted from bloggers' expansion of argument pools in the Trent Lott case invite a reversal of Anderson's metaphor. Some remoras maintain a relationship with their hosts based on mutualism, cleaning parasites from their hosts and thus facilitating the smoother operation of their biological systems. Needless to say, that twist of the metaphor is far more sympathetic to a symbiosis between blogging and the institutional press.[119]

A second example of boundary work between journalists and bloggers further underlines how journalists articulate themselves to the discovery model of invention. In 2008, *Salon* blogger Glenn Greenwald criticized an interview by CNN reporter John King, prompting an email from King that Greenwald subsequently published on his blog: "I don't read biased uninformed drivel so I'm a little late to the game.... The portion [of the interview criticized by Greenwald] you cited was aired by one of our programs—so by all means it is fair game for whatever 'analysis' you care to apply to it using your right of free speech and your lack of any journalistic standards or fact checking or just plain basic curiosity. You clearly know very little about journalism. But credibility matters."[120] In just a few offhanded sentences, King affirms that journalists are trained professionals, unbiased, informed, analytical, fact-oriented, and credible—central features of the informationist model of invention premised on the supposed discovery of external truths. Bloggers, on the other hand, are marked by the lack of these virtues. Is the difference between blogging and journalism so great? I think not, at least when it comes to how invention of arguments actually occurs. For both bloggers and journalists, invention is a social act, animated by engaging the ideas of others, not discovering some fixed external truth that speaks for itself. But in many cases, members of the traditional press hold on to the notion that they alone work with a discovery model of invention and thus should have their reports elevated above all others.

Despite tensions between bloggers and the traditional press, the evolution of the Lott story actually hinted at a potentially collaborative relationship. Between Tuesday, December 10, and Wednesday, December 11, Trent Lott's Senate office fielded 288 media calls.[121] By December 12 and 13, the institutional media caught up with blogs in covering the Trent Lott story. Coverage in the *New York Times* is indicative of the overall treatment of the Lott story. On December 13, the controversy started receiving a special section, "Divisive Words," which centralized coverage of the fallout from Thurmond's birthday party. Lott's initial reluctance to entertain resigning as Senate majority leader softened as his popularity eroded throughout the week of December 13–20. He eventually yielded to immense public and elite pressure and resigned his leadership post on December 20.

To draw a straight line from bloggers' rhetorical activities to the downfall of Trent Lott obviously simplifies complex pathways of communicative influence. Yet bloggers clearly deepened argument pools that subsequently shaped the broader public debate about Lott's appropriate fate. Most importantly, in terms of establishing bloggers as key actors in the networked rhetorical imaginary, bloggers' communicative power was identified as a significant factor in follow-on reflections about Lott's resignation. From the left, Paul Krugman called Josh Marshall's *Talking Points Memo* "must reading for the politically curious" and "responsible for making Trent Lott's offensive remarks the issue they deserve to be."[122] From the right, John

Podhoretz claimed that the "drumbeat that turned this story into a major calamity for Lott, and led directly to President Bush's welcome disavowal of Lott's views yesterday, was entirely driven by the Internet blogosphere."[123] Arianna Huffington, who would later found the influential blog hub *The Huffington Post*, noted that blogs "continued hammering away at the story, and eventually succeeded in moving it out of the shadows into the political spotlight."[124] Even Cass Sunstein cites the Trent Lott affair when he writes that "bloggers appear to have influenced the public stage, driving media coverage and affecting national perceptions of national questions."[125] Trent Lott, in his autobiography, blamed blogs for sparking the firestorm of criticism.[126] All this positive attribution accelerated blogging's reputation as a site for rhetorical invention, drawing the blogosphere deeper into contemporary circuits of public deliberation. Marshall himself attributed many of the developments to the intercast of the blogosphere, claiming, "I'm certain that the web generally—and particularly a lot of different weblogs—kept this story in front of people and forced attention to it long enough that it became impossible to ignore."[127] By generating so many novel arguments, bloggers were able to shape attention and thus public opinion on a major controversy for the first time.

Invention and the Networked Public Sphere
(Thinking with Habermas Against Habermas)

What does the Lott case suggest about the significance of invention in the networked public sphere? Democratic deliberation requires not just conversation among citizens, but conversation circulating *novel* opinions that stimulate innovation and change in public controversies. The alternative is stagnation, falling into a deliberation trap that features the eternal return of the same old arguments. A particular piece of public discourse is inventive if it destabilizes traditional attention patterns, as inventive rhetoric defamiliarizes routine ways of apprehending an issue. By making the familiar strange, rhetors invite audiences to think about situations anew, to see old controversies with fresh eyes, and to transform understandings of the possible. In this case, the dominant narrative of Lott as a harmless good old boy faded as his checkered past was brought to public attention in a more sustained and detailed way. When put in the context of his most recent offense, Lott's cultural politics could not be legitimated.

Fitting the blogosphere into extant theories of public deliberation would appear, at first blush, to be fairly easy. If, as Habermas argues, independence of media organizations and communicative reflexivity of citizens are the preconditions for deliberative legitimation processes, than the blogosphere should fare well as a democratic intermediary.[128] After all, the blogosphere, in the early years at least, sat outside of the institutional corporate media and relied on looping iterations of public argument advanced by citizens. Bloggers engage in critical argumentation practices that would be more or less recognizable to the inhabitants of Habermas's bourgeois public sphere. Indeed, blogs are explicitly analogized to this prior rhetorical imaginary, reviving "the coffee house model of textual circulation."[129] Bloggers thematize issues of public concern and use their broad reasoning faculties to argue about them. The blogosphere links citizens together in crisscrossing social networks, circulates arguments capable of forging publics, congeals public opinion, and legitimizes action. Bloggers' critical—even vituperative—orientation makes them "the new pamphleteers," politicizing issues much like the partisan press and small publishers of the early modern era.[130] Even the pseudonymity of some blogs is analogous to the status bracketing that formed part of the bourgeois rhetorical imaginary.

Bloggers do not only approximate the argumentation practices of their bourgeois antecedents detailed in Habermas's early historical work; in the Trent Lott case, their communicative activity hewed closely to Habermas's later, more comprehensive account of contemporary public deliberation outlined in *Between Facts and Norms*. Habermas's mature theory of law and democracy acknowledges that the political economy of the mass media in late modern culture tamps down inventive arguments coming from the periphery. The mass media, like the institution of the state, tends toward well-established routines: predictable interview subjects, obvious lines of inquiry, and formulaic norms of presentation. Habermas explains that these "settled routines" of bureaucracy are destabilized when a conflict materializes.[131] As controversies unfold, increased communicative activity from the periphery "is characterized by a consciousness of crisis, a heightened public attention, an intensified search for solutions, in short, by *problematization*. In cases in which perceptions of problems and problem situations have taken a conflictual turn, the attention span of the citizenry enlarges, indeed in such a way that controversies in the broader public sphere primarily ignite around the normative aspects of the problems most at issue."[132] Habermas foreshadows the contemporary concern with attention by identifying it as the catalyst for public deliberation. The linchpin of Habermas's mature theory of deliberation is a defense of unorchestrated, free, spontaneous, and attention-getting communication from actors on the periphery flowing toward the core administrative actors of the state.[133] The spontaneous communication that emanates from the periphery is, ideally for Habermas, a rhetorically inventive stratum that hosts a "processing of 'exhaustive' proposals, information, and reasons."[134]

Since actors on the periphery are closer to the lifeworld, they can more powerfully thematize problems in their everyday experience. But communicative power can supplant undemocratic social and administrative power only "to the extent that the periphery has both (a) a specific set of capabilities and (b) sufficient occasion to exercise them."[135] Habermas clarifies that the specific set of capabilities in (a) includes the abilities to "ferret out, identify, and effectively thematize latent problems," a rigorous requirement that requires actors to produce communication that is "both attention-catching and innovative."[136] These are essentially challenges of invention. But (b), the occasion to exercise these critical capabilities, Habermas claims, is an even tougher criterion to meet. Since the political economy of the mass media restricts public discourse, Habermas is rather sanguine about the ability of traditional civil-society agents to focus attention. He explains that "the signals they send out and the impulses they give are generally too weak to initiate learning processes or redirect decision making in the political system in the short run."[137] This signaling problem is a serious one for contemporary deliberation, for if citizens are able to exercise their voices but are locked into a circulation pattern that keeps them on the periphery, then legitimation processes are doomed to stall.

Given these criteria, the blogosphere seems a neat fit for Habermas's later theories of deliberation. In the Lott case, and in many episodes since then, bloggers created a sense of crisis by more thoroughly problematizing an issue than the institutional mass media had. On the periphery of established communication networks, they used the specific affordances of blogging—quick publication, hyperlinked and interthreaded discourse, and conversation across space and time—in attention-getting ways to spur opinion formation. As the issue received attention in the blogosphere, it spilled over to the institutional mass media and from there followed more conventional pathways of influence to the core administrative actors who eventually abandoned their support of Lott. The historical "signaling problem" of civil-society actors is lessened when bloggers flood the zone and unleash lots of novel, attention-getting arguments from multiple perspectives. Instead of *signaling*, a metaphor that evokes broadcast media, networked intermediaries *relay* layers of messages through hyperlinks. Bloggers promote and transform novel posts from the periphery of the blogosphere, drawing an ever-greater share of attention as public argument spirals through nodes and hubs of escalating size. Since any fragment of discourse on the internet is only a hyperlink away, nodes on the periphery can quickly become more central to the network and consequently unsettle the attention routines of mass media and administrative actors. While the structural affordances of the blogosphere are no guarantee of influence, in at least some cases the combination of networked media and inventive argument provides the means for citizen critics to mobilize public opinion.

In thinking with Habermas's early and late theories of public deliberation, I have made the case that the blogosphere meets his normative requirements for democratic legitimacy by evading the corporate media and enhancing citizen reflexivity. This sets the stage to think against Habermas, who has thus far declined to take the blogosphere, and the networked public sphere more generally, as a site of meaningful deliberation. In more recent work, Habermas specifically negates the value of increased inventional activity occurring through digitally networked intermediaries by claiming that the internet ushers in a "welcome increase in egalitarianism . . . [which] is being paid for by the decentralisation of access to unedited contributions. In this medium the contributions of intellectuals lose the power to create a focus."[138] In Habermas's telling, the increase in participation fueled by the internet creates an information glut that hides the wheat with the chaff, for only the traditional "voluntary associations of civil society" maintain the focalizing power to make sense of it all.[139] There are at least two problems with Habermas's critique of networked publics: (1) the power of intellectuals and other agenda-setters in established civil-society associations to focalize public debate is accompanied by significant risks in artificially narrowing the agenda, and (2) networked intermediaries are also capable of focusing public deliberation.

First, the elevation of certain agenda-setters as privileged focalizers of public debate runs into a critique that many bloggers lodge against the traditional news editor. In practice, editors become resistant to novel interpretations from the periphery. How can the responsibility of focusing public debate—picking the "best" news and opinion to highlight, publish, and circulate—not be accompanied by the hubris of the tastemaker? The focalizing power of the traditional broadcast news leaves much to be desired, given that the institutional press often leavens stories of tragic environmental disaster and sobering legislative contests with segments on flying squirrels and the celebrity life cycle (ascent, marriage, divorce, death). Before networked media, citizens attempted to "send a signal" strong enough to challenge or countermand the agenda-setting through protests, boycotts, or letters to the editor. Although occasionally effective, the intensity of contemporary gatewatching practices performed by bloggers and other networked intermediaries creates more sustained pressure on mass media agenda-setting.

Second, bloggers, alongside other actors in the networked public sphere, can operate as focalizers of public debate. Both Glenn Reynolds and Josh Marshall regularly (re)published insights from readers' emails, other blogs, and the traditional press. Aren't bloggers, then, organizing opinions by sifting through heterogeneous arguments introduced by readers and commenters? Habermas takes discourse mediated by the internet as an undifferentiated mass of communication, assuming that there are "unedited contributions" to public discourse by internetworked intermediaries. They are not unedited; they are edited differently. Rather than the prepublication editing that defines the broadcast press, networked intermediaries engage in postpublication filtering of argument. This postpublication filtering is more spontaneous, self-organized, and organic than the prepublication filtering executed by an editor, which suggests that the networked public sphere conceivably meets Habermas's criteria for deliberative legitimation processes better than the historical bourgeois public sphere or the model he constructs in *Between Facts and Norms*. Habermas seems to assume that the blogosphere is an evenly distributed network, with equally sized nodes and equally strong ties between nodes, ensuring that every contribution receives an equal share of attention. However, one of the frequent criticisms of the blogosphere's democratic pretensions, the ossification of an "A-list" of bloggers, demonstrates how bloggers perform the focalizing function needed to structure public discourse. Clay Shirky's early explanation of the power laws of blogging revealed that the top 100 blogs tend to accumulate the lion's share of links.[140] These top blogs focus debate by attending to whatever happens to be roiling the networked public sphere at the moment, thus shaping the attention patterns of bloggers lower down the chain of attention. Although there is a power law that unevenly distributes attention, the networked architecture of the blogosphere makes it more open than the modern mass-mediated public sphere to the communicative signals from the periphery. So when bloggers not on the A-list flood the zone on an issue, they can gain attention as the arguments move around the periphery of the networked public sphere and into more central nodes.[141]

Habermas's criticism of focalization is situated within a larger fragmentation thesis that resembles Sunstein's fear of deliberative enclaves. Habermas marshals this fragmentation *topos* by explicitly limiting the influence of internetworked communication in liberal democracies:

> [C]omputer-mediated communication in the web can claim unequivocal *democratic* merits only for a special context: It can undermine the censorship of authoritarian regimes that try to control and repress public opinion. In the context of liberal regimes, the rise of millions of fragmented chat rooms across the world tend instead to lead to the fragmentation of large but politically focused mass audiences into a huge number of isolated issue publics. Within established national public spheres, the online debates of web users only promote political communication, when news groups crystallize around the focal points of the quality press, for example, national newspapers and political magazines.[142]

Habermas goes on to suggest that bloggers perform only a "parasitical role" that offers modest benefit, as when the bloggers at *Bildblog.de* sent a bill for 2,088 euros to the tabloid *Bild.T-Online* for corrections and fact-checking services.[143] This was a media prank designed to draw attention to the critical deficits of the institutional media, but Habermas apparently takes it as a signature demonstration of what the blogosphere contributes to public deliberation.

Habermas's conceptualization of the internet here is deeply flawed. The internet is, quite obviously, more than a series of chat rooms. While chat rooms were, along with email, a prominent element of the 1990s-era internet, the "vernacular web of participatory media" has proliferated far beyond these humble beginnings.[144] Habermas's claim that the internet's democratic merit lies in the evasion of censorship by authoritarian regimes is certainly reasonable, especially given the centrality of networked media in the Arab Spring of 2011. However, to limit the internet's efficacy in other polities ignores the growing body of literature suggesting that internetworked communication does, at least occasionally, activate change in advanced liberal democracies as well.[145] Equally troubling, Habermas situates networked media as merely reactive (or "parasitic") to the communication that comes from the dominant, agenda-setting institutional media.

But, as the Lott case shows, the flow of information from the broadcast media to the public is often reversed in the networked public sphere, with bloggers breaking stories or inventing novel interpretations that are later drawn upon by the institutional media.

Finally, as Axel Bruns explains, the fragmentation critique "ignores or rejects the reality that especially online, individual publics are multiply connected both implicitly through shared membership and explicitly through a network of hyperlinks connecting postings right across the boundaries" of different forums.[146] The criticism that networked publics are uniquely susceptible to fragmentation ignores the possibilities that communicative coalitions encouraged by networked media serve as a centripetal force during outbreaks of deliberation. Despite the centrifugal potential of public discourse in internetworked forums, there are, following Yochai Benkler, "mechanisms and practices that generate a common set of themes, concerns, and public knowledge around which a public sphere can emerge."[147] Flooding the zone, by producing copious amounts of attention-getting and attention-transforming public argument, is such a practice. That bloggers can generate argument around certain events suggests that their activity should not be seen as mere fragmentation, but rather as a type of communicative differentiation that accommodates hypercomplexity. In some cases, bloggers' generation and development of public argument are so compelling that their communication migrates from more reticulate enclaves, where they incubate arguments, to more general media. Such a process meets Sunstein's condition for wider circulation of enclave-generated argumentation and Habermas's demands for focalization of public debate.

One explanation for Habermas's failure to consider the networking of the public sphere robustly is that the conceptual model of deliberation from *Structural Transformation* still drives his theory, despite the changed cultural conditions and media system. Habermas's commitment to the role of the "quality" press, voluntary associations, writers' groups, and public interest organizations in focusing public discourse lingers. Such groups played an important role in the bourgeois public sphere by managing sheaves of criticism generated by the public. Like Sennett and Putnam, Habermas forecloses the possibility that alternative forms of deliberative organizing—organizing without organizations—can perform some of the democratic functions traditionally conducted in associational contexts.[148] But a more fundamental problem lies in what William Outhwaite identifies as Habermas's increasingly fundamental distinction between the context of discovery and the context of justification.[149] Habermas's late theory of deliberation maintains that "the publics of parliamentary bodies are structured predominantly as a *context of justification*. These bodies rely not only on the administration's preparatory work and further processing but also on the *context of discovery* provided by a procedurally unregulated public sphere that is borne by the general public of citizens."[150] This model expresses commitments to informationist models of communication that presume citizens in the lifeworld "discover" problems that are subsequently amplified by the mass media to the relevant stakeholders.

Given the critique of the discovery model of invention developed throughout this chapter, this distinction is especially tendentious. The context of discovery/context of justification distinction originates in the early twentieth century from logical positivism, an informationist intellectual movement committed to conceptualizing science as "an autonomous enterprise" not affected by the social or by language.[151] The context of discovery is supposed to be an objective one: experimental data speak for themselves, uninhibited by words or relationships, to reveal some fundamental truth about nature. Following whatever scientific revelation comes to light in the context of discovery, the significance and implication of the discovery moves to the context of justification: a scientist explains a finding to fellow scientists in the lab, grant funders, engineers pursuing applications, or public bodies. This move to seal science off from so-called nonobjective forms of understanding was a crucial step in elevating it as *the* metadiscourse of the twentieth century. But the distinction is a dubious one, roundly critiqued by scholars like Michael Polanyi and Thomas Kuhn because, as my account of informationism suggests, facts never speak for themselves. Whenever symbols are employed to convey facts, the rhetor is always already in the realm of interpretation and justification by shaping how we pay attention to the thing "discovered." The popular story of Isaac Newton recognizing the universal law of gravitation after an apple fell on his head illustrates this blurred process well. The fact of the apple's falling becomes embedded in justification as soon as Newton starts asking why it happened. John Lyne argues that taking invention seriously as a rhetorical act draws attention to how justification pervades the "discovery" process, as when "the reasoner tests an intuition against facts or internalized norms, thinks of a skeptical colleague, [or] structures research with an eye toward public presentation."[152] There is simply no escaping justification, just as, in the terms of invention, there is no escaping generativity.

The nuances of the debate over the contexts of discovery and justification are far more detailed, but for my purposes it is enough to simply cast doubt on the existence of two discrete contexts in science. If the distinction between discovery and justification is a dubious one in scientific discourse, then it is doubly dubious in deliberative discourse about moral controversies. Citizens do not just "discover" social problems and then demand redress in contexts of justification; they problematize a certain phenomenon *as* requiring attention. Social problems, like truth, are not found but made.[153] This is particularly the case with regard to moral issues, like Lott's potential segregationist sympathies. The evidence for this was not initially obvious, instead requiring interpretation of code words and documents obscured by the passage of time. Even if these can be made conceptually distinct, in practice there is a high level of recursive back-and-forth movement between discovery and justification, with the lines demarcating the two constantly shifting. Bloggers went looking for evidence of Lott's past racism with an eye already turned toward problematizing his comments. There was no realm of "objective" facts or exigencies just waiting to be discovered; at every step along the way, rhetorical choices generated meaning.

The distinction between contexts is not an inconsequential conceptual error, for this presupposition requires Habermas to develop a way to move a message from contexts of discovery to contexts of justification. He relies, consequently, upon a series of transmission metaphors that assume a broadcast system of media. Habermas writes in *Between Facts and Norms* that the "political public sphere [is] a sounding board for problems . . . to this extent, the public sphere is a warning system with sensors that, though unspecialized, are sensitive throughout society . . . the public sphere must, in addition, amplify the pressure of problems."[154] Sounding board, warning system, and amplification: these metaphors import a terminology, and thus assumptions, more appropriate to a broadcast system of media. They appear to be holdovers from *Structural Transformation*, where Habermas also describes the public sphere as a "sounding board" that involves the "transmission and amplification of the rational-critical debate of private people assembled into a public."[155] The contemporary understanding of the sounding board, as a person to test an idea on, obscures its origins as a structure put behind a pulpit or podium. Common in preelectronic times when a speaker addressed a large audience, the sounding board amplified the volume of the voice. The warning system metaphor works similarly. Citizens in the lifeworld (the context of discovery) act as sensors, detecting exigencies that demand address (in the context of justification). Alternatively, Habermas refers to citizens as having "appropriate antennae" capable of detecting the systemic deficiencies of everyday life and, mediated by the public sphere, transmitting them toward more central actors skilled in the arts of justification.[156]

By conceptualizing the public sphere as a sounding board and warning system, Habermas limits the functionalities of the contemporary (networked) public sphere. These mechanistic metaphors of transmission and amplification replicate the conventional informationist assumption that arguments simply need discovery and then circulation. But, as my metarhetorical history of invention and reading of the Lott case shows, public deliberation is not so simple. Deliberation produces meaning through iterations of rhetorical activity over time. Rhetoric does not just transmit and amplify opinion; it *transforms* opinions by changing the ways in which publics attend to issues. The persistence of the conceptual system of *Structural Transformation*, even in late Habermasian theory, forecloses opportunities to consider the potential for public deliberation beyond a mass media–dominated system. This is unfortunate, as the networked public sphere is reinvigorating three core rhetorical concepts—*kairos*, agonism, and copiousness—related to invention with the capacity to activate deliberative legitimation processes.

The speed of blogging makes the blogosphere a rich site of invention. Speed is related to *kairos*, one of the key words for the Sophists and other classical rhetoricians. The instant reply, quick quip, and timely rejoinder were praised in classical times and are newly salient in our own. Bloggers utilize the instantaneousness and continuousness of digital publication to fashion timely responses to arguments instead of waiting for the daily, weekly, or monthly publication of press organs. They do not wait for editorial feedback to clear a news item. Continuous publication also makes flooding the zone on timely issues easier for digitally networked intermediaries than for the press. In contrast to the newspaper, which even in the digital era is committed primarily to daily publication, bloggers are able to post as the story unfolds, sometimes—like Glenn Reynolds—tens or even hundreds of times in a single day. Together, the instantaneousness and continuousness of blogs increase the speed at which public argument is developed and circulated in internetworked public cultures, quickly populating the field of argument by proliferating possible *topoi* to be scrutinized. This speeds the summoning of evidence and enumeration of possible arguments, which lets public deliberation keep pace with the sociopolitical acceleration that contemporary public cultures face.[157] The blogosphere provides an alternative to the slower, sequential character of traditional public deliberation, where speakers must take turns to listen and then respond to arguments—a process, as the Senate filibuster shows, that is often laborious.[158] The blogosphere provides a better balancing of sequencing and simultaneity than the institutional press. However, to adapt the old driving safety warning, speed can kill. The acceleration of public deliberation creates modest challenges for deliberation, like the spread of rumor, and more fundamental ones, like departing from what Ron Greene calls "the preferred temporality of rhetorical deliberation."[159]

The *agonism* of the blogosphere also fuels invention. Agonism is often used to dismiss contributions from the blogosphere *in toto*, for if blogging merely breeds fragmentation and discord, then it hardly deserves special consideration as a site of democratic deliberation. Agonism, though, can be recuperated by appreciating how it fuels inventional processes—the great insight of the Sophists and the *dissoi logoi* fragment. As Thomas Sloane explains, "the inventive process in rhetoric is not only dialogic but controversial, even disputatious in nature."[160] The blogosphere encourages disputatiousness by directing, through hyperlinks, attention to others' arguments. Richard Lanham's claim that "hypertextual linking can move us from one world of discourse to another, and this kind of voyaging has always stimulated creativity" reflects the rhetorical activity of Atrios, Marshall, and Reynolds as they integrated others' commentary into their own.[161] In the information-rich environment of the internet, bloggers easily collect, parse, post, and stitch together fragments circulating throughout the media ecosystem. What makes the agonism of blogs distinct from that of the traditional press is that they often make public what Peter Simonson calls the "media of invention," the "enabling contexts and communicative forms through which rhetorical invention occurs."[162] The social situations, personal relationships, conversations, blog posts, and other material that nourish an act of invention are often publicly articulated. Hyperlinked attributions reveal the media of invention to a public audience and thus expose these constituents of public argument to scrutiny by others.

Invention is also aided by the *copiousness* of digitally networked intermediaries. Copiousness is an abundance of thought or resourcefulness borne of preparation, as the well-known anecdote about Erasmus's inventional strategy shows.[163] Erasmus engaged in the process of *copia* by writing 147 variations of the sentence "Your letter pleased me very much," and settling on the best one. Such a process parallels the blogosphere's proliferation of discourse through postings and comments that can expand the range of arguments and how they are articulated. The often-rowdy process of argumentation in the blogosphere invites bloggers to riff on each other's postings in a way that constantly generates new vantage points for criticism. To be clear, more is not necessarily better; however, as James Crosswhite argues in defense of copiousness, "the more arguments we have, from the more perspectives, the better chance criticism has of producing valuable results."[164] That is an elegant defense of the networked public sphere.

However, bloggers, if they are to be considered successful, cannot simply reproduce copious amounts of public discourse from other bloggers. They must *distill* observations from other sources. Thus, in the blogosphere, copiousness is in a dialectical relationship with concision. The condensation of the copious into the concise is one way that public opinion gets bundled in digital communication networks, downplaying some angles and highlighting other elements to manage information abundance. The proliferation of discourse in the networked public sphere may well drown out the focalizers of public debate *if* certain *topoi* are not crystallized into condensed, quality arguments capable of organizing deliberation. Sometimes, as in the Lott case, bloggers do this well, while at other times their ability to concentrate the key arguments is more difficult, and thus their influence on a particular controversy is muted. The life cycle of any deliberative episode moves like an accordion, expanding and contracting argumentative *topoi* as it iterates through communication nodes. When the deliberative accordion is carefully calibrated between too much and too little public discourse, diverse opinions are drawn into public conversation, new possibilities are generated, and judgments with legitimacy are made through the process of inventive argument.[165]

The *kairotic* speed, agonism, and copiousness of bloggers are signs of what journalism scholars Lewis Friedland, Thomas Hove, and Hernando Rojas call *"systematically increased communicative reflexivity."*[166] With networked media technology, they speculate, "perhaps for the first time in history, the informal public sphere has a medium that in principle allows for large-scale expression of mass opinion in forms that *systematically* affect the institutional media system."[167] This rise in communicative reflexivity addresses some of the core weaknesses of the broadcast press that Esther Scott identified in her postmortem of the Lott affair. The ignorance of reporters about historical events is now countered by the ability of bloggers to discover and interpret evidence. Pack journalism is countered by the bevy of gatewatchers focused on mass media agenda-setting. The absence of immediate response is countered by a host of networked critics ready to pounce. It would be a mistake to conclude that the contemporary synthesis of blogging and the traditional press mirrors or betters some kind of nostalgic public sphere; however, such a tiered, interconnected, and critically oriented media system does create more opportunities for digitally networked intermediaries to propel deliberative legitimation processes through inventive rhetorical argument. Perhaps Dewey's "shadowy and formless" public has, with a new medium that supports many-to-many communication and new modes of attracting attention (like flooding the zone), a way to prevent its regular eclipse.[168]

Co-optation of Flooding the Zone

Although bloggers, and now other networked intermediaries, often flood the zone in order to activate the inventional energies of citizens, administrative organizations also recognize that they can use strategies of flooding the zone to co-opt or blunt spontaneous communication from the periphery, putting a networked spin on traditional astroturfing practices. Information management efforts by the military in the wake of 9/11 show how administrative institutions adopted flooding the zone as a communication strategy. After 9/11, the Pentagon created the Office of Strategic Influence (OSI), whose "stated purpose was simple: to flood targeted areas with information."[169] Later, during combat operations in Iraq, Department of Defense outlets produced overwhelming amounts of information emphasizing how well the military operations and subsequent occupation were going. As Torie Clark relates in a chapter called "Flood the Zone" from her memoir chronicling her years as the Pentagon spokesperson, flooding the zone was a key element in the Pentagon's efforts to influence perceptions of the war.[170] More recently, a study by James Kinniburgh and Dorothy Denning written for the Joint Special Operations University contemplates Pentagon efforts to become more actively involved in the blogosphere. As the report's authors explain, "sometimes numbers can be effective; hiring a block of bloggers to verbally attack a specific person or promote a specific message may be worth considering."[171] Alternatively, they suggest that military branches might consider supporting homegrown blogs that appear independent but actually funnel on-message talking points from the Pentagon. Though this report does not indicate that the Pentagon undertook these specific steps to influence public argument in the blogosphere, the Department of Defense did establish a regular "Bloggers Roundtable," which provided "source material" and access to military officials in live chats.[172]

In the 2004 election cycle, bloggers got on candidate payrolls in a few high-profile races to flood the zone. These orchestrated efforts to create the impression of unorchestrated argument are reminiscent of old "payola" scandals in the music industry. Markos Moulitsas Zúniga (of *DailyKos*) and Jerome Armstrong were paid by Howard Dean's campaign while writing blog posts that praised his politics. They eventually disclosed that they were on Dean's payroll, but the suspicion of *quid pro quo* persisted.[173] At the same time, John Thune, in a heated race with Tom Daschle for a Senate seat in South Dakota, hired two bloggers to critique negative press and create positive buzz for his campaign. The bloggers did not reveal that they were on the payroll of the Republican nominee, though Thune's campaign account eventually revealed that the bloggers were being paid.[174] In 2006, Wal-Mart created a blog called *Working Families for Wal-Mart*, which positioned itself as a grassroots advocacy group designed to rebut critics of Wal-Mart. It was, in fact, a joint effort between Wal-Mart and its public relations firm, Edelman, to counter Wal-Mart's bad press.[175]

Flooding the zone is achieving the status of gospel for public relations firms working on political campaigns, owing in part to what is now known as "Macacagate." In August 2006, Virginia's George Allen was in the midst of a reelection campaign for his Senate seat. One of his opponent's aides, S. R. Sidarth, followed Allen around to each campaign stop in what has become standard operating procedure for campaigns' opposition research. On a sunny day in Breaks, Virginia, Allen singled out this aide, who was filming every minute of Allen's visit, by referring to Sidarth, who traces his heritage to the Indian subcontinent, as a "macaca" ("macaca" is a racial slur, meaning "monkey," widely used in Francophone Africa). The video circulated wildly on video-sharing websites like YouTube and spread through blogs, emails, and social networking sites. Allen eventually lost the election, in part because of the negative publicity from this videotaped moment. In the wake of the controversy, one campaign strategist recommended that the Allen campaign should have flooded the zone to overwhelm curious searchers looking for the "macaca video."

> To flood the zone, upload dozens and dozens of random videos which have absolutely nothing to do with the clip you're trying to make "disappear." The real strength of the clips you're uploading isn't to respond directly to the video, but to confuse the YouTube user and make it impossible for them to find the video they're looking for. The one thing every campaign can count on is that any web user

has a slight case of undiagnosed ADD (attention deficit disorder). If they don't find what they're looking for seconds after the search has begun, they'll tire, and give up the search.[176]

This strategy is becoming widespread, with public relations firms now offering to flood the zone with their specially trained "blog warriors" to "put your talking points on the blogosphere 24/7," because "today's blog attacks can be tomorrow's news."[177]

In at least some instances, bloggers identify astroturfing and neutralize artificial opinion cascades, usually at some expense to the credibility of the organizations that were attempting to manipulate public debate. "Public opinions that can acquire visibility only because of an undeclared infusion of money or organizational power," Habermas argues, "lose their credibility as soon as these sources of social power are made public."[178] These critical interventions expose where "publicity attempts to hide itself, pretending to come from the people through what have come to be called 'astroturf' groups, that is, organizations that purport to be 'grassroots' but that are actually funded and operated by hidden organizations."[179] Astroturf resists being peeled back, and despite some successes, bloggers cannot claim to catch all instances of astroturfing. However, when astroturf blogs *are* smoked out, the criticism lodged against them underlines the value of bloggers' participation in public deliberation: namely, as coalescers of spontaneous communication coming from peripheral nodes of a public culture. The expansion of the rhetorical imaginary with the term "flood the zone," then, manifests both the potential and the threat of communication in internetworked times. The term can be used as a normative benchmark to demarcate organic processes of spontaneous communication from artificial attempts by institutions to overwhelm communicative power with money.

The growth of the blogosphere as a site for public argument was, in part, a response to a corporate institutional press that had partially abdicated its role in detecting signals from civil-society actors and sluicing them toward decision makers. The trope "flooding the zone" signifies the capacity of bloggers and other digitally networked intermediaries to invent arguments that shape public deliberation. As this case study shows, the internetworked blogosphere in the Lott case allowed deliberators to focus attention and generate communicative power that dislodged Trent Lott from his perch at the top of the Senate. This early episode of blog-borne public argument funneled inventive spontaneous communication from the periphery to more general-interest media. But, as blogs become more "institutionalized," theorists and critics of networked media must ask whether some of the political economy problems of the broadcast media are being imported into these new media forms. Is a gradual narrowing of viewpoint diversity inevitable in any media form, or does the architecture of the networked public sphere prevent pathways of influence from gradually hardening? That question is a crucial one in working out the complex connections between networked media and democratic legitimation in future episodes of public deliberation.

4

AMBIENT INTIMACY IN SALAM PAX'S *WHERE IS RAED?*

In the wake of the Lott case, members of the institutional press turned their attention to the emergent genre of blogging. Words related to "emotion" were invariably invoked in these press accounts. "Blogs are cyber reality shows," one commentator noted, "widely read diaries that publicly detail the social drama and fluctuating emotions of young lives."[1] Early adopters of blogs used them "to do what they once did through personal diaries, phone conversations and hangout sessions: cementing friendships with classmates, seeking new friends, venting, testing social limits, getting support and getting all emo ('highly emotional' in blog-speak)."[2] Reports underlined how "the defining characteristic of blogging is its highly personal nature."[3] Press commentators situated blogs as highly subjective sites for self-expression: "like a journal, 'blogs' tend to be highly personal, running the gamut from short musings to angst-filled rants."[4] Consequently, "online journals have a bad reputation: emotional train wrecks and narcissistic ramblings plastered on the Web for all to see."[5] The danger, according to some critics of blogging, is that these expressions of youthful exuberance were habituating citizens to hyperemotional patterns of public discourse. To wit, some critics alleged, "the way we argue now has been shaped by cable news and Weblogs; it's all 'gotcha' commentary and attributions of bad faith. No emotion can be too angry and no exaggeration too incredible."[6] Sometimes the emotional nature of blogs was compared to more "objective" modes of journalism: "The blogs and the 'citizen journalism' are all opinion, emotion, and reaction, not news. Someone still has to tell people what is going on. It takes skills to do that. It requires the ability to quickly analyze mounds of data to figure out what is most important; to focus on an event, not one's own reaction to it; and to tell a story in a clear, concise and powerful way. In other words, it requires journalists who have honed their craft through practice and training."[7]

But commentators from the institutional press were not entirely pessimistic about the emanations from the blogosphere. Many noted the different emotional register of blogs by drawing on the metaphor of voice. Blogs were "a forum for fresh voices and viewpoints" that were "powerful tools in two ways: as one-stop clearinghouses of information and links, and—in the case of blogs emanating from a war zone—as unfiltered, up-to-the-minute sources of firsthand observation."[8] Like new media in prior war zones, blogs provided "a different voice to coverage of the war against Iraq."[9] This association with voice occupied the popular imagination: "bloggers are often eloquent in the way that those who are not self-consciously polished often are—raw, uncensored, and energized by the sound of their newly awakened voices."[10] Scholars like Henry Jenkins and David Thorburn also employ the language of voices by noting that "the current diversification of [digital] communication channels . . . is politically important because it expands the range of voices that can be heard in a national debate, ensuring that no one voice can speak with unquestioned authority."[11] Whether critics see emotion in the blogosphere as a positive or a negative, they surely agree that one major consequence of blogging has been, in Trish Roberts-Miller's phrasing, to "facilitate the expressive public sphere."[12]

Many of these claims about emotion and voice were connected to Salam Pax, a blogger living in Baghdad before the war in Iraq. Salam Pax, a pseudonym taken from the Arabic and Latin words for peace, began his blog, *Where is Raed?*, as a way to stay in touch with his friend Raed who was studying abroad.[13] Salam's writing coincided with "a deep dissatisfaction with Big Media, a hunger for connection and community, and a yearning for political passion and for the writer's voice."[14] Salam Pax's blog offered "a personal account of the war from the Iraqi capital, unencumbered by reporting restrictions."[15] According to press accounts, the blog "put a personal face on the war"[16] through Salam's "idiosyncratic personal descriptions of Baghdad."[17] Readers of the blog learned about Salam Pax's personal, professional, and public life. He had spent a considerable amount of time living overseas. He liked red wine. His musical tastes were eclectic. His English was impeccable, equaled by his command of popular culture and wry humor. He worked in an architecture design firm. Early blog posts focused on complaints about his job and social engagements with friends and family. But as war clouds gathered, Pax concentrated his blogging on tidbits about life in prewar Iraq.[18] For a time, *Where is Raed?* was the only English-language blog coming from inside Iraq that narrated life under the specter of invasion.[19] Salam Pax's weblog became the most linked-to blog in the brief history of the blogosphere.[20] Popularity in the blogosphere translated to mass media press coverage; he became the "virtual personification of Iraq," identified as the Anne Frank of the war *and* its Elvis.[21] Eventually, Salam Pax netted a book deal to compile his blog posts and a fortnightly column in *The Guardian*.

Salam Pax's blogging is an opportunity to consider how the rational-critical sensibilities embedded in the modern rhetorical imaginary bump up against new sensibilities in the networked public sphere. While the structure of feeling that dominated modern sensibilities was grounded in the objective, dispassionate, impartial norms of public reason pitted against the subjective vicissitudes of emotion, the networked public sphere revalues norms of subjectivity, passion, and partiality.[22] Pax's rhetorical interventions contest the dominant liberal-modern conceptualization of citizenship as an impartial, reason-driven enterprise bound by nation, drawing attention to the complexities of life in Iraq during late 2002 and early 2003. The case of Salam Pax thus underlines how the expression of *pathos* afforded by the blogosphere creates public feeling, forges intimate relationships, and fashions imagined communities.

I analyze this challenge to the traditional model of the rational-critical public sphere by exploring Salam Pax's enactment of cynicism and melancholy. These two affects are often invoked in the press as stereotypes of blogging's emotional range: bloggers are essentially cynical actors trying to gain attention and fame and/or they are melancholic social isolates living in their parents' basements.[23] Two scholarly books extend these critiques. Geert Lovink's *Zero Comments: Blogging and Critical Internet Culture* argues that cynicism is the dominant emotion of the blogosphere and that, as a result, bloggers populate public discourse with critique unmoored from action. Michael Keren's *Blogosphere: The New Political Arena* posits that melancholy is the dominant emotion of the blogosphere and that bloggers are verbal fetishists disengaged from social structures that mediate real change. Lovink's and Keren's critiques are welcome antidotes to the triumphalism that accompanied early reflection on blogging; they are, moreover, astute in directing attention to the emotional implications of this new media form. Their diagnosis is at least partially on point, for cynicism and melancholy *are* present in Salam Pax's blogging. However, both Lovink and Keren greatly oversimplify the affective registers that prevail in the blogosphere. The articulation of human experience is simply too rich and varied for a single affect to dominate any particular medium.

Bloggers constantly experience and articulate, consciously and not, a range of feeling-states.[24]

Instead of trying to document the broad range of emotional expressiveness on blogs, I adopt a rhetorical perspective on Salam Pax's blogging that recuperates both cynicism and melancholy by situating them as two *political tones* that have specific rhetorical effects useful to networks of informal public deliberation.[25] Deliberation is always already embedded in a field of affects, and cynicism and melancholy canalize these affects to focus attention. I interpret the critiques lodged by Lovink and Keren as betraying an allegiance to a particular structure of feeling—a felt preference for objectivity, dispassion, rationality, embodiment—that dominated the modern social imaginary.[26] But if the networking of the public sphere is accompanied by a change in the structure of feeling, they are attempting to import norms of deliberation from one public culture to another. As I argue in this chapter, perpetuating the split between reason and emotion creates deliberation traps by marginalizing certain rhetors, styles, and topics. Instead, we ought to see cynicism and melancholy as rhetorical interventions that draw attention to strangers in the lifeworld.

To make this case, I explore how rhetorical theory has conceptualized the relationship between emotion and reason. Like invention, emotion has long been caught in a binary. It is either thought to compete with reason or be somehow complementary to it. A metarhetorical tracing of the metaphors that reflect this relationship between reason and emotion lays the groundwork for a more detailed examination of Lovink's and Keren's critiques. I ultimately make the case that the attention-shaping power of affect and emotion plays a vital role in deliberation and that increased cycling of affect into public life through blogs and other networked media produces "ambient intimacy." The concept of ambient intimacy adds to our understanding of the networked rhetorical imaginary by identifying how the circulation of affect facilitates the formation and transformation of potentially global publics.

Emotion Between Competition and Complementarity

The language of desire, passion, feeling, emotion, and affect—words that attempt to express a foggily understood visceral intensity—lends itself to highly metaphorical accounts. The dominant metaphors for this kind of bodily experience reflect different configurations of reason, emotion, publicity, and intimacy throughout history. Once again, classical Greece provides a starting point, as the tensions between Plato and Aristotle on the relationship between *logos* and *pathos* constitute the basic template for considering the relationship between reason and emotion. These themes are so familiar they need only a sketch: Plato believed that the *hoi polloi* were motivated more by uncontrollable *pathē* than elegant *logoi*. Since poets and artists appealed to the emotions of the lowest common denominator, they had no place in a Republic.[27] Rhetoricians fell into the same category, for what they taught was linguistic trickery geared to rousing an audience emotionally rather than engaging in a dialectical process that revealed real knowledge. For Plato, these kinds of base appeals distract from more proper ways to govern by competing with *logos* for the direction of the soul. Plato's allegory of the charioteer in the *Phaedrus* outlines the nature of the tripartite soul through the metaphor of a charioteer, who represents *logos*, being pulled by two horses. One horse is white, well-made, and spirited in all the right ways, responding to "the word of command and by reason."[28] The other horse is ill-formed, insolent, and black in color. These equine representations of the higher and lower passions are reined in by the *logos* of the charioteer. The charioteer can steer a virtuous path so long as the black steed's impulsiveness remains subordinated to the white steed's more refined sensibilities. In *The Republic*, Plato switches up the beastly metaphor: a regal, law-and-order–loving lion and a chaotically pleasure-seeking, multiheaded hydra represent the soul's desires. The "just man" seeks to forge an alliance with the lion to sublimate the hydra's pushes and pulls.[29] Plato's metaphors are certainly evocative, drawing attention to the sometimes wild intensities of our bodies and our ability to draw on cognitive abilities empowered by *logos* to work with, suppress, or overcome them.

Aristotle, in contrast, linked *pathos* to cognitive processes usually associated with *logos*. According to him, "the emotions are those things through which, by undergoing change, people come to differ in their judgments and which are accompanied by pain and pleasure."[30] As emotional intensities surrounding an issue are changed, so are people's opinions. Feeling unsafe on a dark street at night is an experience of bodily intensity that wisely cues one to be cautious. Aristotle's teachings presume "a contoured world of emotional investments" that charge language with meaning.[31] Thus, to move people cognitively requires mobilizing them emotionally, which makes appealing to *doxa* (public opinions, commonplaces, and shared feelings) essential to the activity of persuasion. *Logos* and *pathos*, in Aristotle's formulation, are not necessarily at odds, especially—and this is crucial—given rhetoric's capacity to challenge and enlarge received *doxa*. Rhetoric acknowledges received attention patterns but is not bound to them. By redirecting attention to more ethical and practical considerations, rhetoric broadens the horizon of an audience. Aristotle's thesis on the complementarity of *pathos* and *logos* was both more realistic, in that it taught students how to think about persuasion according to how people were actually moved, and richer, in that it offered substantially more resources for persuasion.

Aristotle's dominant metaphors for emotion are oriented not around suppression but mediation. Aristotle prefers to see a temperate person, in Marlene K. Sokolon's translation, as having "his [sic] appetites in symphony (*symphōnia*) with his reason."[32] The *pathetic* appetites could be brought into harmony with *logos* through positive or negative reinforcement and through speech itself. When mobilized effectively, emotion motivates the action that rhetoric inspires. Two other metaphors underline the symphonic conception of emotion. First, the idea of *metekhousa* suffuses Aristotle's writings on emotion and reason.[33] The term implies partnership, or partaking, hinting at the mutual interpenetration of emotion and reason. Second, emotion is likened to the impulses of childhood: potentially wild, but also educable. Aristotle stresses in the *Nicomachean Ethics* that "the appetitive part of us should be ruled by principle, just as a boy should live in obedience to his tutor."[34] Each of these metaphors—symphony, partnership, tutor—reinforces Aristotle's thesis that emotion and reason can be brought together in a way that advances civic virtue.

Aristotle's observations are, however, relegated to a minority view in the dominant history of Western civilization. Cicero referred to followers of Aristotle's complementarity thesis as "feeble and unmanly," highlighting the historically gendered nature of emotion.[35] Why, asks the Roman rhetorician, would any dosage of emotion be useful if emotion was itself a flaw or deficiency? Cicero's adaptation of Greek teachings on emotion, garnished with a Stoic twist, resulted in another metaphor: feeling was a kind of sickness that the rational faculties could cure.[36] The emotion-as-illness metaphor is grounded in the etymology of *pathos* itself, as the root of *pathos* refers to "suffering" or "disease"; contemporarily, the study of disease is known as pathology.

This tension between *pathos* and *logos* stretches into modern times, receiving, in "emotion" and "reason," terminological updates that narrowed the capaciousness of the earlier Greek terms. Etymologically, the sense of reason as "thinking in a logical manner" originated in the 1590s, and the conception of emotion as a "strong feeling" originated in the 1650s.[37] The early modern age is replete with metaphors for emotion. Descartes referred to emotions as the heated excitations of the soul in *The Passions of the Soul*; Kant upped the ante by calling them tempests of the soul in *Metaphysics of Morals*; Hume situated reason as slave and passion as master in *The Treatise on Human Nature*; Hugh Blair linked passion to contagion in *Lectures on Rhetoric and Belles Lettres*; Madison thought that the passions could be inflamed or kindled in *Federalist* 10; Darwin had his nerve-force in his lesser-known *Expression of Emotion in Man and Animal*; Lippmann hinted that the emotions were produced by the clang and clatter of free association in *Public Opinion*; and so on and so forth through modern history.

The implications of these metaphors could certainly be mined for further insight, but the more interesting development in the early modern rhetorical imaginary is how reason and emotion became articulated to the new social categories of public and intimate. According to Habermas, the early modern era established the categories of public (the literary and "political"), private (the economic), and intimate (the conjugal family) as organizing principles for bourgeois culture and, by extension, their norms of deliberation. As the *oikos* prepared the ancient Greeks to participate in the *polis*, so the intimate sphere was considered to be a site where public selves might be better cultivated.[38] Yet the intimate sphere's cultivation of feeling and emotion was not, in the bourgeois self-conception at the time, to spill over into rational-critical debate—except as the general facilitator of humanist principles like love and freedom, which provided a *telos* for public deliberation. It was a spatial, not temporal, kind of complementarity: emotion and reason could coexist so long as they operated in separate locations. Bring them together, and the preferred rational norms of the bourgeois public sphere would be exposed as fictions built on feelings.

This spatial complementarity worked for citizens just beginning to exercise their critical faculties in forming public opinion. As Lauren Berlant interprets this process, "persons were to be prepared for their critical social function in what Habermas calls the intimate spheres of domesticity, where they would learn (say, from novels and newspapers) to experience their internal lives theatrically, as though oriented toward an audience."[39] This audience-centeredness was increasingly important as ever-more-heterogeneous publics began to meet and persuade each other on a larger scale. The evolution of letter writing, then a relatively new mode of expression, marks how intimacy constituted a subject ready to participate in public life. At first, the postal service primarily circulated letters that conveyed basic happenings from afar. Later, "scholarly communication and familial courtesy" dominated letters.[40] But as the self-conception of the bourgeois consolidated, letter writing became a site for emotional outpourings. Through letter writing, Habermas emphasizes, "the individual unfolded himself in his subjectivity." The gendered pronoun here underlines the liberal, masculine self-conception of an autonomous, unified subject thought to be independent from capital and thus capable of "entering into 'purely human' relations" with their fellow bourgeois.[41] Letters were an "'imprint of the soul,' a 'visit of the soul'; letters were to be written in the heart's blood, they practically were to be wept."[42] It is hard to imagine a more vivid account of the sentimentalism that ripened in the bourgeois intimate sphere.

While the intimate sphere created fellow feeling, the public sphere demanded norms of reasoned argumentation designed to reconcile competing opinions. The individual experience of emotion, though an important part of bourgeois subjectivity, was too subjective to provide a basis for collective decision making. Reconciling competing emotions through language was complicated, if not impossible, so the more impartial instrumentality of public reason was developed with increasing sophistication to generate a comparatively more objective method for judgment. As a consequence, citizens toggled between two mutually reinforcing subjectivities: a private one steeped in intimate feeling and a public one committed to rational-critical argument.[43] Retrospectively, the strong preference for impartiality and reason at the birth of the bourgeois public sphere can be charitably interpreted as a necessary correction for centuries of aristocratic rule based on indecipherable whims and feelings.[44] Yet, as the modern imaginary congealed, the bourgeois fetishization of reason created a deliberative trap by entangling public rhetoric within a system of oppressive social relations. Take gender, for example: the development of the public use of reason came while significant transformations in gender relations were occurring. The enhanced critical power of the citizenry was purchased by systematically devaluing expressions of emotion, which became linked with women's work in the intimate sphere. Though the modern social imaginary professed to be cultivating intimate ties based on the common humanity of all people, the bourgeois public sphere was in reality "a camouflage for male domination."[45] Though women often learned the norms of public reason through letter writing and literature, they were formally excluded from participating in rational-critical debate in the early bourgeois public sphere. This historical fact exposes the internal inconsistency of a bourgeois public sphere supposedly premised on inclusivity. Women did participate in rhetorical activities of many types, and even occasionally gained entry into public arenas, but the sharp lines between what was appropriate behavior in public and in private served to rationalize their exclusion and justify their regulation by more privileged actors.

Who gets to talk is not the only stake in this cultural development, for the restriction of the public use of reason to propertied white men unintentionally privileged their communicative norms—thus shaping the *how* of talk as well. Masculine communication styles became articulated to norms of publicity, thus privileging impartiality, disinterestedness, and objectivity. In this way, actors in the modern imaginary gradually came to equate publicity and reason with masculinity and intimacy and emotion with femininity. The preference for certain ways of speaking subtly but powerfully empowers those acculturated to privileged codes of speech, reentrenching inequities that were supposedly bracketed by the bourgeois public sphere.[46] The communicative norms articulated to public reason often silence those on the periphery, and not just along the axis of gender but also along axes of ethnicity, nationality, class, sexual orientation, and species. As social categories, public and private historically function as fields of argument that privilege certain ways of communicating. To some extent this is inevitable—and even desirable. Not every private feeling warrants equal consideration in public debate, and, conversely, sometimes reason is a useful instrumentality even in extraordinary domestic spaces. But democratic legitimacy finds purchase in establishing an appropriate relationship between public and private communication, not endorsing one to the exclusion of the other.

The early press, whose boisterous partisanship further calls into question the assumption of a public sphere free of emotion, eventually faded in favor of a national press that claimed to institutionalize the norms of impartiality, disinterestedness, and objectivity. Publishers found it more profitable to abandon their previously partisan inclinations in favor of a "neutral" approach to the news that attracted more advertising dollars.[47] Like the early bourgeois public sphere, which paraded masculinity as neutrality, the presupposition of press impartiality simply concealed institutional biases.[48] Despite the lionization of the norms of abstraction, impartiality, and objectivity in the press, broader cultural changes exposed them as untenable fictions. A core animating principle of many social movements in the 1960s and 1970s was a reconsideration of the traditional norms dividing public from private.[49] The feminist slogan "the personal is political" encapsulates a fundamental challenge to the modern social imaginary. This slogan materialized from efforts by midcentury feminists to politicize inequities borne largely out of the public eye.[50] In politicizing these inequities formerly considered nonpolitical, new social movements made the public-private divide more permeable and articulated an alternative relationship between the two that broadened the possibilities for social justice. Along with the politicization of previously "private" issues came a set of revaluations of women's public communication capacities. Though it would be a stretch to say that women, or any historically marginalized group, are on equal deliberative ground in a public arena dominated by masculine, white, and class-privileged norms and codes, the patrolling of rhetorical space that was so indicative of the nineteenth and twentieth centuries is less prevalent in the twenty-first. That such disciplinary activity is quickly identified and critiqued signals a loosening of traditional norms that previously restricted public deliberation to Reason instead of just reasons.[51]

New media technologies, by changing processes of publication, inevitably reconfigure these received notions of public and private. That blogs are often called "public diaries" demonstrates this blurring line between public and private, as a diary has historically been an intimate document only. Kris Cohen identifies this shift by noting that "blogs appear to be shifting the balance of personality and impersonality in the operation of publics and in the production of public subjects."[52] While the terms that cluster around objectivity are figured as fundamental values of twentieth-century journalism, partiality, emotion, and intimacy are more acceptable norms in the blogosphere. As journalist Antony Loewenstein points out, "the finest bloggers are much more transparent about their biases. . . . Such moves increase reader respect and contribute to the development of a democratic media ideal."[53] The traditional press's commitment to objectivity and the blogosphere's commitment to subjectivity need not be placed into an antagonistic relationship. Each performs a valuable democratic service. As Robert Hariman and John Lucaites assert, "print media's virtues of disembodied assertion, systematic organization of ideas, and dispassionate tone," while effective in circulating information in a democracy, are often "insufficient to motivate collective action."[54] The partiality and passion present on blogs, on the other hand, might well move people to participate more fully in democratic public life.⁵⁵ However, I read the critiques lodged by Geert Lovink and Michael Keren as declining to see the potential of this synthesis in the broader networked public sphere, instead preferring the structure of feeling associated with modern informationist sensibilities. I turn now to relating a brief history of cynicism, examining the charges leveled by Lovink, and then reinterpreting cynicism conveyed through Salam Pax's blog within a rhetorical frame before following a similar path for melancholy and Keren's critique.

The Cynical Salam Pax

Although popular invocations of cynicism connote bitterness, negativity, and withdrawal, there is a richer history of cynicism that does not tilt inevitably toward a toss-your-hands-up nihilism. If cynicism can be said to have a beginning, then that beginning is with Diogenes of Sinope in the Greece of the classical rhetoricians. Diogenes was a Cynic and an itinerant who frequented the Athenian agora to challenge the high theory of Plato with what Peter Sloterdijk terms "'dirty' materialism."⁵⁶ Rather than working out a philosophy of the true, good, and just, Diogenes celebrated the pleasures of the body. In one famous anecdote, Diogenes farts in response to Platonic theory. Another recalls Diogenes responding to Plato's "subtle theory of eros" by masturbating in the public square.⁵⁷ This kind of dirty materialism as an argument strategy was built upon a cheeky repudiation of the overly intellectualized idealism of Plato. Rather than rationalize social convention and custom, those who followed the Cynics lived like the animals they recognized themselves as being. They were, above all, to be true to themselves. Their rhetorical interventions, though, received decidedly mixed reviews. On the one hand, there was obvious interest and excitement by Athenians in following the idiosyncratic meanderings of Diogenes: what would this master of orchestrating attention do next? But the Cynics' rejection of the culturally acceptable norms of speech narrowed their potential audience and their ultimate appeal. The cynical rhetor is a recurring one that, according to Ted Windt, reasserted itself in the countercultural protest movements of the 1960s.⁵⁸ These protest movements, like Diogenes, resisted the conformity of organizational culture in mid-twentieth-century America and western Europe. Thus, one strategy of the protest movements was to contest the conventions of public address. New social movement protestors emphasized that their concerns about social justice and public life could not be neatly translated into the dominant rational-critical idiom represented by highly formalized modes of speech.[59]

Are bloggers, then, just the most recent iteration of the Cynics? Yes, according to Geert Lovink's *Zero Comments: Blogging and Critical Internet Culture*. Lovink begins his book with a long epigraph from a blogger that inspires his title and prefaces his connection between blogging and cynicism: "Blogging is a form of vanity publishing. You can dress it up in fancy terms, call it 'paradigm shifting' or a 'disruptive technology,' the truth is that blogs consist of senseless teenage waffle. Adopting the blogger lifestyle is the literary equivalent of attaching tinselly-sprinkles to the handlebars of your bicycle. In the world of blogging '0 Comments' is an unambiguous statistic that means absolutely nobody cares. The awful truth about blogging is that there are far more people who write blogs than actually read blogs."[60] Succinctly, Lovink's thesis is that "blogs zero out centralized meaning structures and focus on personal experiences, not, primarily, news media" (1). Immediately, the legitimacy of the public-private distinction materializes in *Zero Comments* as a structuring assumption.

Lovink aims to identify the common undercurrents that shape this new media form, finding that blogging involves "a techno-affect that cannot be reduced to the character of the individual blogger" (xxiii).[61] This techno-affect is fundamentally a cynical one. Lovink rightly acknowledges how the interplay between the broader cultural milieu and the technological affordances of networked communication produces this cynical techno-affect: "It is the general culture that has become cynical. What is important to note is the Zeitgeist into which blogging as a mass practice emerged. Internet cynicism in this case would be a cultural spin-off from blogging software, hardwired in a specific era. This techno-attitude results from procedures such as login, link, edit, create, browse, read, submit, tag, and reply" (12–13). What does Lovink mean when he opaquely asserts that the fundamental procedures of blogging—the software functionalities— produce a techno-attitude of cynicism? The basic processes of blogging involve linking to other content and reacting to it. These reactions are often critical, lodging a disagreement with the primary source or adding some nuance by appending additional commentary. Perhaps it is this critical attitude that so easily turns one cynical.[62] Alternatively, perhaps cynicism is simply a side effect of information abundance. To attract or sustain attention, Lovink proclaims, blogging necessarily descends into a kind of spectacular one-upping designed to produce traffic and thus advertising revenue. Lovink is at least partially correct that *some* bloggers and commenters do engage in crude efforts to acquire attention by updating Diogenes with—to be frank—digital farts (trolling) and digital masturbation (self-indulgent drivel).

In contrast to the early internet, which was shaped by a strong countercultural influence, Lovink links blogging to the post-9/11 world conditioned by postmodern anomie, lack of institutional credibility, and a consumer-capitalist imperative that reduces motivation to the almighty dollar.[63] Again, part of Lovink's argument is perceptive; he develops an early critique of the political economy of networked media. "New Economy" gurus latched onto blogging as a micro–public relations tool that aided businesses in developing profitable relationships with customers.[64] As the blogosphere became more popular, there was pressure on individual bloggers to distinguish themselves from the hordes of people rushing, lemming-like, into this new media form. The predictable result was a rash of "How to Cash in on Blogging" artifacts: books, articles, and entire blogs that recommended building an audience through punchy headlines, short entries full of passion, and keyword-heavy (thus search engine–optimized) words. These guides to blogging mimic the role that rhetorical handbooks have long played in distilling communication strategies for popular audiences. As Lovink puts it in *Zero Comments*, "the ideal blog post is defined by zippy public relations techniques" (4). Blogs, for Lovink, are so singularly focused on gathering attention that they end up favoring the spectacular over the deliberate. Of course, critiquing the ways in which the commercial imperative dumbs down communication is grasping at pretty low-hanging fruit. Lovink's critique might have more traction if it were tailored to for-profit blogging. Yet he insists on eliding the differences among all blogs by arguing that "instead of focusing on the quality of the content, and the culture of writing, diary keeping, and reflection, blogs have become more of a rat race for maximum attention, measured in links and friends" (xxiv). Without a doubt, some blogs are surely vulnerable to this criticism. At the same time, quality and quantity are not automatically antithetical, and many bloggers happily blog even with zero comments.

Instead of critique, "blogs offer a never-ending stream of confessions," Lovink contends, "a cosmos of micro-opinions attempting to interpret events" (17). He adds, "bloggers rarely add new facts to a news story. They find bugs in products and news reports, but rarely unmask spin, let alone come up with well-researched reports" (8). Although the Trent Lott imbroglio and countless episodes since then provide counterexamples, Lovink asserts that "what bloggers often lack is an ability to do thorough research and investigative journalism" (38). Lovink's assessment of blogging presumes a narrow interpretation of research and investigation that maps onto the historical distinction between public and private: can revelations of private experience ever become more than confession for Lovink? Could personal experience ever inform public argument? For Lovink, the only communicative consequence of blogs is to create a "dense cloud of impressions" (8) and "broad associations, a people's hermeneutics of news events. The computable comments of the millions can be made searchable and visually displayed, for instance, as buzz clouds" (15). Blogs are more Monet than Rembrandt—and as a good Dutch national, Lovink is apparently compelled to favor the latter in his discounting of the value of impressionistic representations.

Lovink extends his critique by arguing that the teleology of blogs involves dismantling old meaning structures:

> Blogs bring on decay. Each new blog is supposed to add to the fall of the media system that once dominated the 20th century.... What is declining is the "Belief in the Message." That is the nihilist moment, and blogs facilitate this culture as no platform has ever done before. Sold by the positivists as citizen media commentary, blogs assist users in their crossing from truth to nothingness. The printed and broadcasted message has lost its aura. News is consumed as a commodity with entertainment value. Instead of lamenting the ideological color of the news, as previous generations have done, we blog as a sign of the regained power of the spirit. As a micro-heroic, Nietzschean act of the pajama people, blogging grows out of a nihilism of strength, not out of the weakness of pessimism. Instead of repeatedly presenting blog entries as self-promotion, we should interpret them as decadent artifacts that remotely dismantle the mighty and seductive power of the broadcast media. (17)

This passage underlines the central problematic of Lovink's pan-blogospheric theorizing. While some bloggers may intend to undermine the existing media system, not all blogs intend to do so. If blogs are supposed to dismantle Big Media, then what are we to make of the fact that the *New York Times* now hosts numerous in-house blogs to complement traditional reporting? Similarly, to assert that bloggers do not focus on the ideological leanings of news sources is as hasty as implying that this was a bread-and-butter critique of previous generations. Many blogs are fervently dedicated to exposing the "liberal" or "conservative" bias in the news.

So what is to be made of Lovink's argument that the "Belief in the Message" is declining? The mass media's historical role in circulating messages is now challenged by blogging's "creative nihilism... [which] openly questions the hegemony of mass media" (1). Lovink defines nihilism as "not the absence of meaning but a recognition of the plurality of meanings" (22). Since bloggers can present multiperspectival accounts, they moot the "centralized meaning structures" that could otherwise organize public life (1). The decline of the institutional media's "aura" no longer grants them authority to make Messages with a capital M, which makes for chaos.[65] "Questioning the message is no longer a subversive act of an engaged citizenry," Lovink intuits, "but an *a priori* attitude, even before the TV or PC has been switched on" (22). In more gentle hands, this observation could easily be framed as laudable: we now have a culture of critical thinkers! But Lovink worries instead that the contemporary hermeneutic of suspicion overshoots the sweet spot between too much and too little questioning. If we are skeptical of everything, then how are we supposed to find any common ground from which to act politically? If the newspaper and other broadcast media can no longer forge imagined communities, where meanings are circulated in a discernible, legible fashion, how are we to coordinate collective action? Without the aura of authority, what use are newspapers at all? What is the work of the broadcast media in an age of bloggable reproduction?

The obvious objection to this whole line of Lovinkian observation is that these centralized meaning structures—grand narratives, transcendent values, and organizing institutions—are relics of the modern age, offering increasingly diminishing returns over the past several decades. These useful fictions may have brought a veneer of cohesion to the modern social imaginary, though, as fictions, they were never as central or as meaningful as Lovink assumes. Yes, the development of centralized meaning structures like the newspaper was essential to bourgeois self-conception, but that meaning was meaningful only for a very partial slice of the populace. With the decline in the salience of organizing grand narratives associated with the postmodern condition, it is difficult to imagine how these traditional, centralized meaning structures could adequately ground public life today, especially under the circumstances of hypercomplexity. Lovink's critique presupposes an informationist model of communication where broadcast media circulate Messages—knowledge, facts, and information—while networked media only circulate messages—mostly conjecture, opinion, and confession.

In *Zero Comments*, Lovink doubles down on informationist assumptions by comparing blogging to an idealized vision of dialogue, stressing "the pushy tone is what makes blogs so rhetorically poor. What lacks in the software architecture is the very existence of an equal dialogue partner" (35). This postulation of an equal partner betrays a commitment to a particular vision, initiated by Platonic theory and revalorized by the bourgeois public sphere, of communication occurring on perfectly even dialogical grounds.[66] Absent this dialogical structure, blogging becomes a shallow practice where the mindset that "a link will do" replaces "knowledge" (24). In the quick circulation of blog posts, swimming with everything else in the complex datastream, Lovink opines that "the art of homemade rhetoric and the roughness of instant interpretation are what matter to bloggers" (24–25). And here we get to the real point: the problem with blogging is that it is so . . . rhetorical. Blogs aren't *really* interested in sustaining conversations because they're *really* about pushing their own opinion on others through overwrought bloviation. Bloggers get so invested in their "homemade rhetoric" that they sacrifice any real knowing—which rather begs the question of whether the alternative of overly processed "store-bought rhetoric" from the institutional mass media is that much better. Rather than engaging the real, Lovink states, the "tendency to remain on the surface, touch a topic, point to an article without even giving a proper opinion about it apart from it being worth mentioning, is widespread and is foundational to blogging. How many of the postings . . . are Socratic questioning?" (30). Once again, dialectic is made the enemy of rhetoric. Needless to say, if Socratic questioning is the gold standard, then most communication is doomed to be found severely lacking—including, it must be said, the monological form of a book like Lovink's.

What if, instead of seeing cynicism as a techno-affect built into the blogosphere, we saw it as a political tone with rhetorical consequences related to attention? Conceiving of cynicism as a tone offers a more subtle reading of how a blogger's voice adapts to particular situations for particular effects. Cynical tones are a stylistic resource that focuses attention on a particular issue, but not in the "thin" way that Lovink critiques. Instead, cynicism promises to rearrange perspectives more fundamentally. Some of the Cynics in ancient Athens sought to redeem fellow citizens through diatribes that, as Windt shows, "dramatize[d] their criticism of society."[67]

The diatribe contests some basic notions about public discourse. Whereas public speeches usually appeal to common assumptions, beliefs, and logical forms in an attempt to forge bonds of identification with an audience, practitioners of the diatribe reject these strategies as kowtowing too much to social norms. In contrast, "the diatribe... is moral dramaturgy intended to assault sensibilities, to turn thought upside-down, to turn social mores inside-out, to commit in language the very same barbarisms one condemns in society."[68] Diatribes often feature long monologues, fables and fabulations, jokes and ridicule, absurdities and inversions. Diatribes speak from personal experience rather than trade in publicly ratified myths.

The diatribe finds its way into virtually every medium, as talk radio and cable news attest. The diatribe also found a home in the blogosphere, given the possibility of push-button publishing of personal pet peeves. Sometimes, bloggers explicitly cue their audience that a diatribe or a rant is coming. Readers are, presumably, supposed to take those posts with a grain of interpretive salt. On Monday, March 16, 2003—four days before major military operations by the United States were to commence in Iraq—Salam Pax's blog explicitly used this cueing strategy by capitalizing and bolding the word "RANT" before beginning the post "No one inside Iraq is for war (note I said 'war,' not a 'change of regime')."[69] In the first sentence, Salam Pax situates himself clearly. He is no patsy of Saddam Hussein. His parenthetical explanation is a gentle rebuke to some proponents of the war who suggested that questioning the rationale for war necessarily meant an endorsement of Saddam Hussein's brutal rule. He continues, "No human being in his right mind will ask you to give him the beating of his life—unless you are a member of Fight Club, that is—and if you *do* hear Iraqis (in Iraq, not expat) saying 'Come on, bomb us!' it is the exasperation and ten years of sanctions and hardship talking. There is no person *inside* Iraq who will be jumping up and down asking for the bombs to drop. We are not suicidal, you know—not all of us in any case."[70] Three allusions operate in concert to support the central point Salam is making about how no one in Iraq wants war. First, the reference to the late 1990s film *Fight Club* operates as an analogy that, given the popularity of the film and the likely readership of the blog, functions as a recognizable commonplace of global popular culture that signifies the brutality of violence and the sickness that invites it. Second, the parenthetical aside "not expat" distinguishes Iraqi expatriates from citizens living in Iraq, suggesting that Iraqi émigrés who argue for invasion speak from a position of privilege, since they do not have to live through the bombing. The figures of Ahmed Chalabi—the Iraqi expat, consummate Washington, D.C., insider, and longtime advocate for intervention—and Salam Pax, billed as an ordinary Iraqi on his book cover, could not be more different. That difference, Salam argues, should shape the way readers interpret the credibility of war commentators. He is there, on the ground, taping his windows shut to prevent incoming bombs from shattering glass into his family's home, while deep-pocketed neoconservatives at a fancy Washington, D.C., fundraiser were feting Chalabi.[71] Finally, the last sentence is a not-so-subtle nudge to those who stereotype all "Arabs" as "terrorists." These allusions amplify the central hypothesis being advanced by Salam Pax—that no humans want violence visited upon their community.

With this setup, Salam moves into the body of the rant, a simmering exposition of the history of Iraq and the failures of the international community after the first Gulf War in the early 1990s. He reveals his judgments in very personal terms:

> I think that the coming war is not justified (and it is very near now, we hear the war drums loud and clear—if you don't, then take those earplugs off!). The excuses for it have been stretched to their limits they will almost snap. A decision has been made sometime ago that "regime change" in Baghdad is needed and excuses for the forceful change have to be made. I do think war could have been avoided. Not by running back and forth the last two months, that's silly. But the whole issue of Iraq should have been dealt with differently since the first day after Gulf War I.[72]

Salam articulates a widely held view among opponents of the war that the pretexts for invasion were flimsy justifications for a decision arrived at shortly after the events of September 11, 2001. War was being waged not for human rights, but to pursue some hidden imperative of oil, empire, or revenge. This paragraph begins a complex analysis of post–Gulf War Iraq, blaming the "international community" for a sanctions regime that perversely consolidated Hussein's power and stalled democratic movements.[73] While this type of historical analysis is important, and certainly relevant, it is not clear what Salam Pax hopes to achieve by this excursus. After all, knowing the path that led to this moment was unlikely to silence war's drumbeat. No audience could right the wrongs of the last decade. In the context of a rant, though, this decision is sensible. Salam Pax is not attempting to propose a course of action; he is aiming to jolt his readers by introducing underrepresented perspectives in public debate about the war.

Shock is precisely the purpose of the diatribe. This shock is not for self-aggrandizement. Rather, it is "the first step towards rearranging perspectives."[74] Salam Pax highlights hypocrisy in an attempt to further surprise: "What is bringing on this rant is the question that has been bugging me for days now: how could 'support democracy in Iraq' come to mean 'bomb the hell out of Iraq'? Why did it end up that democracy won't happen unless we go thru war? Nobody minded an un-democratic Iraq for a very long time. Now people have decided to bomb us into democracy? Well, thank you! How thoughtful."[75] The first question, about how "supporting democracy" became equated with "bomb Iraq" in public discourse, invokes the doublespeak popularized by another famous cynic, George Orwell. Salam draws attention to the rhetorical somersaults required to create democracy, a method for sustaining peace, through war, the ultimate agency of violence. He underscores how the international community propped up Hussein for years to counterbalance Iran's regional power, with no concern for the internal democracy of Iraq. In his view, democracy promotion was not an actionable reason for intervention over the past decades, so Iraqis were rightfully suspicious about why *now* was a good time for military action to depose Hussein. Salam Pax is reacting to a flashpoint of cynicism—hypocrisy. A cynic, in the tradition of Diogenes, cannot stand quietly by when others say one thing and do another, preferring one to just do what one will do and make no apologies for it. For Salam Pax, the invocation of human rights and democracy as rationales for war smack of double standards. The international community doesn't wage war on every nation-state that abuses a citizenry, so human rights rhetoric in this case likely masks other, more pernicious, intentions.

The line "now people have decided to bomb us into democracy? Well, thank you! How thoughtful" is not to be read flatly. There is an attitude inscribed in these sentences, which appears on blogs across a wide spectrum of genres, best described as "snark." Snark, a portmanteau that collapses "snide" and "remark," is often used to characterize quick witticisms that puncture an argument or offer a dismissive aside. Lovink cites the online *Urban Dictionary* for a definition of snarky language: "quips or comments containing sarcastic or satirical witticisms intended as blunt irony. Usually delivered in a manner that is somewhat abrupt and out of context and intended to stun and amuse."[76] The term became popularized in blogging communities, capturing the often terse and pointed nature of some blog commentary. Jim Brown explains that snark is a kind of defense mechanism for networked interlocutors, delivering "jabs and opinions in a knowing tone, attacking the opposition coldly or preemptively insulating the author against attacks and trolling."[77] Snark can be interpreted as a stylistic marker of a cynical tone. The opposite of snark for Lovink is emo (shorthand for "emotional"), a style that is closely related to melancholy and which I detail shortly.

This particular rant by Salam highlights the problems with the international community's approach to Iraq after the first Gulf War. By suggesting that "the situation in Iraq could have been solved in other ways," he identifies the semiautonomous region of northern Iraq as an option that could have been tried in southern Iraq.[78] He also gives a lengthy indictment of economic sanctions as tools of foreign policy. Salam emphasizes that "sanctions made the Iraqi people hostages in the hands of this regime; tightened an already tight noose around our necks. A whole nation, a proud and learned nation, was devastated not by war, but by sanctions."[79] Ostensibly, the sanctions were supposed to prevent Saddam Hussein's regime from acquiring so-called dual-use commercial products (like fertilizers or pesticides) that could be adapted to military ends. Salam delivers the following retort: "And can anyone tell me what the sanctions really did about weapons? Get real. There are always willing nations who will help; there are always organizations which will find his money sweet. Oil-for-Food? Smart Sanctions? Get a clue. Who do you think is getting all those contracts to supply the people with 'food'? Who do you think is heaping money in bank accounts abroad? It is *his* [Hussein's] people, *his* family, and the people who play *his* game."[80] In this passage, Salam Pax reveals another recurring *topos* of cynicism, the opposition between human nature and social institutions.[81] Institutions, for the cynic, are self-serving creatures interested only in their own perpetuation.[82] Cynics like Salam Pax found fertile material in dissecting institutional prerogatives and profit motives in the controversial Oil-for-Food program, which sold Iraqi oil to raise revenue for alleviation of the humanitarian crisis in Iraq. In this case, Salam labels the program as an enormous shell game, which, given the scandals associated with Oil-for-Food, was close to the mark. Though the Oil-for-Food program was set up by the United Nations to provide some relief from economic sanctions, Salam sees it as just another way in which Saddam Hussein, the "he" who is not named in this excerpt, was able to game the system. The skepticism of Salam Pax and other Iraqis about their impending "liberation" is more understandable with this backdrop, since past interventions by the international community only tightened Hussein's authoritarian grip.

Despite Salam Pax's reasons for being doubtful about the impending invasion, critics of military intervention were caught in a difficult rhetorical situation. Those who argued against intervention were often painted as supporters of Hussein's regime, which meant that the onus was on opponents of war to suggest how to resolve the "Hussein problem." Salam Pax navigates this difficult rhetorical situation by blogging, "do support democracy in Iraq, but don't equate it with war. What will happen is something that could/should have been avoided. Don't expect me to wear a 'I ♥ Bush' T-shirt."[83] In this passage, Salam pithily severs the purported tie between democracy and military intervention, providing an opening for critics of the impending war to likewise disaggregate their disdain for war from support for Hussein. More ominously, this part of the post provides a rejoinder to then vice president Dick Cheney's hopes that invading soldiers would be greeted as liberators.

Salam winds up this blog post by writing, "to end this rant, a word about Islamic fundis/wahabisim/qaeda and all that."[84] He concludes:

> Do you know when the sight of women veiled from top to bottom became common in cities in Iraq? Do you know when the question of segregation between boys and girls became red hot? When tribal law replaced THE LAW? When "Wahabi" became part of our vocabulary? It only happened *after* the Gulf War. I think it was Cheney or Albright who said they will bomb Iraq back to the Stone Age.... Well, you did. Iraqis have never accepted religious extremism in their lives. They still don't. Wahabis in their short *dishdasha* are still looked upon as sheep who have strayed from the herd. But they are spreading.... They call it *al hamla al imania* ("the religious campaign"). Of course, it was supported by the Government: pumping them with words like "poor in this life, rich in heaven" kept the people quiet. Or the other side of the coin is getting paid by Wahabi organizations. Come pray and get paid—no joke, dead serious. If the Government can't give you a job, run to the nearest mosque and they will pay and support you. This never happened before. It's outrageous. But what are people supposed to do? Their government is denied funds to pay proper wages and what they get is funneled into their pockets. So please stop

telling me about the fundis—never knew what they are never would have seen them in my streets. RANT ENDS.[85]

Compacted into this one blog post is a powerful mélange of cynically valenced arguments about cultural realities, social performances, historical events, and personal affliction. Salam Pax's diatribe created a complex moral dramaturgy that effectively drew global attention (recall that he was the most linked-to blogger in the short history of the blogosphere). But beyond gathering attention and opening up the potential for a subsequent rearrangement of perspectives, Windt observes, "the diatribe diminishes in usefulness. People demand serious remedies, seriously treated. Moral dramaturgy must give way to conventional rhetorical forms."[86] As a genealogy of events, Salam's diatribe provides context for how we got here, but it does little to suggest what we should do now that we *are* here. From one direction, Lovink's critique of cynicism fits neatly here, as Salam's personalized history of Iraq might be accused of being pushy, idiosyncratic, naïve, and self-promotional. But Lovink's critique must be balanced with a recognition of how Salam Pax's passionate cynicism usefully highlighted hypocrisy, the inadequacies of institutional reasoning, and humanist values of nonviolence.

What, then, can be said about the effect of all this cynical rhetoric? The function of the diatribe, for Windt, is "to reduce conventional beliefs to the ridiculous, thereby making those who support orthodoxy seem contemptible, hypocritical, or stupid. Each seeks laughter, but not for its own sake. Rather, laughter serves as a cleansing force to purge pre-conceptions about ideas, to redeem ignored causes, to deflate pomposity, to challenge conventional assumptions, to confront the human consequences of ideas and policies."[87] Effective diatribes expose the ridiculousness of social convention, the absurdity of certain beliefs, and the contours of power. As Sloterdijk elaborates, cynics "provoke a climate of satirical loosening up in which the powerful, together with their ideologists of domination, let go affectively—precisely under the onslaught of the critical affront."[88] Rhetorical interventions by cynics, then, produce a more open affective moment that enables alternative, sublimated, or underappreciated feelings to find purchase.

Adducing effect is notoriously difficult, especially given the proliferation of networked publics with idiosyncratic reception strategies. But if the coverage of Salam Pax's blog in the traditional news media is any sign, then his blogging succeeded in loosening up the rhetorical atmosphere and introducing a counter-narrative of war. His writing was lauded for the "strength of its voice, the fluency of its wit and the even-handed scabrousness of its political invective."[89] Salam Pax was "amusing, cynical, worldly and passionate . . . perhaps the best example of the power the Internet wields: in this media culture dominated by massive corporate news organizations, the reporting convention of one-to-many can be subverted by a personal, global conversation."[90] Some commentators picked up on the fact that the blog showed that "Pax didn't fit into the stereotype of the Iraqi. . . . He seemed just like us. He was gifted in English, wrote freely about his CD collection (including an obsession with David Bowie and Coldplay), was as critical of Saddam's regime as he was about the US-led invasion . . . [and] writes with a disarmingly jaunty campness of style."[91] Salam's accounts of the war were "riveting"[92] and a fresh alternative to the "sanitized network TV coverage."[93] His posts were described as "fascinating and haunting in their detail."[94] *Where is Raed?* was described as a collection of "compelling musings" that drew a large audience to the blog.[95] The blog "gained a cult following before the war as increasing numbers of internet readers turned to him for a fresh and revealing perspective of life in Baghdad."[96]

Salam Pax's cynical cheekiness drew attention to the deadly realities of war. As one commentator noted, "beneath the jokey tone . . . is an underlying fear that is one of the great strengths of the diary. Pax lets us know exactly what it was like waiting for the bombs to drop."[97] It would be too easy to argue that the visceral, personal nature of Salam Pax's blogging transformed public discourse about the war. It didn't, at least not totally. What it did do was draw attention to another aspect of the war in Iraq— not the political wranglings between the Bush administration and the Hussein regime and the United Nations and other allies; not the military personnel and potential strategies and new weapons; not the economic benefits and oil resources and geopolitical implications at stake. Instead, the blog represented one person's struggle to make sense out of the ongoing chaos, a real-life allegory that painfully demonstrated the human costs of war. Cynicism can be recuperated from Lovink's critique by situating it as a political tone that responds to specific rhetorical situations with the aim of producing an appreciation for individuals fenced in by institutions. The cynical tone allowed Salam Pax to tack between critiques of the Bush administration's case for war and Saddam Hussein's authoritarian rule. This evenhandedness created an opening for more complex considerations about war and peace, providing a counter-narrative to the impending war and drawing attention to the daily struggles of Iraqis. While mere attention is no guarantee for the rearranging of perspectives that is the hoped-for effect of cynical rhetoric, it is certainly a necessary beginning to any such process.

The Melancholic Salam Pax

Like cynicism, melancholy is a contested term that runs the gamut from quiet self-reflection to sadness, pensiveness, gravity, sobriety, and even debilitating grief. Melancholy, too, traces back to classical Greek culture. However, unlike cynicism, the rhetorical features of melancholy—its purpose, form, *topoi*, styles, figures, and effects—are relatively undertheorized.[98] Melancholy never inspired a collective of thinkers to do what the Cynics did for cynicism, perhaps explaining its underappreciated history as a unique set of affects.[99] To address the lacunae of theoretical work on melancholic rhetoric vis-à-vis Salam Pax's blogging, I first sketch a brief history of melancholy and then delve into Keren's diagnosis of the melancholic blogosphere.

Efforts to understand the complex of affects that float under the sign of melancholy were first developed in classical Greece. Aristotle (or a close follower of Aristotle's—precise authorship is disputed) noted in the *Problemata Physica*, "Why is it that all those who have become eminent in philosophy or politics or poetry or the arts are clearly of an atrabilious temperament, and some of them to such an extent as to be affected by diseases caused by black bile?"[100] The classical ideal was to achieve balance between the four humors of black bile, yellow bile, phlegm, and blood. Melancholia, the literal translation of "black bile," was thought to contribute to excellence in philosophy, politics, and other arts if present in excess. For the writer of the *Problemata*, melancholics are particularly adept at translating their quiet interior moments into incisive perceptions. This assumption coheres with the persistent stereotype that true artists occupy some very dark corners necessary for their brilliance (the so-called Woody Allen gene).[101] Humoral theory, though antiquated now, presented a plausible explanation for contrasting personalities and health until the advent of modern medicine proved otherwise. With the displacement of humoral theory, melancholy became a cultural rather than a biological disposition.

In cultures influenced by classical Greek thought, melancholy is often considered a "necessary" emotion that, in conjunction with other mature affective responses, produces a balanced person at the mean of emotional life. Melancholy deepens the sense of one's self and one's social world. It functions, as Emily Brady and Arto Haapala explain, as an educative emotion because "rather than being an immediate response to some object that is present to perception, melancholy most often involves reflection on or contemplation of a memory of a person, place, event, or state of affairs."[102] In this spirit, Keats referred to melancholy as "the wakeful anguish of the soul" in "Ode on Melancholy" in 1819.[103] This wakeful anguish signals the key tension of melancholy: alertness to the world is often pitted against the anxiety of knowing. Social creatures crave awareness of the world, but knowledge is only power if it doesn't collapse one in a heap of jelly at the bottom of the bed. Thus, the feeling of melancholy can oscillate dramatically between intensified perception of social realities and political quietism. "Melancholy," philosopher Max Pensky postulates, "is a source of critical reflection that, in its ancient dialectic, empowers the subject with a mode of insight into the structure of the real at the same time as it consigns the subject to mournfulness, misery, and despair."[104] Melancholy thereby produces a "heightening or intensification of a certain power of spiritual perception or insight into the nature of the world."[105] Melancholy is not an inhibition to activism but a kind of reflectiveness that can undergird and motivate collective struggle.[106]

This isn't to fetishize melancholy, especially as it slides along the spectrum toward depression. Nor is it to uncritically celebrate the melancholic's perception of "the Real," which from a rhetorical perspective is not as firm as Pensky intimates. Rather, it is to situate melancholy as a reflection-inducing mood that, by encouraging fullness of preoccupation with an object, invites the development of a rich and evocative rhetorical palette.[107] In this conception of melancholy, melancholics develop more sophisticated insights into their social world by generating a more nuanced vocabulary for their reflections. This process between interior thought and exterior publication, the "dialectical vigor" of melancholy, is characterized by Pensky as "the representation of the simultaneity of otherwise rigorous heterogeneous properties of the human experience of the world."[108] A melancholic senses, in a heightened way, a problem inherent in the art of rhetoric: every attempt at representation oversimplifies, and thus does violence to, the richness of the lifeworld, yet it is necessary to generate contingent insights required to coordinate human activity.

Freud's pathologization of melancholy in the early part of the twentieth century muted this dialectical dynamic. Freud understood melancholia in contradistinction to mourning, which was a natural process characterized by "the reaction to the loss of a loved person, or to the loss of some abstraction which has taken the place of one, such as one's country, liberty, an ideal, and so on. In some people the same influences produce melancholia instead of mourning and we consequently suspect them of a pathological disposition."[109] For Freud, mourning is work that the ego must do to detach itself from loss to go on with life, whereas melancholy occurs when this process of detachment persists beyond a reasonable time. Melancholy includes "cessation of interest in the outside world," "inhibition of all activity," and a "lowering of the self-regarding feelings to a degree that finds utterance in self-reproaches and self-revilings."[110] This Freudian interpretation set late modern public culture down a crooked path that led to the medicalization of melancholy (and the consequent mood-managing drugs).

Michael Keren's *Blogosphere: The New Political Arena* extends the Freudian pathologization of melancholy to the blogosphere. Keren perceives blogging as an evolution of "life writing," a genre that contains "autobiographies, memoirs, confessions, spiritual quests, meditations, personal essays, travelogues, autobiographical short-stories and novels; portraits, complaints, conceptual writings, works of humor, and family histories."[111] Such a wide range of generic forms effectively, if inexhaustively, shows the plurality of expression on blogs. For Keren, life writing potentially functions as an emancipatory process of self-revelation and connection with others, as it did for the bourgeois public sphere caught up in the world of letters (8). Keren explicitly speculates that blogs may connect individuals to the "public arena" in the same way that salons and coffeehouses did (10). He even acknowledges that bloggers in the Trent Lott affair and Salam Pax appeared to have "direct political impact" (6).

However, Keren then sounds a cautionary note. The similarities between blogging and the bourgeois public sphere do not flow down to the norms and practices of each, for the blogosphere is an "arena in which new political modes, norms, and forms of action and inaction are emerging" (10). These modes, norms, and forms—constituents of a new imaginary—embrace a melancholic attitude that short-circuits what Keren considers to be effective democratic politics. "This new arena," Keren writes, "can be characterized by a unique combination of the fresh voice of emancipation and a deep sense of withdrawal and rejection" (11–12). Rather than the kind of enlightenment that the break with Church doctrine represented for the bourgeois public sphere, the emancipation provided by blogging ushers in melancholy. Melancholy, for Keren, is the "'unappeasable attachment to an ungrievable loss'" (12).[112] He cites Freud's description of melancholics as shameless talkers about their own condition: "Shame before others . . . is lacking in him [sic], or at least there is little sign of it. One could almost say that the opposite trait of insistent talking about himself and pleasure in the consequent exposure of himself predominates in the melancholiac" (12).[113] The implications for bloggers are obvious. Keren goes on to claim that "melancholy is not only a psychological condition but can also be seen as a form of social withdrawal stemming from the loss of a solid normative base, especially the solid base provided by the universalized 'I' of the enlightenment" (12).[114] The assumption that only the liberal unified subject can enact collective political action conveys Keren's commitment to modern sensibilities.

The networked citizen, for Keren, severs the melancholy dialectic between withdrawal and insight. As he attests in *Blogosphere*, this "critical insight [into the real] is not, as in the case of the enlightened person, constructive and active but destructive and passive" (13). Keren's totalizing indictment of blogging is premised on informationist assumptions:

> The politics of blogosphere is melancholic not because it lacks joy, triumph, and exultation but because when these emotions, like any other feelings, thoughts, or activities are present, their relation to real life is incidental. Blogosphere involves journalism without journalists, affection without substance, community without social base, politics without commitment. It replaces action by talk, truth by chatter, obligation by gesture, and reality by illusion. Millions of individuals write their lives while giving up on living them, if only because of the long hours they spend at their computers. . . . Bloggers assert an individuality that gets lost in the need for approval by others, for it requires quite an effort to get one's blog posted on other bloggers' lists of favorites. They speak the truth without clear standards about what speaking truth on the Internet means, do good and refrain from evil in virtual reality, and often turn into political activists without leaving home. (14–15)

Keren crystallizes several prominent informationist critiques of blogging in this short passage. The lack of institutional structure makes blogging a token of real change; bloggers are virtual, not real; they engage in fluff, not stuff; they yearn for attention, not truth; they type away their lives rather than living them; they are self-promotional sycophants and armchair activists; they are alien to the political order.¹¹⁵ I submit that Keren's indictment of blogging functions as an indictment of human communication in general. Hours spent watching television (even if it is the "news"), talking on the phone (even if it is about "politics"), or listening to the radio (even if it is "public") fritter away civic potential. That these communicative modes might have positive effects in strengthening the social fabric of a group or in clarifying one's own position is ignored. Keren's zero-sum approach to blogging ignores the fact that communication, inevitably mediated and often multiply remediated, *sometimes does* and *sometimes does not* trade off with other types of political engagement. Public communication emanating from the blogosphere, like all communication, produces a variety of complex affective and cognitive effects that engage people in a multiplicity of ways and to a variety of ends.

The type of politics that Keren prefers becomes evident as he continues: "This notion of civil society stands in contrast to melancholic politics as it emerges in the blogosphere. The latter is filled with nicknames rather than people, a fetishism of ideas rather than a presentation of interests, solipsistic discourse rather than an orderly exchange, and a lack of clear frameworks of social obligation and political responsibility" (15–16). The end result? "Political passivity," "fake communal relations," and "verbal fetishism" (16). Blogging is the new false consciousness. In response to those who situate internetworked public discourse as a site for public deliberation, Keren writes, "society is not a 'great debate' but a concrete network of relations steered by political elites, bureaucratic routines, economic interests, and cultural industries. None of these is significantly affected by online or offline discourse" (151). And so Keren finally comes clean. "The political" is neatly severed from discourse; it is a hermetically sealed field of power relations that requires exclusive attention to materialist practice and can safely ignore discourse as part of the superstructural epiphenomena that do not—cannot—impact the structural phenomena of politics itself (which Keren operationally defines very narrowly). For Keren, rhetoric's attention-steering properties have no impact on material reality.

Keren's detection of melancholy in the blogosphere *is* an apt diagnosis of Salam Pax's blog, as Pax certainly has melancholic moments. But Salam Pax's excuse was a good one, as he was literally waiting for the most powerful military in the world to attack his country with the promise of shock and awe. These melancholic moments can be read, *contra* Keren, as employing a particular tone to draw attention to the grim realities of warfare as experienced by those civilians in war zones. But what are the rhetorical features of a melancholic tone? If the diatribe is the conventional form to express cynicism, then what is the conventional form for melancholic rhetoric? What are the central *topoi* of melancholic rhetoric? Are there recurring rhetorical figures utilized by a melancholic tone? What is the purpose of adopting it? Does it have a particular style? Finally, what effect does it have on audiences?

The form that melancholic rhetoric most often takes is the lament.[116] In the classical Greek tradition, ritual laments were dedicated to gods, fallen heroes, destroyed cities, and the dead.[117] They were often formal, collective, and concentrated speech acts that aided mourners in their transition through the cycle of grief while solidifying a culture's collective memory. Contemporary laments reflect the post-parenthetical norms of networked culture. Salam Pax's laments are comparably informal, individually produced, and dispersed throughout his blog posts. His lamentations are not done for an explicitly ritual purpose; they are, if anything, lamentations of the everyday. Some of the most melancholic moments occur when Salam Pax describes the regular hardships endured by Iraqis. Occasionally he writes a passage that underlines the dramatic conditions in Iraq: "For how much would you sell your kidney? Salah sold his for $250. His fiancée sold hers as well, for the same price. They've been engaged for a while and they needed the $500 (that's equivalent to a million Iraqi dinars) to build two extra rooms in his parents' house for them to live in. I know this because a relative of mine was the buyer. Breathe in. Change the subject."[118] Though the sanctions-induced economic and medical hardships of Iraqi citizens were well documented, Salam Pax's blog reveals a more personal side to these affronts to human dignity. The closer war came, the more melancholic Salam became. In November, Salam writes, "my favorite headline until now is from Reuters: WORLD SEES CHANCE FOR PEACE; IRAQ MUM ON UN VOTE. Funny, the world sees peace, while I have to prepare a bomb shelter in my house. If you need me, I'm hiding under my bed until this is over."[119] Later that month, he makes his concern for the future of Iraq clearer, invoking images of a Baghdad-yet-to-be: "I worry about what will happen during the attacks and I worry more about what will happen afterwards. I take walks in parts of the old city and I can't stop thinking 'Will this be still there this time next year?' You are right; on an emotional level I cannot and will not accept a war on Iraq."[120] Pax declines a logocentric defense of his reaction, explicitly acknowledging that his emotional response is his only justification and assuming his audience will understand why that is enough.

Like the diatribe, which is intended to shock the sensibilities of listeners to facilitate the rearranging of perspective, these laments are jolting. They provide a dramatic image to many blog readers of what life was like in Iraq during this time. One purpose of melancholic rhetoric is thus to provide a concrete counter-narrative to the abstract discourses that often dominate public discourse during wartime. This was a role of the lament in ancient Greece. Ritual lamentation by women was "seen as a potential threat to the orderly functioning of the male public sphere and as undermining the heroic male code of military glory" by reminding the broader culture of the all-too-real human costs of violence.[121] The networked lament serves an analogous role. Contemporary broadcast news often reports war as what journalism scholar Jim Hall calls a "clinical game" focusing on abstract numbers and new weaponry, whereas "personal accounts insist that their readers make those painfully banal but crucial connections" about the human costs of war.[122] Hall explains that citizens who use networked media to report on their own experience of war counter the "seamless narrative carapace" constructed by governments and corporate news by introducing conflicting accounts, inviting "news consumers [to] become aware of the language that is employed to construct" stories about war.[123]

One way in which Salam Pax's blog provided a counter-narrative about the impending war was by following the traditional *topoi* of the lamentation. Linda Austin identifies these *topoi* as "exclamations of ineffability and the *ubi sunt*, often together. As the *ubi sunt* catalogs the losses, the ineffability (or inexpressibility) *topos* inscribes our confrontation with the idea of death and absence. Both may register shock and grief through a language of trauma."[124] Ineffability, the inability to articulate some phenomenon in language, is exhibited in the colloquialism "words fail us." In the passage above, when Salam concludes the story of Salah's selling a kidney on the black market with "breathe in, change the subject," he is performing the inexpressibility of injustice. In another post, he explicitly states his expressive inabilities to his friend Raed:

> Raed, I'm sorry but David Bowie's song "I'm Afraid of Americans" is stuck in my head and I can't think of anything else to write. Actually . . . there is a lot to write about, but it doesn't matter. . . . Light a candle for me will you, Raed? Keeping myself together takes effort the last two days . . . and do you know what else I read in the *New York Times*? The American troops they are studying how the Israeli

army fought in Jenin. *Jenin*. Remember how Jenin looked like after the siege? How comforting is that? Excuse me, but I need to listen to some angry-boy-music and bang my head against a wall and bleed; it will make me feel better, I'm sure. Have I told you already that I hate the world? P.S. Raed, don't even think about coming to Baghdad the next couple of days/weeks. You might not be able to go back to Jordan. Besides, I don't want you here the next couple of days. I am planning on spending them in a drunken haze. I do not want you near me.[125]

Here, that unique melancholy produced by living on the precipice of war is on full display with the ineffability *topos*. First, Salam Pax disparages his own attempts at blogging by noting that he can't think of anything to blog about, and that writing would be meaningless anyway. Secondly, he invokes Jenin as the apparent analogue for Iraq's future, invoking the macabre visual evidence that he and Raed likely shared after Israel's deadly military operation in that Palestinian city in 2002. Rather than explicitly articulating the details of Jenin, he lets the argument operate enthymematically with his intended audience of Raed and his imagined global audience, who were only an internet search away from better understanding the unspoken premise. Even Salam's difficulty in expressing the ineffable is affecting.

The second *topos* of the lament, the *ubi sunt*, refers to an often-nostalgic recollection of another time that appears as a catalog of the disappearance of valued people, artifacts, or moments. While the traditional *ubi sunt* prefaced a longer, more in-depth lamentation, it is more distributed in Salam Pax's blog, the entirety of which could be perceived as a running catalog of injustices. There are, however, some blog posts that perform the *ubi sunt* in a more conventional manner. When the comments function on *Where is Raed?* was still active, a commenter in favor of invasion responded to one of Salam Pax's posts by writing "now SHUT THE F— UP and learn to appreciate us a little!!!"[126] Salam responds:

> OK. Let us all have five minutes of silence to do some appreciation.
> I appreciate the dropping of tons of bombs on my country.
> I appreciate the depleted uranium used in those bombs.
> I appreciate the whole policy of dual containment, which kept the region constantly on the boil because it was convenient for the US.

> I appreciate the support the US government shows to all the oppressive governments in the region only to dump them after they have done what was needed of them.
> I appreciate the US role in the sanctions committee.
> I appreciate its effort in making me look for surgical gloves and anaesthetic on the black market, just to get a tooth pulled out—because these supplies are always being vetoed by the sanctions committee.
> I appreciate the policies of a country which has spent a lot of time and effort to sustain economic sanctions that punished the Iraqi people, while it had no effect on Saddam and his power base, turning us into hostages in a political deadlock between the Iraqi government and the US government.
> I appreciate the role these sanctions had in making a country full of riches so poor.
> I appreciate watching my professors having to sell their whole personal libraries to survive, and seeing their books being bought by UN staff who take them home as souvenirs.
> I have so much appreciation it is flowing out of my ears.[127]

This fusillade of injustices amplifies the rhetorical intensity of the *ubi sunt* formula that piles on plaint after plaint. Pax's *ubi sunt* is probably more aggressive than traditional laments, but similarly logs losses due to war and suggests a counterfactual narrative of how things could have been.

Working in tandem with the *topoi* of ineffability and the *ubi sunt* is the rhetorical figure of allusion. Classicist Margaret Alexiou submits that "part of the artistic economy in the language of folk tradition is the allusive method, by which a fact or idea is expressed indirectly but concretely, through symbols."[128] In Greek culture, allusions were usually made to widely recognized natural phenomena. Thus, in the ritual laments of the Greeks, there would often be references to light, trees, water, and nature's cycles as symbolic referents of life's passage into death.[129] These allusions ground the mourning process in everyday phenomena, gaining persuasive power because they draw on common experiences of the natural world. Though allusions to these natural phenomena still abound today in melancholic rhetoric, allusion in highly mediatized cultures just as often refers to the artifacts of late capitalism like film, music, and popular links on the internet.[130] This is a strategy used to full effect by Salam Pax, who regularly references global popular culture artifacts in his blog posts.

His obsession with David Bowie songs was matched only by his interest in the band Coldplay. On October 3, he blogs that he is "spiralling down fast. I have been listening to Coldplay's 'Politik' non-stop since 9 a.m. Either the world is not worth commenting on or I am just plain lazy."[131] Such a withdrawal from even talking about the world is a signature move of the melancholic—precisely the type of disengagement that Keren so roundly critiques. Yet this post should not be dismissed as mere withdrawal so quickly.[132] While it is problematic to interpret Salam's choice of music as some sort of revelation about his inner thoughts, neither can this single track be totally dismissed, especially since Salam regularly interprets lyrics for what they mean to him. Salam Pax's lyrical obsessions underline Steven Himmer's observation that "every weblog can be considered literary in the sense that it calls attention not only to what we read, but also to the unique way we read it."[133] Imagine Salam sitting in front of an old computer at the design firm he worked at, with these lyrics from Coldplay's "Politik" looped:

> Look at the earth from outer space
> Everyone must find a place
> Give me time and give me space
> Give me real, don't give me fake
> Give me strength, reserve control
> Give me heart and give me soul
> Give me time, give us a kiss
> Tell me your own politik
> And open up your eyes
> Open up your eyes
> Open up your eyes
> Just open up your eyes.[134]

Time, space; real, fake; strength, control; heart, soul: there may not be more traditional themes for melancholics. The chorus, "open up your eyes," suggests melancholics' superior perceptive capacities and others' inability to see what was going on around them. As revelatory as this passage may be, it easily falls into the category of emo, noted earlier by Geert Lovink as the opposite of snark.[135] Emo stands for emotional or emotive; "'I'm sad' is the most common definition associated with emo."[136] Emo represents not just being in touch with emotions, but being in touch with the sensitive, melancholic side of one's emotional life. Emo is a cultural style strongly associated with a particular genre of music, which is often "moody, melodic and marked by an obsession with doomed relationships."[137] The caricatures of emo overlap significantly with the caricatures of blogging. Both are ridiculed as the province of lonely, overprivileged teenagers with nothing better to do than wallow in their own self-indulgent emotions. But emo is also a rhetorical style that, like snark, finds a unique outlet on blogs.

Salam's posts became increasingly emo as the war began. On Friday, March 21, 2003, al-Jazeera broke the news that nine B-52 bombers were apparently heading to Iraq. As the bombers were flying in, Salam's family gathered around a map of Iraq, trying to "figure out what is going on in the south" of Iraq.[138] The closer the United States moved to initiating military action, the more popular Salam Pax's blog became, eventually forcing Google to create a mirror site to prevent the site from crashing.[139] With increased attention from institutional media and the rest of the nascent blogosphere, there were increased queries about his identity. He received a series of emails asking if he was "for real," to which he responded "please stop sending e-mails asking if I am for real. Don't believe it? Then don't read it. I am not anybody's propaganda ploy—well, except my own. Two more hours until the B-52s get to Iraq."[140] After this post, three days passed before Salam Pax posted again—the war had begun, and his internet connection was no more.

Eventually, Salam Pax began posting again, though somewhat erratically and often with the assistance of an intermediary, Diana, a blogger from the United States who befriended Salam Pax through interactions in the blogosphere. His family weathered the military storm of the first few days, and, as was reported on the blog, was safe if perpetually anxious. Trapped in the house, Salam and family watch movies: "In the oh-the-irony-of-it-all section of my life I can add the unbelievable bad luck that when I wanted to watch a movie, because I got sick of all the news, the only movie I had which I have not seen a hundred times is *The American President*. No joke. A friend gave me that video months ago and I never watched it. I did last night. The American 'presidential palace' looks quite good. But Michael Douglas is a sad ass president."[141] Later, he writes, "I am still trying to ignore the 24-hour, non-stop TV bombardment. News just ups my level of paranoia. I'm living in my headphones or watching silly videos. *Ice Age* has become a house favourite."[142] Salam's retreat to the house during the heat of the military campaign is understandable, given the dangers of being outside. But a later admission confirms Keren's suspicion that bloggers are apolitical melancholics: "I confess to the sin of being an escapist. When reality hurts, I block it out—unless it comes right up to me and knocks me cold. My mother, after going out once after Baghdad was taken by the US army, decided she is not going out again—not until I promise it looks kind of normal and OK. So I guess the Ostrich manoeuvre runs in the family."[143] However, in what amounts as a rejoinder to Keren, Salam un-ostriched himself after major combat operations and joined the Campaign for Innocent Victims in Conflict (CIVIC), trying to assess the damage on the ground. He blogged about his experiences with CIVIC, as well as some translation jobs he did for journalists in the area. Toward the end of major combat operations, his blogging at *Where is Raed?* began to slow down, until it eventually stopped completely.[144]

Among many other emotional registers, Salam Pax employed melancholic rhetoric to draw attention to the grim realities of everyday life under the threat of war. The form his melancholic rhetoric took was the lament; the *topoi* included claims of inexpressibility and a cataloguing of injustice, a dominant rhetorical figure was allusion, and his style could be characterized as emo. But what were the effects of this melancholic voice? Did a melancholic tone, with its characteristic dialectical vigor, actually establish better insights into what was happening? Was withdrawal and reflection an aid to more penetrating observations? The answer could never be as simple as "yes" or "no." But the commentary from the press about Salam Pax indicates that his popularity as a blogger could be attributed to his ability to craft a compelling narrative about the conflict. This portal into the daily life of Iraqis provided "better insight" than the institutional press.[145] One journalist said that there is "an authority to this witness that no foreign correspondent can match."[146] His blogging "made hearts flutter with his idiosyncratic personal descriptions of Baghdad before and after the war."[147] The power of his accounts meant that "suddenly this two-finger typist was linked all over the blogging world, written up in mainstream media and used as an official information source. He was the 'insider' describing his country's descent into chaos."[148] As compared to other media accounts of the war, Salam Pax's blog provided "personal insight that bypassed the sanitizing Cuisinart of big-media news editing."[149] Blogging is an appealing medium, especially during times of war, because the "proximity to events, spurious or not, is very attractive to audiences trying to acquire an honest feel of the story and the sense of temporal immediacy amplifies it."[150] This proximity, and the extraordinary if melancholic detail that Salam Pax shares, explains the broad circulation of his blog posts.

Emotion in the Networked Public Sphere
(What's Affect Got to Do with It?)

Commentators often put Salam Pax's blogging in the context of the dramatic changes internetworked media were having on global communication, as bloggers were, for the first time, circulating firsthand, immediate, and regular updates on life in a war zone to a global public. The *Washington Post* columnist Howard Kurtz reflected on this phenomenon: "[F]or all the saturation coverage of the invasion of Iraq, this has become the first true Internet war, with journalists, analysts, soldiers, a British lawmaker, an Iraqi exile and a Baghdad resident using the medium's lightning speed to cut through the fog of war. The result is idiosyncratic, passionate and often profane, with the sort of intimacy and attitude that are all but impossible in newspapers and on television. . . . The strength of this new form of communication is the sheer variety of voices."[151] What makes this assertion by Kurtz noteworthy is not his observation about the quantity of newly heard voices populating the blogosphere, but the ability of those blogging voices to convey qualitative dimensions of intimacy and attitude.[152] Salam Pax's blogging is indicative of the revalorization of emotional-intimate communication in the networked rhetorical imaginary. Vertically organized modern societies produced an imaginary that positioned the private sphere as providing a large pyramidal base of experience that the public sphere at the top drew upon, sorted, and rationalized. The slowness of mass media provided a natural buffer between public and private spheres that is lost with the immediacy of networked media. A shift to a more horizontally organized culture, with a medium capable of publicizing feelings at low cost, thus challenges modern conceptions of public and private.[153] But if this reorganization of our imaginary destabilizes the traditional lines between public and private, how should we understand the renewed prevalence of emotion in democratic public life?

Lovink's and Keren's critique of emotional-intimate communication in the blogosphere is a reminder of how new rhetorical imaginaries coalesce only in fits and starts. The influence of older civic engagement models that question the value of personal disclosure and emotion remains prominent. But this historically contingent model of public deliberation cannot drive considerations of networked communication working with dissimilar cultural conditions, or the deliberation trap that historically marginalized citizen participation will open up once again. Neither can emotional-intimate communication be uncritically valorized or allowed to supplant reason as a method for decision making, lest we pave the way for incommensurable clashes of emotional expressions or, worse, the kind of base propaganda that characterized the twentieth century's world wars. How to navigate between these poles? Much as rhetorical invention lies on the bias between discovery and generativity, so do rhetorical theories of emotion occupy the middle ground between assumptions that emotions simply compete with reason or that emotions ought to be embraced *in toto*. Reason and emotion, strictly bifurcated in the modern imaginary, are increasingly understood as entwined and connected—networked—through attention processes. To draw out the relationship between affect and attention, I will develop my position that cynicism and melancholy are political *tones* before turning to my exegesis of "ambient intimacy" as another consitutent of the networked rhetorical imaginary.

While tone usually evokes aural dimensions of speech, it is not limited to vocalization. Emails and text messages are regularly misinterpreted precisely because of a mismatch between intended and interpreted tone. All language carries a tonal register. Even the supposedly unemotional journalistic voice attempts to strike a tone of dispassion and objectivity in order to comport with the informationist norms it adheres to. Although journalistic tones carefully cultivate an air of impartiality, journalists are social creatures using language that is inescapably charged with emotion. Taking tone seriously as an analytical category offers a way to see how emotion is always already encoded in language. This is the insight that the participants in the rational-critical debate of the bourgeois public sphere missed. Language does not just report affect; language itself is affective.[154] Language is not reducible to data transmission, as the informationist model of communication presupposes; rather, it is embedded in a deeply social and emotionally resonant world. "I can't wait to see what the cafeteria will serve today" produces divergent meanings, depending on whether those words are spoken with a hopeful or sarcastic tone. Listeners cannot but be affected by hearing this sentiment, although they may well not cognize their level of affectedness. This is a crucial point that the concept of affect clarifies: communication does not require cognition for it to have impact. Following Eric Shouse, affect is a bodily reaction to some experience, a prepersonal sensation that only sometimes climbs the ladder of consciousness.[155] Being on the receiving end of hate speech or listening to an inspiring public address often invites this kind of visceral response: the blood boils in the former, and goosebumps pop up in the latter. Goosebumps are not cognitively generated. They are nonconscious bodily reactions to being affected by one's environment. The body absorbs and reacts to all sorts of stimuli all the time, only a small bit of which becomes thematized through cognition and language. A *feeling*, then, is what happens when an affect begins to be cognized. We make sense of affective responses through comparison to prior experiences. Feeling is biographical. An *emotion* is the rhetorical expression of that feeling, based on socially constructed labels that attempt to reflect recurring feeling-states.

Computers do not respond to the affective residues of language, because a 1 or a 0 is a 1 or a 0 is a 1 or a 0. Affect, the bodily experience of intensity, is a mark of sentience that carries with it a latent ability to assist in the navigation of the social world. As Shouse details, "affect is what makes feelings feel. It is what determines the intensity (quantity) of a feeling (quality), as well as the background intensity of our everyday lives (the half-sensed, ongoing hum of quantity/quality that we experience when we are not really attuned to any experience at all)."[156] As political scientist George Marcus elucidates, "emotion processes, processes that precede conscious awareness, shape what we pay attention to and how we pay attention."[157] In other words, the intensity of affect shapes what we pay attention to by making something stand out against the background. If people had no affective reactions, it would be impossible to direct attention, for everything would be equally weighted and we would face unbelievable problems in sorting out which phenomena to address. In an affectless world, falling in love would be as meaningful as falling out of a chair. This relationship between affect, feeling, emotion, and reason blurs the traditional distinction between the cognitive and the noncognitive. Emotion and reason are not intractably opposed; instead, they are entwined with each other in a kind of symbiotic double helix.[158] Affective reactions, in a nod to the Aristotelian tradition, direct cognitive attention. This insight is what makes the assessments by Lovink and Keren so impoverished. You can't stop affect—you can only hope to direct it.

The tonal qualities of rhetoric are, for Benjamin Barber, how we move each other to action: "through words we convey information, articulate interests, and pursue arguments, but it is through tone, color, volume, and inflection that we feel, affect, and touch each other."[159] Tone is a conduit for affect. Facts do not move people, but the valences that accompany interpretation do. Walter Lippmann famously argued that citizens responded to the complexity of the modern world by relying on stereotypes that created predictable identities, scripts, and routines.[160] This is one way to address information abundance, but stereotypes serve us poorly when they fail to acknowledge the richness of the social world. Emotion, though, works a disruptive magic. Outpourings of emotion are, following George Marcus, picked up by an individual's neural surveillance system, shifting attention to the "intrusive stimuli" and inhibiting prior habits of mind to activate a process of cognition that accounts for the new phenomenon.[161] This is a somewhat clinical but effective way to describe Salam Pax's meteoric rise in the blogosphere. The outpouring of cynical and melancholic affects through his blog pivoted a global public that traditionally received its news about the war from broadcast media, with their predictable war-coverage scripts, toward a new voice. By producing anxiety, cynicism and melancholy shift our cognitive efforts from reliance on habit to "open consideration of new alternatives."[162] Salam Pax's cynicism and melancholy performed a rhetorical interruption that reshuffled attention routines.[163]

The modulation of affect through "bread and circus," especially orchestrated by powerful institutions, could be a harbinger of ever more sophisticated control used to keep populations in check.[164] But the increased circulation of affect into public life also promises to vitalize stranger sociability, that particular form of intimacy that defines democratic public cultures.[165] As citizens encounter each other through the networked public sphere, affective ties form through the circulation of commodities, texts, bodies, and personae.[166] This circulation generates patterns of identification that strengthens collective public life. Marcus explains how affect expands attention economies toward specific issues: "Getting people to share in the concerns of others, to take an interest in a problem, crisis, or issue that is not part of their intimate lives, depends on making a specific connection between the observed grievance and one's emotional response."[167] This observation is doubly true in the context of international relations. Networked media invite more nonelite interest in public, and especially foreign, affairs.[168] Salam Pax's book tour led him to argue that the role of blogs in producing global intimacy was unparalleled: "With blogging in the developing world, you get to feel people are listening to you, you can discuss things in a way you otherwise cannot. I mean look at Chinese and Iranian weblogs. Where else could you get such insight into daily life in those countries?"[169]

Have we witnessed a parallel process before? Arguably. Benedict Anderson's *Imagined Communities* identifies how the early circulation of the novel and the newspaper created a "consciousness of connectedness" that produced the nation-state.[170] The increased circulation of newspapers and novels created a sense of belonging for groups of national peoples with common experiences—belonging that was strengthened with continual reference to their collective past. Newspaper readers, seeing the same newspaper *also* being read by fellow citizens at social gathering spots throughout the day, were "continually reassured that the imagined world is visibly rooted in everyday life."[171] This useful fiction about participating in a larger collective conversation was paramount to the bourgeois public sphere's self-conception as a public that knew about itself. An analogous movement is now taking place to accommodate the expansion of social life to a global plane. There may not yet be a global public sphere *per se*, but the networked public sphere contains global dimensions.[172] The internet is a medium through which global publics intercommunicate. Just as the novel gave readers a glimpse of the intimate lives of others in the nation, and thus created a sense of social belonging, blogs crack open the intimate spheres of global others. This sense of intimacy is not isomorphic with the intimacy created through the novel. The novel dispenses intimate moments in discrete narrative chunks, whereas the intimacy created by blogs is, like the humming of background noise, ambient.

The term "ambient intimacy" emerged organically as bloggers and observers of networked media tried to explain the blurring of the private into public and the resulting *un*sequestration of emotional-intimate discourse from the private sphere. This latent feature of the networked rhetorical imaginary was explicitly thematized in the wake of social networking sites like MySpace, Facebook, and the microblogging site Twitter. *Wired* magazine writer Clive Thompson's early forays into Twitter made him wonder if it was just "blogging taken to a supremely banal extreme" because of the "stupefyingly trivial" posts about the minutiae of people's lives.[173] But Thompson came to appreciate Twitter as a kind of "proprioception, your body's ability to know where your limbs are. That subliminal sense of orientation is crucial for coordination. . . . Twitter and other constant-contact media create *social* proprioception. They give a group of people a sense of itself, making possible weird, fascinating feats of coordination."[174] Media, from the voice to novels and the newspaper to blogs and microblogs, might be seen as a kind of social proprioception that accommodates complexity.

Blogger Leisa Reichelt coined "ambient intimacy" in the context of Twitter microblogging, extending the concept to many other forms of social networking sites. She writes,

> I've been using a term to describe my experience of Twitter (and also Flickr and reading blog posts and Upcoming). I call it Ambient

Intimacy. Ambient intimacy is about being able to keep in touch with people with a level of regularity and intimacy that you wouldn't usually have access to, because time and space conspire to make it impossible. Flickr lets me see what friends are eating for lunch, how they've redecorated their bedroom, their latest haircut. Twitter tells me when they're hungry, what technology is currently frustrating them, who they're having drinks with tonight.[175]

It is all too easy to dismiss much of the private detail publicized through these digitized social networks as narcissistic claptrap—who cares that you're drinking coffee? that you like this song? that you can't sleep? that your pets and kids are astonishingly cute? For the small worlds of networked publics, quotidian information like this *might* matter. Knowing Salam Pax's penchant for red wine or David Bowie appears unnecessary, or even goofy, but this kind of sharing of everyday intimacies is a way of connecting to others who may not be physically present. While ambient intimacy signifies the accelerated blurring of public and private, it is also convenient shorthand for the nature of rhetoric, which ambiently carries intimacy through tone.

Ambient intimacy continues a historical trajectory noticed in Habermas's study of familial closeness in the bourgeois intimate sphere. The rise of the bourgeois middle class brought about what Habermas called "permanent intimacy," which replaced the occasional intimacy experienced by aristocratic families with spacious abodes and irregular contact with one another.[176] Middle-class norms cultivated a new attitude about the role of the family as a site of nurturing fellow feeling, with parents (or at least mothers) taking a more active role in child-rearing. Ambient intimacy is "perpetual" intimacy, an evolution marked by the rise of so-called helicopter parents who use digital technology to stay in constant contact with their children. The evolution of mobile media is a crucial dimension in this process, as it allows us to be always on/always available, intimately tethered to our past selves and our social networks.[177]

New media always produce new ways to work through affects with consequences for the role of emotion in public life. For Habermas's bourgeois, the letter deepened their sense of subjectivity and expressivity. Brent Malin similarly describes the development of close-up photography as creating "a new capacity (or, perhaps, mandate) for emotional expressiveness," as the candid photo encouraged people to be shown smiling.[178] Television created new forms of "affective ambiance" surrounding live events: catastrophes, wars, celebrity weddings, and sporting events.[179] Networked media, too, constitute "extensive networks and technologies for the inspection, confession, governance, and transformation of affect."[180] As Jodi Dean explains, "every little tweet or comment, every forwarded image or petition, accrues a tiny affective nugget, a little surplus enjoyment, a smidgen of attention that attaches to it, making it stand out from the larger flow before it blends back in."[181] Blogs and related media genres are a substantial network of communication devoted to assessing, judging, and relating ever-smaller affective judgments. For Nigel Thrift, new technologies take "what was formerly invisible or imperceptible," like affect, and constitute it "as visible and perceptible through a new structure of attention which is increasingly likely to pay more than lip-service to those actions which go on in small spaces and times."[182] Note the connection to attention: making affective reactions visible, as Salam Pax did through his blog, creates new objects of attention, sparking public conversation and deliberation about issues which were heretofore concealed by the structure of feeling and top-down architecture of the broadcast mass media.

Blogs thus reintroduce communication richness—deep affective detail—into large-scale communication matrices.[183] Blogging and similar genres produce rich discourse that explains strangers (even those strangers that are kin) to each other. Since networked media embrace richness rather than standardization, blogs become sites where difference is encountered, negotiated, affirmed, denied, or deferred. In January 2004, Salam Pax's blog came under fire for playing the "Western" cultural game rather than participating in the Arabic-language Iraqi blogosphere. Raed, in a rare blog post, came to the defense of his friend in a way that reveals the underlying purpose of the blog:

> [W]hat I want to say is that we seem to have lost the middle ground. When I met Ted Koppel the first time he said that he needed a cultural interpreter. And this is exactly what this blog and the rest of the blogs in the Iraqi Blogosphere, in all its variety, has been providing. The things the reviewer saw as negatives, "irreligious, western educated, and has spent half his life outside Iraq," are really the basis for the common things between us. You and me, we have this dialogue because of them. In a world growing apart by the day it is absolutely wonderful to find that everybody can go on about the food they like on an Iraqi blog [check out the comments] and for a moment forget

all the politics. This reminds us that we *do* have things in common and not everybody is out to cut the others' throat. I do not feel ashamed of standing in the middle anymore; actually I am proud of it. The Iraqi Bloggers show that we *can* talk. You think some of us are too ungrateful and critical? Habibi at least we are talking about it, you really have not met the people who are really truly unhappy with the whole situation here. BUT . . . we are still playing the [dominant/subordinate culture] game. We write in English to communicate with you, we try to establish links and reference points very much relevant to you.[184]

This is a prescient meditation on cross-cultural communication in a globalized world. Raed and apparently Salam recognize the need for cultural interpreters to make sense of indigenous Iraqi attitudes and practices. To maximize their appeal, they admit to consciously making efforts to craft a rhetorical strategy that would appeal to English-speaking readers in the rest of the world. The rhetorical performance of cynicism and melancholy are part of this effort as well, since they are well-recognized emotion-constellations shared across cultural difference. In this way, blogs function as one site of identification where cosmopolitan citizens come together to negotiate alternative frames of reference.[185]

Oversharing in an Ambiently Intimate World

If learning about Salam Pax's work life and overseas experience shows the potential for ambient intimacy to aid identification, the dark side of ambient intimacy is illuminated by the term "dooced." To be "dooced" is to lose one's job because of blogging, usually blogging something deemed inappropriate by employers. The slang term comes from the pseudonym Dooce, which Heather B. Armstrong uses on her blog. "Dooce" became a verb when Armstrong was fired in 2002 from her design job because of what her employer perceived as inappropriate blogging about the workplace and co-workers.[186] Armstrong was certainly not the first person to be fired from a job for a personal website, nor was she likely the first person to be fired specifically because of a blog. Yet her experience garnered significant press attention at a moment when blogging was beginning to gain a foothold in the networked media ecology. Being dooced points to the risks of ambient intimacy. Making the formerly invisible or imperceptible more visible or perceptible, as Thrift describes, can have negative consequences. While the public-private distinction is fading at the level of culture, many institutions are predictably less excited about employees airing private, and possibly proprietary, information. Armstrong's experience is a stark reminder that ambient intimacy creates conditions for communication to spill over contingent but enforced boundaries.

There is a word for this: oversharing. Oversharing, as a named phenomenon, became prevalent in the 1990s with the use of mobile phones. But the growth of blogs, followed by the explosion of social networking sites, makes oversharing a prevalent feature of networked public culture. The overshare, often cringingly replied to with the phrase "too much information," is familiar to anyone engaged in networked media. It is so common, and so common a word, that it was *Webster's New World Dictionary*'s Word of the Year in 2008. Webster's *Word of the Year* blog defined it thus: "overshare (verb): to divulge excessive personal information, as in a blog or broadcast interview, prompting reactions ranging from alarmed discomfort to approval."[187] In a YouTube video announcing the Word of the Year, the dictionary's editor-in-chief, Mike Agnes, reflects on how the word signified both "the tedious minutiae on personal websites and blogs and the accidental slips of the tongue in public."[188] The same video features people-on-the-street interviews that identify classic instances of oversharing—getting drunk and blurting out things they later regret, sharing intimate details about the experience of pregnancy, projecting their life plan for the next ten years on Facebook, using Facebook to give an hour-by-hour schedule for their next week, and changing their mood status every five minutes, for example. Oversharers are "socialholics," addicted to revelatory public proclamations (there's Freud's "shameless talkers about themselves" again).

The disciplinary implications of oversharing are made explicit in the same *Word of the Year* video. One interviewee wondered how high school and university students will face employers with access to "their entire lives" through Facebook. Another interviewee mentions an email about an employer who confronted an employee's work absence with the employee's Facebook status update noting their hungover state. Yet another interviewee reports that a law firm confronted a potential employee with the first interest the person identified on Facebook: "getting wasted." Facebook's quasi-blogging architecture enabled this kind of oversharing, especially as it migrated to mobile devices: "Facebook . . . has clearly been built on the back of the culture of oversharing. Many members broadcast the mundane details of their lives through a 'status update' feature, which lets people—nay, encourages them—to describe the contents of their lunch or the virulence of their bronchitis."[189]

Leisa Reichelt, the blogger who coined the term "ambient intimacy," later expressed qualms about the implications of the shifting sands of public and private by suggesting that the flip side of ambient intimacy was "ambient exposure." Ambient exposure, for Reichelt, identifies "a vulnerability, a risk associated with taking a position that could, potentially, result in loss or harm."[190] Like Dooce, or the tens of thousands of new college graduates who scrub their networked presences their senior year, so much publicity poses potential dangers. As Reichelt clarifies in her blog post on ambient exposure, "essentially, we may not *want* to have the same level of intimacy with some people as we do with others."[191] Networked media are often credited with flattening hierarchies, but sometimes that flattening comes at the expense of control over the circulation of messages. As in the case of Salam Pax, ambient intimacy produces stranger sociability and global publics, directs attention to underrepresented individuals or groups and their stories, and rearranges attitudes by activating strong affective reactions, but it also poses a new set of risks that networked citizens must navigate.

5

SHALLOW QUOTATION ON *REALCLIMATE*

By 2004, networks of blogs had formed densely interconnected, specialized discourse communities. Blogrings of different sizes mushroomed as dedicated sites for engaged discourse about their respective interests. Scientific communities were no exception, as blogs created an informal peer-review process, built social capital for bloggers, and provided a multimodal forum for broad-based scientific discussion. The group blog *RealClimate*, sustained by a network of climate scientists, hosts deliberation about climate science. Why start a blog on climate science? In their introductory post, the bloggers at *RealClimate* declare that they perceive

> agenda-driven "commentary" on the Internet and in the opinion columns of newspapers crowding out careful analysis. . . . Journalists with deadlines and scant knowledge of the field quite often do not know where to go for this context on papers that are being pushed by some of the partisan think-tanks or other interested parties. This can lead to some quite mainstream outlets inadvertently publishing some very dubious and misleading ideas. *RealClimate* is a commentary site on climate science by working climate scientists for the interested public and journalists. We aim to provide a quick response to developing stories and provide the context sometimes missing in mainstream commentary.[1]

Posts focus on issues like "Climate Sensitivity and Aerosol Forcing," "The Acid Ocean—The Other Problem with CO_2 Emission," and "How Much of the Recent CO_2 Increase is Due to Human Activities?"[2] Each post includes numerous links to available scientific literature on the web, causing one reviewer of the site to give it the "footnote frenzy" award.[3] Shortly after the founding of the blog, *RealClimate* began landing on blogrolls and received prominent mass media coverage.

Traditional public sphere actors greeted science blogs uneasily, as demonstrated by a 2006 controversy involving *RealClimate* blogger and paleoclimatologist Michael Mann. Mann and his co-authors had, in a 1998 paper, generated a reconstruction of mean temperatures for the North American hemisphere over the last millennium, producing a widely circulated graph that showed temperatures after 1900 increasing dramatically.[4] The results were visually arresting, producing what would come to be known as the "hockey stick" graph. But the graph also attracted critics who tried to undermine the supporting data. The skeptics' position, represented by a paper that Stephen McIntyre and Ross McKitrick published in *Energy and Environment* in 2003, maintained that a different weighting of certain proxy data straightened out the hockey stick.[5] The ensuing controversy, explored in more detail throughout this chapter, flushed out critics of science blogs who were skeptical about the amount of scientific conversation occurring through new, informally peer-reviewed sites. The Wegman Report, a product of a congressional investigation on Mann's research, included this barb: "much of the discussion on the 'hockey stick' issue has taken place on competing web blogs. Our committee believes that web blogs are not an appropriate way to conduct science and thus the blogs give credence to the fact that these global warming issues are have [sic] migrated from the realm of rational scientific discourse. Unfortunately, the factions involved have become highly and passionately polarized."[6] The Wegman Report's dig at science blogs is understandable, as science blogging does not adhere to the blind peer-review process usually posited as central to validating scientific argument. What the Wegman Report misses, though, is that blogs are usually not used to *conduct* science but rather to provide a platform for *public debate* about scientific claims. This function of science blogs is concealed for the authors of the Wegman Report because they hew closely to the modern normative divide between "rational scientific discourse" conducted by experts and "passionately" partisan discussion by nonspecialists.

The Wegman Report reflects modern political liberalism's reliance on expert competence at the expense of the collective wisdom of the governed. This historical tendency is accentuated in hypercomplex internetworked cultures, with gobs of science and technology controversies creating conditions for experts to become ever more specialized in ways that often foreclose citizen participation. The deliberation trap this sets up is obvious: if experts and the publics they purportedly serve employ variant understandings of scientific and technical problems, decisions made by experts in the public's name are likely to lack legitimacy. While science blogs like *RealClimate* are no panacea, I contend that they provide a contact space for expert discourses to be translated into language more intelligible in the broader networked public sphere. To make this case, I trace the rise of the expert paradigm from classical Greece through the modern era. Once again, metaphors envision a normative role for specialist discourses to assume in public deliberation. I then turn to an analysis of *RealClimate* itself, identifying three categories of scientific discourse that the bloggers interpret for wider publics. As a "translation station," *RealClimate* bloggers practice shallow quotation, the process of borrowing small snippets of technical discourse translated to a more public idiom. Although shallow quotation evades one deliberative trap, it sets up another. In the final section, I look at how shallow quotation can run wild, as it did during an email hacking scandal that implicated several *RealClimate* bloggers.

Expertise Between Pedagogy and Participation

Expertise is not static. The scale of a medium shapes who is considered an expert—and the role that experts play in public deliberation. One-to-one communication, usually mediated by the voice, lends itself to a "counselor model" of expertise like that practiced by Socrates. Counselors may claim special knowledge from individual experience, cultural knowledge, or the tea leaves at the bottom of the glass. They may draw out dormant knowledge in the counseled through questioning, in which case the counselor and counseled co-create knowledge through shared inquiry. One-to-many communication is represented best by the mass media and supports a "broadcast model" of expertise. Public service announcements and the nightly network news demonstrate how this model works, since the message emanates from a single point source and is distributed to many people. Many-to-one communication lends itself to an "advisory model" of expertise. Examples of many-to-one communication include citizens writing letters or emails to public officials and the United States' presidential cabinet.

In each instance, the model of expertise and the dominant medium of communication do not just incidentally coincide, for the cultural use of the medium actually shapes the model of expertise. The familiar face-to-face settings and simpler problems of oral societies invited dialogue as a problem-solving technique. More complex modern societies require more sophisticated ways of acquiring inputs to aid organizational decision making and then circulate expert advice to citizens. The broadcast model of expertise was an efficient way of communicating information to both specialists and masses of people before the advent of digital technologies. Internetworked technologies offer the first credible medium for many-to-many communication, where interlocutors sustain large-scale, interlinked, synchronous and asynchronous contact. The blogosphere is an exemplar of many-to-many communication, alongside *Wikipedia*, Twitter, and a host of other platforms. Notably, the internet hosts many-to-many communication *but also* is a medium that, unlike any other, supports the earlier communication models of one-to-one, one-to-many, and many-to-one.[7] What kinds of changes to the practice and perception of expertise might come about as a result of many-to-many communication?

Just like invention and emotion, expertise is often caught between two polarities. Expertise is either conceived of as "participatory," with co-constructive dialogue figured as the ideal, or as "pedagogical," assuming that a sage on the stage should disseminate knowledge.[8] A rhetorical model of expertise again weaves through the middle by recognizing the importance of both drawing in local knowledge through participation *and* integrating the specialized knowledge gained through experience. Internetworked technologies offer new opportunities for blending these two often-polarized senses of expertise. Networked contexts like *Wikipedia* or discussion forums illustrate how specialized knowledge is made available for wider audiences who refine, synthesize, and alter propositions through iterations of deliberation.[9] The classical Athenian agora and the European bourgeois public sphere, which also attempted to mobilize participation by the many while integrating knowledge held by the few, precede these networked environments. These earlier media cultures, however, were limited by social codes that restricted participation and by technology that prevented efficacious many-to-many communication.

Greek public culture laid the groundwork for many of the norms of Western science by developing the logical forms that were the basis for scientific reasoning and providing institutional support that made sustained scientific inquiry possible.[10] But properly speaking, there were no "experts" in classical Greek culture—the word had not been invented yet. There was a strong Hellenic inclination for polymathic persons (literally, "having learned much"). The Sophists were proud of their ability to speak on any topic whatsoever. Aristotle recognized the interconnection of rhetoric, poetics, metaphysics, physics, ethics, and politics and wrote learned treatises on each subject. Even the democratic structures of classical Athens were designed to circulate knowledge resources across the *polis*. Josiah Ober's work on the legacy of Athenian governance underlines the utility of "a culture of voluntary sharing of knowledge, effective knowledge circulation, and constant mutual instruction."[11] To form this kind of participatory public culture, the Athenians designated 139 *demes*, or self-governing communities, which formed "public assemblies at which all the demesmen could gather to debate and decide upon issues of local concern."[12] The demes habituated citizens into patterns of participatory decision making that accounted for the various perspectives present, bringing individual competencies and knowledge to bear on the problems facing the *polis*.[13] The demes were subsequently organized into a master network that was institutionalized in the Council of 500: "the 500 councilors chosen each year by their fellow demesmen were the human embodiment of the *knowledge resources* of the entire Athenian polis. Their duty as councilors was to bring local knowledge to the center—to participate in open discussions, bringing to bear all the relevant information they possessed."[14] The *polis* was a network connected by the foot and the voice, powered by an open, participatory *telos* that purported to synthesize the best that could be known. Although Athenian public culture recognized the benefits of drawing in proficiencies from a participatory network, other cultural practices drew on a pedagogical model of expertise. Plato's defense of the dialectic-practicing philosopher-king is a protean defense of expertise.[15] And in *Busiris*, Isocrates mentions in passing that those who regularly shift occupations become, as the colloquialism goes, a jack-or-jill-of-all-trades and master of none.[16]

Modern senses of expertise drew on the script established by early religious practice. The religious practice of the ancient Greeks created a hierarchical insider/outsider dynamic, as only the priests were able to enter the temples.[17] Similarly, the early Christian Church preserved sole interpretive authority over the Bible, which was not translated to vernacular languages until the sixteenth century. This backdrop of scribal authority leads Thomas Lessl to attribute to experts a "priestly voice" more comfortable with making pronouncements than engaging in dialogue.[18] In both ancient Greece and early modern Europe, media new to the times destabilized these expert pedagogies. Alphabetic writing moved natural philosophy beyond the scribal-priestly class in classical Greece and, similarly, print culture made religious texts accessible throughout the social networks of the bourgeois public sphere.

Early print culture circulated not just religious texts but texts devoted to science, forging publics devoted to broad-based scientific inquiry. The individual scientist gained "automatic contact" with a broader public through the scientific societies, public lectures, and publications that constituted part of the bourgeois public sphere.[19] Scientists were treated as experts, considered further along in the process of enlightenment than others. Though this position threatened the supposed equality of participants in the bourgeois public sphere, these proto-experts were given a privileged role in enlightening others only, as Habermas points out, "inasmuch as they convinced through arguments and could not themselves be corrected by better arguments."[20] Thus, expertise was figured as a function of the process of argument rather than the product of credentials. But this processual nature of expertise eventually faded in favor of credentialism, as the etymology of the word "expert" demonstrates. "Expert" is a contraction of the French "experienced," originating in the specific context of court trials in the nineteenth century where the authenticity of handwriting was at stake.[21] Handwriting experts were gifted at pattern recognition. Their successful track record of forgery detection gave them an epistemic authority not extended to nonexperts, so they were not expected to exhibit their reasoning publicly, nor could they be challenged by anyone but a fellow handwriting expert. They were thus insulated from public criticism. In subsequent centuries, the word "expert" moved beyond handwriting trials, mutating away from the original sense of a person wise with experience. What replaced it was a model that privileged professional training, credentialing, and peer review as a measure of expertise.[22]

Three key metaphors reflect the refiguration of the science-culture relationship as the twentieth century began to face decisions made by technical experts on a much larger scale: Dewey's "two-way street," early Habermas's "translation," and later Habermas's "autism." Both Dewey and Habermas recognize that technical expertise potentially undermined democratic deliberation by trumping public will with specialized knowledge claims. To sustain democratic oversight in the face of technocracy, they both employ metaphors with a normative vision of how scientific discussion ought to circulate through broader publics. The stakes could not be higher. Scientists are now employed by states, corporations, and universities to develop pharmaceutical drugs, sources of energy, and military weapons. They are called on to improve the healthfulness of food, ameliorate the pollution of rivers, and understand climatic changes. The instrumental applications of science increase the experts' centrality in managing risks produced, ironically, from some of modernity's excesses.[23] Environmental pollution is the most obvious of these excesses, with carbon dioxide–fueled climate change looming as a particularly daunting challenge. The pedagogical approach to expertise, from Plato's *Republic* to Walter Lippmann's notion of "organized intelligence," dictates that decisions about complex issues should be left to people who devote their lives to studying them.[24] What can the public possibly contribute to sophisticated conversations about scientific and technical controversies?

Dewey's defense of a self-governing public addressed Lippmann's contention that complexity, especially regarding scientific and technical issues, outstrips the ability of a public to participate meaningfully in the decision-making process. Dewey argues that the relationship between science and common sense need not be antagonistic, as scientific inquiry takes cues from common sense, verifies or contests commonsense intuitions, and reforges common sense over time. These two systems of knowledge partake in "a unified logic" that holds out the possibility for a "two-way movement between common sense and science."[25] But instead of deliberating about scientific inquiry in wider public venues, as in the science societies of the bourgeois public sphere, "the return road into common sense is devious and blocked by existing social conditions" in the early twentieth century.[26] In Dewey's phrasing, "the paths of communication between common sense and science are as yet largely one-way lanes," putting democratic governance on a path to technocratic decision making uncoupled from the practical needs of a public.[27]

Why is it important to develop a two-way movement between scientific discourses and common sense? One reason is that, as Habermas puts it, "if the discourse of experts is not coupled with democratic opinion- and will-formation, then the experts' perceptions of problems will prevail at the citizens' expense."[28] The public sphere successfully thematizes problems in the lifeworld that demand redress only by taking into account citizen discourses. The absence of this interface between scientists and citizens results in "a technocratic incapacitation of the public sphere" because there is no effective check on technocrats, all too ready to rule without restraint.[29] Technocratic decision making updates representative publicity, with experts supplanting the monarch in being trotted out before a public.[30] Absent public input through democratic channels, advancements in science and technology are likely to serve privileged interests instead of the public interest. Or worse: technocrats, after all, made the trains run on time in Nazi Germany and built atomic bombs in the United States.[31] More robust expert-public interchanges promise to address scientific controversies with more legitimacy and a greater appreciation of the stakes than technocratic pronouncements.

How, then, do decisions about technical controversies gain legitimacy but maintain fidelity to science's best predictions? In *Towards a Rational Society*, Habermas poses two related questions that specifically broach this problem of legitimation: "How is it possible to translate technically exploitable knowledge into the practical consciousness of the social life-world?" and "How can the power of technical control be brought within the range of the consensus of acting and transacting citizens?"[32] The latter question is answered with a little more ease, primarily by encouraging technocrats to be responsive to citizen needs and critiques. From the bottom up, citizens should be given opportunities to set the agenda for scientific inquiry by, for example, identifying polluted rivers and lobbying for research into potential sources of toxins. From the top down, citizens and their representatives should maintain oversight powers so that scientific decision making stays within democratic bounds. These democratic constraints on scientific knowledge production are valuable inasmuch as they check exclusively technocratic reasoning. But can models of public deliberation that simply give everyone a seat at the table sufficiently ground deliberative legitimation processes? Perhaps publics are, in some cases, better situated to make risk calculations more expansively than technocrats working through limited cost-benefit algorithms. But if citizen participation in science and technology controversies is to go beyond risk assessment, citizens must have sites where technical argument is translated into everyday language in a way that supports argument about the finer points of the controversy. If citizens cannot argue successfully on the "front end" of scientific controversies, then their effectiveness at regulating scientific decisions on the "back end" is bound to be weak. The controversy over climate change is a textbook case of this problem. Climate science relies on data from thousands of years, detecting minute yet significant shifts in the overall climate patterns of the earth. The causal relationships of climate models are extremely complex, the jargon seemingly impenetrable, and the points of *stasis* difficult to determine. Citizens must learn the vocabulary of climate science, know the points of *stasis* in the controversy, and be able to judge public arguments about it in order to have a robust role in the broader conversation about climate change.

How, then, might scientific knowledge be converted into commonsense language for publics to use in making judgments? Habermas posits that "conflicts must be decided, interests realized, interpretations found—through both action and transaction structured by ordinary language."[33] Scientific and technical knowledge must move from highly technical, specialized language to a more public idiom. Habermas relies on a translation metaphor, arguing that democracies need methods of "reliable translation of scientific information into the ordinary language of practice and inversely for a translation from the context of practical questions back into the specialized language of technical and strategic recommendations."[34] The forums where technical and ordinary language games intersect are translation stations, where science and common sense meet (perhaps shaking hands, even as they look warily at each other's tickets).

These translation stations are desirable for democratic deliberation, but the idea of translation begs a more fundamental question: *can* scientific claims make the jump from technical jargon to more publicly understandable language? Many experts resist translating their findings into ordinary language, for part of what makes them experts is a mastery of the code, jargon, specialized literature, and complex methodology that constitute their area of expertise. They alone may enter the temple. While scientists often insist that technical language cannot be converted neatly into ordinary language without the massive loss of information, the presence of interfield communication conducted in ordinary language between scientists partially belies this position.[35] Professional journals and conferences often function as translation stations for scientists, who refer to research findings communicated in more ordinary language than the technical language of practitioners in a parallel subfield. The use of less field-specific language is necessary because, as Habermas noted in 1971, scientists, too, face a "rising flood of information."[36] Here again climate science is a textbook case. The increasingly interconnected, multidisciplinary nature of a scientific controversy like climate science amplifies the need for translation. Understanding climatic change "is such a vast undertaking that no single scientist, nor any group of scientists can master anything but a small part of it."[37] No one discipline of knowledge has a monopoly on climate science, making it difficult for experts—never mind more general publics—to make sense of the state of the science when it gets called into question.[38]

There is a deep irony in the nature of translation between scientific publics and more general publics that Habermas identifies: "given a high degree of division of labor, the lay public often provides the shortest path of internal understanding between mutually estranged specialists."[39] Ordinary language, Habermas's term for the idiom of the public, is the "'ultimate metalanguage'" that "circulates throughout society and can be translated into and from every specialized code."[40] Informationist critiques of ordinary language emphasize how the movement away from specialized language shaves away nuance and meaning. Translation, in this sense, is a euphemism for data loss. This is an impoverished conception of translation that a rhetorical perspective corrects for. Rhetoric, historically focused on adapting to situations, audiences, cultures, and forums, can be seen as an art of translation. Translations can dumb down *or* they can elevate and produce new meanings, depending on the situation and the skill of the rhetor. Translation ought not be thought of simplistically as a one-to-one correspondence between words, for the process of moving from one language game to another is fraught with stops and starts, words that shade into each other, culturally weighted meanings, inside jokes, and heuristic shortcuts. The intrinsic roughness of any translation can productively spark continuing conversation about the accuracy, appropriateness, and generativity of different renditions. Translation in this sense may well *add* layers of nuance and meaning by selecting certain ways to pay attention to a word, phrase, or idea. As Burke noted, "every translation is a compromise (although, be it noted, a compromise which may have new virtues of its own, virtues not part of the original)."[41] In any case, some level of translation is inevitable, since addressees never interpret signs precisely as intended.[42]

Habermas's mid-twentieth-century hopes that the generation of more translation stations would create a more rational society were dashed by the steady differentiation of subsystems declining to participate in the conversion of technical discourses into common sense. In *Between Facts and Norms*, Habermas perceives a key juncture for public deliberation in increasingly complex, functionally differentiated, late modern cultures. Either the subsystems self-perpetuate with little regard to intercommunication and democratic oversight, *or* they are coupled with discourse from the public sphere to activate legitimation processes.[43] If theorists of public deliberation resign themselves to the former option, the model of society that develops is essentially autistic in nature: "According to systems theory, all functional systems achieve their autonomy by developing their own codes and their own semantics, which no longer admit of mutual translation. They therefore forfeit the ability to communicate directly with one another and as a result can only 'observe' each other."[44] Habermas's deployment of autism as a metaphor for the (non)interaction of subsystems resonates with depictions of people with autism as not sharing perceptions of a common world. John Durham Peters accentuates this concern by suggesting that autism is the disorder of address in a digitized public culture where individuals, as well as systems, relax the historical impulse to intercommunicate.[45] Though the facts of differentiation make intercommunication between subsystems a challenge, the norms of democracy mandate it. Scientific and technological controversies frequently appear on deliberative agendas, requiring scientists, politicians, citizens, and other interlocutors to find a common language. Thus, in the twentieth century, the Deweyan and Habermasian hope for contact between experts and publics was primarily to be found in public participation meetings and the institutional press. Though these two sites for discussion of scientific issues occasionally contribute to more robust public dialogues about science, both suffer from deep flaws that stunt deliberation about scientific controversies.

The problem with public meetings aimed at motivating citizen engagement with scientific institutions is that they easily become hollow rituals of participation. Administrative agencies in the United States often open their rule making to public comment through face-to-face and electronically mediated forums with the hope of generating legitimacy. However, the inescapable problem of scientific authority in these situations creates a disparity in *ethos* between the scientists, who are often positioned as knowers, and citizens, who are regularly situated as learners. Though the medium of conversation between these two stakeholders is necessarily ordinary language, there is a high likelihood of what Stephen Turner describes as a "discursive asymmetry."[46] Traditional public participation processes thus become "ritualistic endeavors"[47] that are "designed [or are perceived] to shroud an elitist policy making process in the cloak of democracy."[48] When a government agency invites the public to a hearing, the meeting often functions as a rubber stamp for preordained decisions. As Michele Simmons and Jeffrey Grabill note, "citizen participants at a public meeting are often characterized (by government officials, industry representatives, and university researchers) as people who often know nothing and rant emotionally about irrelevant issues."[49] Tweaks in interaction design may well reduce the ritualistic elements of public hearings while increasing deliberative legitimacy. Yet Carol Hager notices how, "even in the absence of domination by one group or faction, the search for the better argument can become a technical search that cuts off political interaction."[50] Institutional responses to the predicament of public-science communication thus have difficulties in managing the problem of authority in technical communication.[51]

The institutional press offers another site in which publics and scientists can meet in the medium of ordinary language. It, too, faces a major problem. The journalistic norm of objectivity and balance, represented by the convention of reporting on "both sides" of a controversy, creates a perverse effect when it comes to scientific issues. Must journalists interview card-carrying members of the Flat Earth Society whenever they cover geological issues? Must they interview advocates who deny the connection between HIV and AIDS when they report on new developments toward an AIDS vaccine? Reporting "both sides" results in some dubious journalism. If the complexity of climate science denies scientists a panoramic view of the issue, then journalists with multiple beats to cover are unlikely to develop the ability to synthesize cutting-edge developments across a number of fields accurately. This failure in discretion often leads journalists to give more credence to lobbyists, front-groups, and fringe views then they deserve. Yet reporters are advised to hedge their bets, because the history of science is littered with moments where the consensus position is overturned by what was previously a minority, even absurd, perspective. Showing both sides, then, serves as a check against false consensus and the premature closure of scientific controversy.

But the press, by institutionalizing the norms and formats of bourgeois rational-critical debate, models a kind of public debate that encourages "smaller, less recognized or less powerful groups to compete on an equal footing with larger, more familiar, or more powerful groups."[52] Skeptics of climate change—in the extreme minority of climate scientists—use this journalistic convention to full effect in gaining attention for their views. One side effect of the balance convention is to reduce political debate from a rich field of subtly variegated opinions into two polarized sides. Using the dramatic case of Holocaust deniers to prove her point, Deborah Tannen maintains that the use of adversarial, "show both sides" formats gives often repulsive or unsupportable minority viewpoints unjustified publicity.[53] For former journalist and climate activist Ross Gelbspan, a proportionalizing approach would be more appropriate than the current model. That is, a journalist should focus on new research findings for 95 percent of an article, "with the skeptics getting a paragraph at the end."[54] The adversarial format of journalism is particularly problematic for science controversies because it imports norms far afield from scientific argumentation. Scientific evidence is argued over for years through measured, written argument, a far cry from broadcast media geared toward the daily publication of spectacle.[55] Scientific argument proceeds by establishing loose "complexes of evidence" that resist reduction to polarized propositions like "Is anthropogenic global warming happening?"[56] Scientists often perceive public debate on issues where there is a lopsided consensus, in face-to-face exchanges or through the mass media, "as an attempt to publicize the heresy and keep it alive scientifically rather than as a serious procedure for arriving collectively at the truth."[57]

The dilemma is a thorny one: translation stations are important for facilitating deliberative legitimation processes related to science and technology controversies, yet efforts by both the state and the institutional press to encourage citizen participation usually produce deliberation traps of ritual or spectacle. Although the reformation of these twentieth-century translation stations may see them eventually having a more potent role, the norms that currently govern these translation stations are problematic from a rhetorical perspective. In contrast, blogs like *RealClimate* encourage the cultivation of public participation while incorporating pedagogical moments, offering an alternative to traditional translation stations in informal networks of public deliberation.

RealClimate as a Translation Station

What sorts of technical issues about climate science do *RealClimate* scientists attempt to translate into ordinary language? *RealClimate* blog posts can be organized into three overarching categories significant to the public conversation about science. The first category deals with scientific issues regarding the state of climate science, such as the impact of aerosols, climate modeling, extreme events, and paleoclimatology. The second category addresses how climate science is discussed in the broadcast media, with a special focus on responding to common contrarian arguments. The final category considers scientific practice itself by delving into meta-issues like the significance of peer review and the meaning of consensus. These three broad categories mark distinct layers where *RealClimate* performs a translation function.

Category 1: The Science of Climate, in Which the Dummies' Guide Becomes a Universal Hermeneutic

The hockey stick is a powerful visual argument that underlines how skeptics' criticisms are minor quibbles that fail to challenge the linkage between accelerated carbon dioxide emissions and climate change. Although most of the peer-reviewed literature ratifies the hockey stick reconstruction, questions linger about the model. This uncertainty prompted Michael Mann to write "Myth vs. Fact Regarding the 'Hockey Stick,'" identifying four (later updated to five) myths regarding the controversy.[58] In the conventional "myth vs. fact" format, Mann counters persistent misconceptions with a bevy of links to peer-reviewed articles, visual images, and publicly available scientific reports.[59] While a compelling post, it presumes that norms of peer review carry the same significance in public contexts as they do in scientific ones. Still, Mann goes into far more depth than a newspaper article would, revealing more insider information than a journalist could know and with a command of the secondary literature on the hockey stick that only someone with extensive experience in climate science could muster.

Mann's post performs a light translation of science, but more extensive engagement with public audiences is required if *RealClimate* is to operate as a deep translation site that blends participation with pedagogy. *RealClimate* does serve this deeper translational function through a structural feature of blogs: comments. In February 2005, Gavin Schmidt and Caspar Amman produced a "Dummies Guide to the Latest 'Hockey Stick' Controversy" that is an exemplar of deep translation. They begin their post acknowledging their translational task by writing, "due to popular demand, we have put together a 'dummies guide' which tries to describe what the actual issues are in the latest controversy, in language even our parents might understand."[60] The term "Dummies' Guide," alluding to the popular line of books that simplify complex subjects, is code for the process of turning technical language into more accessible modes of communication. In this spirit, Schmidt and Amman focus on the methodological issues at the heart of McIntyre and McKitrick's critique of Mann et al.'s 1998 "hockey stick" paper. They initially offer two links to *RealClimate* blog posts with more technical descriptions of the material they cover.[61] Two more links to other *RealClimate* posts on "the wider climate science context" and the "relationship to other recent reconstructions (the 'Hockey Team')" are then provided.[62] This preface by the *RealClimate* bloggers offers links to a buffet of topical posts that fall along a sliding scale of difficulty and specialization. The Dummies' Guide itself is presented in a question-and-answer format, split into two parts. In "Technical Issues," Schmidt and Amman explicate the method used by Mann et al., going into detail about the significance of what is called Primary Component Analysis (PCA). The second part of the post deals with the application of that method to the 1998 hockey stick paper and the critique by McIntyre and McKitrick.

The main point of this second part is that Mann et al.'s choice of PCA analysis was (a) appropriate given their object of study and (b) correctly applied. To prove that Mann et al. conducted the analysis correctly, Schmidt and Amman produce a series of graphs that show the poorer "validation statistics," or "skill," of McIntyre and McKitrick's modified study.[63] Their analysis leans toward more technical language in this part, but is still largely intelligible to nonspecialists. Schmidt and Amman's technical writing is greatly aided by the graphical depictions of the hockey stick that compare competing interpretations of the data. After this detailed explanation, though, Schmidt and Amman summarize their Dummies' Guide by writing, "So does this all matter? No. If you use the MM05 convention and include all the significant PCs, you get the same answer. If you don't use any PCA at all, you get the same answer. If you use a completely different methodology (i.e. Rutherford et al, 2005), you get basically the same answer. Only if you remove significant portions of the data [as McIntyre and McKitrick did] do you get a different (and worse) answer."[64] The post concludes with a graphical representation that puts Mann et al.'s 1998 reconstruction together with numerous other separate, and similar, reconstructions, each using different methods of analysis. Again, the hockey stick figure appears as a spike around 1850 that coincides with the acceleration of the industrial era. In the end, Schmidt and Amman argue that, despite the critique of McIntyre and McKitrick, the preponderance of evidence indicates that the hockey stick was an accurate depiction.

How did Schmidt and Amman fare as translators of highly technical material? Were they successful in converting their modes of scientific proof to ordinary language? The comments on this post offer differing opinions about the effectiveness of the translation. Several comments underlined the successful translation of the methodological issues. Commenter Garry Culhane writes, "Congratulations. Now you can break out a bottle of the good stuff. . . . Of course, it is still a little on the high end, but I can see it is very difficult to condense and digest to such a point that material can be thrown up in sports page language. But this piece really is a big jump forward in expository style and content."[65] John S. comments, "I must congratulate you on a much clearer presentation of the current issues than has previously been set out."[66] Commenters like Lynn Vincentnathan create additional layers of translation, condensing the post further:

> I probably need the Complete Idiot's Guide, but what I get out of this is, using the mean of the whole data set (if it does have an actual hockey stick shape) as zero creates a higher horizontal line from which all the data vary in various amounts & it tends to "pull up" the negative differences & makes the positive differences look not so big (or it makes all the data look on average equally large in distance from the mean, both in pos & neg directions), making the whole thing look like nothing much is happening, aside from cyclical changes. Whereas, using the past (lower) data to establish a mean gives us a lower horizontal line from which data vary—making the past data look fairly cyclical (except for that mini-ice age), and the recent data look like it's going into new and higher territory.[67]

Schmidt and Amman did not please all readers with their translation. Commenter Florens de Wit submitted, "I agree that this presentation is quite a good read, even for someone who has no prior knowledge of PCA; I doubt if my mother would understand it however. :-)"[68] Greg Johnson wrote, "Ugh. This is so horribly written as to require a dummies guide to your dummies guide."[69] Steven Corneliussen commented, "I don't blame the *RealClimate* scientists for their often-stated preference simply to report scientific facts and to leave actual political debating to others. And I too use my mom as a calibration for keeping technical readability at the right level. But I have to say, it would heavily stretch my mom's and my capacities to apply this dummies' guide to what's been asserted this morning in what may be the world's most influential newspaper [the *Wall Street Journal*] for denying *RealClimate*'s scientific facts."[70] The differing opinions about the satisfactory nature of the dummies' guide indicate the range of scientific knowledge among readers of *RealClimate*.

Differing familiarity with scientific concepts makes translating key terms challenging, for how do experts recognize success in translating their technical claims into ordinary language—besides, apparently, asking one's parents? (Note how the term "parents" in the original *RealClimate* blog post has been converted to "mom" in the comments section. The invocation of the "mom test" pinpoints the gender biases that implicitly code technical language as masculine and translational efforts as less intense, thus more accessible to "moms.") The affordances of the blog format address this problem of translation. Through the comments extending off each blog post, readers participate in direct communication with authors and, importantly, other readers and commenters. The many-to-many communication infrastructure of the blog thus supports the incorporation of a more participatory model of expertise, where citizens put pressure on more pedagogically oriented translational efforts. Concepts that are poorly translated, or simply need more amplification, receive treatment in the comments section. Comment number 29 on the Dummies' Guide post illustrates how citizens challenge the *RealClimate* bloggers' foothold in common sense and how the bloggers then interact with broader publics. In this comment, Mat McClain pushes the *RealClimate* bloggers to clarify some fuzzy concepts. I quote this comment in full to show how multiple areas of confusion received clarification through inline comments (in square brackets, preceded with "Response") by Gavin Schmidt:

> Your dummies guide has confused me in an exponential sense even before I achieved a satisfactory base understanding of your theorem. In the first section, You use the ambiguous term "noisy records." Can you define "noisy records" for my mom?
>
> [Response: A data record that has a signal (that you are interested in), and "noise" that you aren't. Like listening to a static-filled radio station.]
>
> From the second section please explain the following: Please explain in a geo-metaphysical sense, the relationship between "climate data applications" and "the physics" of a given algorithmic situation. Please explain this so my mother could understand it.
>
> [Response: Think of a swing in a kid's playground. It can move in a number of ways (or modes) (back and forwards, twisting, side to side) that can be predicted based on the physics (the length of the ropes, how far apart they are, the weight of the seat etc.). Now take a time series of the motion of a random swing. Numerically I can try and see what the most important patterns of movement are by doing a PC analysis. It's likely (but not certain) that the first few

individual PCs will resemble the modes I would have predicted based on the physics. But sometimes they won't (if for instance someone was pushing the swing in a particular way). Thus the answers from the PC analysis *may* have a distinct physical meaning, but they don't necessarily. When looking at climate data, the PCs may each have a distinct physical meaning, but not necessarily.]

From Section 3: Explain the "Monte Carlo" simulation for us "dummies" before you apply it to your empirical position. Please do it in a way that my mom could understand.

[Response: Monte Carlo is famous for it's [sic] casinos. There, many games of chance are played that depend on random numbers (i.e. the sequence of roulette plays). Many methods in mathematics or statistics that use large amounts of random numbers to estimate whether something is coincidental or significant are therefore called Monte Carlo methods. For example, from many, many Monte Carlo simulations we know that rolling a normal die gives a 6 about 1/6th of the time. If instead, a die gave you a 6 a third of the time (over a long enough period) you would judge that significant and might therefore suspect it was loaded.]

From Section 4: If your methods are objectively scientific, explain your "a priori" parameters so my mom could understand them.

[Response: The question really is do any "a priori" assumptions affect the final result?' The answer is no.]

This should keep your plate full. I will wait with baited [sic] breath for your response that will, no doubt, assimilate nicely with invective for the truth, and the scientific method.

[Response: Let me know how your mom gets on. -gavin][71]

Whether or not this is a serious query on McClain's part, or a cheeky bit of trolling, Schmidt clarifies obscure elements of the original blog post, primarily through metaphor ("static-filled radio station," "swing in kid's playground," "Monte Carlo methods"). As Schmidt's response reveals, the bloggers at *RealClimate* often rely on metaphors to do the explanatory heavy lifting for their technical claims.[72] One of the affordances of the many-to-many environment is to create a public back-and-forth between interlocutors, which identifies and clarifies potentially obscure claims or insufficient evidence.

This Dummies' Guide rehabilitation of the hockey stick metaphor was useful for citizens aiming to make sound public arguments, especially as they learned from each other in the many-to-many forum of the comments. Take commenter Raymond Pierrehumbert, who elaborates that "there is a legitimate reason for putting so much energy into defending it. The 'hockey stick' is an excellent educational tool. Much of the evidence and theory is complex and hard to explain. We are short on scientifically respectable arguments that can be immediately grasped by the public."[73] Joseph O'Sullivan responds, "Raymond Pierrehumbert has provided some crucial information. I wondered why the 'hockey stick' was being singled out, and his comment explains alot [sic]."[74] The interactive nature of comments means that fellow citizens often translate the import of particular scientific arguments for each other, a crucial dimension of social learning that takes place in the networked public sphere.

Category 2: Climate in the Media, in Which Contrarians Get Taken to Task

Part of *RealClimate*'s mission is to critique poor representations of climate science in the institutional media. Thus, responses to artifacts of public culture regularly appear on the blog. Two of these posts, on Michael Crichton's novel *State of Fear* and an editorial published in the *Wall Street Journal*, demonstrate the refutational capacities of the blogosphere.

Michael Crichton's novel *State of Fear* is about a wily band of do-gooders thwarting ecoterrorist plots aimed at drawing attention to climate change. Throughout the novel, Crichton's protagonists digress into long explanations of why climate science is untrustworthy. Scientific graphs pepper this piece of literary fiction. *State of Fear* was exceptional, in the purely descriptive sense of that word, in that it produced a bibliography of published articles that questioned theories of anthropogenic climate change. The list of citations at the end of the book lends the arguments made in the text a patina of credibility. It was this bibliography, rather than the narrative quality of *State of Fear*, that received press coverage.[75] Gavin Schmidt's review of *State of Fear* for *RealClimate* identifies where Crichton cherry-picks evidence about the scientific uncertainty surrounding global warming. Schmidt's catalog of Crichton's errors shows an advantage of scientists' involving themselves with the artifacts of popular culture. Experts often know where the soft spots of an argument lie, and blogs now provide a public venue where those areas are vigorously pressed. Schmidt identifies three key lines of argument where Crichton mischaracterizes the scientific evidence:

- *Crichton identifies times and places where cooling trends are present, which presumably undercuts the assumption that the globe is warming.* Schmidt responds by noting that localized cooling in the Northern Hemisphere between 1940 and 1970 is from alternate causes, which, when controlled for, still indicate a warming trend. He goes on to note, "global warming is defined by the global mean surface temperature. It does not imply that the whole globe is warming uniformly (which of course it isn't). (But that doesn't stop one character later on (p. 381) declaring that ' . . . it's [sic] effect is presumably the same everywhere in the world. That's why it's called global warming')."[76] Another character declares that the cooling of Antarctica proves that global warming isn't happening. In response, Schmidt links to a prior *RealClimate* post titled "Antarctica Cooling, Global Warming?" that expounds on how climate change produces not just overall warming but regionally specific climate oscillations. As Schmidt makes this argument, he adds hyperlink extensions to more conclusive summaries of specific issues that *RealClimate* bloggers had already addressed.
- *Crichton uncharitably and selectively reads testimony by prominent climate scientist James Hansen.* A character in Crichton's novel says, "Dr. Hansen overestimated [global warming] by 300 percent."[77] James Hansen, probably the foremost citizen-scientist at the vanguard of the public debate over the certainty of climate science, is reduced to the hyperventilating and sadly erroneous scientist. Schmidt's explanation of the genesis of the 300 percent figure usefully connects some dots for those unfamiliar with the backstory of Hansen. He first links to the paper in question by Hansen et al. in 1988 that posited three future scenarios for global warming: one with significantly more carbon dioxide emissions, one that stays the course, and one that presumes no more carbon dioxide emissions after 2000. After noting that Hansen's predictive model correctly accounted for the following ten years of global warming, Schmidt then defuses the 300 percent claim: "The '300 percent' error claim comes from noted climate skeptic Patrick Michaels who in testimony in congress in 1998 deleted

the bottom two curves in order to give the impression that the models were unreliable."[78] Schmidt's knowledge of the history of this debate, with a link to NASA's GISS page that demonstrates Michaels's error, provides a panoramic perspective on the origin of this particular error.

- *Crichton homes in on the Urban Heat Island Effect (UHIE) and the unreliability of satellite data as impediments to scientific certainty about climate change.* Questioning the instruments of measurement for temperature or sea-level rise is a common strategy of those who deny anthropogenic climate change. In this case, Crichton asserts that the Urban Heat Island Effect, a theory that temperature increases are attributable to urbanization, is the real cause of global warming. In response, Schmidt links to a *RealClimate* post that addresses the UHIE issue, and he discloses that recent scholarly papers further corrected for the effect, which will increase confidence in temperature assessments. Similarly, Crichton questions the satellite data about rising sea levels in a dialogue between two characters: "[Sea level is] rising faster, satellites prove it." "Actually, they don't."[79] Schmidt admits that satellite data can be problematic, but that Crichton's conclusion overstates the degree of uncertainty on this point.

Though there is more to the review of *State of Fear*, these are the essential points of *stasis* that Schmidt identifies and the general gist of his response.

Based on the commenters' reactions, this post excelled in dissecting and translating some of the scientific assertions in Crichton's novel. One reader wrote, "Fascinating. So glad that now I won't have to read Crichton's loopy book. Many thanks for putting up this blog, it's a tremendous resource."[80] Joseph Steig underlines the pedagogical value of the post by noting, "this is exactly the sort of analysis to which I will be so happy to point the readers of Crichton's work that I will inevitably meet over the coming months."[81] *RealClimate*'s review was linked to by numerous other websites, including the well-known blog *Pharyngula*,[82] the Union of Concerned Scientists, and the Natural Resources Defense Council. Even *Time* magazine weighed in by reporting, "the Internet wasn't invented for *RealClimate* specifically, but it's hard to imagine a site more in line with the Web's original purpose: scientific communication. An assembly of climate researchers gives readers what's lacking virtually everywhere else—straightforward presentation of the physical evidence for global warming, discussed with patience, precision and rigor, and, quite often, length, such as in a 2,300-word evisceration of Michael Crichton's work of fiction, *State of Fear*."[83] Not everyone was convinced of Schmidt's analysis. One commenter expresses reservations: the "point that comes across in the book is that these models shouldn't be trusted without significant empirical evidence, particularly when policy is being based on them. And I tend to take the book's side on this perspective." The comment received an inline response that directed further queries about modeling to chapter 8 of the IPCC report on climate.[84] Though perhaps a product of a well-moderated comments section, the discussion that followed on the post tended to be quizzical reactions that were supplemented by inline responses directing interested readers to other sources that supported the points made in the review. In this way, the *RealClimate* scientists extended the conversation through hyperlinking conventions rather than foreclosing more dialogue by waving their credentials.

In another case of responding to contrarian currents in the institutional press, *RealClimate* bloggers took on the editorial board of the *Wall Street Journal*, a famously skeptical band of climate contrarians. *RealClimate*'s collaboratively authored "The *Wall Street Journal* vs. The Scientific Consensus," published on June 22, 2005, responded to an editorial, "Kyoto by Degree," in the *Wall Street Journal* a day earlier (see fig. 2).[85] *RealClimate*'s response demonstrates the capacity of blogs to perform line-by-line refutation, an argumentative technique with roots in the process of formal debate.[86] In a formal debate, interlocutors aim to refute their opponent through rigorous attention to each individual argument made. The norms of the institutional media are generally not as detailed, as competing experts regularly talk past each other's arguments instead of directly refuting each other's points. Blogging's elevated place in the networked media ecology is deserved precisely because bloggers so easily interpose their own refutations between parts of an original digital text.

RealClimate's refutation of the editorial further shows how the accumulative nature of their previous posts deepened their arguments—and how shallow quotation of these posts allows the bloggers to piece new arguments together. For every misrepresentation in the *Wall Street Journal* editorial, the bloggers link to past *RealClimate* articles that more thoroughly delve into the controversy. Figure 2 is a screenshot from the middle of this post. Though just a small portion of the entire post, it shows how

The editorial then returns to the issue of paleoclimate reconstructions and the so-called "Hockey Stick", repeating literally each of RealClimate's documented "Hockey Stick" myths:

> Then there's the famous "hockey stick" data from American geoscientist Michael Mann. Prior to publication of Mr. Mann's data in 1998, all climate scientists accepted that the Earth had undergone large temperature variations within recorded human history.

The actual prevailing view of the paleoclimate research community that emerged during the early 1990s, when long-term proxy data became more widely available and it was possible to synthesize them into estimates of large-scale temperature changes in past centuries, was that the average temperature over the Northern Hemisphere varied by significantly less than 1 degree C in previous centuries (i.e., the variations in past centuries were small compared to the observed 20th century warming). This conclusion was common to numerous studies from the early and mid 1990s that preceeded Mann et al (1998). The Mann et al (1998) estimates of Northern Hemisphere average temperature change were, in fact, quite similar to those from these previous studies (e.g. Bradley and Jones, 1993; Overpeck et al, 1997), but simply extended the estimates a bit further back (from AD 1500 to AD 1400). In reality, the primary contribution of Mann et al (1998) was that it reconstructed the actual spatial patterns of past temperature variations, allowing insights into the complex patterns of cooling and warming in past centuries. In fact, regional temperatures changes (e.g. in Europe) appear to have been significantly larger, and quite different, from those for the Northern Hemisphere on the whole. Neglecting the significance of the large regional differences in past temperature changes is another classic pitfall in the arguments put forward by many climate change contrarians (see Myth #2 here).

The WSJ editorial continues,

> This included a Medieval warm period when the Vikings farmed Greenland and a "little ice age" more recently when the Thames River often froze solid.

The sentence, first of all, perpetuates two well-known fallacies regarding the so-called "Medieval Warm Period" and "Little Ice Age". See the RealClimate discussions of the Little Ice Age and Medieval Warm Period for explanations of why both the Viking colonization of Greenland and the freezing of the River Thames actually tells us relatively little about past climate change.

The actual large-scale climate changes during these intervals were complicated, and not easily summarized by simple labels and cherry-picked anecdotes. Climate changes in past centuries were significant in some parts of the world, but they were often opposite (e.g. warm vs. cold) in different regions at any given time, in sharp contrast with the global synchrony of 20th century warming.

The WSJ then continue with a statement that is problematic on several levels,

> Seen in that perspective, the slight warming believed to have occurred in the past century could well be no more than a natural rebound, especially since most of that warming occurred before 1940.

Firstly, the overall warming of the globe of nearly 1 degree C since 1900 is hardly "slight". That warming is about 1/5 of the total warming of the globe from the depths of the last Major Ice Age (about 20,000 years ago) to present.

Secondly, the argument that the climate should have naturally "rebounded" with warming during the 20th century defies the actual peer-reviewed scientific studies which, as discussed earlier, suggest that the climate should have actually *cooled* during the 20th century, not warmed, if natural factors were primarily at play. Anthropogenic greenhouse gases are required to explain the observed warming. Also, it is incorrect that most of the warming occurred before 1940; in contrast, the warming since 1970 is larger than that up to 1940.

The WSJ proceeds with the claim that key scientific findings that are common to numerous independent studies (specifically that late 20th century hemispheric warmth is anomalous in the context of past centuries) can somehow be pinned on one particular research group or even individual (see Hockey Stick Myth #1 here):

> Enter Mr. Mann, who suggested that both the history books and other historical temperature data were wrong. His temperature graph for the past millennium was essentially flat until the 20th century, when a sharp upward spike occurs — i.e., it looks like a hockey stick. The graph was embraced by the global warming lobby as proof that we are in a crisis, and that radical solutions are called for.

This is patently incorrect.

Fig. 2   Screenshot of *RealClimate* post

bloggers respond, on point, to specific claims while adding hyperlinks to buttress their detailed analysis. The *RealClimate* post goes on like this at some length, creating a 2,100-word response to a 500-word editorial. Some of the refutations are particularly compelling, as when they respond to the *Wall Street Journal*'s citation of a 2003 Soon and Baliunas study. Ironically, the *RealClimate* bloggers gleefully point out, this study was thoroughly discredited in the *news* section of the *Wall Street Journal*.

Though the blog post focused on the scientific claims made in the *Wall Street Journal* editorial, the comments following the post show how quickly science and politics interpenetrate. A number of commenters produced contrary evidence, which was rebutted by other commenters and occasionally the *RealClimate* bloggers. Again, the commenters observe the translation function being performed. Edward Meyer writes, "thank you for the piece by piece rebuttal of the WSJ op-ed. This is one for sons, friends who don't normally concern themselves with these matters, and my brother. But the detailed rebuttal is more: it characterizes as nothing else could have done the depth of anti-science ideology that is at work behind the scenes in government policy setting today."[87] John Monro wrote, "as usual, a lucid, concise and unarguable (for those who care to listen) debunking of the standard global warming sceptics' arguments. I have already linked your site to my homepage."[88] "Bravo for Real Climate," began Wayne Davidson, "much needed in responding to ignorance like this WSJ article which seem to thrive on apathy and a low sense of esteem for the scientific community."[89] Some commenters even urged readers to take action by circulating a link to this *RealClimate* post to local civil-society organizations.[90] Regular commenter Dano theorizes *RealClimate*'s broader role: "Information moves both horizontally (out to you and me) and vertically (up to policy-makers). Ideas are shared on the Internets [sic], and as a result scientists are becoming more effective at distributing useful information upwards. This site is on the cusp of this information movement, and can be said to be both emergent and adaptive; both of these terms we should become more familiar with, BTW."[91] Dano's comment registers both the more continuous flow of scientific information and how networked media spur translations of that information to broader publics. Commenters like Dano add their own vernacular conjectures about *RealClimate*'s function because they detect an underlying disturbance in the rhetorical imaginary; the presence of a new circulatory matrix for distributing and discussing scientific controversies was an exigency that invited sense making of new deliberative practices by participants.

Category 3: The Practices of Science, in Which the Importance of "Going Meta" Becomes Apparent

In response to the *RealClimate* review of Michael Crichton's *State of Fear*, one commenter suggested that the current public debate about climate change was stale. This commenter identified Crichton's book as the epiphenomenon, when "the real problem is a lack of understanding about science and its process."[92] This comment points to the dearth of metadiscussion about the norms of science and science communication in venues with a broad public audience. How many television news stories cover the intricacies of peer review? When was the last radio show on framing scientific issues? Do newspaper accounts of scientific discoveries often reveal details about the scientific process? Much of this debate over the practice, norms, and communication of science is trapped in disciplinary journals or conferences. This is a departure from the earlier, thicker interpenetration of science and culture represented by the science societies of the eighteenth century, which generated, reviewed, revised, and affirmed norms of science. *RealClimate* retrieves part of this function from science's past, tweaking it with contemporary communicative norms and internetworked media. Science blogs do not simply offer translation of the latest scientific developments and rapid refutation of what they perceive as poor representations of science in the mass media; they function as sites where the very norms of science are discussed through public argument between citizens and scientists. From the standpoint of the broader climate science controversy, debates about scientific norms like peer review and communicating scientific findings are needed because the climate controversy often becomes bogged down in these issues. Two instances illustrate how *RealClimate* creates opportunities for discussion about meta-issues in science.

On January 20, 2005, Michael Mann and Gavin Schmidt wrote "Peer Review: A Necessary But *Not* Sufficient Condition." The post begins by acknowledging that the scientist-bloggers of *RealClimate* privilege peer-reviewed science, linking to an explanation of peer review by science journalist Chris Mooney. Mann and Schmidt confirm peer review's utility, but then note the following conditions in which peer review is not sufficient:

> (i) the work is submitted to a journal outside the relevant field (e.g. a paper on paleoclimate submitted to a social science journal) where the reviewers are likely to be chosen from a pool of individuals lacking the expertise to properly review the paper, (ii) too few or

too unqualified a set of reviewers are chosen by the editor, (iii) the reviewers or editor (or both) have agendas, and overlook flaws that invalidate the paper's conclusions, and (iv) the journal may process and publish so many papers that individual manuscripts occasionally do not get the editorial attention they deserve.[93]

Mann and Schmidt's explanation of the uses and limitations of peer review previews the direction of their argument: given the ability of both sides to invoke peer-reviewed science, advocates on each side of the climate science controversy must develop a further justification to determine *which* peer-reviewed science should receive more credence. This additional layer tends to point to quality markers of particular publications: while contrarian climate scientists claim peer-reviewed results, much of the research the skeptics rely on tends to be in journals with lower standards of peer review.

This *RealClimate* blog post relates the details of a key moment when peer review underperformed at weeding out poor science. Willie Soon and his co-authors published an article in the journal *Climate Research* that purported to show a warming trend in the medieval period, thus proving that warming cycles were unlinked to human carbon emissions. Mann and Schmidt use the Soon case to share three specific details related to peer review standards: (1) that the *Climate Research* editor Chris de Frietas had a controversial history;[94] (2) that the chief editor and three additional editors resigned over the way the Soon paper was handled, and (3) that the publisher of *Climate Research* admitted that the findings of the Soon paper could not be derived from the data. Mann and Schmidt charge that "another journal which (quite oddly) also published the Soon et al study, 'Energy and Environment,' is not actually a scientific journal at all but a social science journal."[95] This kind of line drawing smacks of disciplinary turf battles and the historical marginalization of the social sciences in favor of the so-called hard sciences. (Let's not imagine where the humanities rest in this formulation!) Fair enough; however, Mann and Schmidt produce a more incisive tidbit by noting that the editor of *Energy and Environment*, Sonja Boehmer-Christiansen, admitted to a science journalist in the *Chronicle of Higher Education*, "I'm following my political agenda—a bit, anyway. But isn't that the right of the editor?"[96] Mann and Schmidt continue in this vein about the suspect reputations of other outlets that regularly publish the research of skeptics, detailing (with a litany of links) other research articles, initially hailed as peer-reviewed science by contrarians, that were later discredited.

The Soon study displays a key problem with mass-mediated reportage on scientific matters. Mann and Schmidt: "The study was summarily discredited in articles by teams of climate scientists (including several of the scientists here at *RealClimate*), in the American Geophysical Union (AGU) journal *Eos* and in *Science*. However, it took some time [for] the rebuttals to work their way through the slow process of the scientific peer review. In the meantime the study was quickly seized upon by those seeking to sow doubt in the validity behind the scientific consensus concerning the evidence for human-induced climate change (see news articles in the *New York Times*, and *Wall Street Journal*)."[97] Again, the political economy of the mass media creates conditions for "the impression that scientific progress consists of a series of revolutions where scientists discard all their past thinking each time a new result gets published. This is often because only a small handful of high-profile studies in a given field are known by the wider public and media, and thus unrealistic weight is attached to those studies."[98] The differential punctuations of the daily press looking for splashy headlines vis-à-vis the slower scientific peer-review process meant that the Soon paper shaped public discourse even though it was fundamentally unsound. The implication of this blog post is that citizens should be skeptical when so-called bombshell papers that supposedly disprove anthropogenic warming are trumpeted in press accounts. Partially for this reason, science blogs like *RealClimate* are thought to usefully supplement traditional peer-review processes in a faster-paced media environment.[99] Mann and Schmidt nest their theory of peer review in an incrementalist view of science, maintaining that "any new study will be one small grain of evidence that adds to this big pile, and it will shift the thinking of scientists slightly."[100] Is this the last word on peer review? Of course not. But in thematizing peer review, the scientists at *RealClimate* provide openings for critics to introduce their objections dialogically.

Commenters at *RealClimate* appreciated this explanation of peer review. Dano observed, "this essay demonstrates the value of *RealClimate*. It has been realized on this entry. Well done."[101] Steven Corneliussen wrote, "thanks for this discussion and for its important applicability to all the rest of science."[102] Brian C confesses, "at the risk of sounding like a fan-boi, this is a great piece of writing for people like me who have some knowledge of climate science, but don't always fully understand how seriously to take the contrarians."[103] Peter Wetzel, self-identified as a scientist working on climate prediction models, comments, "this post provides excellent insight into the realities (imperfections) of the checks and balances that the scientific peer review system intends to impose on papers which reach the public. It is the best system yet devised to assure credibility in the discourse among scientists."[104] Commenter John Hunter magnified the testimony of Mann and Schmidt with revelations about his recent engagements with Boehmer-Christiansen at *Energy and Environment* that confirmed the journal's lax peer review standards.[105]

RealClimate bloggers thematize issues close to the heart of scientific inquiry, like peer review, but they also introduce posts about communicating scientific argument to public audiences. Under the category "Communicating Climate" are a number of posts concerning the rhetorical challenges involved with articulating technical claims.[106] Gathered here are posts on journalistic convention, the art of press releases, framing scientific issues, public understanding of science, and other issues arising when technical and public discourses intersect. In taking up these rhetorical issues involved in communicating climate science, the bloggers show a high level of self-reflexivity with regard to the public-technical interface. In one post, "How Not to Write a Press Release," Gavin Schmidt critically analyzes how a recent scholarly paper was cited in press coverage as predicting global warming as high as 11 degrees in the coming decades.[107] In reality, the paper in question produced a range of possible results, with 11-degree warming being a very low likelihood. Yet the press release that accompanied the paper included this unlikely number, which the press predictably ran with ("Mega-warming coming, scientists say!"). Schmidt fears that this kind of alarmism sensationalizes climate science, and he wonders whether the sensationalism was "because the scientists were being 'alarmist,' or was it more related to a certain naivety in how public relations and the media work? And more importantly, what can scientists do to help ensure that media coverage is a fair reflection of their work?"[108]

Schmidt identifies three rough spots in mass media–driven translation efforts. First, the actors in the institutional media "like a dramatic statement, and stories that say something is going to be worse than previously thought get more coverage than those which say it's not going to be as bad."[109] Second, most journalists read the press release instead of the paper, which diminishes the caveats and calibrations that might otherwise temper sensationalist headlines. Finally, media frames funnel science stories into predetermined sluices.[110] Schmidt insists that traditional press organs "have a small number of preconceived frames into which they will place the story—common ones involve forecasts of possible disasters, conflict within the community (the more personal the better), plucky Galileos fighting the establishment, and of course anything that interacts directly with politics, or political interference with science. This can be helpful if the scientific story fits neatly into one [of] the boxes, but can cause big problems if the story is either more complex or orthogonal to the obvious frames."[111] Schmidt concludes that scientists must exercise more control over the way in which their research is framed in press releases.

This post sparked 258 comments. Remarkably, the very scientists and press officers involved with the paper and press release coming under Schmidt's scrutiny posted a comment that rebutted the suggestion that they sensationalized their findings in the press conference.[112] Posted by Myles Allen, the comment contains emails that asked members of the press who were at the original press conference whether the scientists had sensationalized their findings, or whether they were appropriately cautious in postulating that runaway warming of 11 degrees was unlikely. This parallel account provided by Allen suggested that the fault lay not with the scientists, but with sloppy journalists somewhere down the publication line. Whether the press release and the subsequent criticism by Schmidt was on point or not is less relevant than the fact that a tight feedback loop formed, where the scientists involved in this episode could quickly respond with a behind-the-scenes explanation and more detailed interpretation of their side of the controversy.

In another example of how *RealClimate* scientists thematize issues relating to the communication of science, blogger Rasmus Benestad posted about a conference he attended on Communicating Science and Technology.[113] Benestad's post received a flurry of comments over the coming days. One of the most interesting sets of comments on this post involves the relationship between the "deficit model," which presumes that scientists perform a pedagogical role in informing the public, and the "engagement model" of communicating science, which encourages public participation. Regular commenter Steve Corneliussen responded:

> To what extent did your conference engage the important contrast between the deficit model and the engagement model? In my experience too many scientists assume, without even realizing it, that science communication must be improved only under what some people call the "deficit model"—the name refers to the deficit in public knowledge about science—to the exclusion of what's been called the "engagement model." . . . In fact, it's my impression that many scientists aren't even remotely aware of the contrasting approaches.

> But maybe that problem is diminishing. It seems to me, for example, that *RealClimate*.org itself represents a breakthrough in the relation of science and society precisely because *RC* balances engagement-model benefits with deficit-model necessities.[114]

In this comment, *RealClimate* is situated as a third way that synthesizes both the deficit and engagement approaches. Later, Corneliussen adds another comment: "A problem, though, is that deficit-model communication tactics—useful and important as they are—don't account for all the dimensions of the communications challenge. Consider a particularly virulent dimension, a tactic that I believe I'm seeing increasingly employed against climate science: sarcasm."[115] He then provides an extended rhetorical analysis of the use of sarcasm in argument over climate science, with the conclusion that scientists need a richer view of communication to account for how scientific argument is conducted outside of field-specific sites. Corneliussen's view reflects a rhetorical perspective on language and argumentation that is often underrepresented in scientific forums. Just as importantly, he identifies *RealClimate* as a site that probes this rhetoricity by drawing public participation into this interactive discussion.

The bloggers at *RealClimate* adopt a self-reflexive attitude about their own orientation toward communicating climate science. In a post called "The Missing Repertoire," Gavin Schmidt linked to a report published by the Institute for Public Policy Research (IPPR), a think tank based in the United Kingdom, called "Warm Words: How Are We Telling the Climate Story and How Can We Tell It Better?"[116] As Schmidt describes, the "basic point of the report was to present a textual analysis of the kinds of language ('repertoires') used in the media when discussing climate and to associate the different repertoire with the advocacy position of the users and the likely effectiveness of that language in swaying opinion."[117] Repertoire is an intriguing way to characterize competing ways of communicating climate science, suggesting as it does a broad array of argumentative styles, modes of proof, and aesthetics of performance. The IPPR report identifies three distinct repertoires that accept the basic presumptions of contemporary climate science: alarmism, techno-optimism, and small actions save the world. The report lists considerably more denialist repertoires: "It'll be alright"-ism, comic nihilism, rhetorical skepticism, free marketism, expert denialism, and the ultra-contrarian attitude that "warming is good." Each of these orientations is associated with familiar arguments, unique commonplaces, and peculiar stylistic conventions.

But Gavin Schmidt identified *RealClimate* as participating in a repertoire that was missing from the IPPR report: "it strikes me that there is a huge missing category—and indeed one in which I think *RealClimate* might fall (along with some of the best reporting on the issue—Andy Revkin's [environment writer for the *New York Times*] pieces for instance). That category is the straight 'It's serious (and interesting) but don't panic' repertoire. This is the language most often heard at scientific conferences and it surprises me that the IPPR authors didn't find enough examples to give it a description all it's [sic] own."[118]

Schmidt's description of these rival repertoires underlines the stylistic gap between scientific communities and public spheres. *RealClimate*'s rigorous, sober scrutiny displays engaged expertise that presents an alternative to the more "excited style of journalism."[119] The genesis of this collective persona of sobriety is probably due to the demands of forging a credible style when one lies at the intersection of technical and public fields of argument. In serving as a translation station where experts and nonscientific publics meet, *RealClimate* bloggers bridge two divergent discourse communities. This bridging requires a high level of self-reflexivity about style, proof, and jargon. Blogger Henry Farrell, situating *RealClimate* in the broader context of science blogging, speculates that a regularized interface between scientific and public discourses transforms them both: "Scientists who are dismayed at the sloppy treatment of science in the media have set up group blogs including the *Panda's Thumb* (evolution), *RealClimate* (global warming and climate science), and *Cosmic Variance* (physics).... All of those blogs weave back and forth between the specialized languages of academe and the vernacular of public debate. They are creating a space for dialogue between the two, connecting them together, and succeeding, to a greater or lesser degree, in changing both."[120] Science blogs like *RealClimate* are authored for technical and popular audiences, requiring bloggers to keep the needs of *both* audiences in mind while posting. As a result, the sensationalist excesses of the mass-mediated public sphere and the excesses of insularity familiar to the technical sphere are both reduced, because the presence of either would alienate part of their audience. What really regulates the translational process is the commenters, who introduce critiques of blog posts from anywhere along the spectrum of public to technical objections. If the *RealClimate* bloggers are getting too technical, or playing too fast and loose with translation, a commenter often brings it to attention, spurring clarifications and emendations.

Expertise in the Networked Public Sphere
(Building Translational Bridges to Everywhere)

Admittedly, crafting discourse that meets the exacting standards of scientists while maintaining intelligibility for public audiences is a difficult rhetorical task. However, based on reactions to *RealClimate* circulating in the institutional mass media and the blogosphere, the bloggers make great strides in translating scientific discourse to a public idiom. On a *New Republic* blog, Bradford Plummer writes, "for a more thorough look at the IPCC's sea-rise predictions, and why they're likely underestimates, this RealClimate post is a good place to start. (It's readable, even for non-experts.)"[121] A *Salon* article references *RealClimate* by arguing, "there are few things the blogosphere excels more at than debunking revisionist lies about global warming."[122] A story in *The Guardian* says that *RealClimate* "nail[s] the myth that scientists struggle to communicate their work."[123] *RealClimate* bloggers "get into the nitty-gritty of climate research, interacting earnestly with fans as well as foes in long strings of reference-rich commentary."[124] These meta-reflections confirm *RealClimate*'s success at creating a networked public sphere that hybridizes public-technical argumentation.

RealClimate's entrance into the citational economy of blogs, letters to the editor, and news stories as a trusted source for intelligible commentary on climate science further underlines the effectiveness of this translational function. Bloggers often link to *RealClimate*, as in this post: "As usual, you can get most of what you need at *RealClimate*. Here's the most pertinent piece. The short version is that a combination of changes to ocean currents and airflow around Antarctica mean that warming there was always expected to lag far behind the rest of the planet."[125] Those who deny anthropogenic climate change are referred to "accessible blogs on climate change, such as www.celsias.com or www.realclimate.org."[126] A letter to the editor notes, "where do these hopeful skeptics get the idea that they are the only ones trying to find chinks in the body of climate change evidence? The real climate scientists make a living looking for alternative explanations (www.realclimate.org)."[127] A *Newsweek* article concludes, "it is wrong to think that the 'skeptics'' arguments have gone unanswered. One group of climate researchers does this very well, at http://www.realclimate.org/."[128] These comments signal *RealClimate*'s success at stimulating a robust debate about climate science in the networked public sphere.

RealClimate and similar science blogs create a counter-trend to the so-called autistic tendencies of complex subsystems that decline to intercommunicate. Indeed, the blog's performance as a translation station is consistent with Habermas's declaration that, though boundaries may appear to separate distinct fields of argument from interacting, "one can always build hermeneutical bridges from one text to the next."[129] *RealClimate* is a hermeneutical bridge that participates in what Habermas calls "multi-level translations" between expert knowledge claims and civil society.[130] This kind of bridging rhetoric involves the translation of the norms, arguments, evidence, and implicit understandings of one discourse community to another.[131] Hermeneutical bridge building between expert and lay publics is not entirely new, as the established genre of popular science writing attests. Yet, as networked media expand the ability of niche discourse communities to develop their own language games, more intense hermeneutical bridge building is required to accommodate complexity and differentiation during deliberative episodes. In this way, the rhetorical ability to bridge discourse communities is a power with "new power" in the networked public sphere.[132]

One of the signature elements of blogging, the offset pull quote, facilitates this rhetorical bridge building between networked publics. When bloggers respond to others' texts, as in the *RealClimate* rebuttal to the *Wall Street Journal* editorial, they often excerpt quotes and then provide commentary. In the other case studies, the pithy terms "flooding the zone" and "ambient intimacy" rose organically from bloggers' homegrown theorizing about communicative practice. Translation, too, is a prominent native trope about science blogging. Although the word "translation" does some work in identifying a part of the networked rhetorical imaginary, a term taken from argumentation theory—"shallow quotation"—usefully reflects the communicative activity that undergirds all translation. Shallow quotation is a citation of others' views that does not deeply borrow. Argumentation scholar Charles Willard articulated shallow quotation as the process through which claims migrate between argument fields. Willard's development of shallow quotation attempted to counter the supposition that discourses emerging from different language communities were invariably incommensurable. For Willard, critics and theorists need not worry about accepting certain positions or ideas wholesale, for "the depthless quotation of positions and theories might help ideas across field boundaries."[133]

As the posts throughout this chapter show, *RealClimate* deftly, if shallowly, quotes relevant portions of scholarly scientific research to support the group's arguments. *RealClimate* bloggers manage the complexity of the climate science knowledge network by paraphrasing or selecting only the key quotes from lengthier and more sophisticated research reports.[134] This is a useful alternative to posting full research papers, or lengthy segments from published articles, which would tax most readers' attention. Of course, there is a risk to shallow quotation.[135] As Willard contends, "'Shallow' alerts us to the fact that we are doing something risky—something, indeed, that we often encounter in mistakes. . . . The risk, then, is the incompetence of the non-native: One borrows an idea without understanding its context and thus misuses it."[136] This is the critique of nonexpert journalists writing on science issues: they incompetently perform shallow quotation. Sometimes bloggers, too, summarize a scientific paper poorly, or cherry-pick unrepresentative quotes, which sparks recriminations and clarifications throughout the blogosphere. Thus, shallow quotation invites reflexivity about the depth and faithfulness of any pull quote. In broadcast media, this ability to argue over the shallowness or depth of a quotation is limited in comparison to internetworked media. Television anchors inevitably give one of their dueling experts "the last word." On blogs, there is theoretically *never* a last word. Blogs are able to continually deepen the contextualization of their quotations—as in the *RealClimate* bloggers' exchange with commenters on the hockey stick post—with as much sophistication as the situation or audience warrants.

How do the translational capacities of the blogosphere function in the broader networked public sphere? C. P. Snow observed that the late modern era saw a gradual separation between the two cultures of the scientific and the literary.[137] John Brockman extended Snow's own thinking on a possible "third culture" that could harmonize the scientific and the literary by identifying how late twentieth-century scientists were assuming the roles of public intellectuals by writing books aimed at popular audiences.[138] With sites like *RealClimate*, the networked public sphere expands the forums that support this "third culture" where scientists and publics directly interact. John Lyne stipulates that a "rhetorically informed third culture" would be

1. Constituted by both experts and nonexperts;
2. Marked by a shared interest in the social reception of technical knowledge;
3. Characterized by the presence of arguers who assume that they are addressing, ultimately if not immediately, an audience that includes both experts and nonexperts;
4. Brought into focus by the presence of distinct voices;

5. Hospitable to rhetorical argument, narrativity, and persuasive representation; [and]
6. Constituted in such a way that effective participation requires accepting the legitimacy of both empirical and interpretive methods.[139]

RealClimate convincingly meets the first four criteria Lyne explicates. It is a site for experts and nonexperts who are invested in the broader cultural implications of technical knowledge. Interlocutors assume a mixed audience of climate science specialists and nonspecialists. There are distinct voices. *RealClimate* bloggers may not conceptualize their own interventions as rhetorical, nor do they place empirical and interpretive methods on the same plane—but they cannot avoid metaphor in explaining scientific concepts or dodge the inevitability of interpretation. A third culture provides an alternative to the conventionally conceived interface between scientists and publics by eschewing the informationist pedagogical-deficit model in favor of one that reintegrates rhetorical sensibilities and draws in public participation. This rhetorically informed third culture does not, however, cut science and scientists down to size by reducing science to just one discourse among many equals. Instead, it draws scientific argument into public deliberation in the context of informal many-to-many communication. The informality of the third culture is important, as institutional efforts to spur interaction between scientists and nonexpert publics are likely to replicate the pedagogical model of expertise that risks ritual or spectacle. Sites like *RealClimate* encourage the greening of the networked public sphere by providing information about environmental controversies, providing mechanisms for discussion and debate about those controversies, and elevating the "reflexive learning potential of both the state and civil society."[140] Perhaps, with a bolstered third culture, Dewey's one-way lanes might finally be expanded into two-way streets able to support robust traffic between science and the broader public culture.

Shallow Quotation Gone Wild: When Hackers Attack

In mid-November 2009, a hacker broke into the server of the Climatic Research Unit (CRU) at the University of East Anglia in the United Kingdom and downloaded more than 800 megabytes of private emails, documents, and software code. A portion of this download, about 61 megabytes, was posted on the blogs and discussion forums of climate science skeptics right before the fifteenth United Nations climate change conference in Copenhagen. Climate skeptics pointed to private emails between *RealClimate* blogger Michael Mann and Phil Jones, the head of the CRU, as well as other prominent climate scientists as evidence that the science on climate was cooked.[141] Quickly dubbed "Climategate" by skeptics, the scandal lit the blogosphere afire and eventually lit up the institutional media. Two specific quotations from the emails at the center of the controversy bear scrutiny as signifiers of shallow quotation gone wild.

An email by Phil Jones from November 16, 1999, included the sentence "I've just completed Mike's *Nature* trick of adding in the real temps to each series for the last 20 years (ie, from 1981 onwards) and from 1961 for Keith's to hide the decline." Jones was not emailing about a forthcoming publication in a scientific journal. He was instead trying to create a diagram for the cover of a World Meteorological Organization report on climate. Nonetheless, climate skeptics interpreted the quote as demonstrative of how climate scientists fudge scientific data to fuel a politically driven agenda. A shallow read of this shallow quotation does appear damning, featuring as it does an acknowledged "trick" to "hide the decline" in temperatures shown by some of Keith Briffa's data (the "Keith" in the quotation). This is the shallow read many skeptics preferred. Former Alaska governor and vice presidential candidate Sarah Palin, in an editorial for the *Washington Post*, proclaimed that "the e-mails reveal that leading climate 'experts' deliberately destroyed records, [and] manipulated data to 'hide the decline' in global temperatures."[142] Longtime skeptic Senator James Inhofe (R-OK), in his comments at the Copenhagen climate conference, invoked the Climategate scandal as evidence that the science of climate was relentlessly manipulated. He suggested that the Climategate emails ratified his skepticism, reading the Jones quote about the "Mann trick," which he followed up with "of course he means hide the decline in temperatures, which caused another scientist [in the leaked emails], Kevin Trenberth, to write: 'The fact is we can't account for the lack of warming, and it's a travesty that we can't.'"[143] This latter quote from Trenberth, the head of the Climate Analysis Section at the National Center for Atmospheric Research (NCAR) in the United States, often accompanied Jones's email as the two "bombshells" that supposedly discredited the conventional view of anthropogenic climate change.

Is it surprising to see politicians gleefully glom on to little rhetorical fragments like this, which seem to so obviously confirm their skepticism? No. In the migration of these fragments of discourse from the technical sphere to the public sphere, the worst fears of those who question the public's capacity to comprehend scientific discourse are confirmed. In the hands of nonexperts, scientific discourses can get handled sloppily, especially if intense political motivation is at work. The main sloppiness in the reasoning of Inhofe and Palin, whose claims are representative of the public discourse circulating through sites of climate science contrarianism, is elision, an argumentation fallacy of omission. Inhofe's statement suggested that the initial email by Jones about using "tricks" *caused* Trenberth to note the "travesty" of not being able to account for the lack of warming. Even by butterfly-effect theories of causation, this is a stretch. These two emails are separated in time by ten years, yet Inhofe links them in a temporally collapsed sequence to magnify their rhetorical significance. Both Inhofe and Palin rely on another elision in their interpretation of the Jones email quotation: reading the "trick" and "hide the decline" parts of the email together without recognizing the deeper, specialized meaning of each concept for the climate science community.

While the commonsense valence of the word "trick" implies manipulation, falsification, chicanery, or artifice, the term is often used in the sciences to refer to clever, but ethical and routine, ways of reconciling data sets that may use different measures. Jones was referring to how Mann reconciled instrumental data from the last 150 years, when temperature data began to be recorded systematically, with the proxy data gathered from temperature reconstructions acquired through tree-ring data. A press release from the CRU puts the use of "trick" in this context: "To produce temperature series that were completely up-to-date (i.e. through to 1999) it was necessary to combine the temperature reconstructions with the instrumental record, because the temperature reconstructions from proxy data ended many years earlier whereas the instrumental record is updated every month. The use of the word 'trick' was not intended to imply any deception."[144] The trick is not much of one: to make the data consistent in terms of unit of time (months and years), climate scientists must tweak the data a bit. The tweak doesn't fundamentally change the data, but it does change how the data are represented and organized. The *RealClimate* bloggers, responding to the initial wave of criticism based on the hacked emails, clarify "the 'trick' is just to plot the instrumental records along with reconstruction so that the context of the recent warming is clear. Scientists often use the term 'trick' to refer to a 'a good way to deal with a problem,' rather than something that is 'secret,' and so there is nothing problematic in this at all."[145] Despite this rhetorical shortcut employed by

Jones, climate science skeptics fixated on the term as proof of climate scientists' rhetrickery. Little clarification could soothe the concerns of these skeptics, which casts doubt on the capacity for technical discourses to move into more public arenas without losing some of their essence. The editors at *Nature*, no less, absolved Jones by noting that "the term 'trick'—slang for a clever (and legitimate) technique" was simply a hammer for political opponents of climate science to wield against the scientific consensus.[146] If Jones had said, instead of "trick," that he had mimicked Mann's clever method of reconciling two data sets, this particular shallow quotation of a private email would not have run so wild.

The "hide the decline" part of Jones's email is similarly justifiable. Jones admitted that "hide the decline" was a phrase "written in haste,"[147] admitting later that they were "poorly chosen words."[148] "The decline" refers to what is more commonly known in climate circles as the "divergence problem" emanating from Keith Briffa's tree-ring proxy data. Briffa's research indicates that tree-ring data strongly correlates with temperature from the nineteenth century until about 1960, when it begins to diverge from the temperature data. The problem of accounting for this divergence is a vexing one for climate scientists, because there appears to be an unknown variable at work that makes the tree-ring data unreliable after 1960. Climate scientists recommend not using the post-1960 tree-ring data as a result. The *RealClimate* bloggers, in their initial response to the hacking incident, underline this point: "Those authors [Briffa et al] have always recommend not using the post 1960 part of their reconstruction, and so while 'hiding' is probably a poor choice of words (since it is 'hidden' in plain sight), not using the data in the plot is completely appropriate, as is further research to understand why this happens."[149] The climate skeptics' critique is unlikely to be assuaged by this explanation, despite the fact that even if the Briffa data are fabricated outright, a host of other data will still confirm the basic hockey stick model (the aforementioned "hockey team").

Phil Jones used the CRU web page to expand on the broader context of the major cherry-picked phrases.[150] "Context" was a key word for Michael Mann, too, who noted that climate denialists are "'taking these words totally out of context to make something trivial appear nefarious.'"[151] Kevin Trenberth, the scientist cited by Inhofe, echoed Jones and Mann by indignantly proclaiming, "I'm appalled at the very selective use of the e-mails, and the fact they've been taken out of context."[152] Trenberth, in a statement on NCAR's website, gave the appropriate context:

In my case, one cherry-picked email quote has gone viral and at last check it was featured in over 107,000 items (in Google). Here is the quote: *"The fact is that we can't account for the lack of warming at the moment and it is a travesty that we can't."* It is amazing to see this particular quote lambasted so often. It stems from a paper I published this year bemoaning our inability to effectively monitor the energy flows associated with short-term climate variability. It is quite clear from the paper that I was not questioning the link between anthropogenic greenhouse gas emissions and warming, or even suggesting that recent temperatures are unusual in the context of short-term natural variability.[153]

Trenberth's explanation about short-term variability does not, in his estimation, undermine the long-term trends represented by the hockey stick. In each of these instances, Jones, Mann, and Trenberth rely on one defense: critiquing the skeptics for too shallow a reading of their hacked emails. Fortunately for these three accused scientists, the affordances of networked media gave them opportunities to interpret the widely circulating shallow quotations with a little more depth. Compared to the institutional broadcast media, the benefits of networked media for adding context are much greater. Phil Jones's refutation of the most cherry-picked phrases from the email on the CRU website, the *RealClimate* bloggers' response, and even *Wikipedia*'s coverage of the controversy provide incredible depth that traditional newspapers could not match. *Wikipedia*'s entry on the incident is an outstanding example of the kinds of hyperlinked context that networked media excel at providing.[154]

A number of independent commissions examined the Climategate controversy: the House of Commons Science and Technology Committee, Independent Climate Change Review, and International Science Assessment Panel in the United Kingdom, along with the Pennsylvania State University (Michael Mann's institutional home), the Environmental Protection Agency, and the Department of Commerce in the United States. Each of the reports largely absolved the scientists from any charge of data manipulation or political machination, though there were some sternly worded suggestions about openness and playing nice with skeptical scientists. The Environmental Protection Agency's assessment of the controversy is nicely summative, stating that skeptics drawing on these hacked emails "have routinely misunderstood or mischaracterized the scientific issues, drawn faulty scientific conclusions, resorted to hyperbole, impugned the ethics of climate scientists in general, characterized actions as 'falsification' and 'manipulation' with no basis or support, and placed an inordinate reliance on blogs, news stories, and literature that is often neither peer reviewed nor accurately summarized in their petitions. Petitioners often 'cherrypick' language that creates the suggestion or appearance of impropriety, without looking deeper into the issues or providing corroborating evidence that improper action actually occurred."[155] Is this a satisfying response for climate permaskeptics? Unlikely. Instead, the concurrence of all of these so-called independent commissions is simply interpreted as a sign of the depth of the conspiracy—more evidence of how many institutions have sampled the anthropogenic climate change Kool-Aid.

Despite being cleared of the most damning charges, the Climategate scandal shows how powerful the influence of the institutional media remains. The page A1 news that "climate scientists fudge data!" attracts far more attention and traction than do the corrective and sober findings of the independent commissions, dutifully reported months later on A14. And for all the influence that the blogosphere and related networked media acquired through the first decade of the twenty-first century, enough citizens are still tuning into broadcast news reports that inevitably shallowly quote the shallow quotations of shallow quotations. As one study showed, Climategate deeply hurt public trust in climate scientists, faith in the actual science of climate change, and belief in anthropogenic climate disruption.[156] According to this study, almost half of those who followed the Climategate story said that it made them less likely to believe that global warming was happening. There are, indeed, risks in a rhetorical culture of shallow quotation—just as there always have been.

6

THE PROSPECTS OF NETWORKED RHETORICS

The advent of digital media technology recasts the historical tension between rhetorical and informationist models of communication. After many centuries of conceptualizing the mind as a machine, with inputs feeding into the turning gears of mental cogitation, the dominant metaphor for informationism now is the brain-as-computer. The brain is figured as an information-processing machine, absorbing data and using neural algorithms to make decisions. Rivaling the brain-as-computer metaphor is what I would assert to be rhetoric's key metaphor, both historically and contemporarily: the network. Rhetors are situated in a network of cultural influences and they function as points of articulation for that network. Through their communication, they reshape and transform the activity and topology of the network. The network trope assumes a central role in this book, modifying media, rhetoric, rhetorical imaginary, and the public sphere in order to highlight the renewed salience of this organizational form.

The elevation of the network form promises to strengthen public rhetoric and public deliberation, even in the face of the informationist hopes that accompany the ascendance of Big Data. Whereas hierarchical structures often thwart democratic practices, robust networks of communication are the basis for democratic legitimacy. The closer an imaginary hews to informationist norms—by favoring invention from established corporate interests rather than citizen actors, cordoning off emotion from the public sphere, and insulating scientific discussion from broader publics—the more likely rhetorical challenges related to invention, emotion, and expertise will become deliberative traps that curtail public participation and weaken democratic legitimacy. The openness of the new, networked system of mediation destabilizes the informationist communication norms of late modernity. The revaluation of rhetoric is not yet complete, but, because of the necessity of a revitalized art of attention in an era of information abundance, the promise of building a stronger rhetorical culture is palpable.

Rhetorical theorists and critics—in and beyond the university—have a valuable role in building this networked rhetorical culture by making sense of communication practices afforded by networked media. There are, of course, many ways to do this. *Networked Media, Networked Rhetorics* builds a lexicon for networked communication practices by taking seriously the native tropes of flooding the zone, ambient intimacy, and shallow quotation. Each of these tropes, which identify new modes of publicity, solidarity, and translation, respectively, mark ways in which networked intermediaries draw on rhetorical sensibilities to shape attention in an era of information abundance. The notion that invention is just a process of discovery is undermined by the significance of flooding the zone, which generates meaning out of information from the clash of many different perspectives. Ambient intimacy undermines the presumed competition between reason and emotion by suggesting that that there is an inescapable, complex, and rich interaction between affect, feeling, emotion, and cognition. Though experts still lean on their credentials in order to assume a pedagogical stance in teaching citizens about science, networked media create conditions for an emergent third culture that is far more participatory because of interlocutors' reliance on shallow quotation of technical discourses. It is not just that the generativity of invention, the complementarity of emotion, and the participatory senses of expertise are uncritically valorized in the networked public sphere, but that citizens' networked rhetorical practices weave between the discovery-generation, competitive-complementary, and pedagogical-participatory poles.

Throughout *Networked Media, Networked Rhetorics*, I suggest that networked media help activate deliberative legitimation processes. But, as the analysis in each case study has detailed, flooding the zone can be easily co-opted by administrative actors, ambient intimacy can too easily slide into oversharing, and shallow quotation can run amok. These three potential deliberative traps are signs of surplus publicity, or, as I will call it, hyperpublicity.

Hyperpublicity; or, In Defense of Playful Public Argument

Rhetorical cultures embrace symbol play. If there are many ways of attending to a thing symbolically, then there is some value in playing with these different ways in order to see which is most useful, or most humorous, or most poignant, and so on. This is why rhetorical pedagogy draws on *dissoi logoi*, or the two-sidedness of argument, by encouraging students to defend a position they do not believe in. This kind of experimentation illuminates the dynamism of the controversy for students and facilitates the identification of common ground that can help depolarize argument about an issue. "Seeing argument as play," Cate Palczewski submits, "induces a comic frame where mistakes are inevitable, where those who disagree are not spurred by evil intentions, but by errors, and where any decision is always provisional, contingent, and uncertain. . . . [W]hen playing, not only must we consider those who disagree as possibly in error, but we must also entertain the possibility that we, too, are in error."[1] Play can be serious, and as the case studies highlighted in this book indicate, sometimes playfulness can interact with publicity in ways that enrich argumentation. The bloggers in the wake of the Lott toast were playing with different perspectives and interpretations and histories; Salam Pax's punchiness was reflective of another kind of play; and the *RealClimate* bloggers often exude playfulness as they engage with their commenters.

But in the penumbra of publicity always lurks disciplinary power. This is Foucault's major criticism of Habermas's defense of publicity, and it is one that can be escalated, given how internetworked media kinetically amplify publicity processes. The term "hyperpublicity" captures a condition of public culture marked by ubiquitous recording technologies and networked circulation patterns. It signals an expansion in the capacity of personal media to record, archive, make searchable, and circulate opinions, events, and interactions in publicly accessible databases. Hyperpublicity hints at how more of life and culture is becoming *public* life and *public* culture. On the one hand, this increased level of publicity produces new methods of deliberative legitimation processes elucidated in this book. However, hyperpublicity also risks curtailing the possibilities for a democratic public culture to play with possibilities. Specifically, I will argue that the ubiquity of recording media, alongside the decline of the bound audience in favor of the potentially unbound network, threatens play in a way that potentially undermines the rhetorical renaissance otherwise under way.

At the beginning of the twenty-first century, a suite of gadgets would be required to do what a single smartphone does today: take pictures and video, capture audio, and, importantly, play back, edit, and circulate all these media. The documentary impulse of the human species leverages these advances in recording technologies toward the mapping of the lifeworld at a finer and finer grain of representation. Although we are only on the cusp of this emergent phenomenon, Aaron Barlow predicts that "one day, no major event will occur anywhere in the world without people recording it on cell phones and broadcasting it on a blog."[2] That day, if it has not already arrived for intensively internetworked cultures, is not far off. Barlow's point can be extended further, for sometimes it seems that no *minor* event goes unreported either. What Martin Dodge and Rob Kitchin describe as the coming "age of pervasive computing" promises to provide another uptick in the recording of everyday life.[3] Extrapolating from current trends, Dodge and Kitchin predict the emergence of "lifelogs," unified archives that capture every action, event, and conversation in one's life.[4] Lifelogs would be generated by wearable computing devices that continuously and passively record video and audio while measuring interior states of the body (like heart rate) and exterior environmental factors (like pollution).[5] These devices, presumably, would not be full-body suits but instead would be small and non-intrusive, uploading captured information to a networked repository. This sounds like the stuff of science fiction, but it is not so far-fetched—the documentary features of blogs and social networking sites make them proto-lifelogs, patchy only by the current limitations of technology.[6] Admittedly, there would be lots of advantages to lifelogging: imagine never forgetting what you had for lunch yesterday, or never misremembering what your significant other got you for your birthday last year, or knowing that your heart rate drops every time you see a tomato. Among more serious benefits, there would be drawbacks. Lifelogs would store quarrels with loved ones, forever preserving nastiness hurled in a fit of anger. Embarrassing moments would be permanently saved on your lifelog and potentially on others' lifelogs. In light of these developments, Dodge and Kitchin argue for an "ethics of forgetting."[7] Forgetting can be a good thing, for human relationships are too fragile to be sustained in a world of perfect memory. As Oscar Wilde incisively noted, "one should absorb the colour of life, but one should never remember its details. Details are always vulgar."[8]

What complicates pervasive computing, from the perspective of rhetorical experimentation, is how internetworked media transform the nature of the audience. The history of media technology might be cast as a gradual loosening of the bounds of an audience. As technologies change, the breadth and depth of publicity expands. The speeches of the Greeks fell on the ears of a relatively bounded audience: you were either in the agora, or you had to settle for a secondhand account of the rhetorical meanderings of Aristotle or Diogenes. Writing, and then print, loosened this bond. No longer did one have to be present at the point of oral articulation, for the circulation of text faithfully reconstructed a rhetor's words. Electronic media further sped up this circulatory matrix, though national boundaries largely contained the flow of messages. Networked media unbind the artifact of communication from national audiences. It is possible now for any fragmentary collection of symbols to traverse the globe within seconds of publication. Even the most intimate details are only a blogger away from being public. The term "audience" may no longer be a terribly useful organizing concept, rooted as it is in the sense of an assembly of listeners. Rhetors no longer publish to a bounded and knowable audience; they publish to a network. That network may well be predictable, but it is always already an open assemblage of nodes that can shift, re-form, circulate, or consolidate ties with any act of communication. For example, although people often post status updates on social networking sites to be circulated to a group of people they have preselected to be in their social network (what may resemble a traditional audience), these messages often circulate to broader networks. Particularly hilarious or absurd status updates often get screen-captured and posted to other sites like Reddit or Lamebook, major hubs that in turn relay messages to yet other networks. Most of this, admittedly, is more or less harmless, and indeed this fear of discourse escaping the intended audience is a very old one. One of Plato's criticisms of writing is that the written text is likely to roll around to audiences with limited understanding of the context of the discourse. Plato's fear seems even more salient in a media era where networks of communication can circulate symbol fragments with even greater ease and fidelity across artificial boundaries of time and space. This intensification of publicness *in potentia* threatens to colonize the entirety of the social field.[9]

An example from the 2008 presidential primary campaign illustrates how hyperpublicity constrains experimentation and playfulness of argument in the maturing networked public sphere. A heated primary campaign for the Democratic presidential nomination between Senator Barack Obama of Illinois and Senator Hillary Clinton of New York was being debated in the intercastings of a matured blogosphere. By then, advertisement- and donation-funded blog hubs like *The Huffington Post*—a politically left site that integrates numerous blogs into continuous commentary on breaking stories—had become clearinghouses for civic news. Founded by political activist Arianna Huffington, *The Huffington Post* was one of the most popular sites throughout the 2008 election. As part of its coverage of the 2008 campaign, *The Huffington Post* set up a series called "Off the Bus," which was a separate section of the site featuring commentary from citizens (as opposed to the press corps and pundits, who often ride "on the bus" with the candidates).

On April 11, 2008, Mayhill Fowler, a semi-retiree who had taken up citizen journalism, posted an extensive report in *The Huffington Post*'s Off the Bus section about a speech that presidential candidate Barack Obama made to a group of fundraisers in San Francisco. Fowler, a regular blogger at *The Huffington Post*, was following the Obama campaign as the primary race finished up with voting in Pennsylvania, Indiana, and North Carolina. She happened to be in attendance at the fundraising speech with an audio recorder. In her blog post, she quoted Obama extensively:

> "You go into some of these small towns in Pennsylvania, and like a lot of small towns in the Midwest, the jobs have been gone now for 25 years and nothing's replaced them," Obama said. "And they fell through the Clinton Administration, and the Bush Administration, and each successive administration has said that somehow these communities are gonna regenerate and they have not. And it's not surprising then they get bitter, they cling to guns or religion or antipathy to people who aren't like them or anti-immigrant sentiment or anti-trade sentiment as a way to explain their frustrations."
>
> Obama made a problematic judgment call in trying to explain working class culture to a much wealthier audience. He described blue collar Pennsylvanians with a series of what in the eyes of Californians might be considered pure negatives: guns, clinging to religion, antipathy, xenophobia.[10]

Predictably, Fowler's report launched a flurry of conversation about the implications of Obama's comments. From one perspective, this confirmed the perception that Obama was, in the words of a famous 2004 political advertisement, a Volvo-driving, latte-drinking, sushi-eating, *New York Times*–reading, East Coast liberal elitist who was condemning conservative lifestyle choices to a group of San Francisco funders. From another perspective, Obama's comments reflect what had become common sense for Democratic strategists: Republicans had mastered the ability to get citizens to vote against their economic interests by amping up culture war wedge issues.[11] Either way, the story presented a significant challenge to the Obama campaign, and the development of the story in the networked public sphere reveals the normalization of blogging in the contemporary media ecology.

After publication on *The Huffington Post*, Fowler's blog post was picked up throughout the blogosphere and by the institutional media with considerably less lag time than earlier in the blogosphere's history. "*The New York Times, The Los Angeles Times, The Washington Post, CNN.com*, the Associated Press, Fox News, Reuters, Politico, the *Lou Dobbs Show, Hardball, Olbermann's Countdown, The Atlantic.com, The DailyKos, TalkingPoints-Memo* and myriad other outlets" all covered the story.[12] Cable television news latched on, as did talk radio. The original story at *The Huffington Post* almost instantly collected over 5,000 comments. Parallel sites like the left-leaning *DailyKos* and the right-leaning *RedState* picked up on these comments and debated their implications. Millions of voices on blogs, social networking sites, video portals, and other networked media magnified the scale and depth of frenzy over Obama's comments, soon dubbed "Bittergate." Many professional journalists argued that Fowler violated traditional press norms that kept fundraisers off the record, which she later confessed to not realizing.[13] Others defended Fowler's approach as useful precisely because it *did* contravene the staid norms of the press corps. Marc Cooper claimed that Fowler "violates almost all of the conventions of traditional reporting (though not its ethical code) and that's what makes it all so damn interesting."[14] He coupled that observation with a note on the emerging symbiosis between the institutional press and the blogosphere by reveling in how "it's also quite a bit of fun to see how a report like hers can actually set the agenda for the entire national press."[15] Fowler was both credited and elided as breaking the story in various outlets, showing how bloggers' reporting contributions are still often marginalized even as they gain prominence as journalistic stimulants for public deliberation.[16]

Should Fowler, an avowed Obama supporter, have published these comments, knowing the firestorm they were likely to ignite? Should she have respected the semiprivate nature of the fundraiser? Should she have been allowed to bring an audio recorder to the talk? From her perspective, a statement articulated in private by Obama betrayed some unwarrantable assertions about small-town America, and she used her blog to put those issues on the public agenda. Indeed, the regulative logic of publicity suggests that Obama should have been taken to task for his comments, since they were arguably the kinds of private reason-giving that norms of the public sphere are designed to hinder. However, that the Fowler-Bittergate story shows how hyperpublicity serves democratic ends is too simple a conclusion to draw from the episode. The comments of some observers at the fundraiser Fowler attended suggest how hyperpublicity constrains rhetorical experimentation. David Coleman, a *Huffington Post* blogger who also attended the San Francisco event, added context worth quoting at length:

> Rather than seizing the opportunity to recite stump-worn talking points at that time to the audience—as I believe Senator Clinton, Senator McCain and most other more conventional (or more disciplined) politicians at such an appearance might do—Senator Obama took a different political course in that moment, one that symbolizes important differences about his candidacy. The response that followed sounded unscripted, in the moment, as if he were really trying to answer a question with intelligent conversation that explained more about what was going on in the Pennsylvania communities than what was germane to his political agenda. I had never heard him or any politician ever give such insightful, analytical responses. The statements were neither didactic nor contrived to convince. They were simply hypotheses (not unlike the kind made by de Tocqueville three centuries ago) offered by an observer familiar with American communities. And that kind of thoughtfulness was quite unexpected in the middle of a political event. In my view, the way he answered the question was more important than the sociological accuracy or the cause and effect hypotheses contained in the answer. It was a moment of authenticity demonstrating informed intelligence, and the speaker's desire to have the audience join him in a deeper understanding of American politics.[17]

Coleman explains that Obama's comments were essentially unscripted, veering away from talking points and stump speeches in a refreshingly spontaneous manner. His use of "disciplined" to describe the more tightly scripted campaigns of Clinton and McCain invites a Foucauldian understanding of traditional campaign discourse that was, however momentarily, contravened by Obama's more free-spirited comments.

Obama likely felt more comfortable speaking off the script because he was confident that the members of the audience were allies and that what was said in the room would more or less stay in the room. Marc Cooper, one of the editors of Off the Bus, confirmed this unscriptedness by noting, "Obama was indeed more loose-lipped than usual," though he followed up that observation with what is now the *sine qua non* of political campaigning: "He should be more careful in his choice of words when he is staring into so many video cams, no matter who is holding them."[18] Obama's explanation was "that I just mangled it, which, you know happens sometimes. The point that I was making was actually two separate points that got conflated. Number One, that people who had felt abandoned by Washington and political leaders when it comes to an economy that's falling apart, [and Number Two, that] they find stability in those things that they count on—their faith, the traditions that have been passed down generation to generation and in many rural communities that includes hunting, their family, their community—those are positive things."[19] One can see this maneuvering as just that: an able politician participating in the cynical game of word-parsing in order to wiggle out of a tough spot. However, a more charitable read is that Obama is being honest in confessing that, in a moment of unscripted exploration, he poorly chose his words. In the twenty-first century, though, Obama is stuck with the life he speaks—and he learned this lesson. Four years later, in the presidential election race against Mitt Romney, a video leaked of Romney at a private fundraiser saying that 47 percent of U.S. citizens were "dependent on government," saw themselves as "victims," and were thus inevitably going to vote for Obama.[20] The parallels with Bittergate in 2008 were not lost on commentators, who noted that even behind closed doors, Obama was hewing to his stump speech, toning down attacks on Romney, and requiring attendees to leave their mobile phones and cameras at the door.

These incidents are not rare examples of someone's being tripped up by the ubiquitous presence of recording devices. The George Allen "Macacagate" episode, recounted at the end of chapter 3, precedes Bittergate and "47%-gate." "There was no question in anyone's mind," reporter Tom Zeller claims in his reflection on Macacagate, "that the YouTube culture—in which every public moment can be clipped, cropped and distributed instantly across the globe by anyone at any time—had changed the rules of the game."[21] In a review of the implications of this "YouTube Election," *New York Times* reporter Ryan Lizza wondered whether "candidates [would] be pushed further into a scripted bubble," becoming "more vapid and risk averse than ever."[22] Republican strategist Matthew Dowd bemoans how "[p]oliticians can't experiment with messages.... They can't get voter response. Seventy or 80 years ago, a politician could go give a speech in Des Moines and road-test some ideas and then refine it and then test it again in Milwaukee.... It's taken some richness out of the political discourse."[23]

The ubiquitous presence of recording devices on the campaign trail makes candidates increasingly risk averse. Any slip up immediately becomes the gaffe-of-the-moment, parsed by a legion of bloggers and amplified through the institutional broadcast media. A candidate's evolution on issues becomes evidence of flip-flopping, with before and after video clips spliced together in damning juxtaposition. No longer can a candidate successfully adapt to a specific audience without risk of being called out for saying one thing to a particular audience and another thing to another audience. To be clear, this situation is not entirely bad. Catching politicians in contradictions and publicizing occasions where they over-pander to an audience in private are incredibly useful exercises in a democratic system that depends on citizen oversight.

But hyperpublicity is a double-edged sword, and the concern that politicians must now become more scripted and take fewer risks on the campaign trail threatens the vibrancy of dialogue about collective public life. Why is spontaneity and experimentation to be valued in democratic politics? Why is risk taking important in the democratic process? Though these might not appear to be the paramount values of deliberation, play, experimentation, spontaneity, and risk taking are central features of healthy public argument and a vibrant rhetorical culture.[24] Arguments so often become quarrels because arguers are not willing to undergo the mutual transformation that might occur as a result of risk-taking exchange. Indeed, for argumentation to be fruitful, interlocutors must be open to changing their own opinions on an issue, or be open to the possibility that the locus of a disagreement might be transformed through the process of argumentation. Even on the presidential campaign trail, candidates must be willing to listen and engage citizens through arguments that change according to the dictates of the rhetorical situation. Yet if candidates are unwilling to do so because their attempts at engaging citizens might backfire in wider spheres of public deliberation, then they have every incentive to resort to canned stump speeches.[25] The predictable result is that public dialogue becomes increasingly prepackaged, with candidates reticent to wander beyond safe zones marked off by bland and preplanned talking points.

Presidential politics offer an extreme example of the potential for hyperpublicity to reduce risk taking and experimentation, but it potentially presages parallel developments in other arenas of human life. The lesson that Allen, Obama, and Romney learned about the risks of spontaneous public discourse is repeated on smaller scales across networked media—as anyone who has ever been called to account for a poorly thought-out blog post, status update, or tweet can surely attest. The classroom provides another salient example of hyperpublicity stunting playfulness. Often considered a safe space, or what Rosa Eberly calls a proto-public, classrooms have long been idealized as a location where students and instructors are encouraged to experiment with ideas before engaging in the citizenship practices expected of graduates.[26] But instructors are increasingly wary that what they say, or wear, or assign will end up on RateMyProfessor, student blogs, or Facebook pages, on various so-called watchdog sites that monitor academia, or as fodder for state legislatures looking to slash the final scraps of support for higher education. Consequently, instructors have become even more careful about decisions made, things said, and actions taken in the classroom. Again, in many cases, this is all to the good—publicity surely works to improve pedagogy in some ways. Yet teaching is, by design, full of failed experiments, spontaneous remarks, and accommodations of specific situations. Can teaching thrive in a space where public scrutiny is directed at everything said and done in the classroom? Is it possible to encourage a playful spirit of inquiry when broader publics have a tendency to judge immediately what is happening in a situation in which they have no part? Do spaces of perpetual judgment undermine understanding? Are people willing to risk themselves and experiment as much if they realize that their rhetorical production might be circulated to virtually any audience?

Informal, semipublic atmospheres facilitate mutual risk taking, though I do not mean to foreclose the possibility that even in hyperpublic situations co-arguers do occasionally take risks. But taking risks is far more enticing when there is an imperfect record. Hyperpublicity forecloses the dissipation of speech, the ephemerality intrinsic to oral communication. That speech dissipates after utterance, receding into listeners' memories, means that historically there has been no perfect account of communication. Speech, as a medium, encourages misrememberings, partial hearings, and imperfect accounts as a resource for future invention. Prenetworked media—writing, print, and electronic—could provide at best a patchy record. While there are undoubtedly benefits to having a crisper public record of what was said by who and when, there may be times when democratic legitimacy would benefit by a fuzzier accounting of what has happened in the past in order to make it easier to work out what should be done in the future. Perhaps, then, alongside Dodge and Kitchin's "ethics of forgetting," we ought to encourage an "ethics of experimentation."

Perhaps such an ethics will emerge organically, as citizens adapt to new circumstances, become more forgiving of communication preserved on networked media, and are habituated to understanding networked rhetorics as intrinsic sites of play. Perhaps—but the viability of such an ethics of experimentation can only be enhanced by a broad-based rhetorical pedagogy that makes the case for the value of spontaneity, risk, and play.

Six Challenges for Networked Rhetorics

What are the broader prospects for theorizing networked rhetorics? A scholarly research agenda that develops networked rhetorical theory might well strengthen the position of rhetorical models of communication over informationist ones. More importantly, such an account of networked rhetorics promises to open new pathways for citizen participation, strengthen deliberative legitimation processes, and extend dignity, freedom, and justice in contemporary public cultures. At this point, early in the history of networked media, I propose a set of common challenges for scholars of networked rhetorics. Though I believe that these six challenges form a useful core for the future study of internetworked rhetorics, I want to register their openness by focusing primarily on questions prompted by each capacious theme. The work required to further inquiry into networked rhetorics is so variegated and rich that, rather than making pronouncements about the nature of future research, an interrogatory mode is more appropriate. Of course, the questions I ask are themselves just preliminary interrogations that must be expanded, revised, and perhaps addressed in future research.

Networked rhetorical theory must account for the attention challenges of information abundance. Part of the claim developed in *Networked Media, Networked Rhetorics* is that attention has always been at the center of rhetoric. Lanham's refiguration of rhetoric as an art of attention in an era of information abundance is a bold step toward thinking through the relationship between the two; I have complemented his approach with the rhetorical theories of Kenneth Burke, who may turn out to be the most significant twentieth-century theorist of attention. Rhetorical theory could benefit from paying more sustained attention to attention, a project that this book begins only modestly. What role does attention assume, and what model of attention is presumed, in different historical and contemporary rhetorical theories? Are there older assumptions about attention that ought to be reclaimed? Or, alternatively, do vestiges of untenable assumptions about attention lurk in contemporary rhetorical theory? How might our rhetorical theories of attention be complicated and extended by unfolding research on the human body? How does attention connect to other terms in the rhetorical lexicon, such as invention, emotion, and expertise, as well as audience, judgment, *kairos*, and decorum? Is attention essentially finite, or is it a fungible resource that can be expanded through rhetorical activity? What is the relationship between attention, communication routines, and defamiliarization of experience? How does attention shape relationships, subjects, and ideologies—and vice versa—in particular situations?

Another layer of questions can be asked about rhetoric, attention, and mediation. How do new forms of mediation shape attention? How will the networked attention economy change interpersonal, organizational, and public communication? What are the implications of networked media reflexively capturing attention through hits, comments, most emailed, most blogged, and most re-tweeted? This latter question points to the rise of a new kind of attention structure: the algorithm. Traditionally, humans functioned as attention gatekeepers. Whether the wizened sage or the newspaper editor, *people* have usually been the ones involved in making choices about what information is circulated. While people are still involved at various levels in designing algorithms, they have a diminished day-to-day role as attention gatekeepers in an era where complex computer systems filter large-scale information flows. Search engines are the quintessential example of a reflexive algorithm that functions as an attention gatekeeper: by tracing which links people click on for specific queries, search engines amass huge amounts of metadata, in turn reshaping the order in which links appear in search results. This seems to be a subtle manipulation of attention, because they are aggregated from thousands or millions of decisions by presumably neutral third parties. But the consequence of this manipulation is anything but subtle, for the first-page real estate of a search query is crucial for attention.[27] Algorithms increasingly shape everyday experience in internetworked media. They produce search results, recommend books, music, and movies, shape what updates appear on social networking sites, and so on, leading Ted Striphas to theorize that deeply networked public cultures are increasingly algorithmic cultures.[28] Algorithms function according to code, but because code (so far) has a hard time judging quality, it defers to crude attention markers grounded in quantity, like hits. But the popular is not always the correct or the just, and algorithms have a tough time telling the difference.[29] If rhetoric is an art of attention, then it can also be an art of inattention. Algorithms complicate detection of how attention and inattention are crafted, for they are usually concealed behind layers of proprietary trade secrets. Google's search algorithm is a deeply guarded secret, as is the Facebook algorithm that determines how status updates are ordered. Although the impact of algorithms on the shaping of culture is significant, decisions about the shape of attention patterns are being made with little democratic accountability. There is, consequently, a political project as well as a rhetorical one in understanding how algorithms shape attention.

Networked rhetorical theory must document and theorize the kinds of rhetorical performances that prevail in networked media. Media enable and constrain human expressivity; thus, as media change, human expressivity changes. Networked rhetorics must register the communicative changes occurring on the right side of what I reframed as the Gutenberg Comma. The tradition of rhetorical scholarship, focused on individuals speaking to relatively bound audiences, can guide—but must not overdetermine—new modes of performance mediated by internetworked technology. Part of this surely involves simply taking networked media artifacts as objects of study. This is inevitable, as internetworked sites of rhetorical production continue to expand (indeed, there may come a time when virtually all rhetorics are networked rhetorics, at which point "networked" may simply fade away as an adjectival term). But theorists and critics of networked rhetorics must not judge the new rhetorics by the measures of the old. As networked rhetorics become more prevalent, we can expect a transformation of rhetorical theories, not just modest modifications. Although the "add internetworked media and stir" approach (taking old rhetorical theories and applying them to new forms of communication) may occasionally pay dividends, looking for more native explanations will likely better account for communicative phenomena afforded by networked media. The approach taken in *Networked Media, Networked Rhetorics* is to identify and unpack three tropes emerging organically from the early blogosphere, interpreting them as signals of the new rhetorical norms of networked public culture. Such a strategy can be usefully extended to other dimensions of the networked public sphere. Building a vocabulary that successfully hybridizes, innovates, and transforms received rhetorical theories to reflect contemporary communicative practices is a crucial task.

Networked rhetorical theory must account for many-to-many communication. Internetworked technologies support many-to-many communication through a variety of platforms.[30] Be they blogs, *Wikipedia*, discussion boards, or some other collaborative software platform, networked media provide the first credible structure to aid many-to-many communication. Networked many-to-many communication is heralded as "a new form of communication that allows for different forms and styles of communication,"[31] allowing a multiplication of "new forms of cooperation and relationships across spatiotemporal distances."[32] The diminution of the role of institutional attention gatekeepers means that many-to-many communication has "the potential to collapse the social and political spheres by creating forms of discourse outside the ambit of traditional politics and which deal with such matters as global justice, environmentalism, intimate relationships, different sexualities, frailty and personal risk, and which prioritize lay experience over professional expertise."[33] Many-to-many communication is unsettling to received rhetorical theory not only because of an expansion in the kinds of topics that can become thematized for public deliberation, but because it requires negotiating multiple, unbound audiences at the same time. Given the conditions of hyperpublicity, rhetors are constantly faced with the possibility that their public communication will be intercepted and circulated to multiple audiences simultaneously. Rhetoric's long concern with audience adaptation may well provide unique resources to grapple with this latent problem of many-to-many communication. A sophisticated account of many-to-many communication might also provide an alternative to the staid and roundly critiqued sender-receiver model. When thinking of communication in terms of networks, it is easier to see any particular node as a point of articulation rather than an atomized point source producing information. However, as James Bohman points out, "many-to-many communication may increase interactivity without preserving the essential features of dialogue, such as responsive uptake."[34] Here is another wrinkle related to attention: with so much information flowing in digitally networked environments, public deliberation can easily devolve into the mere registration of opinions rather than a transformative exchange of opinion.[35]

Networked rhetorical theory must refigure the rhetorical canons. Any new rhetoric must maintain the productive elements of the traditional rhetorical canons while making accommodations to account for networked media.[36] This refiguration of the canons is different from the call by Laura Gurak and Smiljana Antonijević to "assert a new canon."[37] Their revisioning of the canons would elevate concepts like speed, reach, anonymity, interactivity, *kairos*, and collaboration. These may well be keywords of the networked age, but they cannot provide the same kind of guidance for rhetorical production that invention, arrangement, style, memory, and delivery have for millennia. Rhetorical theorists have long acknowledged how the different canons dynamically interact; for example, stylizing discourse requires an inventional process of choosing between rhetorical figures, and certain performative styles are conducive to specific particularities in delivery. However, the different phases can be disentangled for analytical purposes. This analytic disentanglement usually implies a particular linear sequence that a rhetor moves through: begin with a creative spark, organize arguments so that others can follow them, stylize in an attention-sustaining fashion, memorize the speech, and deliver it orally. This sequence is quite sensible for rhetoric in the speech tradition, for if oral communication is the endpoint of rhetorical production, then the creative process can be backmapped within the norms of orality.

This linear process is complicated because the available means of persuasion—Aristotle's definition of invention—must include a survey of media beyond the voice. The medium of delivery shapes the possibilities of inventive expressivity: rhetors will invariably draw on different resources if they are producing a video than if they are speaking in front of a crowd. Aristotle was wise to this necessity, discussing the differences between spoken and written discourse in *The Rhetoric*, but the expansion of "delivery systems" in the contemporary media ecology provides more options to consider. The rhetorical canons might be reconfigured, then, by inverting the traditional sequence and considering the medium of delivery first. Or perhaps the canons might be envisaged as more cyclical, with rhetors beginning consideration of production at any point in the cycle and refining their ideas as they move through the circuit several times. Or perhaps the canons ought to be seen as a star, with invention at the center and arrangement, style, memory, and delivery as points that a rhetor considers as moments in the creative process that admit of situated choice making. Rhetors might use these different configurations of the canons in tandem, as thought experiments to multiply the array of productive possibilities. In order to destabilize the conventional account of the rhetorical canons, I will offer tentative ways to reconsider each step in the productive process, beginning with a reframing of "delivery" and "memory."

- *Delivery should be reframed as "articulation" and acknowledge new dimensions of speed, reach, and interactivity.* In most modern rhetorics, both delivery and memory were considered primarily technical questions related to publication. Questions of delivery are more foregrounded with networked media, as James Porter explains: "There is considerable rhetorical difference between a wiki, a blog, an email discussion list, and a synchronous chat room—and there are considerable ethical, editorial, and political decisions involved in setting up and maintaining any of these types of forums."[38] Moreover, for Ben McCorkle, rhetorical theories of delivery must increasingly account not just for the "text" itself, but for the "extra-textual or paratextual features of the 'performing' text."[39] The term "delivery" connotes a transmission/informationist model of communication—it is, in Collin Brooke's memorable example, "stuff," like pizza and books, that is delivered.[40] Perhaps, then, thinking through delivery in the networked era might be more compelling if we considered it under the sign of "articulation." Articulation, as a term that can reference oral communication, pays homage to rhetoric's roots in the speech tradition while acknowledging both cultural and network theory that situates rhetors as points of articulation (and points articulating, or connecting, symbols) in larger webs of influence. These processes of articulation are quick, they spread far, and they re-articulate through the interactive processes of networked media.

- *Memory is resurgent with the remediation of oral forms, but it might be made more "active" by reframing it as "memorability."* Digital *aides de mémoire* would seem to make memorizing large chunks of text even less necessary—the bloggers in *Networked Media, Networked Rhetorics* are doing very little memorizing before articulation. However, the increased presence of live video through the internet may lend some new heft to this old canon, as the oral fluency that accompanies strong capacities for recall is likely accompanied by an increase in persuasive power. In contexts where recall is *not* as important, rhetors might reframe memory as "memorability." Although rhetoricians have long sought for memorable speeches, memorability is usually thought to be a function of invention, arrangement, style, or delivery. Given the attention demands in an information-abundant public culture, rhetors must think more strategically about what memorable "meme" (the etymological family resemblance is not accidental) they want to put into circulation. The meme—a rhetorically enticing bit of information that is easily portable and usually catchy—is an evolution of what was called in earlier eras a maxim, *sententia*, conceit, or sound bite. These eloquent formulations persist in the memory and thus communication of others, shaping attention patterns even as the meme evolves over time.

- *Style must accommodate changes in technology and culture.* New media technologies inevitably produce new ways of executing style at a micro level (thus, hyperlinks can be seen as metonyms; networked rhetorics often draw on visual metaphors). But style can be considered on a more macro level, as well, acknowledging how the aesthetic dimensions of a performance are shaped by technological affordances. Snark, emo, and trolling, for example, are styles uniquely emboldened by networked media. Moreover, cultural differences are often coded as differences in style; networked rhetorics must, then, acknowledge cultural pluralism and integrate insights from contemporary cultural and rhetorical theory to push style beyond the Greco-Roman-Eurocentric tradition.

- *Arrangement might pay more careful attention to the interaction between different modes of communication and take seriously the possibilities of rearrangement.* Everyday citizens have, for most of human history, usually been in the position of arranging oral, written, or printed communication. Only a small group of people engaged in televisual and film media, which blend audio and visual modes, have had to consider the interaction between different modes in the arrangement of their material. Yet, as media technologies have become more available, and as they have converged through the digital medium, citizens are now experimenting with new ways to arrange symbols for persuasive effect. Some of these new arrangement practices fall into the category of banal but important, like figuring out where images ought to go in a blog post or web page, but some of these arrangements are more novel as new genres emerge that seamlessly blend visual, audio, and even tactile dimensions of communication. Moreover, citizens are involved in the process of *re*arranging, or remixing, extant symbol fragments. In many ways, remixing is that most rhetorical of acts—a nod to the intertextual roots of rhetoric.[41] While usually thought of as the province of electronic DJs, remixing occurs across all sorts of networked media. A blog "remixes" a news story by linking to it and excerpting a paragraph, following it with the blogger's interpretation. More attention to the dynamics and rhetorical effects of remixing as a kind of rearrangement will fruitfully expand the canon of arrangement to account for new communication practices.

- *Invention can be reconsidered through the collaborative and interactive possibilities of networked media.* Internetworked media are conducive to creating environments where invention thrives. In contrast to print culture, which largely individuated the process of creation and reception, invention of networked rhetorics is often a social process drawing on communication between the many to proliferate new perspectives and possible meanings. The sociality of invention is complemented by the juxtapositional logics of networked media technology. The interactivity (between citizens, and between citizens and communicative artifacts) provided by blogs, wikis, databases and other networked interfaces yields a continuing conversation that holds out the possibility of perpetual invention. A key challenge for rhetors in the networked age, as opposed to the modern era, is to see invention as a process and not a product. Unlike a finished book, there is an openness and contingency to any act of networked invention. Invention is always a work in progress, revisable and extendable by self and others. Seeing the goal of invention as producing conditions for more inventive symbol use to materialize is a quintessentially rhetorical sensibility.

Networked rhetorical theory must develop a conception of cosmopolitan citizenship. Rhetoric has long been tied to citizenship. In Athens, citizens used the art of rhetoric to make a case, and even now citizens use rhetoric to make entreaties to their representatives, to each other, and increasingly to globally networked publics. Robert Asen's "discourse theory of citizenship" is amenable to thinking through citizenship at a global level because it decenters the act of (local or national) voting as the *sine qua non* of citizenship in favor of a range of deliberative activity.[42] This is an important precursor for any theory of cosmopolitan citizenship, especially given the absence of an international body responsive to democratic voting. But Asen's examples of citizenship acts are congressional testimony and debate, petitions directed at legislatures, trauma survivors' demonstrations, anti-fur protests, bus tours, and buying local—all of which assume the context of *embodied* interaction. Yet interaction with global others is, for most people, not likely to privilege embodiment. Until recently, the rhetorical imagination largely centered on acts of citizenship at the national and subnational level. But with a global medium supporting a global networked public sphere, we might—must, even—begin theorizing the practices and prospects of cosmopolitan citizenship. How does one enact cosmopolitan citizenship? Does engaging in microloans through Kiva.org qualify as an act of cosmopolitan citizenship? How about participating in global organizations? What about commenting on blogs by citizens active in the Arab Spring movements? Following a Chinese dissident on Twitter? How does cosmopolitan citizenship fit in with other allegiances to nation, state, region, and locale? Are there particular norms and values that must adhere to a cosmopolitan vantage point, or is it simply a vague signifier that one knows other places exist? How can cosmopolitan citizenship be "thickened" through a concentrated pedagogy that takes place in schools, the arts, and public culture? These questions, long in the background of rhetorical theory, must move to the center with networked rhetorics.

Networked rhetorical theory must focus its critical edge on how societies of control are communicatively justified, extended, and maintained. Foucault's articulation of disciplinary power is intimately linked to the rise of modern institutions. As those institutions are transformed through new cultural, economic, and technological practices centered on the network form, their power is redeployed in creative ways. The French philosopher Gilles Deleuze theorized the emergence of "societies of control" as intensifications of disciplinary power; the conditions for control societies accompany new technologies from surveillance tools to genetic manipulation. Control societies interconnect previously disparate disciplinary enclosures. For example, the spread of the home computer, and later handheld devices, make working from home possible and thus connect two sites where power operates, so that we are simultaneously subjected to an intensification of multiple sites of disciplinary power. While disciplinary enclosures like the school or factory "mold" individuals, control societies exert their power through "*modulation*, like a self-transmuting molding continually changing from one moment to the next."[43] There is an opening for rhetoricians to investigate the modulations in control societies, for Deleuze claims that "style is a set of variations in language, a modulation."[44] While style can forge resistant publics, as I detail in chapter 4, it can also operate as modulating vehicles for control, manipulating our affective states in order to embed us further in power relationships that deny human dignity and freedom.[45]

Raymie McKerrow's introduction of the idea of "critical rhetoric" to the field of rhetorical studies was instrumental in opening the field to Foucauldian interpretations of disciplinary power necessary to understand the operation of power and discourse in late modern societies.[46] Rhetorical studies might now repurpose critical rhetoric toward understanding rhetorics of control. How are logics of control rhetorically justified, extended, and maintained? How are rhetorics of control subtly embedded in public and popular culture? Do certain cultural practices habituate citizens into accepting patterns of decision making in the new control societies? How do algorithms exercise control over the circulation of information? How does the coming era of pervasive computing extend the potential for control? The focus of *Networked Media, Networked Rhetorics* on the software of blogging is warranted, given the power that software historically exerted and still continues to exercise. But as digital media technology has developed in the decade since blogging became mainstream, advances in hardware—particularly the development of wearable computing—pose some challenging questions in the context of control. Of course, issues of surveillance are involved here, as are more subtle questions about augmented-reality technologies like Google Glass, which promises heads-up visual displays on eyeglasses. What kinds of control are possible with technologies that mediate the senses so intimately? How might a digital overlay in one's field of vision be used to control perception, movement, and interaction? How do activity trackers that monitor steps, calories burned, sleep, and bodily processes create new conditions for self-control and governmentality?

What new modes of resistance might accompany these efforts at control? Where there is control, there will be manifold modes of resisting the dominant logics of hyperpublicity and networks. Deleuze theorized one mode of resistance that seems apt for an era of information abundance: "The problem is no longer getting people to express themselves, but providing little gaps of solitude and silence in which they might eventually find something to say. Repressive forces don't stop people from expressing themselves, but rather, force them to express themselves. What a relief to have nothing to say, the right to say nothing, because only then is there a chance of framing the rare, or ever rarer, the thing that might be worth saying."[47] Slow down, opt out—at least occasionally. Doing so offers the critical distance that aids eloquence and invention, stimulates novel ways of attending to issues of public life, and, at least occasionally, facilitates judgments with high degrees of legitimacy.

Although the term "networked rhetorics" necessarily implies a plural project, these six loci provide a core set of challenges for rhetoricians to work through. And work through them we must: the quality of public deliberation, the potential for citizen engagement in civic affairs, and thus the very shape of our democratic future depends on strengthening the rhetorical norms of networked public culture.

NOTES

Chapter 1

1. Axel Bruns and Joanne Jacobs, "Introduction," in *The Uses of Blogs*, ed. Axel Bruns and Joanne Jacobs (New York: Peter Lang, 2006), 5.

2. See Carolyn R. Miller and Dawn Shepherd, "Blogging as Social Action: A Genre Analysis of the Weblog," and Kevin Brooks, Cindy Nichols, and Sybil Priebe, "Remediation, Genre, and Motivation: Key Concepts for Teaching with Weblogs," both in *Into the Blogosphere: Rhetoric, Community, and the Culture of Weblogs*, ed. Laura J. Gurak, Smiljana Antonijević, Laurie Johnson, Clancy Ratliff, and Jessica Reyman, June 2004, http://blog.lib.umn.edu/blogosphere/blogging_as_social_action_a_genre_analysis_of_the_weblog.html and http://blog.lib.umn.edu/blogosphere/remediation_genre.html. Blogging is a genre of networked discourse with recurring features like reverse chronology postings, link-heavy posts, and more personal interpretations of unfolding events. Blogs are further categorized into three primary genres: the "filter blog," collecting links from around the web; the "personal blog," featuring the blogger's thoughts; and the "knowledge blog," synthesizing fragments of social knowledge. See Susan Herring, Lois Ann Scheidt, Sabrina Bonus, and Elijah Wright, "Weblogs as a Bridging Genre," *Information Technology and People* 18, no. 2 (2005): 142–71. As the blogosphere matured, each of these three genres splintered into more distinct sub-genres. For example, personal blogs are now further categorized as "mommy blogs," "travel blogs," or "food blogs."

3. Jill Rettberg, *Blogging* (Cambridge: Polity Press, 2008), 68–70. The occasional speculation about whether or not blogging is "dead" does not mark the end of a genre; rather, it implicitly acknowledges the normalization of the blog architecture that is everywhere and so sometimes seems nowhere. Clay Shirky predicted this normalization: "weblog technology will be seen as a platform for so many forms of publishing, filtering, aggregation, and syndication that blogging will stop referring to any particularly coherent activity. The term 'blog' will fall into the middle distance, as 'home page' and 'portal' have, words that used to mean some concrete thing, but which were stretched by use past the point of meaning." See "Power Laws, Weblogs, and Inequality," *Clay Shirky's Writings about the Internet* (blog), February 8, 2003, http://www.shirky.com/writings/powerlaw_weblog.html.

4. Henry Jenkins, *Convergence Culture: Where Old and New Media Collide* (New York: New York University Press, 2006).

5. Quoted in Geoff Brumfiel, "The First Web Page, Amazingly, Is Lost," National Public Radio, May 22, 2013, http://www.npr.org/2013/05/22/185788651/the-first-web-page-amazingly-is-lost.

6. Early uses of new media genres are rhetorical antecedents that shape the genres' subsequent development. In this way, early blogging episodes structure the generic features of contemporary blogging in the same way that, for example, past inaugurals shape current ones. See Kathleen M. Jamieson, "Antecedent Genre as Rhetorical Constraint," *Quarterly Journal of Speech* 61, no. 4 (1975): 406–15.

7. Some scholars critique the overemphasis on blogs participating in civic conversations, contending that a subtle bias advantages traditionally masculine topics and male bloggers at the expense of a more well-rounded view of blogging; see Susan Herring, Inna Kouper,

Lois Ann Scheidt, and Elijah L. Wright, "Women and Children Last: The Discursive Construction of Weblogs," in Gurak et al., *Into the Blogosphere*, http://blog.lib.umn.edu/blogosphere/women_and_children.html. As Stella Minahan and Julie Wolfram Cox document, knitting blogs supply guidance for a renewed do-it-yourself ethic to many young women (and some men) who find social and aesthetic value in meeting together for what are called "Stitch'nBitch" sessions; see their "Stitch'nBitch: Cyberfeminism, a Third Place, and the New Materiality," *Journal of Material Culture* 12, no. 1 (2007): 5–21. Melissa Gregg underlines this point by noting, "within blogging culture, the phenomenon of 'LiveJournal bashing'—mocking the interests of online journal writers—arises from the assumption that the personal chat of young people is trivial in comparison to the weighty political content discussed on pundit-style blogs." See Gregg, "Posting with Passion: Blogs and the Politics of Gender," in Bruns and Jacobs, *Uses of Blogs*, 155.

8. On "inflection points," see Peter F. Cowhey and Jonathan D. Aronson, *Transforming Global Information and Communication Markets: The Political Economy of Innovation* (Cambridge, Mass.: MIT Press, 2009).

9. Seyla Benhabib, "Democratic Iterations: The Local, the National, and the Global," in *Another Cosmopolitanism*, ed. Robert Post (Oxford: Oxford University Press, 2006), 45–82.

10. William T. Quick, "I Propose a Name," *Daily Pundit* (blog), January 1, 2002, https://web.archive.org/web/20021112212531/http://www.iw3p.com/DailyPundit/2001_12_30_dailypundit_archive.html. The term *logos* connotes a range of meanings in the ancient Greek, including "word," "argument," "proof," "reasoning," and "thought." See Susan Wells, "Logos," in *The Encyclopedia of Rhetoric*, ed. Thomas Sloane (Oxford: Oxford University Press, 2001), 456–68. The multiple meanings of *logos* square nicely with the wide range of communicative activity present on blogs. Quick popularized the term "blogosphere," but credit widely goes to Bradley Graham, an early blog pioneer, for coining the term. See Bradley Graham, "It's Peter's Fault," *The Bradlands* (blog), September 10, 1999, http://www.bradlands.com/weblog/comments/september_10_1999/.

11. *Logos, pathos,* and *ethos* can be used to guide the production of rhetoric, but they can also be employed to analyze invention, emotion, and expertise at more macro levels of culture and governance. Michael Leff makes an extremely compelling case for the close association between rhetoric as a productive art and rhetoric as an interpretive lens in "The Idea of Rhetoric as Interpretive Practice: A Humanist's Response to Gaonkar," in *Rhetorical Hermeneutics: Invention and Interpretation in the Age of Science*, ed. Alan G. Gross and William M. Keith (Albany: SUNY Press, 1997), 89–100.

12. Michele H. Jackson, "The Mash-Up: A New Archetype for Communication," *Journal of Computer-Mediated Communication* 14, no. 3 (2009): 730–34.

13. Throughout the twentieth century, the field of rhetorical studies witnessed the development of several "new rhetorics" in response to changing cultural conditions and needs. I. A. Richards generated a new rhetoric in *The Philosophy of Rhetoric* (New York: Oxford University Press, 1936). Marie Hochmuth Nichols found Kenneth Burke's new rhetoric in "Kenneth Burke and the 'New Rhetoric,'" *Quarterly Journal of Speech* 38, no. 2 (1952): 133–44. Chaim Perelman and Lucie Olbrechts-Tyteca, too, framed their *magnum opus* as *The New Rhetoric: A Treatise on Argumentation*, trans. J. Wilkinson and P. Weaver (Notre Dame: University of Notre Dame Press, 1969).

14. See Lisa Gitelman's critique of the idea of "new" media in *Always Already New: Media, History, and the Culture of Data* (Cambridge, Mass.: MIT Press, 2006) and James MacNamara's dissection of the term in "'Emerging' Media and Public Communication: Understanding the Changing Mediascape," *Public Communication Review* 1, no. 2 (2010): 5–6.

15. See Jonathan Sterne on the misnomer of "social media" in "What if Interactivity Is the New Passivity?" *Flow* 15, no. 10 (April 9, 2012), http://flowtv.org/2012/04/the-new-passivity/.

16. See Claire Lauer, "Contending with Terms: 'Multimodal' and 'Multimedia' in the Academic and Public Spheres," *Computers and Composition* 26, no. 4 (2009): 225–39.

17. This unifying term originates with Richard Lanham's "Digital Rhetoric and the Digital Arts," in *The Electronic Word: Democracy, Technology, and the Arts* (Chicago: University of Chicago Press, 1993). Also see James P. Zappen, "Digital Rhetoric: Towards an Integrated Theory," *Technical Communication Quarterly* 14, no. 3 (2005): 319–25.

18. See, for example, James Porter, "Recovering Delivery for Digital Rhetoric and Human-Computer Interaction," *Computers and Composition* 26, no. 4 (2009): 207–24; Jim Ridolfo and Dànielle Nicole DeVoss, "Composing for Recomposition: Rhetorical Velocity and Delivery," *Kairos: A Journal of Rhetoric, Technology, and Pedagogy* 13, no. 2 (2009), http://kairos.technorhetoric.net/13.2/topoi/ridolfo_devoss/intro.html; and Ben McCorkle, *Rhetorical Delivery as Technological Discourse: A Cross-Historical Study* (Carbondale: Southern Illinois University Press, 2012). To some extent, this attention to the long-neglected canon of delivery is overdue. These exemplary works do not naively focus on delivery at the expense of other rhetorical concepts, since the canons are intimately connected to each other; however, an emphasis on delivery risks a focus on the technology of the medium at the expense of invention, arrangement, style, and memory.

19. "To understand the political life of a community," William Connolly observes, "one must understand the conceptual system within which that life moves." See Connolly, *The Terms of Political Discourse* (Lexington, Mass.: D. C. Heath, 1974), 39. Thus, understanding the rhetorical imaginary of networked public culture identifies deeper sensibilities of contemporary public life.

20. Charles Taylor, *Modern Social Imaginaries* (Durham: Duke University Press, 2003), 23.

21. Benedict Anderson, *Imagined Communities: Reflections on the Origin and Spread of Nationalism*, new ed. (London: Verso, 2006).

22. Taylor, *Modern Social Imaginaries*, 23. The idea of a social imaginary resembles Pierre Bourdieu's *habitus*, a connection made more apparent in Taylor's exegesis of Bourdieu in "To Follow a Rule . . . ," in *Bourdieu: Critical Perspectives*, ed. Craig Calhoun, Edward LiPuma, and Moishe Postone (Chicago: University of Chicago Press, 1993), 45–61.

23. Imaginaries play a role similar to the one Donald Bryant ascribed to rhetoric: adjusting ideas to people and people to ideas. See his "Rhetoric: Its Functions and Its Scope," *Quarterly Journal of Speech* 39, no. 4 (1953): 413. The idea of a social imaginary is a useful supplement to Habermasian theory and one that addresses a lacuna both in Habermas's original formulation of the bourgeois public sphere and in rhetorical theory. See Meili Steele, "Hiding from History: Habermas' Elision of Public Imagination," *Constellations*, September 2005, 409–36.

24. Modern political theorizing, as Benjamin Barber observes, adopted a vocabulary grounded in material relationships. The Newtonian preconceptual frame of modernity, as Barber calls it, asserts that space is limited, that individuals necessarily react to each other like billiard balls, that citizens are individual parts plugged into a greater whole, that property is a meaningful extension of the self, and that boundaries and sanctions must be applied to leverage coordination. See Barber, *Strong Democracy: Participatory Politics for a New Age* (Berkeley: University of California Press, 1984), 34–37. The Hobbesian premise "all that exists is body, all that occurs motion" captures the prevailing assumptions of modernity. While materiality metaphors are applicable for industrial conglomerates seeking to maximize profit by competing with rivals over scarce goods, they emphasize the competitive at the expense of the cooperative. The physicality of this vocabulary, for Barber, means that "liberal theory cannot be expected to give an adequate account of human interdependency, mutualism, cooperation, fellowship, fraternity, community, and citizenship" (34–35). Human interaction is richer than any material or spatial metaphor can capture. My point isn't to deny the materiality of human relations, but to understand them as only one part of a dialectical interplay with virtual—that is to say, imagined—processes of communication and cooperation. Today, metaphors of the virtual rival more material metaphors in frequency and descriptive power: the terms "cyberspace," "world wide web," "virtual reality," "knowledge networks," and "information superhighway" all hint at the alternative

conceptual models now used to think about human relations (even as these terms have become outmoded).

The hubbub surrounding peer-to-peer transmission of music, television, and film files announced the most recent clash between material and virtual metaphors. For some artists and large media corporations, peer-to-peer networks represent piracy, a metaphor grounded in a very zero-sum way of thinking about material possessions. The alternative metaphor, much more sympathetic to the phenomenon, emphasizes sharing. The point that file sharers regularly make illustrates the poverty of the pirate metaphor. A pirate, in stealing booty from another, takes sole possession of it, but the digital nature of files obviates this zero-sum relationship. The *potential* for revenue lost through file sharing makes the arguments for criminalizing peer-to-peer transmission of copyrighted material less straightforward than if a pirate walked into a music store and walked out with a compact disc.

25. In Asen, "Imagining the Public Sphere," *Philosophy & Rhetoric* 35, no. 4 (2002): 351.

26. Marshall McLuhan, *Understanding Media: The Extensions of Man*, critical ed., ed. Terence Gordon (1964; repr., Corte Madera, Calif.: Gingko Press, 2003), 127. McLuhan's claim highlights how new media forms displace old intermediaries and spawn pioneering ones, thus rearranging patterns of interaction. Jay David Bolter and Richard Grusin similarly interpret new media as re-mediating functionalities previously provided by other media. See their *Remediation: Understanding New Media* (Cambridge, Mass.: MIT Press, 2000). A middle ground between technological determinism and social constructionist theories of technology is found in the concept of "affordances," explicated by Ian Hutchby in "Technologies, Texts, and Affordances," *Sociology: The Journal of the British Sociological Association* 35, no. 2 (2001): 441–56. An affordance signals the potentiality inherent in any technology—potentiality that is activated by socially situated actors. Lucas Graves extends the concept of affordances to the blogosphere, exploring how technological developments intertwine with sociocultural patterns to produce a complex blogging ecology that serves a range of publics. See Graves, "The Affordances of Blogging: A Case Study in Culture and Technological Effects," *Journal of Communication Inquiry* 31, no. 4 (2007): 331–46. For Graves, blogging affords participants the opportunity to apply open-source methods to news (by drawing on collective knowledge to fact-check narrative accounts), fixity (through the use of archived permalinks), and juxtaposition (in connecting disparate links into a coherent narrative). Kenneth Burke accentuates this point about the affordances of media by emphasizing "how expert practitioners of a given medium may resort to the kinds of contents that the given medium is best equipped to exploit"; see *Language as Symbolic Action: Essays on Life, Literature, and Method* (Berkeley: University of California Press, 1966), 416.

27. Taylor, *Modern Social Imaginaries*, 29.

28. Although the internet was certainly prompting a revision in the (post)modern social imaginary years before blogging became popular, blogging dispersed these networked practices to a larger segment of the population and foreshadowed the intensive networking that shaped the first decade of the twenty-first century. Patrice Flichy's exploration of the "cyber-*imaginaire*" constructed in the 1990s by elite and popular discourses is largely harmonious with Taylor's conception of the social imaginary; see Flichy, *The Internet Imaginaire*, trans. Liz Carey-Libbrecht (2001; repr., Cambridge, Mass.: MIT Press, 2007), 107. One point of tension between Flichy and Taylor, though, is that Flichy sees the internet imaginaire as largely driven by elite discourses that then structure the possibilities of public imagination. For Flichy, ideas about what roles the internet could play in contemporary culture were largely shaped by politicians, industrialists, computer scientists, and hackers, whose "discourses spawned the internet myth that was then popularized for the general public" (107). His examination of texts by Al Gore, Howard Rheingold, William Gibson, and *Wired* magazine shows how imagining about the internet shaped the nascent networked imaginary. Recognizing the role of popularizers in determining how we think about new technologies, I occasionally draw from popular press articles and books to underline the extent to which the grammar of the blogosphere diffused into public discourse.

29. Debra Hawhee and Christa Olson, "Pan-historiography: The Challenges of Writing History Across Time and Space," in *Theorizing Histories of Rhetoric*, ed. Michelle Ballif (Carbondale: Southern Illinois University Press, 2013), 91.

30. Burke, *A Grammar of Motives* (1945; repr., Berkeley: University of California Press, 1969), 77.

31. Periodization carries risks, namely, obscuring the continuities between and diversities within different eras. But, as Tom Pettitt stresses, "insistence on continuity has to acknowledge that change has occurred" over time, to which I would add that appreciation of differences within and across cultures ought to be coupled with recognition of commonalities. See Pettitt, "Bracketing the Gutenberg Parenthesis," *Explorations in Media Ecology* 11, no. 2 (2012): 97. My hope is that a juxtaposition of the classical, modern, and networked produces consideration of similarities and dissimilarities between and within different cultural sensibilities rather than merely flattening different eras. The heuristic power of juxtaposition can be appreciated by contrasting the binarization characteristic of much modern thought with the relationality that pervades the networked era. The modern imaginary is often associated with a binary sensibility, grounded in dichotomies like culture/nature, mind/body, public/private, and action/speech. Although there are certainly exceptions to this binary thinking in early modern thought, signs of these dualisms pervade the ideological tenets of liberalism and their institutional manifestations. If early modern sensibilities were founded on dichotomies, networked sensibilities are grounded in the action of *oscillatio*, the rhetorical figure that Lanham associates most closely with networked media (*Electronic Word*, 43–46.) For Lanham, *oscillatio* captures the dynamism of digital text: one oscillates between looking *at* and *through* the text. The hyperlink demonstrates this oscillation. As one reads a blog post, one can look *through* a hyperlinked fragment as part of a sentence. However, one can also look *at* the hyperlink by clicking on it and following the redirection. This both/and relationship shows how networked sensibilities privilege relationality. The networked imaginary is refiguring the classic modern binaries into oscillating pairs, as the categories of nature/culture, mind/body, public/private, and action/speech are increasingly conceptualized as mutually imbricated. The case studies analyze, respectively, how the modern binaries of discovery/generation, reason/emotion, and pedagogy/participation, which elevated the first element of each pairing, are similarly becoming more intimately intertwined in the networked imaginary. Seeing the interaction between these pairs—rather than their opposition—creates spacious conditions for rhetorical activity, which straddles these polarities to facilitate judgment.

32. See James Carey's "Historical Pragmatism and the Internet," *New Media & Society* 7, no. 4 (2005): 443–55.

33. Burke, *Grammar of Motives*, 59.

34. On using representative anecdotes as a critical method, see Barry Brummett, "Burke's Representative Anecdote as a Method in Media Criticism," *Critical Studies in Media Communication* 1, no. 2 (1984): 161–76; Arnie Madsen, "Burke's Representative Anecdote as Critical Method," in *Extensions of the Burkeian System*, ed. James W. Chesebro (Tuscaloosa: University of Alabama Press, 1993): 208–29, and Robert Wess, "Representative Anecdotes in General, with Notes Toward a Representative Anecdote for Burkean Ecocriticism in Particular," *K. B. Journal* 1, no. 1 (2004), http://www.kbjournal.org/node/54.

35. Critics, like artists, seek to develop a vocabulary that adjusts others to new situations by "stressing such ways of feeling as equip one to cope with the situation." See Kenneth Burke, *Counter-Statement* (1931; repr., Berkeley: University of California Press, 1968), 108.

36. Ibid., 59.

37. This is not to imply that rhetorical terms from other imaginaries do not bear on the networked rhetorical imaginary. It is, instead, to adopt a theoretical attitude supple enough to see the continuities and discontinuities between rhetorical imaginaries, as opposed to the "add networked media and stir into rhetoric" approach provided by theoretic/etic approaches; see Edwin Black, "A Note on Theory and Practice in Rhetorical Criticism," *Western Journal*

of Speech Communication 44, no. 4 (1980): 331–36. I strive to see how indigenous practices transform our understanding of rhetoric in a way that follows the approach some feminist, queer, and visual rhetoricians take in expanding the rhetorical tradition. On this transformative approach, see Barbara Biesecker, "Coming to Terms with Recent Attempts to Write Women into the History of Rhetoric," *Philosophy & Rhetoric* 25, no. 2 (1992): 140–61.

38. Burke, *Grammar of Motives*, 503.

39. See Lakoff and Johnson's *Metaphors We Live By* (Chicago: University of Chicago Press, 1980), 235. The three tropes that are the heart of this book might be considered "dead metaphors," metaphors whose original imagery and associations are lost through repetition. If metaphors slip so easily from the figurative to the literal, than it is no stretch to say that rhetoric, and how norms of rhetorical practice are metaphorically captured in rhetorical theory, crystallizes an imaginary. Taylor underscores that citizens do not explicitly theorize social imaginaries. Instead, contours of an imaginary are "carried in images, stories, and legends" (*Modern Social Imaginaries*, 23), and, I would add, metaphor. Adam Smith's metaphor of the invisible hand of capitalism entailed a bevy of assumptions and prescriptions for the new capitalist economies of modern Europe. These metaphoric suppliers to the social imaginary are repositories of social knowledge and, with their circulation throughout a public, fashion common (and often hegemonic) understandings across multiple cultural sectors. By examining the stories, myths, and metaphors of a particular social imaginary, we better understand the norms and practices of different cultural formations.

40. Robert Ivie's metaphoric criticism showcases the utility of this approach. See his "Metaphor of Force in Prowar Discourse: The Case of 1812," in *Critical Questions: Invention, Creativity, and the Criticism of Discourse and Media*, ed. William Northstine, Carole Blair, and Gary Copeland (New York: St. Martin's Press, 1994), 264–80, and "Cold War Motives and the Rhetorical Metaphor: A Framework of Criticism," in *Cold War Rhetoric: Strategy, Metaphor, Ideology*, ed. Martin Medhurst, Robert Ivie, Philip Wander, and Robert Scott (East Lansing: Michigan State University Press, 1997): 71–80.

Chapter 2

1. Thomas Pettitt, "Before the Gutenberg Parenthesis: Elizabethan-American Compatibilities," paper presented at MIT5: Creativity, Ownership, and Collaboration in the Digital Age, Cambridge, Mass., April 27–29, 2007, web.mit.edu/comm-forum/mit5/papers/pettitt _plenary_gutenberg.pdf.

2. John G. Landels, *Music in Ancient Greece* (New York: Routledge, 1999), 2.

3. See Daniel C. Brouwer and Robert Asen, eds., *Public Modalities: Rhetoric, Culture, Media, and the Shape of Public Life* (Tuscaloosa: University of Alabama Press, 2010).

4. Sian Lewis, *News and Society in the Greek Polis* (Chapel Hill: University of North Carolina Press, 1996), 14.

5. In Perlmutter, *Blogwars* (Oxford: Oxford University Press, 2008), 4–6. Isocrates demonstrated how a political culture could be sustained through writing in addition to speech, pulling the art of rhetoric out of the Assembly and law courts and into broader public arenas. Although framing Isocrates as the first blogger is a bit overwrought, the analogy directs scholarly attention to ways in which blogging and other networked media similarly extend the scope and function of rhetoric.

6. Protagoras's "Great Speech" in Plato's dialogue *Protagoras* explores how socialization processes unite a *polis* around a set of common goals. Similarly, Isocrates's political theory is a kind of "positive interpellation" capable of forging political community. See Michael Calvin McGee, "Choosing a *Poros*: Reflections on How to Implicate Isocrates in Liberal Theory," *(F)ragments*, 1998, http://mcgeefragments.net/OLD/Choosing_Poros.html#3.

7. Most famously documented in Plato's *Symposium*.

8. Lewis, *News and Society*, 19.

9. W. Robert Connor, *The New Politicians of Fifth Century Athens* (Indianapolis: Hackett, 1992), 27.

10. Mogens H. Hansen, *The Athenian Democracy in the Age of Demosthenes: Structure, Principles, and Ideology*, trans. J. A. Crook (1991; repr., Norman: University of Oklahoma Press, 1999), 279.

11. Hannah Arendt, *The Human Condition* (Chicago: University of Chicago Press, 1958), 197.

12. Douglas Ehninger, "On Systems of Rhetoric," *Philosophy & Rhetoric* 1, no. 3 (1968): 132.

13. Arendt, *Human Condition*, 204. Publicity connects speech and blogging, too: "blogging more often than not issues from the experience of the blogger observing, analyzing, and reacting to the world (or at least the blogosphere), and then articulating this in and to a public world." See Gerard Goggin, "Blogging Said," in *Edward Said: The Legacy of a Public Intellectual*, ed. Ned Curthoys and Debjani Ganguly (Carlton, Vic.: Melbourne University Press, 2007), 65.

14. As Josiah Ober characterizes the function of democracy in *Athenian Legacies: Essays on the Politics of Going On Together* (Princeton: Princeton University Press, 2005), 2.

15. Although I depart from Quentin J. Schultze's religiously inflected use of informationism, I agree with his characterization of it as "a non-discerning, vacuous faith in the collection and dissemination of information as a route to social progress and personal happiness." See Schultze, *Habits of the High-Tech Heart: Living Virtuously in the Internet Age* (Grand Rapids, Mich.: Baker Academic, 2004), 26. There is considerable overlap between what I am calling the informationist model of communication and James Carey's transmission model in "A Cultural Approach to Communication," in *Communication as Culture: Essays on Media and Society* (1989; repr., New York: Routledge, 2009), 11–28.

16. Wayne Booth's term, "rhetrickery," is revealing on this point; see *The Rhetoric of Rhetoric: The Quest for Effective Communication* (Oxford: Blackwell, 2004).

17. Claude Shannon and Warren Weaver, *The Mathematical Theory of Communication* (Urbana: University of Illinois Press, 1963).

18. Bill Gates, "My Plan to Fix the World's Biggest Problems," *Wall Street Journal*, January 25, 2013, http://online.wsj.com/news/articles/SB10001424127887323539804578261780648285770.

19. See Dan Schiller, *How to Think About Information* (Urbana: University of Illinois Press, 2007), especially 4–14. Quoting scientist Richard Raymond, Schiller writes that "'consideration of the effects of information storage and information transfer on physical, chemical, biological, psychological, and sociological systems' might 'help in understanding and predicting many aspects of our universe'" (5), citing Raymond's "Communication, Entropy, Life," *American Scientist* 38, no. 2 (1950): 278.

20. Quoted in Quentin Hardy, "Why Big Data Is Not Truth," *Bits* (blog), *New York Times*, June 1, 2013, 8:00 A.M., http://bits.blogs.nytimes.com/2013/06/01/why-big-data-is-not-truth/; also see danah boyd and Kate Crawford, "Critical Questions for Big Data: Provocations for a Cultural, Technological, and Scholarly Phenomenon," *Information, Communication & Society* 15, no. 5 (2012): 662–79.

21. For example, Douglas Hart and Steven Simon recommend blogs as a way to cultivate critical thinking skills and collate knowledge streams among intelligence analysts in "Thinking Straight and Talking Straight: Problems of Intelligence Analysis," *Survival* 48, no. 1 (2006): 49–50.

22. As Kenneth Burke noted, all living things are critics, constantly invited to interpret signs and to "interpret our interpretations." See *Attitudes Toward History: An Anatomy of Purpose* (1937; Berkeley: University of California Press, 1954), 6.

23. Lanham, *Electronic Word*, 62. Lanham utilizes the same formulation in his later book, *The Economics of Attention: Style and Substance in the Information Age* (Chicago: University of Chicago Press, 2006), 137–42.

24. Herbert Spencer, *The Philosophy of Style*, 2nd ed., ed. Fred N. Scott (Boston: Allyn and Bacon, 1892), 4.

25. Richards, *Philosophy of Rhetoric*, 11.

26. Edward Schiappa, *Defining Reality: Definitions and the Politics of Meaning* (Carbondale: Southern Illinois Press, 2003).

27. Jeffrey St. John, "Communication as Failure," in *Communication As . . . : Perspectives on Theory*, ed. Gregory Shepherd, Jeffrey St. John, and Ted Striphas (Thousand Oaks, Calif.: SAGE, 2006), 249–56.

28. Kenneth Burke, *A Rhetoric of Motives* (1950; repr., Berkeley: University of California Press, 1969), 43.

29. Ibid., 19.

30. Farrell, *Norms of Rhetorical Culture* (New Haven: Yale University Press, 1993), 182–86.

31. *Say Anything*, dir. Cameron Crowe (Century City, CA: 20th Century Fox, 1989).

32. Lanham, *Economics of Attention*, 9.

33. This is certainly true in the early modern context, where museums and libraries were founded to manage the greater flows of information. See Thomas Hapke, "Roots of Mediating Information: Aspects of the German Information Movement," in *European Modernism and the Information Society: Informing the Present, Understanding the Past*, ed. W. Boyd Raymond (Surrey: Ashgate, 2008), 307–28, Ann M. Blair, *Too Much to Know: Managing Scholarly Information Before the Modern Age* (New Haven: Yale University Press, 2010), and James Gleick, *The Information: A History, a Theory, a Flood* (New York: Pantheon Books, 2011).

34. By 2007, 295 exabytes were being stored in technological devices (an exabyte is 1 billion gigabytes). By 2009, 500 exabytes were being stored. By any standard, this is an enormous amount of information—swamping any library. Martin Hilbert, who coordinated a study on the amount of global digitized information, noted, "You could say the digital age started in 2002. It continued tremendously from there," indicating that the jump in information abundance coincided with the advent of blogging. See Brian Vastag, "Exabytes: Documenting the 'Digital Age' and Huge Growth in Computing Capacity," *Washington Post*, Feb 10, 2011, http://www.washingtonpost.com/wp-dyn/content/article/2011/02/10/AR2011021004916.html, and the original study, Martin Hilbert and Priscilla López, "The World's Technological Capacity to Store, Communicate, and Compute Information," *Science* 331 (April 2011): 60–65. See also Josh Catone, "How Much Data Will Humans Create and Store This Year?," *Mashable*, June 28, 2011, http://mashable.com/2011/06/28/data-info graphic/ for a demonstrative infographic estimating that 1.8 zettabytes (3 more zeroes than an exabyte) were circulated and replicated in 2011. That number is expected to double every two years for the foreseeable future.

35. Lazarsfeld and Merton, "Mass Communication, Popular Taste, and Organized Social Action," originally published in *The Communication of Ideas*, ed. Lyman Bryson (New York: Institute for Religious and Social Studies, 1948); republished in *Mass Communication and American Social Thought: Key Texts, 1919–1968*, ed. John Durham Peters and Peter Simonson (Lanham, Md.: Rowman & Littlefield, 2004), 235.

36. See Neuman, *The Future of the Mass Audience* (Cambridge: Cambridge University Press, 1992), 114.

37. Clive Thompson's excellent write-up of interruption science is a useful overview of some key findings. See "Meet the Life Hackers," *The New York Times*, October 16, 2005, http://www.nytimes.com/2005/10/16/magazine/16guru.html.

38. As Nicholas Carr calls it in *The Shallows: What the Internet Is Doing to Our Brains* (New York: W. W. Norton, 2010).

39. Lev Manovich, *The Language of New Media* (Cambridge, Mass.: MIT Press, 2001), 76–77.

40. Ibid., 77–78.

41. This is not the only conceptual problem with Manovich's use of the term "rhetoric." While it is true that rhetoric was of great importance in early print culture, it was first fully

developed in classical Greece as an *oral* art. Just as Manovich wonders whether rhetoric can survive with the new digitally networked medium, so, too, did early critics of writing and print ponder the fate of rhetoric. Rhetoric is a resilient art, however—and fortunately so, since people are always looking to bury it. Manovich does not recognize the essential bivalence of rhetoric: it is a two-sided art. It can be used to distract, it can be used to focus; it can be primarily ornamental, it can generate substance; it can be used for ill, it can be used for right. There is no essentialist theory of rhetoric. Acknowledging the bivalence of rhetoric underlines how Manovich overgeneralizes about the uses of hyperlinks. Whether hyperlinks distract from or support an argument depends on unique, situational features of the hypertext itself and not just the presence of a type of code.

42. As James G. Webster notes, "The hyperlinked environment can be thought of as a virtual marketplace in which the purveyors of content compete with one another for the attention of the public." See Webster, "Structuring a Marketplace of Attention," in *The Hyperlinked Society: Questioning Connections in the Digital Age*, ed. Joseph Turow and Lokman Tsui (Ann Arbor: University of Michigan Press, 2008), 23. The metaphoric shift from the "marketplace of ideas" to the "marketplace of attention" signals a shift from modern to networked sensibilities.

43. Lanham, *Economics of Attention*, xi. Herbert Simon formulated the predicament of information abundance similarly: "a wealth of information creates a poverty of attention, and a need to allocate that attention efficiently among the overabundance of information sources that might consume it." See Simon, "Designing Organizations for an Information-Rich World," in *Computers, Communication, and the Public Interest*, ed. Martin Greenberger (Baltimore: Johns Hopkins University Press, 1971), 41.

44. Lanham, *Economics of Attention*, xii–iii.

45. Jonathan Beller, *The Cinematic Mode of Production: Attention Economy and the Society of the Spectacle* (Lebanon, N.H.: University Press of New England, 2006), 28.

46. Todd Oakley, *From Attention to Meaning: Explorations in Semiotics, Linguistics, and Rhetoric* (New York: Peter Lang, 2009), 189, emphasis in original.

47. *The Rhetoric*, 1415a. Also see Susan Bickford, "Beyond Friendship: Aristotle on Conflict, Deliberation, and Attention," *Journal of Politics* 58 (May 1996): 398–421. Aristotle was not alone in his interest in attention. Isocrates, in giving advice to those who would read his written speeches aloud to others, implored the speaker to "fix their attention even more on what is to be said than on what has been said before . . . [and] not to seek to run through the whole of it at the first sitting, but only so much of it as will not fatigue the audience." See *Antidosis*, 312.11–12, in *Isocrates*, vol. 2, trans. George Norlin (Cambridge, Mass.: Harvard University Press, 1929), 191–93.

48. James Albert Winans, *Public Speaking* (New York: The Century Company, 1915), 50, 111. Winans draws on psychologist William James's theory of attention, approvingly citing James's adage that "what holds attention determines action" (191).

49. In Campbell, *The Rhetorical Act* (Belmont, Calif.: Wadsworth, 1982), 169.

50. Burke, *Permanence and Change* (1935; repr., Berkeley: University of California Press, 1984), 141, emphasis in original.

51. Winifred Gallagher develops this point excellently in *Rapt: Attention and the Focused Life* (New York: Penguin, 2009).

52. Lanham, *Economics of Attention*, 19.

53. Quoted in Derrick Schneider, "As Wine Blogs Mature, What's the Impact?," *San Francisco Chronicle*, February 21, 2010, http://www.sfgate.com/food/article/As-wine-blogs-mature-what-s-the-impact-3199405.php.

54. Argumentation is central to bloggers' self-conception and, as Aaron Barlow hypothesizes, it distinguishes these networked intermediaries from actors in other kinds of media: "argument (as more than a spectator sport) . . . wakes in people desires that lead to their direct participation in both the public sphere and political life. Without their argumentative side, the blogs would eventually sink into the mire that the commercial news media has found itself stuck in." See Barlow, *The Rise of the Blogosphere* (Westport, Conn.: Praeger, 2007), 179.

55. Quoted in Deborah Solomon, "Kos Célèbre," *New York Times Magazine*, March 19, 2006, http://www.nytimes.com/2006/03/19/magazine/319wwln_q4.html.

56. Jürgen Habermas, *The Structural Transformation of the Bourgeois Public Sphere: An Inquiry into a Category of Bourgeois Society*, trans. Thomas Burger (Cambridge, Mass.: MIT Press, 1989), 4.

57. Ibid., p. 7–12.

58. This attribution is likely a historical inaccuracy nonetheless made plausible by theories of the divine right of monarchs; see Peter Burke, *The Fabrication of Louis XIV* (1992; repr., Bath, U.K.: The Bath Press, 1999), 9–10.

59. The term *öffentliches Räsonnement*, translated as "public use of reason," has connotations unique to German language and culture: "simultaneously the invocation of reason and its disdainful disparagement as merely malcontent griping" (*Structural Transformation*, 27). There is, then, a sense in which the use of "public reason" is always doubly valenced for Habermas, as it has the potential to cover many senses of public talk. In a footnote after this clarification of the doubleness of *öffentliches Räsonnement*, Habermas situates his conception of public reason in line with Hegel's sophistic understanding of reasoning instead of Kant's, who used the term "reasoning" "naively in the Enlightenment sense" (256n1). Habermas is clearly distancing himself from simplistic assertions that rational argumentation yields verifiably good results. It is this doubleness in Habermas's work that makes his overarching theory of publicity amenable to rhetorical approaches; though Habermas is often criticized for not leaving any room for rhetoric's play, it is important to note that his sophistic sense of reasoning is more hospitable to rhetorical approaches than is usually assumed. Moreover, it intimates that malcontent griping—a category which blogging is often accused of falling into—is the necessary flip side to more formal reasoning, providing an opportunity to consider the benefits that such "griping" holds for public deliberation.

60. James Bohman's explanation of publicity parses this complex term: "Publicity works on three levels: it creates the social space for deliberation, it governs processes of deliberation and the reasons produced in them, and it provides a standard by which to judge agreements." See Bohman, *Public Deliberation: Pluralism, Complexity, and Democracy* (Cambridge, Mass.: MIT Press, 1996), 37–38.

61. Following this line of argument, critics question whether the blogosphere is a public sphere, based on the fact that the ideals of the public sphere, like open access and bracketing of status, are not realized through blogging. See Andrew Ó Baioll, "Weblogs and the Public Sphere," in Gurak et al., *Into the Blogosphere*, http://blog.lib.umn.edu/blogosphere/weblogs_and_the_public_sphere.html.

62. Farrell, *Norms of Rhetorical Culture*, 199.

63. Craig Calhoun, "Introduction: Habermas and the Public Sphere," in *Habermas and the Public Sphere*, ed. Craig Calhoun (Cambridge, Mass.: MIT Press, 1992), 37. Filters like these are to some extent necessary, for not every private opinion merits circulation to wide public audiences.

64. Arthur Lupia, "Can Online Deliberation Improve Politics? Scientific Foundations for Success," in *Online Deliberation: Design, Research, and Practice*, ed. Todd Davies and Seeta Peña Gangadharan (Stanford, Calif.: Center for the Study of Language and Information, 2009), 63; available at https://web.archive.org/web/20111118164233/http://odbook.stanford.edu/static/filedocument/2009/11/10/ODBook.Full.11.3.09.pdf. Nick Couldry, Sonia Livingstone, and Tim Markham note that "no amount of communication, however stylish and informative, will engage people in politics, unless they are paying attention, at least some of the time"; see their *Media Consumption and Public Engagement: Beyond the Presumption of Attention* (New York: Palgrave Macmillan, 2007), 3.

65. Following Michael Warner's line that "a public is constituted through mere attention," in *Publics and Counterpublics* (New York: Zone Books, 2005), 87–89.

66. Jürgen Habermas, *Between Facts and Norms: Contributions to a Discourse Theory of Law and Democracy*, trans. William Rehg (Cambridge, Mass.: MIT Press, 1996), 362.

67. James Bovard, *Attention-Deficit Democracy* (New York: Palgrave Macmillan, 2005).

68. Bohman, *Public Deliberation*, 27.

69. Wayne Brockriede, "Arguers as Lovers," *Philosophy & Rhetoric* 5, no. 1 (1972): 1–11.

70. Karl R. Wallace, "The Substance of Rhetoric: Good Reasons," *Quarterly Journal of Speech* 49, no. 3 (1963): 239–49.

71. David Mathews articulates how deliberation reveals choices and forges common ground for citizens to work with and through their differences; see his *Politics for People: Finding a Responsible Public Voice* (Urbana: University of Illinois Press, 1994).

72. John Keane theorizes public spheres as "the sites in which citizens question the pseudo-imperatives of reality and counter them with alternative experiences of time, space, and interpersonal relations," in "Structural Transformations of the Public Sphere," *Communication Review* 1, no. 1 (1995): 10.

73. Habermas reflects his Frankfurt School origins in this intellectual period by absorbing the Culture Industry hypothesis advanced by Theodor Adorno and Max Horkheimer in "The Culture Industry: Enlightenment as Mass Deception," in *Dialectic of Enlightenment: Philosophical Fragments*, ed. Gunzelin Schmid Noerr, trans. Edmund Jephcott (Stanford: Stanford University Press, 2002): 94–136.

74. Habermas's most significant emendations concerning the culture industries are in "Further Reflections on the Public Sphere," in Calhoun, *Habermas and the Public Sphere*, 421–61. Communication and cultural studies scholars challenged Adorno and Horkheimer's culture industry thesis that audiences were dupes of capital; key works in this vein include Stuart Hall, *Encoding and Decoding in the Television Discourse* (Birmingham, U.K.: Center for Contemporary Culture, 1974); John Fiske, *Television Culture* (London: Methuen, 1987); and Janice Radway, *Reading the Romance: Women, Patriarchy, and Popular Literature* (Chapel Hill: University of North Carolina Press, 1991).

75. Richard Sennett, *The Fall of Public Man* (New York: Alfred A. Knopf, 1974); Robert Putnam, *Bowling Alone: The Collapse and Revival of American Community* (New York: Simon & Schuster, 2000).

76. Putnam, *Bowling Alone*, 216.

77. See Postman, *Amusing Ourselves to Death: Public Discourse in an Age of Show Business* (New York: Penguin, 1985). Kurt Cobain, "Smells like Teen Spirit," on *Nevermind* (DGC Records, 1991).

78. Lizabeth Cohen, *A Consumers' Republic: The Politics of Mass Consumption in Postwar America* (New York: Alfred A. Knopf, 2003), 289. See also Gary Gumpert and Susan Drucker, "From the Agora to the Electronic Shopping Mall," *Critical Studies in Media Communication* 9, no. 2 (1992): 186–200.

79. Putnam, *Bowling Alone*, 179.

80. The classic text on the myths of the town hall as an idealized public sphere is Jane J. Mansbridge, *Beyond Adversary Democracy* (Chicago: University of Chicago Press, 1980).

81. Barbara Kaye draws on the uses and gratifications research tradition in media studies to identify ten motivations of bloggers: providing an information-rich presentation, finding personal fulfillment, enabling affiliation, seeking information, pursuing intellectual and aesthetic stimulation, offering an alternative to traditional media, guiding opinion formation, being a convenient source of information, aiding in surveying the political world, and contributing to fact-checking. See her "Blog Use Motivations: An Exploratory Study," in *Blogging, Citizenship, and the Future of Media*, ed. Mark Tremayne (New York: Routledge, 2007), 134–36.

82. Manuel Castells, "Informationalism, Networks, and the Network Society," in *The Network Society: A Cross-Cultural Perspective*, ed. Manuel Castells (Northampton, Mass.: Edward Elgar, 2004), 19. See also his *Internet Galaxy: Reflections on the Internet, Business, and Society* (Oxford: Oxford University Press, 2001), and *The Information Age: Economy, Society, and Culture*, 3rd ed., vols. 1–3 (Oxford: Blackwell, 2003). The idea of social networks far precedes their encoding in the language of social networking sites. As Armand Mattelart convincingly argues, the networking of the world is a consequence of print and then electronically mediated communication; see his *Networking the World, 1794–2000*, trans. Liz

Carey-Libbrecht and James Cohen (Minneapolis: University of Minnesota Press, 2000). I often deploy the term "internetworked" alongside "networked" as a reminder that traditional networking is now often mediated by the internet.

83. Castells, *The Rise of the Network Society* (Oxford: Blackwell, 1996), 469.

84. I am persuaded by Castells's observation that all societies are in some way information or knowledge societies. Although it is also true that all societies can be seen as networks, Castells's explanation of the network form as an increasingly central social morphology and logic makes a reference to a network society apt. Moreover, the term "network" foregrounds the communicative dimensions of this new configuration in a way that "information" and "knowledge" do not. Rather than participating in the fool's errand of divining a clear transition point between modern and networked public cultures, we would be better advised to think about the span from the late 1960s to the early part of the twenty-first century as featuring a clash between modern and networked sensibilities. On the gradual but dramatic transition between the modern and the networked, see Michael Vlahos, "The Politics of a Network World: A Speculation," in *The Civic Web: Online Politics and Democratic Values*, ed. David Anderson and Michael Cornfeld (Lanham, Md.: Rowman & Littlefield, 2003), 185–202.

85. It should be noted that because many bloggers gradually monetized their blogs, obnoxious advertisements are no longer the exclusive property of large media organizations.

86. Bimber, *Information and American Democracy: Technology in the Evolution of Political Power* (Cambridge: Cambridge University Press, 2003), 90–91.

87. Michael Calvin McGee, "Text, Context, and the Fragmentation of Contemporary Culture," *Western Journal of Speech Communication* 54, no. 3 (1990): 284. McGee's recognition of the import of these new networks of communication resonates strongly with the ascendance of blogging: "[t]he communication revolution, however, was accompanied by a knowledge explosion. The result is that today no single finished text could possibly comprehend all perspectives on even a single human problem, let alone the complex of problems we index in the phrase 'issues of the day.' The only way to 'say it all' in our fractured culture is to provide readers/audiences with dense, truncated fragments which cue *them* to produce a finished discourse in their minds. In short, *text construction is now something done more by the consumers than by the producers of discourse*" (288, emphasis in original.) McGee might as well be describing blogging. What does a blogger do if not produce dense (hyperlinked), truncated (pithy), fragments (posts) of public discourse that are assembled in a bricolage by their readers? Blog readers, for their part, attempt to create some sort of narrative synthesis among all these fragments as they weave the posts together in an effort to make sense of it all. Modern sensibilities presumed that fragments would be discovered through scientific inquiry; postmodern sensibilities assumed that fragments were always already shards of power/knowledge; networked sensibilities approach artifacts as being assemblable through digital recombination. I'm indebted to G. Thomas Goodnight for this latter insight.

88. This isn't to say that assertions of a homogeneous culture aren't frequently made. They are, however, often critically interrogated in a way that is unimaginable in a prior rhetorical imaginary. Richard Weaver's explanation of the "uncontested term" in culturally homogenous cultures mirrors McGee's observations here; see "The Spaciousness of Old Rhetoric," in *The Ethics of Rhetoric* (1953; repr., Davis, Calif.: Hermagoras Press, 1985), 169–70.

89. Castells, "Informationalism, Networks, and the Network Society," 19. Also see Alain Touraine, *A New Paradigm for Understanding the World* (Cambridge: Polity Press, 2007).

90. On *The Simpsons*, Moe Szyslak famously defined postmodernism as "weird for the sake of being weird," which may account for much of postmodern art but loses heuristic value in other contexts. While I recognize the endlessly proliferating strains of critique that floats under the sign of postmodernity, and the resistance of postmodernity itself to definition, it is useful to recall the deep ties between this intellectual movement and computerization. Jean-François Lyotard's *The Postmodern Condition: A Report on Knowledge* (1979; repr., Manchester: Manchester University Press, 1984) can be profitably reread in the context of

internetworked culture. In *The Postmodern Condition*, he situates what he calls postmodernism as an outgrowth of "the computerization of society" (7), which produces subjects that are nodes in a broader network which itself is constituted by an endless proliferation of language games (17). Lyotard defines modernity in the context of its Enlightenment roots as "any science that legitimates itself with reference to a metadiscourse of philosophy that appeals to some grand narrative, such as the dialectics of Spirit, the hermeneutics of meaning, the emancipation of the rational or working subject, or the creation of wealth. For example, the rule of consensus between sender and addressee of a statement with truth-value is deemed acceptable if it is cast in terms of a possible unanimity between rational minds: this is the Enlightenment narrative, in which the hero of knowledge works toward a good ethico-political end—universal peace" (xxiii–xxiv). *Post*modernism, then, keys in to the general "incredulity towards metanarratives" (xxiv). This decline in the salience of metanarratives is directly related to "an effect of the blossoming of techniques and technologies since the Second World War" (37) and "the redeployment of advanced liberal-capitalism" (38). Technology and globalization are thus implicated in the denial of any language game's metaprescriptive force; that is, no language game *now* has the authority to automatically trump others, as in prior eras. Discourse communities are simply too splintered for the kinds of legitimation that occurred in prior eras to operate, which is a key part of Lyotard's critique of Habermas's theories of consensus and legitimation, a point I return to in chapter 5.

91. John Thompson's *The Media and Modernity: A Social Theory of Media* (Cambridge: Polity Press, 1995) connects print media to the onset of the modern age. See also David Harvey's *The Condition of Postmodernity: An Enquiry into the Origins of Cultural Change* (Oxford: Blackwell, 1989) on the time-space compression of modernity as compared to postmodernity.

92. Castells, "Informationalism, Networks, and the Network Society," 5, emphasis in original.

93. Lars Qvortrup, *The Hypercomplex Society* (New York: Peter Lang, 2003).

94. Alice Crawford, "The Myth of the Unmarked Net Speaker," in *Critical Perspectives on the Internet*, ed. Greg Elmer (Lanham, Md.: Rowman & Littlefield, 2002), 89–104. The social is increasingly shaped by the additional, crosscutting axis of information. Educational and technological access (experience with information), rhetorical efficacy (facility in framing information), and ability to make sound judgments (negotiating competing information) now interact in profound ways with traditional social identities.

95. Castells, "Informationalism, Networks, and the Network Society," 3.

96. Ibid., 9.

97. "Essentially free," because most bloggers work well within the bandwidth limitations imposed by blog hosting services or their internet service providers. Those with higher bandwidth needs are able to outsource file storage to sites like YouTube or other free data-hosting sites.

98. Though these efforts are occasionally effective in blocking access to sites, the Chinese proverb "you can dam a river forever, but not the mouths of the people," hints at the problems of state censorship keeping pace with technological developments, like proxy IP addresses and anonymizing software. Svetlana V. Kulikova and David Perlmutter explore how bloggers in authoritarian regimes strategically use their relative anonymity in "Blogging Down the Dictator? The Kyrgyz Revolution and *Samizdat* Websites," *International Communication Gazette* 69, no. 1 (2007): 29–50.

99. See Evgeny Morozov's *The Net Delusion: The Dark Side of Internet Freedom* (London: Penguin, 2011) on cyber-utopianism. "Web apologetics" is a clever term borrowed from Chris Lehmann in "An Accelerated Grimace: On Cyber-Utopianism," *The Nation*, March 2, 2011, http://www.thenation.com/article/158974/accelerated-grimace-cyber-utopianism.

100. Gaonkar, *Alternative Modernities* (Durham: Duke University Press, 2001).

101. See Castells, *The Network Society*; also see Manuel Castells and Gustavo Cardoso, eds., *The Network Society: From Knowledge to Policy* (Washington, D.C.: Johns Hopkins Center for Transatlantic Relations, 2006).

102. See Brian Jarvis, *Postmodern Cartographies: The Geographical Imagination in Contemporary American Culture* (New York: St. Martin's Press, 1998), 21, for a concise explanation of how the postindustrial economy of the United States is purchased at the expense of (often unregulated) industrialization abroad.

103. Quoted in "Books of the Year 2003," *The Economist*, December 4, 2003, http://www.economist.com/books/displaystory.cfm?story_id=E1_NNGVRJV.

104. Castells, "Informationalism, Networks, and the Network Society," 22.

105. Kevin DeLuca and Jennifer Peeples offer the "public screen" as one post–public sphere term, though they entwine it with traditional public sphere theory, in "From Public Sphere to Public Screen: Democracy, Activism, and the 'Violence' of Seattle," *Critical Studies in Media Communication* 19, no. 2 (2002): 125–51.

106. John Durham Peters dissects the different meanings inspired by competing translations of *Öffentlichkeit* in his "Distrust of Representation: Habermas on the Public Sphere," *Media, Culture, and Society* 15, no. 4 (1993): 542–44.

107. Even critics of the idea of the public sphere often concede that something like publicity is necessary; see G. Thomas Goodnight's treatment of this issue in his "Opening up 'The Spaces of Dissension,'" *Communication Monographs* 64, no. 3 (1997): 271–72.

108. Stefan Nowotny, "The Condition of Becoming Public," *Transversal*, December 2003, http://www.eipcp.net/transversal/1203/nowotny/en.

109. Burke, *Grammar*, 21.

110. See Barbara Becker and Josef Wehner, "Electronic Networks and Civil Society: Reflections on Structural Changes in the Public Sphere," in *Culture, Technology, and Communication: Towards an Intercultural Global Village*, ed. Charles Ess and Fay Sudweeks (Albany: SUNY Press, 2001), 67–86, and Michael A. Froomkin, "Habermas@Discourse.net: Toward a Critical Theory of Cyberspace," *Harvard Law Review* 116, no. 3 (2003): 749–871.

111. Benkler, *The Wealth of Networks: How Social Production Transforms Markets and Freedom* (New Haven: Yale University Press, 2006), 212.

112. Ibid., 13. John Kelly's fascinating study explores the linkages between these new intermediaries and how they shape attention; see "Pride of Place: Mainstream Media and the Networked Public Sphere," in *Media Re:Public* (Cambridge, Mass.: Berkman Center for Internet and Society at Harvard University, 2008), http://cyber.law.harvard.edu/sites/cyber.law.harvard.edu/files/Pride%20of%20Place_MR.pdf. Henry Jenkins predicts that "new knowledge communities will be voluntary, temporary, and tactical affiliations, defined through common intellectual enterprises and emotional investments . . . they are held together through the mutual production and exchange of knowledge;" in *Fans, Bloggers, and Gamers: Inside Participatory Culture* (New York: New York University Press, 2006), 137.

113. Ibid., 225, 230.

114. Michael Xenos, "New Mediated Deliberation: Blog and Press Coverage of the Alito Nomination," *Journal of Computer-Mediated Communication* 13, no. 2 (2008): 500. I explore the cozy relationship between the press and institutional sources in chapter 3.

115. Benkler, *Wealth of Networks*, 12, 258.

116. Or, as Merlyna Lim and Mark E. Kann frame it, the fact that networked deliberation does not adhere to traditional, idealized, modern norms does not preclude its having democratic effects. See their "Politics: Deliberation, Mobilization, and Networked Practices of Agitation," in *Networked Publics*, ed. Kazys Varnelis (Cambridge, Mass.: MIT Press, 2008), 100.

117. Pettitt, "Gutenberg Parenthesis," 3.

Chapter 3

1. Aristotle, *Rhetoric*, 1356a; in *On Rhetoric: A Theory of Civic Discourse*, trans. George Kennedy (Oxford: Oxford University Press, 1991), 38.

2. Or, as Richard McKeon calls it, an architectonic productive art. See McKeon, *Rhetoric: Essays on Invention and Discovery*, ed. Mark Backmann (Woodbridge, Conn.: Ox Bow Press, 1987), especially chapter 1, "The Uses of Rhetoric in a Technological Age: Architectonic Productive Arts."

3. Benkler, *Wealth of Networks*, 263.

4. See Richard Young and Yameng Liu, "Introduction," in *Landmark Essays on Rhetorical Invention*, ed. Richard Young and Yameng Liu (Mahwah, N.J.: Lawrence Erlbaum, 1994).

5. Brockriede, "Arguers as Lovers."

6. See Burke on recalcitrance in *Permanence and Change*, 255–59.

7. Debra Hawhee, "Kairotic Encounters," in *Perspectives on Rhetorical Invention*, ed. Janice Lauer and Janet M. Atwill (Knoxville: University of Tennessee Press, 2002), 17. Moving along the spectrum from discovery to generation increases the rhetoricity of deliberation. The most rhetorical discourse occurs when there are no demonstrable facts, and meaning is negotiated by debating probabilities and ethics.

8. John Muckelbauer, *The Future of Invention: Rhetoric, Postmodernism, and the Problem of Change* (Albany: SUNY Press, 2008), xi, emphasis in original.

9. "Dissoi Logoi," in *The Older Sophists: A Complete Translation by Several Hands of the Fragments in "Die Fragmente der Vorsokratiker,"* ed. Rosamund Kent Sprague (1972; repr., Indianapolis: Hackett, 2001).

10. Valerie Peterson, "Beyond Dichotomy: The Sophists' Understanding of Antithetical Thought," *Advances in the History of Rhetoric* 1, no. 1 (1998): 1–8.

11. Quoted in John Poulakos, "Toward a Sophistic Definition of Rhetoric," *Philosophy & Rhetoric* 16, no. 1 (1983): 36.

12. Michael Billig, *Arguing and Thinking: A Rhetorical Approach to Social Psychology* (1987; repr., New York: Cambridge University Press, 1996), 75–76, 141.

13. I am deeply indebted to John Poulakos for this insight and my broader understanding of the Sophists. See his *Sophistical Rhetoric in Ancient Greece* (Columbia: University of South Carolina Press, 1995).

14. In Dewey, *Human Nature and Conduct: An Introduction to Social Psychology* (New York: Henry Holt, 1922), 300. Nathan Crick's work connects John Dewey's pragmatism with sophistic thought in *Democracy and Rhetoric: John Dewey on the Arts of Becoming* (Columbia: University of South Carolina Press, 2010).

15. Plato, *Phaedrus*, trans. W. C. Helmbold and W. G. Rabinowitz (New York: Macmillan, 1956), 32. Socrates's line condenses a far more detailed version of invention that is related in *The Republic's* Myth of Er. According to Plato, death releases the immortal soul to drift through the realm of the ideal Forms, glimpsing streaks of Reality that become imprinted upon the soul. Each soul, however, pauses at the river Lethe on its way to reincarnation. Drinking water from the river obscures what the soul saw in the realm of ideal Forms (*lethe* translates as forgetfulness or concealment.) When the soul is born into the material world again, it begins a long process of recovering the knowledge of the Forms that is innate in the soul. Some souls drink heavily from the river Lethe, which means they forget more and are able to recover less, whereas others' more modest sippings equip them to better (re)discover knowledge.

16. Karen LeFevre, *Invention as a Social Act* (Carbondale: Southern Illinois University Press, 1987), 11–12.

17. Aristotle, *Rhetoric*, 1355b; trans. Kennedy, *On Rhetoric*, 36.

18. Walter Ong, *Ramus, Method, and the Decay of Dialogue* (London: Oxford University Press, 1958), 114. Stephen Mailloux's "Rhetorical Hermeneutics Still Again: or, On the Track of *Phronesis*" traces visual metaphors in Aristotle's theory of *phronesis*, in *A Companion to Rhetoric and Rhetorical Criticism*, ed. Walter Jost and Wendy Olmsted (Malden, Mass.: Blackwell, 2004), 457–72. No wonder that Aristotle was drawn to visual metaphors in his depiction of invention, for the ocular is central to how we describe understanding and common ground. We often ask "do you see what I mean?" and hope to "see eye-to-eye."

19. Aristotle, *Rhetoric*, 1397a; trans. Kennedy, *On Rhetoric*, 171.

20. Aristotle, *Topics*, trans. W. A. Pickard-Cambridge (Stilwell, Kans.: Digireads.com Publishing, 2006), 92.

21. Lawrence Prelli hints at the topological metaphor for invention, especially in his description of invention as occurring from contrasting vantage points. See Prelli, *A Rhetoric of Science: Inventing Scientific Discourse* (Columbia: University of South Carolina Press, 1989), 66–68.

22. Two related concepts from thinkers deeply influenced by Aristotle extend and clarify this topographical metaphor. Kenneth Burke's notion of transcendence (etymologically, "to climb over or beyond") incorporates the topographical; for Burke, transcendence is "the building of a *terministic bridge* whereby one realm is *transcended* by being viewed *in terms of* a realm 'beyond it.'" See his *Language as Symbolic Action*, 187. Burke's adaptation of Hegelian dialectic and Socratic transcendence (*Grammar of Motives*, 420–30) for rhetorical purposes is a novel extension of Aristotle's theory of invention. Similarly, Hans-Georg Gadamer's hermeneutic theory relies on the topographical metaphor of "horizon." For Gadamer, when people encounter each other, their prejudices and assumptions are brought into question. The process of trying to understand another transforms one's own horizon—how one perceives the world. As Gadamer explains, "the horizon is the range of vision that includes everything that can be seen from a particular vantage point. Applying this to the thinking mind, we speak of narrowness of horizon, of the possible expansion of horizon, of the opening up of new horizons, and so forth." See Gadamer, *Truth and Method* (1975; repr., New York: Continuum Books, 2004), 301. Gadamer describes a person with no horizon as having a narrow circumference of concern or understanding, whereas having a horizon means "not being limited to what is nearby but being able to see beyond it" (ibid.).

23. Cicero, *De Oratore*, 2.147; in *De Oratore, Books I–II*, trans. Edward W. Sutton and Harris Rackham (Cambridge, Mass.: Harvard University Press, 1942), 305.

24. Quintilian, book 5, chapter 10, 20–22, in *Institutio Oratoria*; quoted in Carolyn Miller, "The Aristotelian *Topos*: Hunting for Novelty," in *Rereading Aristotle's Rhetoric*, ed. Alan G. Gross and Arthur E. Walzer (Carbondale: Southern Illinois University Press, 2000), 139–40.

25. William Eamon, *Science and the Secrets of Nature: Books of Secrets in Medieval and Early Modern Culture* (Princeton: Princeton University Press, 1994), 284. Eamon identifies a knowledge/*metis* pairing that maps onto the discovery/generative model of invention. *Metis* is practical knowledge or conjectural practice; it is cunning intelligence rather than absolute truth. Carlo Ginzburg locates the venatic metaphor as a generative alternative to Platonic conceptions of knowledge—since any hunt necessarily requires conjecture and speculation—in "Clues: Roots of an Evidential Paradigm," in *Clues, Myths, and the Historical Method*, trans. John and Anne C. Tedeschi (Baltimore: Johns Hopkins University Press, 1989), 105.

26. Augustine, *On Christian Doctrine*, 2.32.50. All quotations are from the J. F. Shaw translation of *On Christian Doctrine* (Mineola, N.Y.: Dover, 2009).

27. Ibid., 2.31.48.

28. Ibid., 3.1.1.

29. As George A. Kennedy writes, "Proof in Christian rhetoric derives from the authoritative utterances in the sacred texts and from the moral authority of the speaker, not from argumentation." See Kennedy, *Classical Rhetoric and Its Christian and Secular Tradition from Ancient to Modern Times*, 2nd ed. (Chapel Hill: University of North Carolina Press, 1999), 181.

30. Elizabeth Eisenstein, *The Printing Press as an Agent of Change* (Cambridge: Cambridge University Press, 1979), 120–21.

31. See Lawrence Lessig, *Free Culture: The Nature and Future of Creativity* (New York: Penguin, 2005), and Kembrew McLeod, *Owning Culture: Authorship, Ownership, and Intellectual Property* (New York: Peter Lang, 2001) and *Freedom of Expression: Resistance and Repression in the Age of Intellectual Property* (Minneapolis: University of Minnesota Press, 2007).

32. See *Arguments in Rhetoric Against Quintilian: Translation and Text of Peter Ramus's "Rhetoricae Distinctiones in Quintilianum" (1549)*, ed. James Murphy, trans. Carole Newlands (1986; repr., Carbondale: Southern Illinois University Press, 2010), 27–28.

33. Hugh Blair quoted in *The Rhetoric of Blair, Campbell, and Whately*, ed. James L. Golden and Edward P. J. Corbett (1968; repr., Carbondale: Southern Illinois University Press, 1990), 32.

34. Giambattista Vico, *On the Most Ancient Wisdom of the Italians* (1710), trans. L. M. Palmer (Ithaca: Cornell University Press, 1988), 104.

35. In *The Portable Nietzsche*, ed. and trans. Walter Kaufmann (New York: Viking Press), 46.

36. The Wingspread Conference in 1970, under the auspices of the "Report of the Committee on the Nature of Rhetorical Invention," initiated much of this reconsideration of invention. The report's authors advise considering invention along the lines of a cosmological metaphor. They note that rhetoricians "conceive of a universe of arguments and persuasive tactics, and of galaxies within the universe which are formed by relationships and clusterings among the rhetorical materials. These galaxies have centers, which may be called world-views or stances or originating positions . . . the point and assumption of this perspective is that inventional resources may vary radically from one galaxy to another. There may also be important elements of commonality or similarity, such as recurrent patterns of reasoning and symbolizing." Robert L. Scott, chairman, with James R. Andrews, Howard H. Martin, J. Richard McNally, William F. Nelson, Michael M. Osborn, Arthur L. Smith, and Harold Zyskind, "Report of the Committee on the Nature of Rhetorical Invention," in *The Prospects of Rhetoric*, ed. Lloyd Bitzer and Edwin Black (Englewood Cliffs, N.J.: Prentice Hall, 1971), 233.

37. As the Society for Professional Journalists Code of Ethics describes their mission at http://www.spj.org/pdf/ethicscode.pdf.

38. Lloyd Bitzer defends journalism thus: "It is necessary for them [journalists] to affirm and safeguard this commitment to truth, which is their central virtue, else they confuse themselves with politicians or entertainers and risk losing the public's trust." See Bitzer, "Rhetorical Public Communication," *Critical Studies in Mass Communication* 4 (1987): 427.

39. Richard Weaver, in his classic reading of Plato's *Phaedrus*, makes the case that the ideology of journalism is actually at odds with the ends that journalism purports to pursue: "the techniques of the base lover, especially as exemplified in modern journalism, would make a long catalogue, but in general it is accurate to say that he [sic] seeks to keep the understanding in a passive state by never permitting an honest examination of alternatives. Nothing is feared more by him than a true dialectic, for this not only endangers his favored alternative, but also gives the 'beloved' . . . some training in intellectual independence." See Weaver, *Ethics of Rhetoric*, 11–12. Weaver's diagnosis may be too harsh; as we know, no ideology functions perfectly, and plenty of journalists do function with a spirit of inquiry that Weaver idealizes. Yet plenty of journalists, as the case study shows, also display the attitude identified by Weaver.

40. Michael Schudson establishes the contingency of these norms, codified in the early twentieth century, to distinguish what was deemed the quality press from the tabloid journalism popular at the time, in *Discovering the News: A Social History of American Newspapers* (New York: Basic Books, 1978).

41. Here, I follow Robert Rowland's pragmatic theory of argument: "when we say that a view is true, we really mean that a given symbolic description consistently solves a particular problem. Thus, the statement 'the sun will come up tomorrow,' is considered 'true,' despite ambiguities that a postmodern might point to in regard to the meaning of *sun* or *tomorrow*, because it usefully and consistently solves a particular epistemic problem." See Rowland, "In Defense of Rational Argument: A Pragmatic Justification of Argumentation Theory and Response to the Postmodern Critique," *Philosophy & Rhetoric* 28, no. 4 (1995): 355. Public argument is more about bargaining than truth—there is no true definition of a word, or true value that trumps all others, or true policy action. Instead, public argument is a series

of bargains about definition and interpretation, fact and value, what to pay attention to and how to pay attention to it. Thinking about public argument as a process of rhetorical bargainings rather than competing truth claims is far richer for participants and critics, because it orients us to considering who or what a particular interpretation is useful *for*.

42. This distinction is a crucial one in argumentation theory, for a focus on arguments-as-products neglects the important social dimension of argumentation-as-process. See Daniel O'Keefe, "Two Concepts of Argument," *Journal of the American Forensic Association* 13, no. 3 (1977): 121–28. The affordances of digital media technology—revisability, republishability, updatability—lend themselves to a more processual orientation.

43. In Beck, *The Cosmopolitan Vision* (Cambridge: Polity Press, 2006), 80.

44. See Zygmunt Bauman, *Liquid Modernity* (Cambridge: Polity Press, 2000); Arjun Appadurai, *Modernity at Large: Cultural Dimensions of Globalization* (Minneapolis: University of Minnesota Press, 1996), 33; and Manuel Castells, "The Space of Flows," in *Rise of the Network Society*. Although there does seem to be an uptick in liquid metaphors associated with networked media, such metaphors are actually common frames for information abundance. Robert Lynd and Helen Lynd, in their classic sociological study of Middletown, underlined "the significance of such a *ceaseless torrent* of printed matter in the process of diffusing new tools and habits of thought"; quoted in Peters and Simonson, *Mass Communication and American Social Thought*, 61, emphasis added.

45. Cass Sunstein, *Republic.com* (Chicago: University of Chicago Press, 2001). See Lincoln Dahlberg, "Rethinking the Fragmentation of the Cyberpublic: From Consensus to Contestation," *New Media & Society* 9, no. 5 (2007): 827–47, for a broader overview of this debate; see L. A. Adamic and N. Glance, "The Political Blogosphere and the 2004 U.S. Election: Divided They Blog," Annual Workshop on the Weblogging Ecosystem, WWW2005, Japan, http://www2.scedu.unibo.it/roversi/SocioNet/AdamicGlanceBlogWWW.pdf, and Eric Lawrence, John Sides, and Henry Farrell, "Self-Segregation or Deliberation? Blog Readership, Participation, and Polarization in American Politics," *Perspectives on Politics* 8, no. 1 (2010): 141–57, for direct application to the blogosphere.

46. Azi Lev-On and Bernard Manin, "Happy Accidents: Deliberation and Online Exposure to Opposing Views," in Davies and Gangadharan, *Online Deliberation*, 105–22, http://odbook.stanford.edu/static/filedocument/2009/11/14/Chapter_7._Lev-On_and_Manin.pdf.

47. See his "'I Was Gone on Debating': Malcolm X's Prison Debates and Public Confrontations," *Argumentation and Advocacy* 31, no. 3 (1995): 117–37.

48. Margaret Zulick and Anne Laffoon, "Enclaved Publics as Inventional Resources: An Essay in Generative Rhetoric," in *Argument in Controversy: Proceedings of the Seventh SCA/AFA Conference on Argumentation*, ed. Donn Parson (Annandale, Va.: Speech Communication Association, 1991), 251–52.

49. C-SPAN, "Sen. Strom Thurmond (R-SC) 100th Birthday Celebration," C-SPAN web site, Real Player media file, 1:00, originally aired December 5, 2002, http://web.archive.org/web/20021207064833/www.c-span.org/politics/. On file with the author. Lott later confessed that Senator Bob Dole had, in the previous speech, taken most of his material—forcing him into ad-libbing. See his autobiography, *Herding Cats: A Life in Politics* (New York: HarperCollins, 2005), 246.

50. Thomas Edsall, "Lott Decried for Part of Salute to Thurmond; GOP Senate Leader Hails Colleague's Run as Segregationist," *The Washington Post*, December 7, 2002, A6, LexisNexis.

51. John Berman, *World News This Morning*, ABC, December 6, 2002, LexisNexis.

52. Bill Kovach and Tom Rosenstiel, *Warp Speed: America in the Age of Mixed Media Culture* (New York: Century Foundation Press, 1999).

53. Ben Bagdikian, *The Media Monopoly* (1983; Boston: Beacon Press, 1997).

54. See Robert McChesney, *Rich Media, Poor Democracy: Communication Politics in Dubious Times* (Urbana: University of Illinois Press, 1999) and *The Problem of the Media: U.S. Communication Politics in the Twenty-First Century* (New York: Monthly Review Press, 2004).

55. Bohman, *Public Deliberation*, 199.

56. Jon Stewart, *Crossfire*, CNN, October 15, 2004, http://transcripts.cnn.com/TRANSCRIPTS/0410/15/cf.01.html (consulted 12 September 2009).

57. Esther Scott, "'Big Media' Meets the 'Bloggers': Coverage of Trent Lott's Remarks at Strom Thurmond's Birthday Party," *Kennedy School of Government Case Program*, 2004, 7, http://web.archive.org/web/20040412233307/http://www.ksg.harvard.edu/presspol/Research_Publications/Case_Studies/1731_0.pdf.

58. Ibid., 11.

59. Thomas Edsall, *The New Politics of Inequality* (New York: W. W. Norton, 1989); Thomas Edsall and Mary Edsall, *Chain Reaction: The Impact of Race, Rights, and Taxes on American Politics* (New York: W. W. Norton, 1992).

60. Timothy Cook, "The Future of the Institutional Media," in *Mediated Politics: Communication in the Future of Democracy*, ed. W. Lance Bennett and Robert Entman (Cambridge: Cambridge University Press, 2000), 182–202.

61. E. Scott, "'Big Media' Meets the 'Bloggers,'" 8.

62. Ibid., 10.

63. Ibid., 12.

64. Rodney Benson, "Bringing the Sociology of Media Back In," *Political Communication* 21, no. 3 (2004): 275–92, and Benson, "News Media as a 'Journalistic Field': What Bourdieu Adds to New Institutionalism and Vice Versa," *Political Communication* 23, no. 2 (2006): 187–202.

65. Pierre Bourdieu, *The Rules of Art* (Stanford: Stanford University Press, 1996), 225. Also see Adrienne Russell, "Digital Communication Networks and the Journalistic Field: The 2005 French Riots," *Critical Studies in Media Communication* 24, no. 4 (2007): 285–302, and Donald Matheson, "Weblogs and the Epistemology of the News: Some Trends in Online Journalism," *New Media & Society* 6, no. 4 (2004): 443–67.

66. "Atrios" is actually Duncan Black, a senior fellow at Media Matters for America. I refer to "Atrios" to maintain the spirit of pseudonymity struck in the early days of the blog *Eschaton*.

67. The public nature of blogging's interthreaded and intertextual trail of permalinks allows critics the unique luxury of being able to track the development of specific arguments back over time. My account is not exhaustive, as the rhetorical activity of these bloggers far outpaces the ability to capture each minute detail. This account does, though, identify the major public arguments from the blogosphere that eventually undermined public support for Lott.

68. As Pierre Levy speculates in the context of internetworked communication, "unanswered questions will create tension . . . indicating regions where invention and innovation are required." See Levy, *Collective Intelligence: Mankind's Emerging World in Cyberspace*, trans. Robert Bononno (1994; repr., New York: Basic Books, 1997), 217.

69. By identifying the time that these bloggers posted, I am also illustrating a substantial acceleration of public argument. For modern social imaginaries, the printed date right below the masthead was the "most significant emblem" on the newspaper, providing clear daily punctuation for public deliberation; see B. Anderson, *Imagined Communities*, 33. Timestamps, which mark the hour and minute on blog posts, are similarly significant in showing the accelerated cycle of public deliberation in a networked media ecology.

70. Atrios, "Trent Lott," *Eschaton* (blog), December 6, 2002, 1:21 P.M., http://atrios.blogspot.com/2002_12_01_archive.html#90022436. Demonstrating their flexibility, blogs often notify readers of updates to the a post by capitalizing UPDATE at the bottom of the post and appending, correcting, or amplifying additional commentary to the initial post, rather than deleting or revising the post entirely.

71. Tim Noah, "Blurted Out Conviction of the Week: Trent Lott; What's a Little Segregationism Among Friends?," *Slate*, December 6, 2002, 1:54 P.M. (PT), http://web.archive.org/web/20021230101827/http://slate.msn.com/?id=2075151.

72. Atrios, "Here Is What Senator," *Eschaton*, December 6, 2002, 6:02 P.M., http://www.eschatonblog.com/2002/12/here-is-what-senator-lott-was-proud-of.html.

73. See Stephen Toulmin, *The Uses of Argument* (Cambridge: Cambridge University Press, 1958), and Giandomenico Majone, *Evidence, Argument, and Persuasion in the Policy Process* (New Haven: Yale University Press, 1989).

74. Benkler, *Wealth of Networks*, 218.

75. Alexander Halavais, "Scholarly Blogging: Moving Towards the Visible College," in Bruns and Jacobs, *Uses of Blogs*, 119.

76. See Robert Merton, *On Social Structure and Science*, ed. Piotr Sztompka (Chicago: University of Chicago Press, 1996), 51; originally published in "Three Fragments from a Sociologist's Notebook," *Annual Review of Sociology* 13 (1987): 6–10.

77. Josh Marshall, "I've Always Thought That . . . ," *Talking Points Memo* (blog), December 6, 2002, 3:20 P.M., https://web.archive.org/web/20120223224726/http://talkingpointsmemo.com/archives/000451.php.

78. Josh Marshall, "Hard-Hitting Coverage?," *Talking Points Memo*, December 7, 2002, 5:55 A.M., https://web.archive.org/web/20121112145749/http://talkingpointsmemo.com/archives/000450.php.

79. Atrios, "I Love Being Right!," *Eschaton*, December 7, 2002, 11:23 A.M., http://atrios.blogspot.com/2002_12_01_archive.html#90025159.

80. Axel Bruns, *Gatewatching: Collaborative Online News Production* (New York: Peter Lang, 2005).

81. Arthur S. Hayes, *Press Critics Are the Fifth Estate: Media Watchdogs in America* (Westport, Conn.: Praeger, 2008).

82. Glenn Reynolds, "Trent Lott Deserves the Shit," *Instapundit* (blog), December 6, 2002, 9:15 P.M., http://www.instapundit.com/archives/005985.php#005985/.

83. Glenn Reynolds, "Flood the Zone!," *Instapundit*, December 8, 2002, 8:41 A.M., http://instapundit.com/archives/006007.php.

84. Glenn Reynolds, "Geitner Simmons Has More," *Instapundit*, December 8, 2002, 10:55 A.M., http://instapundit.com/archives/006008.php.

85. Glenn Reynolds, "Of Course, It's Not as Simple," *Instapundit*, December 8, 2002, 11:07 A.M., http://instapundit.com/archives/006009.php.

86. Glenn Reynolds, "The Center for the Advancement of Capitalism," *Instapundit*, December 8, 2002, 11:10 A.M., http://instapundit.com/archives/006010.php.

87. See Glenn Reynolds, "Flood the Zone!," *Instapundit*, December 12, 2002, 3:00 P.M., http://instapundit.com/archives/006127.php; "Flood the Zone!," *Instapundit*, December 16, 2002, 3:06 P.M., http://instapundit.com/archives/006183.php; and "Flood the Zone!," *Instapundit*, December 16, 2002, 11:02 P.M., http://instapundit.com/archives/006190.php.

88. E. Scott, "'Big Media' Meets the 'Bloggers,'" 13. Marshall's "hitting it" (sometimes a sexual metaphor) arguably betrays masculinist inclinations. While the relationship between masculinity and maleness is often complicated, it is not insignificant that the three bloggers here all self-identify as men. Although flooding the zone as a strategy might be grounded in masculine argumentation styles that prefer overwhelming argumentative foes with the sheer *quantity* of postings, my interpretation of it emphasizes how that strategy at least occasionally improves the *quality* of deliberation.

89. Glenn Reynolds, "Christopher Johnson at the *Midwest Conservative Journal* Thinks Trent Lott Should Step Down," *Instapundit*, December 8, 2002, 3:39 P.M., http://instapundit.com/archives/006016.php.

90. Jack Shafer, "The Tao of Bear: The Paul 'Bear' Bryant Lessons on Leadership Howell Raines Failed to Absorb," *Slate*, May 16, 2003, http://www.slate.com/id/2083025/.

91. Alexandra Marks, "*New York Times* Resignations Signal Industry Turmoil," *Christian Science Monitor*, June 6, 2003, http://www.csmonitor.com/2003/0606/p04s01-ussc.html.

92. Quoted in Ken Auletta, "The Howell Doctrine," *The New Yorker*, June 10, 2002, available at http://www.kenauletta.com/howelldoctrine.html. In this interview, Raines attributes the phrase to then deputy managing editor John Geddes. The phrase is most intimately associated with Raines, however.

93. Shafer, "The Tao of Bear."

94. This is especially true in the case of large "data dumps" by organizations like WikiLeaks. Reporters working in small teams could only slowly work their way through millions of documents, but bloggers can coordinate thousands of their readers to filter through these documents systematically.

95. Marcin Lewiński, "Collective Argumentative Criticism in Informal Online Discussion Forums," *Argumentation and Advocacy* 47, no. 2 (2010): 86–107.

96. Personal communication, February 14, 2008.

97. Ibid.

98. Adam Schiffer, "Blogswarms and Press Norms: News Coverage of the Downing Street Memo Controversy," *Journalism and Mass Communication Quarterly* 83, no. 3 (2006): 494. See also Christina M. Smith and Kelly MacDonald, "The Arizona 9/11 Memorial: A Case Study in Public Dissent and Argumentation through Blogs," *Argumentation and Advocacy* 47, no. 2 (2010): 123–39.

99. Schiffer, "Blogswarms and Press Norms," 506.

100. Manuel Castells, *Communication Power* (Oxford: Oxford University Press, 2009), 247–48.

101. Lurking beyond this point about invention and deliberation, however, is a potentially more sinister ideological agenda. The term blogswarm tends to be used more by actors in the traditional press as a depiction of what happens when bloggers flock to a controversy. This construction casts the blogswarm as fundamentally simple: like bees to pollen, bloggers are facilely drawn to the sweet prize of attention. Since swarm intelligence diverges from the kind of cognitive capabilities humans usually valorize, the blogswarm metaphor does subtle ideological work on behalf of the institutional media by associating activity in the blogosphere with a lesser kind of intellectual work.

102. D. Travers Scott, "Tempests of the Blogosphere: Presidential Campaign Stories that Failed to Ignite Mainstream Media," in *Digital Media and Democracy: Tactics in Hard Times*, ed. Megan Boler (Cambridge, Mass.: MIT Press, 2008), 271–300.

103. Josh Marshall, "I Think that a . . . ," *Talking Points Memo*, December 9, 2002, 9:59 P.M., https://web.archive.org/web/20081012044657/http://talkingpointsmemo.com/archives/000485.php.

104. Josh Marshall, "As We Noted a Few Days Ago . . . ," *Talking Points Memo*, December 12, 2002, 3:38 P.M., https://web.archive.org/web/20080812190552/http://talkingpointsmemo.com/archives/000468.php.

105. Josh Marshall, *Talking Points Memo*, "As You Likely Now Know," *Talking Points Memo*, December 12, 2002, 1:10 A.M., https://web.archive.org/web/20080811121002/http://talkingpointsmemo.com/archives/000472.php.

106. Josh Marshall, "One of the Iconic Events . . . ," *Talking Points Memo*, December 12, 2002, 2:37 A.M., https://web.archive.org/web/20080812004326/http://talkingpointsmemo.com/archives/000471.php.

107. Josh Marshall, "And, of Course, There's . . . ," *Talking Points Memo*, December 11, 2002, 10:55 A.M., https://web.archive.org/web/20080809033323/http://talkingpointsmemo.com/archives/000477.php. Marshall linked to the decision in the legal database Findlaw, directly quoting a paragraph describing Lott's filing (see http://caselaw.lp.findlaw.com/scripts/getcase.pl?court=US&vol=461&invol=574).

108. Josh Marshall, "Is TPM Your Source . . . ," *Talking Points Memo*, December 11, 2002, 12:56 A.M., https://web.archive.org/web/20080809145459/http://talkingpointsmemo.com/archives/000476.php.

109. Trent Lott, "Brief of Congressman Trent Lott Amicus Curiae," submitted November 27, 1981. The original file is no longer hosted by TPM and was not archived by the Internet Archive, but is available at http://www.learningace.com/doc/4320598/0b189b09304541238ea60d570a5dd2cf/lott-bju-amicus-brief and on file with the author. This specific phrase circulated into the general media in the following two daily news cycles, receiving considerable play in the following newspaper articles: Susan Milligan, "Controversy over Lott's Remarks Intensifies," *Boston Globe*, December 12, 2002, LexisNexis; Carl Hulse, "Lott Apologizes

Again on Words About '48 Race," *New York Times*, December 12, 2002, LexisNexis; Times Wires, "As Lott Apologizes, '81 Filing Emerges," *St. Petersburg Times*, December 12, 2002, LexisNexis; Ana Radelat, "Lott Remarks Bring Scrutiny to His Ties to Segregationists," *USA Today*, December 12, 2002, LexisNexis; Dana Milbank and James Vandehei, "President Decries Lott's Comments: Bush Calls for Racial Fairness but Doesn't Call for Senator's Resignation," *Washington Post*, December 13, 2002, LexisNexis; James Kuhnhenn, "Lott's Ideology and Ties Are a Matter of Record," *Philadelphia Inquirer*, December 13, 2002, LexisNexis; Adam Nagourney and Carl Hulse, "Bush Rebukes Lott over Divisive Words," *New York Times*, December 13, 2002, LexisNexis; and Thomas Edsall and Darryl Fears, "Lott Has Moved Little on Civil Rights Issues: Analysts Say Remark, Record Consistent," *Washington Post*, December 13, 2002. The story also made the national magazine press; see Howard Fineman, "Ghosts of the Past," *Newsweek*, December 23, 2002, LexisNexis.

110. Atrios, "When I First Posted . . . ," *Eschaton*, December 13, 2002, 10:16 A.M., http://atrios.blogspot.com/2002_12_08_archive.html#90048556.

111. Atrios, "Some People Have Quibbled . . . ," *Eschaton*, December 14, 2002, 7:48 A.M., http://atrios.blogspot.com/2002_12_08_archive.html#90051916.

112. Nathan Crick identifies this process as the press satisfying "its signaling function by turning its spotlight on what occurs in the blogosphere"; see his "The Search for a Purveyor of News: The Dewey/Lippmann Debate in an Internet Age," *Critical Studies in Media Communication* 26, no. 5 (2009): 487. Crick's observation about how the critical capacity of blogs is stunted by being "locked within the ideology of corporate liberalism" (486) because of their reliance on advertising is both too broad a generalization, as many blogs even today reject advertising, and not as applicable to the early blogosphere, which largely did not feature advertisements.

113. John Solomon, "Lott Expresses Regret for Remarks; Court Filing from 1981 Surfaces," Associated Press, December 11, 2002, LexisNexis.

114. Josh Marshall, "One Other Thing . . . ," *Talking Points Memo*, December 11, 2002, 8:47 P.M., http://talkingpointsmemo.com/archives/000473.php.

115. See Henry Farrell, "Norms and Networks," *Crooked Timber* (blog), May 30, 2006, http://crookedtimber.org/2006/05/30/norms-and-networks/.

116. See Thomas Gieryn's "Boundary-Work and the Demarcation of Science from Nonscience: Strains and Interests in Professional Ideologies of Scientists," *American Sociological Review* 48, no. 6 (1983): 781–95. Gieryn investigates how professional scientists cultivate a rhetorical style that attributes certain desirable characteristics to an in-group by virtue of their belonging to the broader institution of science. Professionally trained journalists, too, identify their own work with the broader credentialing institutions of journalism to demarcate their activities from those of bloggers; see Wilson Lowrey, "Mapping the Journalism-Blogging Relationship," *Journalism* 7, no. 4 (2006): 477–500; David Domingo and Ari Heinonen, "Weblogs and Journalism: A Typology to Explore the Blurring Boundaries," *Nordicom Review* 29, no. 1 (2008): 3–15.

117. John Jordan, "Disciplining the Virtual Home Front: Mainstream News and the Web During the War in Iraq," *Communication and Critical/Cultural Studies* 4, no. 3 (2007): 287–93.

118. Kurt Anderson, "Premodern America," *New York*, March 2, 2005, http://nymag.com/nymetro/news/columns/imperialcity/11465/.

119. This symbiosis is marked by articles like J. D. Lasica, "Blogs and Journalism Need Each Other," *Nieman Reports*, Fall 2003, 70–74, and Jay Rosen, "Bloggers vs. Journalists Is Over," *PressThink* (blog), January 21, 2005, https://web.archive.org/web/20131127010932/http://archive.pressthink.org/2005/01/21/berk_essy.html.

120. Glenn Greenwald, "CNN's John King Responds," *Salon*, January 16, 2008, 4:01 A.M., http://www.salon.com/2008/01/16/king_5/.

121. As disclosed by Trent Lott in *Herding Cats*, 253.

122. Paul Krugman, "The Other Face," *New York Times*, December 13, 2002, LexisNexis.

123. John Podhoretz, "The Internet's First Scalp," *New York Post*, December 13, 2002, LexisNexis. Podhoretz draws the parallel to another "key moment in media history": when Rush Limbaugh, in 1991, broke the story about the no-interest bank utilized by members of the House of Representatives. Limbaugh regularly pushed the story on his radio show, eventually gaining national prominence and turning AM talk radio into a powerful force for populist communication.

124. Arianna Huffington, "Vox Populi Is Heard at Full Volume," *Cleveland Plain Dealer*, December 22, 2002, H5, LexisNexis.

125. Cass Sunstein, *Infotopia: How Many Minds Produce Knowledge* (Oxford: Oxford University Press, 2006), 84.

126. In *Herding Cats*, 243–60. In Lott's acknowledgments for *Herding Cats*, he thanks his press secretary, Ron Bonjean, for "catching all the darts, daggers, and blogs thrown at me" during the Thurmond affair (302).

127. That bloggers were responsible for Trent Lott's downfall was a sentiment so strong that it migrated to the growing Iranian blogosphere. Pejman Yousefzadeh, in an article that expressed hope that the blogosphere would aid the liberalization of Iran, cites the Trent Lott case as a sign of the ability of blogging to effect change: "The Blogosphere has already influenced politics, culture, and society immeasurably. It was the first medium to understand the importance of Trent Lott's infelicitous comments at the 100th birthday of former Senator Strom Thurmond.... Let's hope the Blogosphere, and Iranian bloggers in particular, have the power to influence meaningful and effective change in Iranian culture and society." Quoted in Michael Keren, *Blogosphere: The New Political Arena* (New York: Rowman & Littlefield, 2006), 60.

128. Most recently in Jürgen Habermas, "Political Communication in Media Society: Does Democracy Still Enjoy an Epistemic Dimension? The Impact of Normative Theory on Empirical Research," *Communication Theory* 16, no. 4 (2006): 420.

129. Kathleen Fitzpatrick, "CommentPress: New (Social) Structures for New (Networked) Texts," *Journal of Electronic Publishing* 10, no. 3 (2007), doi:10.3998/3336451.0010.305.

130. Donald J. Kochan, "The Blogosphere and the New Pamphleteers," *Nexus Law Journal* 11 (2006), Chapman University Law Research Paper 08-02, http://papers.ssrn.com/sol3/papers.cfm?abstract_id=908631.

131. Habermas, *Between Facts and Norms*, 357.

132. Ibid..

133. Habermas (ibid., 356) borrows Bernhard Peters's sluicing metaphor (note the aqueous trope) to affirm that legitimacy relies on considered opinions flowing from the periphery to the core. Like the ancient Roman aqueducts, deliberation ushers vital nourishment from the margins toward the center. This linear model of deliberation may not fit all that well given the networked architecture of contemporary deliberation.

134. Ibid., 362.

135. Ibid., 358.

136. Ibid.

137. Ibid., 373.

138. Translated and quoted in Axel Bruns, "Habermas and/against the Internet," *Snurblog* (blog), February 18, 2007, http://snurb.info/node/621 (consulted April 2009).

139. Habermas, *Between Facts and Norms*, 358. The seeds of this claim are planted in Habermas's *Structural Transformation*. By the early eighteenth century, the bourgeois public sphere was facing its own kind of information overload: there was so much oral communication in the coffeehouses and salons, *and* so much printed criticism, that keeping track of it all became a full-time job. The professional art critic thus arose to organize disparate lay judgments in the more formally institutionalized contexts of dedicated periodicals (ibid., 41.) The art critic was perceived as further along in the process of enlightenment, and so could educate others, though the critic had to be reflexive enough to acknowledge that their own insights could be corrected or improved by the arguments of others (ibid., 259n32).

140. See Shirky, "Power Laws, Weblogs, and Inequality." Matthew Hindman similarly argues that the "googlearchy" undermines the democratic pretensions of the blogosphere and networked media more generally; see Hindman, *The Myth of Digital Democracy* (Princeton: Princeton University Press, 2009).

141. As the blogosphere has matured, new kinds of filters function to organize and edit networked communication. Contra Habermas, the elevated reliance on algorithmic filtration makes the overorganization of public discourse a real risk. See R. Stuart Geiger, "Does Habermas Understand the Internet? The Algorithmic Construction of the Blogo/Public Sphere," *Gnovis* 10, no. 1 (2009): 1–29, http://gnovisjournal.org/2009/12/22/does-habermas-understand-internet-algorithmic-construction-blogopublic-sphere/.

142. Habermas, "Political Communication in Media Society," 423, emphasis in original.

143. Ibid., 423. Habermas's dismissal of blogs may reflect the weakness of the German blogosphere. One study of the German blogosphere estimated that in 2007, only 100,000 publicly accessible blogs were updated between May and June 2007; participation in blogging communities as an author or commenter is estimated at about a million, but most of these blogs are not oriented around civic affairs. See Jan Schmidt, "Blogging Practices in the German-Speaking Blogosphere: Findings from the 'Wie Ich Blogge?!' Survey," New Communication Media Research Centre Working Paper 07–02 (June 2007), https://www.uni-bamberg.de/fileadmin/uni/fakultaeten/split_professuren/journalistik/Fonk/pdfs-Veroeffentlichungen/Blogging_practices.pdf. Perhaps the strong press tradition in Germany partially obviates the need for a robust blogosphere; in any event, Habermas (and theorists more generally) ought to be careful in extrapolating global blogging norms based on national blogging practice.

144. Robert Glenn Howard, "The Vernacular Web of Participatory Media," *Critical Studies in Media Communication* 25, no. 5 (2008): 490–513. Habermas appears to interpret the "chat room" metaphor rather literally, envisioning a series of rooms closed off from each other; the network or web metaphor better captures the range of dynamic and interconnected practices without falling into the spatialization trap. However, if chat rooms are perceived as the primary deliberative feature of the internet, Habermas's frustration about their inability to contribute to public deliberation is more reasonable. Harry Weger and Mark Aakhus, in "Arguing in Internet Chat Rooms: Argumentative Adaptations to Chat Room Design and Some Consequences for Public Deliberation at a Distance," *Argumentation and Advocacy* 40, no. 1 (2003): 23–38, identify some key design flaws that frustrate public argument in chat rooms. First, they note that conversational coherence is difficult to maintain, with a scrolling transcript hosting multiple threads all on the same screen (27). Contrast this with the tendency of blogs to focus on a single theme per post. Their study examines how chat rooms, by limiting the number of characters a contributor can post at a single time, result in severely underdeveloped arguments (29). Blogs are (virtually) unlimited in the amount of text that can be posted, while also enabling images, audio, and video clips. Finally, they detail how flaming—the use of *ad hominem* attacks—undermines the civil community needed to advance public deliberation (31). Blogging might not fare better than chat rooms on this count, though that is an issue I leave to further empirical work.

145. Bimber, *Information and American Democracy*, and Peter Muhlberger, "Testing Cyber-realism," in *Democracy Online: The Prospects for Political Renewal Through the Internet*, ed. Peter Shane (New York: Routledge, 2004), 225–38.

146. Bruns, "Habermas and/against the Internet," para. 6.

147. Benkler, *Wealth of Networks*, 256.

148. To borrow Clay Shirky's term. See Shirky, *Here Comes Everybody: The Power of Organizing Without Organizations* (New York: Penguin, 2008).

149. Outhwaite, *Habermas: A Critical Introduction* (Cambridge: Polity Press, 2009), 32. Outhwaite is correct that this distinction plays a large role in *Between Facts and Norms*, but Habermas simply takes it for granted rather than explicitly defending it. Habermas's other work does not dwell on the distinction either, except for a short sentence in *Philosophical Discourses of Modernity*, where he claims that "the researcher, the context of discovery, and

the context of justification are so entwined with one another that they have to be separated procedurally." See *Philosophical Discourses of Modernity: Twelve Lectures*, trans. Frederick G. Lawrence (Cambridge, Mass.: MIT Press, 1990), 130. This would seem to suggest that Habermas was more attuned to the lack of distinction in earlier work, maintaining the distinction for sheerly analytical purposes. Unfortunately, the adoption of the distinction in his later political theory is too naïve to be useful.

150. Habermas, *Between Facts and Norms*, 307.

151. Paul Hoyningen-Huene, "Context of Discovery and Context of Justification," *Studies in the History and Philosophy of Science* 18, no. 4 (1986): 501–15. Hans Reichenbach and Rudolf Carnap were early proponents of the distinction, but the terms can be traced back at least to Kant's distinction between *quid juris* and *quid facti*. In light of that deeper intellectual heritage, it is perhaps less surprising that Habermas, as the most sophisticated contemporary extender of Kant, adopts the distinction as a meaningful one.

152. John Lyne, "Bio-rhetorics: Moralizing the Life Sciences," in *The Rhetorical Turn: Invention and Persuasion in the Conduct of Inquiry*, ed. Herbert W. Simons (Chicago: University of Chicago Press, 1990), 49.

153. That social problems are made rather than found is a condensation of Richard Vatz's rejoinder to Lloyd Bitzer's formulation of the exigence. For Bitzer, an exigence is "an imperfection marked by urgency"; see "The Rhetorical Situation," *Philosophy & Rhetoric* 1, no. 1 (1968): 6. In contrast to Bitzer's conceptualization of imperfections as objectively graspable, Vatz responded that exigencies are made salient through rhetoric. See Vatz's "Myth of the Rhetorical Situation," *Philosophy & Rhetoric* 6, no. 3 (1973): 154–61. In other words, rhetoric shapes how we attend to a phenomenon. The Bitzer-Vatz debate loosely maps onto the distinction between the context of discovery and the context of justification. Drawing on Bitzer, Nathan Crick and Joseph Gabriel support the distinction between discovery and justification in public scientific controversies; see "The Conduit Between Lifeworld and System: Habermas and the Rhetoric of Scientific Controversies," *Rhetoric Society Quarterly* 40, no. 3 (2010): 212–13. For them, the context of discovery is a discrete realm of sensual-aesthetic experience where citizens perceive "need interpretations" (a term drawn from Habermas, *Between Facts and Norms*, 308) more clearly before entering the context of justification represented by the larger public sphere of the press. Yet the very notion of "need *interpretation*" concedes that justification is not so neatly separated from discovery, as citizens inevitably assess their own needs with an eye toward the public case for them.

154. Habermas, *Between Facts and Norms*, 359.

155. Habermas, *Structural Transformation*, 175, 188. See Thomas Hove, "The Filter, the Alarm System, and the Sounding Board: Critical and Warning Functions of the Public Sphere," *Communication and Critical/Cultural Studies* 6, no. 1 (2009): 19–38.

156. Habermas, *Between Facts and Norms*, 365. Figuring citizens as endowed with antennae is evocative of Ezra Pound's quip that artists are the antennae of the human race, especially given Habermas's acknowledgment of how the languages of art, religion, and literature are uniquely able to articulate values and disclose worlds.

157. Hartmut Rosa, "Social Acceleration: Ethical and Political Consequences of a Desynchronized High-Speed Society," *Constellations* 10, no. 1 (2003): 3–33.

158. William E. Scheuerman, "Liberal Democracy and the Empire of Speed," *Polity* 34, no. 1 (2001): 41–67.

159. Ronald Greene, "Rhetorical Pedagogy as a Postal System: Circulating Subjects Through Michael Warner's 'Publics and Counterpublics,'" *Quarterly Journal of Speech* 88, no. 4 (2002): 437.

160. Thomas O. Sloane, *On the Contrary: The Protocol of Traditional Rhetoric* (Washington, D.C.: Catholic University Press, 1997), 30.

161. Lanham, *Economics of Attention*, 25.

162. Peter Simonson, *Refiguring Mass Communication: A History* (Urbana: University of Illinois Press, 2010), 26.

163. Sloane, *On the Contrary*, 65.

164. James Crosswhite, "Awakening the Topoi: Sources of Invention in *The New Rhetoric*'s Argument Model," *Argumentation and Advocacy* 44, no. 4 (2008): 177.

165. This musical instrument metaphor and the careful calibration between copiousness and concision that I am identifying is inspired by Ehninger's famous argument violin, a trope that recommends the fine-tuning of one's argumentative stance to adopt a standpoint between the neutralist and the naked persuader; see "Argument as Method: Its Nature, Its Limitations, and Its Uses," *Speech Monographs* 37, no. 2 (1970): 101–10. Also see Gordon R. Mitchell, "Higher-Order Strategic Maneuvering in Argumentation," *Argumentation* 24, no. 3 (2010): 319–35.

166. Lewis Friedland, Thomas Hove, and Hernando Rojas, "The Networked Public Sphere," *Javnost—The Public* 13 (2006): 18, emphasis in original.

167. Ibid., 19, emphasis in original.

168. John Dewey, *The Public and Its Problems* (1927; repr., Athens: Ohio University Press, 1954), 142.

169. Dennis Murphy and James White, "Propaganda: Can a Word Decide a War?," *Parameters* 37, no. 3 (2007): 23. The press excoriated the OSI for being a propaganda machine, eventually causing the office to be shut down—though Secretary of Defense Rumsfeld later noted that the same goals were simply being pursued under other auspices. See "Secretary Rumsfeld Media Availability En Route to Chile," U.S. Department of Defense News, November 18, 2002, http://www.defenselink.mil/transcripts/transcript.aspx?transcriptid=3296.

170. Torie Clark, *Lipstick on a Pig: Winning in the No-Spin Era by Someone Who Knows the Game* (New York: Free Press, 2006).

171. James Kinniburgh and Dorothy Denning, "Blogs and Military Information Strategy," *JSOU Report*, June 2006, 20. They recognize the dangers in this strategy: "Credibility is the heart and soul of influence operations. In these cases, extra care must be taken to ensure plausible deniability and nonattribution, as well as employing a well-thought-out deception operation that minimizes the risks of exposure. Because of the potential blowback effect, information strategy should avoid planting false information as much as possible" (21–22). See http://www.au.af.mil/info-ops/iosphere/iosphere_summer06_kinniburgh.pdf.

172. DoDLive, "Bloggers Roundtable," http://www.defenselink.mil/blogger/index.aspx. See also "Pentagon to Rework Public Relations Operation," *Washington Post*, October 31, 2006, http://www.washingtonpost.com/wp-dyn/content/article/2006/10/30/AR2006103001336.html

173. K. Daniel Glover, "Bloggers Proliferate on Campaign Payrolls," MSNBC, October 31, 2006, http://www.msnbc.msn.com/id/15498843/.

174. David Paul Kuhn, "Blogs: New Medium, Old Politics," CBS, December 8, 2004, http://www.cbsnews.com/stories/2004/12/08/politics/main659955.shtml.

175. David A. Craig, "Wal-Mart Public Relations in the Blogosphere," *Journal of Mass Media Ethics* 22, nos. 2–3 (2007): 215–28.

176. David All, "Five Essential Tips for the YouTube Campaign Trail," *David All Group Blog* (blog), June 10, 2007, https://web.archive.org/web/20070715082718/http://www.davidallgroup.com/2007/06/10/five-essential-tips-for-the-youtube-campaign-trail/.

177. Advantage Consultants, n.d. Retrieved September 11, 2009, from http://www.advantageconsultants.org; website no longer active but on file with the author.

178. Habermas, *Between Facts and Norms*, 364. Bloggers, by identifying orchestrated efforts to flood the zone, draw attention to the communicative infrastructure needed to sustain legitimation processes. This phenomenon confirms Habermas's thesis of the dual orientation of public sphere actors. This dual orientation involves efforts by civil society actors to "directly influence the political system" while "enlarging civil society and the public sphere as well as . . . confirming their own identities and capacities to act" (370.) Habermas derives this distinction from Jean Cohen and Andrew Arato's theory of social movements, which posits a movement between what they characterize as "defensive" identity-consolidating and "offensive" public-influencing functions; see their *Civil Society and Political Theory*

(Cambridge, Mass.: MIT Press, 1992), especially chapter 10, "Social Movements and Civil Society."

179. Barlow, *Rise of the Blogosphere*, 177.

Chapter 4

1. Rachel Simmons, "Cliques, Clicks, Bullies, and Blogs," *Washington Post*, September 28, 2003, LexisNexis.
2. Janet Kornblum, "Teens Wear Their Hearts on Their Blog," *USA Today*, October 31, 2005, LexisNexis.
3. Antony Loewenstein, "The Blogs of War Conquer a Wider World," *Sydney Morning Herald*, October 21, 2003, LexisNexis.
4. Mark Huffman, "'Blog' Trend Provides Virtual Soapbox,'" United Press International, January 18, 2003, LexisNexis.
5. David Gallagher, "A Site to Pour Out Emotions, and Just About Anything Else," *New York Times*, September 5, 2002, LexisNexis.
6. Alan Wolfe, "The New Pamphleteers," *New York Times*, July 11, 2004, LexisNexis.
7. Kelly Toughill, "'Citizen Journalism' Is Not News," *Toronto Star*, March 3, 2007, LexisNexis.
8. James Herbert, "Alternative Source for War News: Internet 'Blogs,'" *San Diego Union-Tribune*, March 20, 2003, LexisNexis.
9. "War Blogs," *Houston Chronicle*, March 27, 2003, LexisNexis.
10. David Kline, "I Blog, Therefore I Am," in *Blog! How the Newest Media Revolution Is Changing Politics, Business, and Culture*, ed. David Kline and Dan Burstein (New York: CDS Books, 2005), 249.
11. Henry Jenkins and David Thorburn, *Democracy and New Media* (Cambridge, Mass.: MIT Press, 2003), 2.
12. Roberts-Miller, "Parody Blogging and the Call of the Real," in Gurak et al., *Into the Blogosphere*, http://blog.lib.umn.edu/blogosphere/parody_blogging.html.
13. Salam Pax, *Where is Raed?*, http://www.dearraed.blogspot.com. Years later, Salam Pax revealed himself as Salam Abdulmunem, but I will refer to him pseudonymously. His original blog posts are now archived at http://salampax.wordpress.com/.
14. Matt Welch, "Blogworld and Its Gravity: The New Amateur Journalists Weigh In," *Columbia Journalism Review* 42, no. 5 (2003), http://web.archive.org/web/20040201212557/ http://www.cjr.org/issues/2003/5/blog-welch.asp.
15. Peter Thal Larsen, "Bloggers Take the War on Iraq on a Journey into Cyberspace," *Financial Times*, April 2, 2003, LexisNexis.
16. Michelle Delio, "Iraq Blog: Hubbub over a Headlock," *Wired*, March 26, 2003, http://www.wired.com/news/culture/0,1284,58206,00.html.
17. Welch, "Blogworld and Its Gravity."
18. Stanley Miller, "Words of War: Internet Journals Offer Glimpses From Iraq," *Milwaukee Journal-Sentinel*, April 1, 2003, LexisNexis.
19. Many other English-language bloggers followed in Salam Pax's wake. The most prominent of these is Riverbend, the pseudonym of a woman who blogged about life in Iraq from 2003 to 2007 (at http://riverbendblog.blogspot.com/). See Kristen McCauliff's study of Riverbend, "Blogging in Baghdad: The Practice of Collective Citizenship on the Blog *Baghdad Burning*," *Communication Studies* 62, no. 1 (2011): 58–73.
20. As reported by Leo Hickman, "Baghdad Calling," *The Guardian*, March 24, 2003, http://www.theguardian.com/environment/2003/mar/24/ethicalliving.iraq.
21. Nick Denton, "Salam," May 30, 2003, http://web.archive.org/web/20080516082141/ http://www.nickdenton.org/archives/005924.html#005924; Elizabeth Wynhausen, "Salam Pax Succumbs to Unbearable Weight of Blogging," *Australian*, May 20, 2004, 17; Peter Maass,

"How Do I Know Baghdad's Famous Blogger Exists? He Worked For Me," *Slate,* June 2, 2003, http://slate.msn.com/id/2083847/.

22. This is one way to read theorists like Walter Ong in *Orality and Literacy: The Technologizing of the Word* (New York: Methuen, 1982) and Eric Havelock in *The Muse Learns to Write: Reflections on Orality and Literacy from Antiquity to the Present* (New Haven: Yale University Press, 1986), who suggest that electronic media reintroduce features of speech associated with emotional expressivity into modes of electronic writing and, by extension, into digital composition.

23. The stereotype of the pajama-clad, parent's-basement-dwelling blogger is a persistent one. Sarah Palin, the 2008 Republican vice-presidential nominee, explained that most of the criticism of her during the campaign was fueled by "those bloggers in their parents' basement just talkin' garbage." See Julie Bosman, "Palin Defends Herself in Fox Interview," *The Caucus* (blog), *New York Times,* November 10, 2008, http://thecaucus.blogs.nytimes.com/2008/11/10/palin-defends-herself-in-fox-interview/.

24. Two clever information-visualization art projects illustrate the dynamic range of affects present in the blogosphere. We Feel Fine, at wefeelfine.org, culled blogs in 2005 for descriptions of feeling-states. There are thousands of bubbles in the We Feel Fine applet that show almost every imaginable feeling; by clicking on the bubble, a snippet of blog text pops up with a fuller clipping of that emotion in context. The Dumpster, a similar project at http://artport.whitney.org/commissions/thedumpster/, scanned blogs that mentioned recent break-ups of romantic relationships and collected them in a similar fashion to demonstrate the different, swirling feelings that bloggers self-report.

25. See Hariman, *Political Style: The Artistry of Power* (Chicago: University of Chicago Press, 1995). If there are what Robert Hariman calls political styles, then, since tone is one constituent of style, presumably there are also political tones. Rhetoricians have not taken tone seriously, in part owing to the legacy of Peter Ramus, who consigned rhetoric (as I explain in chapter 3) to the study of "the vocal grace of tone." There are two recent exceptions. Roderick Hart, Jay Childers, and Colene Lind's *Political Tone: How Leaders Talk and Why* (Chicago: University of Chicago Press, 2013) excellently covers the multifaceted dimension of tone. However, in identifying tone as "a tool people use (sometimes unwittingly) to create distinct social impressions via word choice" (9), I believe they underplay the more ineffable elements of tone, described in Joshua Gunn's "On Speech and Public Release," *Rhetoric and Public Affairs* 13, no. 2 (2010): 175–216, that I try to account for in this chapter.

26. Raymond Williams describes the structure of feeling as the "felt sense of the quality of life at a particular place and time: a sense of the ways in which the particular activities combined into a way of thinking and living," in *The Long Revolution* (1961; repr., Peterborough, Ont.: Broadview Press, 2001), 63. The idea of a structure of feeling captures the emotional and affective investments of a social and rhetorical imaginary. That the modern social imaginary is built on a structure of feeling that restricts the play of emotion is confirmed by Robert Hariman and John Lucaites, who note that "modern civic order is based on muted affect—that is, on the containment of emotionality, and especially negative emotions, to private life and its institutions of family, church, clinic, and television." See their "Dissent and Emotional Management in a Liberal-Democratic Society: The Kent State Iconic Photograph," *Rhetoric Society Quarterly* 31, no. 3 (2001): 6. Examining the official doctrines, institutional histories, or documents of an era do not reveal structures of feeling. Instead, "unofficial" documentary media forms produced in more personal contexts better illustrate the dominant structure of feeling. As Jennifer Harding and Deirdre Pribram explain, "the constitution of feeling and its part in the creation of subjectivity within contemporary power relations can be traced through an examination of journals, diaries, and other forms of personal writing"; see Harding and Pribram, "The Power of Feeling: Locating Emotions in Culture," *European Journal of Cultural Studies* 5, no. 4 (2002): 421.

27. "Poetic imitation . . . waters and fosters these feelings when what we ought to do is dry them up." In Plato, *The Republic,* 606d; quoted from Plato, *The Republic,* vol. 2, trans. Paul Shorey (Cambridge, Mass.: Harvard University Press, 1935), 463.

28. Plato, *Plato in Twelve Volumes*, vol. 9, trans. Harold N. Fowler (Cambridge, Mass.: Harvard University Press, 1925), 253d.

29. Plato, *The Dialogues of Plato*, vol. 2, trans. Benjamin Jowett (New York: Scribner, Armstrong, 1873), 104, 58bB–592b.

30. Aristotle, *Rhetoric*, 1378a; trans. Kennedy, *On Rhetoric*, 121.

31. Daniel Gross, *The Secret History of Emotion: From Aristotle's "Rhetoric" to Modern Brain Science* (Chicago: University of Chicago Press, 2006), 3. See also W. W. Fortenbaugh, *Aristotle on Emotion* (1975; London: Duckworth, 2002).

32. Marlene Sokolon, *Political Emotions: Aristotle and the Symphony of Reason and Emotion* (DeKalb: Northern Illinois University Press, 2006), 13; quoting *Nicomachean Ethics*, 1119b.

33. Sokolon, *Political Emotions*, 19–20.

34. Aristotle, *Aristotle in 23 Volumes*, vol. 19, trans. H. Rackham (Cambridge, Mass.: Harvard University Press; London, William Heinemann, 1934), 1119b.

35. Marcus Tullius Cicero, *Cicero on the Emotions: Tusculan Disputations 3 & 4*, trans. Margaret Graver (Chicago: University of Chicago Press, 2002), 53.

36. The irony here is that Cicero hesitates to link emotion to sickness as he asserts the Greeks did, suggesting that he would use the more neutral "emotions" than "*pathe*." However, the sickness metaphor proceeds to structure even the subtitles of his treatise (*Tusculan Disputations*, 12.)

37. Thomas Dixon, *From Passions to Emotions* (Cambridge: Cambridge University Press, 2003), especially chapter 4, "The Scottish Creation of 'The Emotions': David Hume, Thomas Brown, Thomas Chalmers." Emotion became a more meaningful category of analysis as it was secularized and made an object of orderly inquiry. The emotions as we understand them, then, are products of the operating logic of modernity itself, whereas a more metaphysical and less tameable conceptualization of the passions previously held sway; see the edited collection by Stephen Gaukroger, *The Soft Underbelly of Reason: The Passions in the Seventeenth Century* (New York: Routledge, 1998), and Susan James, *Passion and Action: The Emotions in Seventeenth Century Philosophy* (Oxford: Oxford University Press, 1997).

38. Habermas, *Structural Transformation*, 47. The classicist Brendan Nagle describes the antecedent for this function of the modern public sphere: "*oikoi* were expected to internalize and reproduce in their own micro-environments the ideology that characterized the constitution or *politeia* of their individual cities." See Nagle, *The Household as the Foundation of Aristotle's Polis* (Cambridge: Cambridge University Press, 2006), 6.

39. Lauren Berlant, "Introduction," in *Intimacy*, ed. Lauren Berlant (Chicago: University of Chicago Press, 2000), 3.

40. Habermas, *Structural Transformation*, 48.

41. Ibid.

42. Ibid.

43. Ibid., 56. Habermas's great intellectual rival Peter Sloterdijk beautifully captures the split subjectivity of the modern bourgeois subject: "by day, colonizer, at night, colonized; by occupation, valorizer and administrator, during leisure time, valorized and administered; officially a cynical functionary, privately a sensitive soul; at the office a giver of orders, ideologically a discussant; outwardly a follower of the reality principle, inwardly a subject oriented toward pleasure; functionally an agent of capital, intentionally a democrat; with respect to the system a functionary of reification, with respect to the *Lebenswelt* (lifeworld), someone who achieves self-realization." See his *Critique of Cynical Reason*, trans. Michael Eldred (Minneapolis: University of Minnesota Press, 1987), 113.

44. As Albert Hirschmann's *The Passions and the Interests: Political Arguments for Capitalism Before Its Triumph* (1977; repr., Princeton: Princeton University Press, 1997) relates, modern political thinkers were interested in constraining the passions of the powerful because they were supposedly better endowed with them, a holdover from the Aristotelian notion that virtues were distributed unevenly (69–70).

45. Marie Fleming, "Women and the 'Public Use of Reason,'" *Social Theory and Practice* 19, no. 1 (1993): 42. Critics like Nancy Fraser explain that the traditional modern division of

public and private that were so central to bourgeois self-conception (as described by Habermas) was erroneously conceived. The categories of public and private ultimately operated as ideological screens that consolidated male/masculine power. The private, intimate realm was not exclusively a realm of self-cultivation, interior development, cultural transmission, and social bond formation. It, like the public sphere, was rife with instrumentalities like money, power, sex, and violence. And the decisions made in the public sphere were not as objective, abstract, and impartial as they were promised to be. Decisions that were framed as for the common good actually served an interest, and these interests often consolidated privilege along gendered lines (among many other possible axes.) The very idea of citizenship is built on a masculine model that shed childrearing responsibilities and thus was capable of participating fully in a public designed with their needs in mind. See Fraser's *Unruly Practices: Power, Discourse, and Gender in Contemporary Social Theory* (Minneapolis: University of Minnesota Press, 1989), 119–28.

46. Megan Boler, *Feeling Power: Emotions and Education* (New York: Routledge, 1999).

47. See Schudson, *Discovering the News*, especially chapter 4, "Objectivity Becomes Ideology: Journalism After World War I."

48. Iris Marion Young provides a compelling critique of this impartiality: "The stances of detachment and dispassion that supposedly produce impartiality are attained only by abstracting from the particularities of situation, feeling, affiliation, and point of view. These particularities still operate, however, in the actual context of action." See Young, *Justice and the Politics of Difference* (Princeton: Princeton University Press, 1990), 97.

49. One of the few unifying themes for nearly all the new social movements is their problematization of the public-private dichotomy. Environmentalism is premised on the assumption that deleterious impacts on the public good accompany private (over)consumption. Similarly, the civil rights movement was grounded in an assumption that a democracy could not deny African Americans and others a voice in public affairs because of private biases.

50. See Carol Hanisch, "The Personal Is Political," in *Notes from the Second Year: Women's Liberation*, ed. Shulamith Firestone and Ann Koedt (New York: Notes from the Second Year Press, 1970), 76–78. Consciousness-raising sessions were efforts to recognize serial links between women's suffering from inequities largely felt in private but resulting from decisions made in public. From wage gaps to domestic violence to unfair educational practices, what earlier generations perceived as "private issues" were politicized and made properly "public."

51. In addition to these cultural changes, economic changes further complicate the historical relationship between public, private, and intimate. The notion of the "home office" illustrates the new haziness between private (economic relations) and intimate (conjugal relations). The home office is an architectural evolution on par with the shift from the centrally located courtyard of premodern times to the backyards of the modern era, which aided the creation of the bourgeois intimate sphere. See Habermas, *Structural Transformation*, 45.

52. Kris Cohen, "A Welcome for Blogs," *Continuum: Journal of Media and Culture Studies* 20, no. 2 (2006): 166.

53. Antony Loewenstein, "Bloggers of the World, Unite," *Sydney Morning Herald*, January 20, 2007, LexisNexis.

54. Robert Hariman and John Lucaites, *No Caption Needed: Iconic Photographs, Public Culture, and Liberal Democracy* (Chicago: University of Chicago Press, 2007), 14. Institutional news media do represent voices through firsthand observers, experts, public intellectuals, opinion writers, and "persons on the street" interviews. Yet the amplification of these voices usually functions merely as a hook or as part of a point-counterpoint with competing voices, thus folding personal reflections back into the objective, dispassionate norms of the institutional media.

55. This coheres with Diane Mutz's conclusions in *Hearing the Other Side: Deliberative Versus Participatory Democracy* (Cambridge: Cambridge University Press, 2006) that

hearing multiperspectival accounts of political controversies stunts political participation, whereas partisan communication networks motivate participation in collective action.

56. Sloterdijk, *Critique of Cynical Reason*, 104–5.

57. Ibid., 101.

58. Theodore Windt, *Presidents and Protesters: Political Rhetoric in the 1960s* (Tuscaloosa: University of Alabama Press, 1990).

59. See Jürgen Habermas, "New Social Movements," *Telos* 49 (Fall 1981): 33–37, and Iris Marion Young, "Social Movements and the Politics of Difference," in her *Justice and the Politics of Difference*, 156–91.

60. Lovink, *Zero Comments: Blogging and Critical Internet Culture* (New York: Routledge, 2007), ix; further references to this work will appear parenthetically in the text. Here Lovink is quoting blogger Randi Mooney, "Zero Comments," *Stodge.org* (blog), May 5, 2005, http://blog.stodge.org/199. The irony of Lovink's tendency to cite bloggers speaks for itself. It is difficult to gauge how serious Mooney is being, for the blog post from which this quote is drawn features his drawing up plans for a business that paid people to comment on others' blogs to prevent the terrible feeling associated with seeing "0 Comments" underneath a blog post.

61. Lovink does concede that blogging "appeals to a wide register of emotions and affects as it mobilizes and legitimizes the personal" (3). However, cynicism is the dominant register. Lovink appears to recognize that the greater emotional range of blogging differentiates it from the institutional mass media, but because those emotions valorize the personal, as opposed to the public, he figures them as problematic.

62. See Ronald Pelias, "The Critical Life," *Communication Education* 49, no. 3 (2000): 220–28, for this connection as part of academic life.

63. Fred Turner, *From Counterculture to Cyberculture: Stewart Brand, the Whole Earth Network, and the Rise of Digital Utopianism* (Chicago: University of Chicago Press, 2008).

64. Robert Scoble and Shel Israel, *Naked Conversations: How Blogs Are Changing the Way Businesses Are Talking to Customers* (Hoboken, N.J.: John Wiley & Sons, 2006).

65. Lovink's deployment of the term "aura" obviously registers Walter Benjamin's famous essay "The Work of Art in an Age of Mechanical Reproduction," which hypothesizes that mass-produced prints lack the same aura as the original oil painting. Lovink's concern about the fading of the aura of the mass media speaks more to the fungibility of the idea of aura than to its actuality: aura is in the eye of the beholder, and critics adhering to an older sensibility usually perceive the aura surrounding their preferred medium being threatened by the new. For Paddy Scannell's compelling interpretation of the loss of aura as an opening for radical democracy, see Paddy Scannell, "Benjamin Contextualized: On 'The Work of Art in an Age of Mechanical Reproduction,'" in *Canonic Texts in Media Research: Are There Any? Should There Be? How About These?*, ed. Elihu Katz, John Durham Peters, Tamar Liebes, and Avril Orloff (Cambridge: Polity Press, 2003), 74–89.

66. John Durham Peters, in chapter 1 of *Speaking into the Air: A History of the Idea of Communication* (Chicago: University of Chicago Press, 2001), dismantles the historical preference for face-to-face dialogue by probing the democratic potential of dissemination.

67. Theodore Windt, "The Diatribe: Last Resort for Protest," *Quarterly Journal of Speech* 58, no. 1 (1972): 7.

68. Ibid., 7–8.

69. Salam Pax, *Salam Pax: The Clandestine Diary of an Ordinary Iraqi* (New York: Grove Press, 2003), 119.

70. Ibid., 119, emphasis in original.

71. Ibid., 113.

72. Ibid., 119.

73. Ibid., 120.

74. Windt, "Diatribe," 8.

75. Pax, *Clandestine*, 120.

76. Lovink, *Zero Comments*, 35.
77. James J. Brown Jr., "Louis C. K.'s 'Weird Ethic': *Kairos* and Rhetoric in the Network," *Present Tense: A Journal of Rhetoric in Society* 3, no. 1 (2013), http://www.presenttensejournal.org/volume-3/louie-c-k-s-weird-ethic-kairos-and-rhetoric-in-the-network/.
78. Pax, *Clandestine*, 120.
79. Ibid., 120.
80. Ibid., 121.
81. Windt, "Diatribe," 4.
82. John Durham Peters prescribes cynicism thusly: "cynicism in the life world is bad, but healthy in the realm of the system," cohering with the traditional cynical impulse to approach institutions (be they formal or informal) with a degree of cheekiness. See Peters, *Courting the Abyss: Free Speech and the Liberal Tradition* (Chicago: University of Chicago Press, 2005), 292, and esp. 275–79.
83. Pax, *Clandestine*, 121.
84. Ibid., 121.
85. Ibid., 121–22.
86. Windt, "Diatribe," 8–9.
87. Ibid., 8.
88. Sloterdijk, *Critique of Cynical Reason*, 103.
89. Sam Leith, "'I Saw Both Sides of the War': A Young Iraqi's Internet Diary Became One of the Most Widely Read Sites on the Web," *Daily Telegraph*, 10 September 2003, 17.
90. Murray Whyte, "Where Is Salam Pax?," *Toronto Star*, 4 April 2003, A10.
91. James Norman, "International Internet Sensation Ready to Get Back to His Day Job," *The Age (Melbourne)*, May 22, 2004, LexisNexis.
92. Bret Stevens, "A War in Three Takes," *Jerusalem Post*, October 10, 2003, LexisNexis.
93. Stanley Millar, "Words of War: Internet Journals Offer Glimpses from Iraq," *Milwaukee Journal Sentinel*, April 1, 2003, LexisNexis.
94. Kali Pearson, "Internet Is Buzzing with Pro- and Anti-War Voices," *The Gazette*, April 8, 2003, LexisNexis.
95. Leo Hickman, "War in the Gulf," *The Guardian*, March 24, 2003, LexisNexis.
96. Alex Massie, "Baghdad Blogger Returns to the Web," *The Scotsman*, May 8, 2003, LexisNexis.
97. Christina Lamb, "'War Sucks Big Time," *Sunday Times (London)*, September 28, 2003, LexisNexis.
98. Barbara Biesecker's "No Time for Mourning: The Rhetorical Production of the Melancholic Citizen-Subject in the War on Terror," *Rhetoric and Public Affairs* 40, no. 1 (2007): 147–69, argues that melancholic rhetoric encourages citizens to cede their agency to the state by invoking the specter of a phantasmagoric disaster to come. Though I find psychoanalytic approaches to melancholy provocative, I assume that one can interpret melancholy without resorting to psychoanalytic accounts—it was, after all, a theorized emotional state that predates Freud and Lacan.
99. The eighteenth- and nineteenth-century Romantics could be to melancholy what the Cynics were to cynicism, but, given their emphasis on feeling in general, theirs is too broad a movement to identify so closely with the single feeling of melancholy.
100. See "Brilliance and Melancholy" in *The Nature of Melancholy: From Aristotle to Kristeva*, ed. Jennifer Radden (Oxford: Oxford University Press, 2000), 57; originally in *Problemata Physica*, 953a10–14.
101. Peter Kramer, "The Valorization of Sadness: Alienation and the Melancholic Temperament," *Hastings Center Report* 30, no. 2 (2000): 15.
102. Emily Brady and Arto Haapala, "Melancholy as an Aesthetic Emotion," *Contemporary Aesthetics* 1 (December 2003), http://www.contempaesthetics.org/newvolume/pages/article.php?articleID=214.
103. A healthy regard for the reflectiveness that sometimes marks melancholy seems a precondition for the rise of the concept of interiority in Habermas's description of the

bourgeois public sphere. The world of letters, with its sluggish circulatory matrix, encouraged the bourgeois to reflect (sometimes, no doubt, to a fault) on a social phenomenon at a remove from the happening itself. The retreat into solitude—in nature, in a study, in a library—was often rationalized as a melancholic retreat from the hustle-bustle to achieve some critical purchase on a quickly changing public culture.

104. Max Pensky, *Melancholy Dialectics: Walter Benjamin and the Play of Mourning* (Amherst: University of Massachusetts Press, 1993), 19.

105. Ibid., 21.

106. José Muñoz, "Photographies of Mourning: Melancholia and Ambivalence in Van Der Zee, Mapplethorpe, and *Looking for Langston*," in *Race and the Subject of Masculinities*, ed. Harry Stecopoulos and Michael Uebel (Durham: Duke University Press, 1997), 355–56. Muñoz is writing in the context of how melancholy functions for communities of people of color, lesbians, and gays by reading how the play of mourning in aesthetic forms offers opportunities for identification and community building. His critique of Freud's implicit heterosexism and overly teleological conception of the play of mourning/melancholy is particularly insightful. Salam Pax's blogging could be seen as an artful expression of queer melancholy. Although one does not need to be gay to express queer melancholy, Salam did not hide his sexuality and press accounts often reported on his gay identity as part of their coverage of the *Where is Raed?* blog.

107. As Kenneth Burke theorized the role of art, the "artist shows his [sic] respect for the subject, not by laying a wreath at its feet, but by the fullness of his preoccupation with it. The soundness of his concerns will be manifested either in exceptional variety or in exceptional accurateness." See *Counter-Statement*, 170.

108. Pensky, *Melancholy Dialectics*, 21.

109. Sigmund Freud, "Mourning and Melancholia," in *The Standard Edition of the Complete Psychological Works of Sigmund Freud*, vol. 14, *1914–1916*, trans. and ed. James Strachey (London: Hogarth Press, 1957), 243.

110. Ibid., 244.

111. Keren, *Blogosphere*, 7; further references to this work will appear parenthetically in the text. See also Vivian Serfaty, *The Mirror and the Veil: An Overview of American Online Diaries and Blogs* (Amsterdam: Rodopi, 2004) for further connections between life writing and blogging.

112. Quoting Rebecca Comay, "Perverse History: Fetishism and Dialectic in Walter Benjamin," *Research in Phenomenology* 29, no. 1 (1999): 51.

113. Quoting Sigmund Freud, "Mourning and Melancholia," in *Collected Papers*, trans. Joan Riviere (London: Hogarth Press, 1971), 157.

114. Keren's political commitments are becoming more clear: here, he identifies the unified liberal subject as the precursor to a normative political environment that activates political engagement. This is a strikingly outdated formulation, given the critique of the unified subject by Foucault and the decline in the ability of grand narratives to ground political commitments described by Lyotard. This *topos* of new media threatening the individual acting subject recalls Habermas's conclusion that bourgeois "interiority was hollowed out by mass media" (*Structural Transformation*, 162).

115. The cover of *Blogosphere: The New Political Arena* quite explicitly makes this latter point, as it is dominated by the figure of an alien with stereotypical oblong head, oval eyes, pallid skin tone, and long fingers hammering away at a keyboard. Bloggers are instantly "otherized" as alien figures resting outside of Keren's preferred realm of the political.

116. Since Salam Pax's ire is directed toward the conditions of war, I situate his blogging in the trajectory of ritual laments of war. However, lamentation is part of a larger category of *plaints*. Kenneth Burke categorized the plaint as a tragic frame of rejection, where "one seeks to develop tolerance to the possibilities of great misfortune by accustoming himself [sic] to misfortune in small doses, administered stylistically," in *Attitudes Toward History*, 44–45. When under the "spell" of the elegiac plaint, "one does not tend to size up his own resources accurately . . . it really *spreads* the disproportion between the weakness of the self and the

magnitude of the situation" (44). Melancholics perceive oppressive structures as so much grander than their own little solitary being, which produces pessimism and passivity in the face of injustice. It is possible to see Salam Pax as traveling the road from the tragic plaint to the comic, as does Kenneth Burke's protagonist in his lone novel *Towards a Better Life;* see Krista K. Betts Van Dyk, "From the Plaint to the Comic: Kenneth Burke's *Towards a Better Life,*" *Rhetoric Society Quarterly* 36, no. 1 (2006): 31–53.

117. Margaret Alexiou, *The Ritual Lament in Greek Tradition* (Cambridge: Cambridge University Press, 1974).

118. Pax, *Clandestine,* 12.

119. Ibid., 35.

120. Ibid., 38.

121. Ann Suter, "Introduction," in *Lament: Studies in the Ancient Mediterranean and Beyond,* ed. Ann Suter (Oxford: Oxford University Press, 2008), 4.

122. Jim Hall, "The First Web War: 'Bad Things Happen in Unimportant Places,'" *Journalism Studies* 1, no. 3 (2000): 397.

123. Ibid., 398.

124. Linda Austin, "The Lament and the Rhetoric of the Sublime," *Nineteenth Century Literature* 53, no. 3 (1998): 280.

125. Pax, *Clandestine,* 22–23.

126. Ibid., 49. Unfortunately, there are no longer any archived comments on Salam Pax's blog; there were originally comments, but Salam Pax either disabled them or erased them shortly after the blog became popular.

127. Pax, *Clandestine,* 49.

128. Alexiou, *Ritual Lament,* 185.

129. Ibid., 187–205.

130. This extends Richard McKeon's observation that "whereas the rhetoric of the Romans took its commonplaces from the fine arts and literature, our rhetoric finds its commonplaces in the technology of commercial advertising and of calculating machines." See McKeon, *Rhetoric,* 34. Also see Burke, *Rhetoric of Motives,* 62–63, on "timely topics."

131. Pax, *Clandestine,* 9.

132. Salam's confessed obsession with music fits quite naturally with the traditional treatment for melancholy, as the author of *Problemata Physica* prescribed music as the essential cure for melancholy.

133. Steven Himmer, "The Labyrinth Unbound: Weblogs as Literature," in Gurak et al., *Into the Blogosphere,* http://blog.lib.umn.edu/blogosphere/labyrinth_unbound.html.

134. Coldplay, "Politik," *A Rush of Blood to the Head,* Capitol Records, B000069AUI, CD, 2002.

135. Lovink, *Zero Comments,* 36.

136. Helen Popkin, "What Exactly Is 'Emo,' Anyway?," MSNBC.com, March 26, 2006, http://www.today.com/id/11720603#.UzQxluvbaLw.

137. Tammy La Gorce, "Finding Emo," *New York Times,* August 14, 2005, http://www.nytimes.com/2005/08/14/nyregion/nyregionspecial2/14njCOVER.html?pagewanted=all.

138. Pax, *Clandestine,* 129.

139. Ibid., 133.

140. Ibid., 129.

141. Ibid., 135.

142. Ibid., 142.

143. Ibid., 163–64.

144. Salam Pax began writing a regular column for *The Guardian* and has started and stopped several blogs in the wake of *Where is Raed?*.

145. Natasha Walter, "The Victor of the News Has Been the Internet," *The Independent (London),* 10 April 2003, 13.

146. Gareth Evans, "The Baghdad Blog," *Time Out,* October 8, 2003, LexisNexis.

147. Welch, "Blogworld and Its Gravity."

148. Samela Harris, "Salam Pax: The Voice of Baghdad," *The Advertiser*, May 22, 2004, LexisNexis.

149. Steven Levy, "Random Access Online: Bloggers' Delight," *Newsweek*, March 28, 2003, LexisNexis.

150. J. Hall, "First Web War," 394.

151. Howard Kurtz, "'Webloggers,' Signing on as War Correspondents," *Washington Post*, March 23, 2003, LexisNexis.

152. Kaye Trammell and Ana Keshelashvili suggest that blogging's ability to reveal the "back stage" of relationships and thought processes is a crucial element of the blogosphere; see their "Examining the New Influencers: A Self-Presentation Study of A-List Blogs," *Journalism and Mass Communication Quarterly* 82, no. 4 (2005): 968–92. Janet Alexanian makes a similar point about the intersections of publicity and intimacy in her "Publicly Intimate Online: Iranian Web Logs in Southern California," *Comparative Studies of South Asia, Africa, and the Middle East* 26, no. 1 (2006): 134–45.

153. The observations of this case study intersect with a number of other phenomena indicating that the barrier between public and private is increasingly porous. The rapid extension of the internet into homes in the early twenty-first century greatly increased the opportunities people had to participate in multiple publics, but from the privacy of their own homes. As the public has bled into the private, so has the private realm seeped into public arenas. Public spaces are awash with what traditionally was discourse confined to the private sphere. Increasingly, as information technology becomes more mobile through cell phones and other transportable devices, the historical division between public and private is eroding; see Mimi Sheller and John Urry, "Mobile Transformations of 'Public' and 'Private' Life," *Theory, Culture & Society* 20, no. 3 (2003): 107–25. It may be the case that public and private eventually lose their usefulness as categories in internetworked cultures—the lack of concern about privacy by many people born after 1990 is indicative in this regard.

154. In many ways, affect is a cipher for what Kenneth Burke called "attitudes." Early in the *Grammar*, Burke builds a theory of attitude with recourse to I. A. Richards's conceptualization of attitude as incipient action. Richards writes in *The Principles of Literary Criticism* that "every perception probably includes a response in the form of incipient action. We constantly overlook the extent to which all the while we are making preliminary adjustments, getting ready to act in one way or another" (qtd. in Burke, *Grammar of Motives*, 235–36). Burke reads Richards to say "if we arouse in someone an attitude of sympathy towards something, we may be starting him [sic] on the road towards overtly sympathetic action with regard to it—hence the rhetoric of advertisers and propagandists who would induce action in behalf of their commodities or their causes by the formation of appropriate attitudes" (236). There is considerable overlap between the way Burke and Richards treated incipient action as a precursor to action-in-the-world and how affect is currently conceived as preceding and informing cognized reactions. This link is underlined more when Burke relates the idea of incipient action to the Aristotelian conception of rhetoric as potentiality (242). Burke articulates how attitudes are formed and re-formed through symbolic action: "this complexity of social attitudes comprises the 'self' (thus complexly erected atop the purely biological motives, and in particular modified by the formative effects of language, or 'vocal gesture,' which invites the individual to form himself [sic] in keeping with its social directives)" (237). For Burke, attitudes occupy a "region of ambiguous possibilities," much like affect (242). For this reason, "the realm of the incipient, or attitudinal, is the realm of 'symbolic action' par excellence; for symbolic action has the same ambiguous potentialities of action" (243).

155. Eric Shouse, "Feeling, Emotion, Affect," *Media/Culture* 8, no. 6, (2005), http://journal.media-culture.org.au/0512/03-shouse.php. Deborah Gould's *Moving Politics: Emotion and ACT UP's Fight Against AIDS* (Chicago: University of Chicago Press, 2009) and Marco Abel's "Intensifying Affect," *Electronic Book Review*, October 24, 2008, http://www.electronicbookreview.com/thread/fictionspresent/immersed, provide unbelievably lucid accounts of the complex relationship between feeling, emotion, affect, and political mobilization.

156. Shouse, "Feeling, Emotion, Affect."

157. George Marcus, *The Sentimental Citizen: Emotion in Democratic Politics* (University Park: Pennsylvania State University Press, 2002), 60.

158. James Kastely explores the dialectical relationship of *logos* and *pathos* in "Rhetoric and Emotion," in Jost and Olmsted, *Companion to Rhetoric and Rhetorical Criticism*, 221–37.

159. Barber, *Strong Democracy*, 187.

160. Walter Lippmann, *Public Opinion* (New York: Macmillan, 1922), especially part 3, "Stereotypes."

161. Marcus, *Sentimental Citizen*, 101.

162. Ibid., 116.

163. Farrell, *Norms of Rhetorical Culture*, 258–60. The problem of information abundance again appears, for how is anyone to negotiate the panoply of networked voices calling out for attention? Ananda Mitra and Eric King Watts strike a Lanhamian chord by suggesting that attention is commandeered by "how eloquently the voice can address the reader's emotion and create a 'proper feeling' about the issue." See their "Theorizing Cyberspace: The Idea of Voice Applied to the Internet Discourse," *New Media & Society* 4, no. 4 (2002): 494. Also see Ananda Mitra, "Using Blogs to Create Cybernetic Space: Examples from People of Indian Origin," *Convergence: The International Journal of Research into New Media Technologies* 14, no. 4 (2008): 460. According to one study, blog users who detect a stronger "voice" report increased trust and satisfaction; see Tom Kelleher and Barbara M. Miller, "Organizational Blogs and the Human Voice: Relational Strategies and Relational Outcomes," *Journal of Computer-Mediated Communication* 11, no. 2 (2006): 395–414.

164. Patricia Ticineto Clough, "Introduction," in *The Affective Turn: Theorizing the Social*, ed. Patricia Ticineto Clough and Jean Halley (Durham: Duke University Press, 2007): 1–33.

165. As Michael Warner explains in *Publics and Counterpublics*, 74–76.

166. This underlines Craig Calhoun's point that publicity is not just about processing arguments but about generating social solidarity; see Calhoun, "Imagining Solidarity: Cosmopolitanism, Constitutional Patriotism, and the Public Sphere," *Public Culture* 14, no. 1 (2002): 148. Jenny Edbauer Rice similarly notes that it is not the signifying functions of communication that stitch a public together, but the affective dimensions inherent in any act of communication. See her "The New 'New': Making a Case for Critical Affect Studies," *Quarterly Journal of Speech* 94, no. 2 (2008): 211. In other words, as Lauren Berlant argues, "public spheres are always affect worlds, worlds to which people are bound, when they are, by affective projections of a constantly negotiated common interestedness"; see "Affect, Noise, Silence, Protest: Ambient Citizenship," *Transformations of the Public Sphere*, posted November 20, 2009, http://publicsphere.ssrc.org/berlant-affect-noise-silence-protest-ambient-citizenship/.

167. Marcus, *Sentimental Citizen*, 86.

168. John Maxwell Hamilton and Eric Jenner, "New Foreign Correspondence," *Foreign Affairs* 82, no. 5 (2003): 137–38.

169. Norman, "International Internet Sensation," 2.

170. B. Anderson, *Imagined Communities*, 56.

171. Ibid., 35–36.

172. The absence of a global institution with binding decision-making power makes the development of a global public sphere aimed at influencing it difficult to conceptualize. Yet global public opinion manifested on a number of occasions, most prominently during the February 2003 global antiwar protests targeted at the Bush administration. Internetworked communication was instrumental in coordinating these protests. See Peter N. Stearns, *Global Outrage: The Impact of World Opinion on Contemporary History* (Oxford: Oneworld Publications, 2005), 176–78.

173. Clive Thompson, "How Twitter Creates a Sixth Social Sense," *Wired*, June 26, 2007, http://archive.wired.com/techbiz/media/magazine/15-07/st_thompson.

174. Ibid., emphasis in original.

175. Leisa Reichelt, "Ambient Intimacy," *Disambiguity* (blog), March 1, 2007, http://www.disambiguity.com/ambient-intimacy/.

176. Habermas, *Structural Transformation*, 44. The changing nature of childrearing here is notable. In aristocratic cultures, there were people for that; in bourgeois cultures, the people for that were the parents.

177. Sherry Turkle, "Always-On/Always-On-You: The Tethered Self," in *Handbook of Mobile Communication Studies*, ed. James Katz (Cambridge, Mass.: MIT Press, 2008), 121–38.

178. Brent Malin, "Communication with Feeling: Emotion, Publicness, and Embodiment," *Quarterly Journal of Speech* 87, no. 2 (2001): 222.

179. Michael Maffesoli, *The Contemplation of the World: Figures of Community Style*, trans. Susan Emanuel (Minneapolis: University of Minnesota Press, 1996), 57.

180. Nick Crossley, "Emotion and Communicative Action: Habermas, Linguistic Philosophy, and Existentialism," in *Emotions in Social Life: Critical Themes and Contemporary Issues*, ed. Gillian Bendelow and Simon Williams (New York: Routledge, 2004), 35.

181. Jodi Dean, *Blog Theory: Feedback and Capture in the Circuits of Drive* (Malden, Mass.: Polity Press, 2010), 95. Dean is skeptical of how the circulation of affect contributes to "communicative capitalism," a condition in which "politics is reduced to communication" (126). Given that Dean acknowledges that Geert Lovink's *Zero Comments* instigated *Blog Theory*, much of my critique of Lovink applies to Dean (vi).

182. Nigel Thrift, "Intensities of Feeling: Towards a Spatial Politics of Affect," *Geografiska Annaler* 86 B (2004): 67. Elizabeth Wissinger makes the connection as well: "since affect is connected to attention (insofar as it directs and channels it), in an economy in which the control of attention has value, the control of affective flow has value as well." See Wissinger, "Always on Display: Affective Production in the Modeling Industry," in Clough and Halley, *The Affective Turn*, 235. Blogs and related networked media are particularly conducive to making affective responses visible. Clay Shirky's observation that "as a medium gets faster, it gets more emotional" holds true in the blogosphere ("Q&A with Clay Shirky," *TED Blog*, June 16, 2009, http://blog.ted.com/2009/06/16/qa_with_clay_sh/). The reduction in time lapse between (re)cognition of affective response and personal publication means that individuals capture more of that initial intensity. The more time passes, the more our affective responses become overly cognized, such that we often shield initial affective reaction in *post hoc* rationalization. Because publishing through networked media is so fast, the gap between affective response and cognition is narrowed. As we publish our affective reactions quickly, blogs—and, even more so, Facebook and Twitter—chronicle our affective lives.

183. Contrast the tension between richness and scale in internetworked public cultures with that same tension in modernity. Felix Stalder explains that standardized print documents were the preferred way to organize modern institutions because they "offered a reduction in communicative complexity which enabled an increase in their scale," in *Manuel Castells: The Theory of the Network Society* (Cambridge: Polity Press, 2006), 182. Modern organizations must rely on documentation for organization and coordination. And this reliance on documentation is effective—it authorizes certain people to drive, or to be doctors. The documents at your local Department of Motor Vehicles are simple, direct, and easy to use as long as the paperwork accounts for your circumstance. If your circumstance is unusual, then the documents, or perhaps more precisely, the people trying to get you to fill out the documents, become increasingly inflexible (or, as the king of modern dread Franz Kafka suggested, alienating). The simplicity necessary to scale up then becomes an impediment to social coordination, as those who don't fit a bureaucratically defined norm are marked as deviant. Information technology networks, though, address the scale issue in a fashion that befits the demands of a networked public culture: "the traditional tradeoff between richness of communication, enabling flexibility and involvement, and reduction of communication, enabling scale and focus, has virtually vanished" (ibid., 183).

184. Raed, "Long Post Alert," *Where is Raed?*, January 25, 2004, http://dear_raed.blogspot.com/2004/01/long-post-alert-you-will-not-be.html.

185. James Bohman, "The Globalization of the Public Sphere: Cosmopolitan Publicity and the Problem of Cultural Pluralism," *Philosophy and Social Criticism* 24, nos. 2–3 (1998):

214. Something like Burke's notion of identification (in *Rhetoric of Motives*) could be used to explore further how these public spheres where global citizens come together function.

186. See Heather B. Armstrong, "Collecting Unemployment," *Dooce* (blog), February 26, 2002, http://web.archive.org/web/20121018035340/http://www.dooce.com/archives/daily/02_26_2002.html.

187. "2008 Word of the Year: Overshare," *Word of the Year* (blog), December 1, 2008, http://wordoftheyear.wordpress.com/2008/12/01/2008-word-of-the-year-overshare/

188. Mike Agnes, "2008 Word of the Year: Overshare," JohnWileySons YouTube channel, November 30, 2008, http://www.youtube.com/watch?feature=player_embedded&v=MMcVd6h8iQI#!.

189. Douglas Quenqua, "Friends, Until I Delete You," *New York Times*, January 29, 2009, http://www.nytimes.com/2009/01/29/fashion/29facebook.html.

190. Reichelt, "Ambient Exposure," *Disambiguity*, April 5, 2008, http://www.disambiguity.com/ambient-exposure/.

191. Ibid.

Chapter 5

1. Group, "Welcome to RealClimate," *RealClimate* (blog), December 9, 2004, http://www.realclimate.org/index.php?p=1.

2. Gavin Schmidt, "Climate Sensitivity and Aerosol Forcings," *RealClimate*, July 6, 2005, http://www.realclimate.org/index.php/archives/2005/07/climate-sensitivity-and-aerosol-forcings/; David Archer, "The Acid Ocean—The Other Problem with CO_2 Emission," *RealClimate*, July 2, 2005, http://www.realclimate.org/index.php/archives/2005/07/the-acid-ocean-the-other-problem-with-cosub2sub-emission/; Group, "How Much of the Recent CO_2 Increase is Due to Human Activities?," *RealClimate*, June 7, 2005, http://www.realclimate.org/index.php/archives/2005/06/how-much-of-the-recent-cosub2sub-increase-is-due-to-human-activities/.

3. Ben Rooney, "Footnote Frenzy," *Weblog* (blog), *Daily Telegraph*, June 9, 2005, http://www.telegraph.co.uk/comment/personal-view/3617507/Weblog.html.

4. Michael Mann, Raymond Bradley, and Malcolm Hughes, "Global-Scale Temperature Patterns and Climate Forcing over the Past Six Centuries," *Nature* 392 (April 1998): 779–87.

5. See McIntyre and McKitrick, "Corrections to the Mann et al. (1998) Proxy Data Base and Northern Hemisphere Average Temperature Series," *Energy and Environment* 14 (2003): 751–71.

6. Congressman Joseph Barton subpoenaed Mann's data in 2005 and in turn formed a committee of supposedly neutral scientists, led by statistician Edward Wegman, to make a judgment about the soundness of Mann's science. Edward Wegman, David Scott, and Yasmin Said, "Ad Hoc Committee Report on the 'Hockey Stick' Global Climate Reconstruction," July 14, 2006, 49, http://scienceandpublicpolicy.org/images/stories/papers/reprint/ad_hoc_report.pdf.

7. Stalder, *Manuel Castells*, 181. This flexibility certainly does not mean that many-to-many communication entirely supplants prior modes, as the prevalence of face-to-face communication, televisual broadcast, and even the occasional written letter demonstrates. Rather than conceptualizing many-to-many contact as the pinnacle of human communicative achievement or the inevitable *telos* of technological development, these different modes of interaction overlap considerably in contemporary media ecosystems.

8. I am using the term "pedagogy" in a way more faithful to the original etymology, rather than adopt more recent, radical perspectives on pedagogy that assume co-creation (as in the pedagogies of Paolo Freire or Jacques Rancière). Pedagogy is from the Greek *paidagogos*, referring to a "slave who escorts boys to school and generally supervises them." The original sense of the term, then, implies a sense of supervision or monitoring with continued traction both in the classroom and, as I argue, in contexts where expertise is deployed.

9. The proliferation of "review culture" shows how expertise is now more distributed and participatory. Examine almost any product on Amazon and there is bound to be a rich discussion of the product's virtues and vices, efficiencies and problems, suggested improvements and potential work-arounds. With the onset of "meta-reviews," where reviews can be further ranked according to helpfulness, accuracy, and other criteria, reflexivity is further worked into the evaluative system.

10. Marshall Clagett, *Greek Science in Antiquity* (1955; repr., Mineola, N.Y.: Dover, 2001), 24–31.

11. Ober, *Athenian Legacies: Essays on the Politics of Going On Together* (Princeton: Princeton University Press, 2005), 36.

12. Ibid., 36.

13. Ibid., 37.

14. Ibid., 38, emphasis in original.

15. Plato's Protagoras, in the great speech of the *Protagoras*, notes the irony of the Assembly's asking shipbuilders for advice when it comes to building ships, but letting any old carpenter or cobbler contribute to the equally complex affairs of state (322a–e).

16. Isocrates, *Busiris*, 16–19; in *Isocrates*, vol. 3, trans. La Rue Van Hook (Cambridge, Mass.: Harvard University Press, 1945).

17. Peter Walsh, "That Withered Paradigm: The Web, the Expert, and the Information Hegemony," in Jenkins and Thorburn, *Democracy and New Media*, 366.

18. Thomas M. Lessl, "The Priestly Voice," *Quarterly Journal of Speech* 75, no. 2 (1989): 183–97.

19. Jürgen Habermas, *Towards a Rational Society*, trans. Jeremy Shapiro (1968; repr., Boston: Beacon Press, 1970), 66–69.

20. Habermas, *Structural Transformation*, 259n32.

21. Recounted in Steve Fuller, "The Constitutively Social Character of Expertise," in *The Philosophy of Expertise*, ed. Evan Selinger and Robert P. Crease (New York: Columbia University Press, 2006), 342.

22. See E. Johanna Hartelius, *The Rhetoric of Expertise* (Lanham, Md.: Lexington Books, 2011).

23. See Ulrich Beck, *Risk Society: Towards a New Modernity* (Thousand Oaks, Calif.: SAGE, 1992), 19–20.

24. See Lippmann, *Public Opinion*, especially part 8, "Organized Intelligence."

25. John Dewey, "On Common Sense and Science," in *John Dewey: The Later Works, 1925–1953*, ed. Jo Ann Boydston, vol. 12 (Carbondale: Southern Illinois University Press, 1990), 101–2.

26. Ibid., 83.

27. Ibid.

28. Habermas, *Between Facts and Norms*, 351.

29. Ibid., 373.

30. Habermas, *Rational Society*, 67.

31. See Frank Fischer's critique of technocratic reasoning in *Citizens, Experts, and the Environment: The Politics of Local Knowledge* (Durham: Duke University Press, 2000), especially 10–28.

32. Habermas, *Rational Society*, 52, 57.

33. Ibid., 56. It is easy to figure "ordinary language" as part of the informationist paradigm, smacking of the Clarity-Brevity-Sincerity model critiqued in chapter 1. Habermas's arhetorical approach to discourse invites such a critique. The charitable read, which I adopt, is to see rhetorical language *as* ordinary language. As this case study demonstrates, when scientists address public audiences, they often use metaphors to describe phenomena. These metaphors loosen the scientists' traditional predilection for jargon and field-specific knowledge, thus connecting their discourse more tightly into the ordinary realm of common sense.

34. Habermas, *Rational Society*, 70.

35. See the volume edited by Randy Allen Harris, *Rhetoric and Incommensurability* (West Lafayette, Ind.: Parlor Press, 2005).

36. Habermas, *Rational Society*, 77.

37. Aynsley Kellow, *Science and Public Policy: The Virtuous Corruption of Virtual Environmental Science* (Northampton, Mass.: Edward Elgar, 2007), 47.

38. See Clark Miller and Paul Edwards, "Introduction," in *Changing the Atmosphere: Expert Knowledge and Environmental Governance*, ed. Clark Miller and Paul Edwards (Cambridge, Mass.: MIT Press, 2001), 8–15.

39. Habermas, *Rational Society*, 77.

40. Habermas, *Between Facts and Norms*, 348.

41. Burke, *Counter-Statement*, 54.

42. Ted Striphas, "Communication as Translation," in Shepherd, St. John, and Striphas, *Communication As . . .* , 232–41.

43. Habermas, *Between Facts and Norms*, 334.

44. Ibid., 335.

45. In "Broadcasting and Schizophrenia," *Media, Culture, and Society* 32, no. 1 (2010): 135, 138. Also see Carolyn L. Kane and John Durham Peters, "Speaking into the iPhone: An Interview with John Durham Peters, or, Ghostly Cessation for the Digital Age," *Journal of Communication Inquiry* 34, no. 2 (2010): 119–33. See my critique of the autism metaphor in Damien Smith Pfister, "'A Short Burst of Inconsequential Information': Networked Rhetorics, Avian Consciousness, and Bioegalitarianism," *Environmental Communication: A Journal of Nature and Culture*, forthcoming (2014).

46. Stephen Turner, *Liberal Democracy 3.0: Civil Society in an Age of Experts* (Thousand Oaks, Calif.: SAGE, 2003), 48. As Turner explains, "Scientists themselves, presumably, speak both the 'languages' of science and common sense, and can translate from one to the other as bilinguals. But the results of translation, such as 'this table is composed mostly of empty space,' lack common sense *credibility*, because the grounds for the claim cannot be expressed in common terms. So translation is not enough. Something more is needed, and the usual solution is to characterize these utterances in terms of the notion of 'authority,' making the problem one of expert *authority*" (50).

47. Susan Senecah, "The Trinity of Voice: The Role of Practical Theory in Planning and Evaluating the Effectiveness of Environmental Participatory Processes," in *Communication and Public Participation in Environmental Decision Making*, ed. Stephen P. Depoe, John W. Delicath, and Marie-France Aepli Elsenbeer (Albany: SUNY Press, 2004), 18.

48. Georgia Persons, "Defining the Public Interest: Citizen Participation in Metropolitan and State Policy Making," *National Civic Review* 79, no. 2 (2007): 121; also John Gastil and Laura Black, "Public Deliberation as the Organizing Principle of Political Communication Research," *Journal of Public Deliberation* 4, no. 1 (2008): 24.

49. In Simmons and Grabill, "Toward a Civic Rhetoric for Technologically and Scientifically Complex Places: Invention, Performance, and Participation," *College Composition and Communication* 58, no. 3 (2007): 422.

50. Carol Hager, *Technological Democracy: Bureaucracy and Citizenry in the German Energy Debate* (Ann Arbor: University of Michigan Press, 1995), 217. Walter Fisher similarly notes that field experts tend to dominate public contexts "by the rational superiority of their arguments. . . . The presence of 'experts' in *public* moral arguments makes it difficult, if not impossible, for the public of 'untrained thinkers' to win an argument or even to judge arguments well." See Fisher, *Human Communication as Narration: Toward a Philosophy of Reason, Value, and Action* (Columbia: University of South Carolina Press, 1987), 71, emphasis in original. Robert Patterson and Ronald Lee critique the notion of balance in regulatory decision making as inherently privileging technical discourse; see their "Environmental Rhetoric of 'Balance': A Case Study of Regulatory Discourse and the Colonization of the Public," *Technical Communication Quarterly* 6, no. 1 (1997): 25–40.

51. Some critics of these weak public participation forums suggest "meta-institutional" efforts that rely not on localized participation by a public with scientists but on efforts by

supposedly neutral third parties to make judgments about sound science. Stephen Schneider recommends developing "science courts" that could make more impartial judgments about science; see Schneider, "Is the 'Citizen-Scientist' an Oxymoron?," in *Science, Technology, and Democracy*, ed. Daniel Lee Kleinman (Albany: SUNY Press, 2000), 112–14. However, this meta-institutional effort to make judgments about science replicates traditional patterns of scientific decision making by an elite cadre rather than through deliberative means. As a top-down approach, meta-institutional solutions cannot capture the legitimacy that accrues through more broad-based translation stations.

52. Ken Broda-Bahm, Daniela Kempf, and William Driscoll, *Argument and Audience: Presenting Debates in Public Settings* (New York: International Debate Education Association, 2004), 25–26.

53. Deborah Tannen, *The Argument Culture: Moving from Debate to Dialogue* (New York: Random House, 1998), 37–38.

54. Ross Gelbspan, *Boiling Point: How Politicians, Big Oil and Coal, Journalists, and Activists Are Fueling the Climate Crisis—and What We Can Do to Avert Disaster* (New York: Basic Books, 2004), 73–74.

55. John Ziman, "Are Debatable Scientific Questions Debatable?," *Social Epistemology* 14, nos. 2–3 (2000): 190.

56. Ibid., 194.

57. Ibid., 195.

58. Michael Mann, "Myth vs. Fact Regarding the 'Hockey Stick,'" *RealClimate*, December 4, 2004, http://www.realclimate.org/index.php/archives/2004/12/myths-vs-fact-regarding-the-hockey-stick/, emphasis in original. The ability of bloggers to go back and update posts demonstrates the "dynamic updating" possibilities inherent in blogging as new understandings and interests are discovered; see Christopher Karpowitz and Jane Mansbridge, "Disagreement and Consensus: The Importance of Dynamic Updating in Public Deliberation," in *The Deliberative Democracy Handbook: Strategies for Effective Civic Engagement in the Twenty-First Century*, ed. John Gastil and Peter Levine (San Francisco, Calif.: John Wiley & Sons, 2005), 237–53. The dynamic updating on blogs is a double-edged sword: while it allows additions, useful modifications, and clarifications, it also allows erasure.

59. Mann, "Myth vs. Fact," *RealClimate*.

60. Gavin Schmidt and Caspar Amman, "Dummies Guide to the Latest 'Hockey Stick' Controversy," *RealClimate*, February 18, 2005, http://www.realclimate.org/index.php/archives/2005/02/dummies-guide-to-the-latest-hockey-stick-controversy/.

61. The first link is to Michael Mann, "False Claims by McIntyre and McKitrick Regarding the Mann et al. (1998) Reconstruction," *RealClimate*, December 4, 2004, http://www.realclimate.org/index.php/archives/2004/12/false-claims-by-mcintyre-and-mckitrick-regarding-the-mann-et-al-1998reconstruction/. This post begins with links from ExxonSecrets.org and the Environmental Defense Fund to pages documenting McIntyre and McKitrick's affiliation with oil companies looking to stall action on climate change. The post explains that their criticism was rejected from the journal *Nature*. The second post, Michael Mann, "On Yet Another False Claim by McIntyre and McKitrick," *RealClimate*, January 6, 2005, http://www.realclimate.org/index.php/archives/2005/01/on-yet-another-false-claim-by-mcintyre-and-mckitrick/, covers similar terrain in extending defenses of the methodology used in the original hockey-stick data. One addendum to this latter post is a link-heavy paragraph that explores how the McIntyre and McKitrick critique was amplified in non-peer-reviewed literature—illustrating how the norms of different discourse communities operate.

62. Stefan Rahmstorf, "What If . . . the 'Hockey Stick' Were Wrong?," *RealClimate*, January 27, 2005, http://www.realclimate.org/index.php/archives/2005/01/what-if-the-hockey-stick-were-wrong/, and William Connolley and Eric Steig, "Moberg et al: Highly Variable Northern Hemisphere Temperatures?," *RealClimate*, February 15, 2005, http://www.realclimate.org/index.php/archives/2005/02/moberg-et-al-highly-variable-northern-hemisphere-temperatures/.

63. Schmidt and Amman, "Dummies Guide."

64. Ibid.

65. Garry Culhane, comment on "Dummies Guide," *RealClimate*, 3:22 P.M., February 18, 2005, http://www.realclimate.org/index.php/archives/2005/02/dummies-guide-to-the-latest-hockey-stick-controversy/#comment-1320.

66. John S., comment on "Dummies Guide," *RealClimate*, 4:44 P.M., February 18, 2005, http://www.realclimate.org/index.php/archives/2005/02/dummies-guide-to-the-latest-hockey-stick-controversy/#comment-1321.

67. Lynn Vincentnathan, comment on "Dummies Guide," *RealClimate*, 3:15 P.M., February 18, 2005, http://www.realclimate.org/index.php/archives/2005/02/dummies-guide-to-the-latest-hockey-stick-controversy/#comment-1319.

68. Florens de Wit, comment on "Dummies Guide," *RealClimate*, 6:09 P.M., February 18, 2005, http://www.realclimate.org/index.php/archives/2005/02/dummies-guide-to-the-latest-hockey-stick-controversy/#comment-1325, emoticon in original.

69. Greg M. Johnson, comment on "Dummies Guide," *RealClimate*, 10:31 P.M., March 15, 2005, http://www.realclimate.org/index.php/archives/2005/02/dummies-guide-to-the-latest-hockey-stick-controversy/#comment-1583.

70. Steven T. Corneliussen, comment on "Dummies Guide," *RealClimate*, 12:48 P.M., February 18, 2005, http://www.realclimate.org/index.php/archives/2005/02/dummies-guide-to-the-latest-hockey-stick-controversy/#comment-1316.

71. Mat McClain, comment on "Dummies Guide," *RealClimate*, 4:28 P.M., March 3, 2005, http://www.realclimate.org/index.php/archives/2005/02/dummies-guide-to-the-latest-hockey-stick-controversy/#comment-1583. I have cleaned up minor typos in this comment for readability.

72. Stephen Schneider contends, "if scientists do not find the metaphors to communicate, most citizens simply will not hear them"; "Citizen-Scientist," 117.

73. Raymond T. Pierrehumbert, comment on "Dummies Guide," *RealClimate*, 6:32 P.M., March 1, 2005, http://www.realclimate.org/index.php/archives/2005/02/dummies-guide-to-the-latest-hockey-stick-controversy/#comment-1448.

74. Joseph O'Sullivan, comment on "Dummies Guide," *RealClimate*, 9:29 A.M., March 2, 2005, http://www.realclimate.org/index.php/archives/2005/02/dummies-guide-to-the-latest-hockey-stick-controversy/#comment-1452.

75. Michael Crichton, *State of Fear* (New York: HarperCollins, 2005). George W. Bush was so taken with the novel that he discreetly invited Michael Crichton to the White House to discuss the finer points of climate science.

76. Schmidt, "Michael Crichton's State of Confusion," *RealClimate*, December 13, 2004, http://www.realclimate.org/index.php/archives/2004/12/michael-crichtons-state-of-confusion/.

77. Crichton, *State of Fear*, 247.

78. Schmidt, "State of Confusion."

79. Crichton, *State of Fear*, 424.

80. Chicago Jason, comment on "Michael Crichton's State of Confusion," *RealClimate*, 11:36 P.M., December 13, 2004, http://www.realclimate.org/index.php/archives/2004/12/michael-crichtons-state-of-confusion/#comment-97.

81. Joseph Steig, comment on "Michael Crichton's State of Confusion," *RealClimate*, 5:58 A.M., December 14, 2004, http://www.realclimate.org/index.php/archives/2004/12/michael-crichtons-state-of-confusion/#comment-104.

82. P. Z. Myers, "Crichton as He Deserves," *Pharyngula* (blog), December 14, 2004, https://web.archive.org/web/20041230235701/http://pharyngula.org/index/weblog/comments/crichton_as_he_deserves/; Union of Concerned Scientists, "Crichton Thriller State of Fear," n.d., http://web.archive.org/web/20131002165734/http://www.ucsusa.org/global_warming/solutions/fight-misinformation/crichton-thriller-state-of.html/; Natural Resources Defense Council, "They Don't Call it Science *Fiction* For Nothing," December 16,

2004, http://web.archive.org/web/20090606073516/http://www.nrdc.org/globalWarming/fcrichton.asp.

83. Eric Roston, "RealClimate," *Time.com*, April 17, 2008, http://www.time.com/time/specials/2007/environment/article/0,28804,1730759_1731034_1732032,00.html.

84. Sanjong, comment on "Michael Crichton's State of Confusion," *RealClimate*, 9:50 P.M., December 20, 2004, http://www.realclimate.org/index.php/archives/2004/12/michael-crichtons-state-of-confusion/#comment-327.

85. Group, "The *Wall Street Journal* vs. The Scientific Consensus," *RealClimate*, June 22, 2005, http://www.realclimate.org/index.php/archives/2005/06/the-wall-street-journal-vs-the-consensus-of-the-scientific-community/. The tendency of bloggers to author collaboratively extends a tradition of social authorship in print culture; see Margaret Ezell, *Social Authorship and the Advent of Print* (Baltimore: Johns Hopkins University Press, 1999).

86. Gordon R. Mitchell and Takeshi Suzuki, "Beyond the *'Daily Me'*: Argumentation in an Age of Enclave Deliberation," in *Argumentation and Social Cognition*, ed. Takeshi Suzuki, Yoshiro Yano, and Takayuki Kato (Tokyo: Japan Debate Association, 2004), 163–64.

87. Edward Meyer, comment on "The *Wall Street Journal* vs. The Scientific Consensus," *RealClimate*, 8:22 P.M., June 22, 2005, http://www.realclimate.org/index.php/archives/2005/06/the-wall-street-journal-vs-the-consensus-of-the-scientific-community/#comment-2632.

88. John Monro, comment on "The *Wall Street Journal* vs. The Scientific Consensus," *RealClimate*, 11:57 P.M., June 22, 2005, http://www.realclimate.org/index.php/archives/2005/06/the-wall-street-journal-vs-the-consensus-of-the-scientific-community/#comment-2642.

89. Wayne Davidson, comment on "The *Wall Street Journal* vs. The Scientific Consensus," *RealClimate*, 1:31 P.M., June 29, 2005, http://www.realclimate.org/index.php/archives/2005/06/the-wall-street-journal-vs-the-consensus-of-the-scientific-community/#comment-2797.

90. Lynn Vincentnathan, comment on "The *Wall Street Journal* vs. The Scientific Consensus," *RealClimate*, 9:13 A.M., June 28, 2005, http://www.realclimate.org/index.php/archives/2005/06/the-wall-street-journal-vs-the-consensus-of-the-scientific-community/#comment-2767.

91. Dano, comment on "The *Wall Street Journal* vs. The Scientific Consensus," *RealClimate*, 12:05 P.M., June 23, 2005, http://www.realclimate.org/index.php/archives/2005/06/the-wall-street-journal-vs-the-consensus-of-the-scientific-community/#comment-2656.

92. Michael Pettengill, comment on "Michael Crichton's State of Confusion," *RealClimate*, 3:08 P.M., December 28, 2004, http://www.realclimate.org/index.php/archives/2004/12/michael-crichtons-state-of-confusion/#comment-461.

93. Michael Mann and Gavin Schmidt, "Peer Review: A Necessary But *Not* Sufficient Condition," *RealClimate*, January 20, 2005, http://www.realclimate.org/index.php/archives/2005/01/peer-review-a-necessary-but-not-sufficient-condition/.

94. See David Appell, "Politics in Peer Review?," *Scientific American*, June 24, 2003, http://www.sciam.com/article.cfm?id=politics-in-peer-review.

95. Mann and Schmidt, "Peer Review,'" *RealClimate*.

96. Ibid.

97. Ibid.

98. Ibid.

99. See "The Web Gets Social," *Nature*, June 2005, 419.

100. Mann and Schmidt, "Peer Review," *RealClimate*.

101. Dano, comment on "Peer Review: A Necessary But *Not* Sufficient Condition," *RealClimate*, 1:23 P.M., January 20, 2005, http://www.realclimate.org/index.php/archives/2005/01/peer-review-a-necessary-but-not-sufficient-condition/#comment-895.

102. Steven Corneliussen, comment on "Peer Review: A Necessary But Not Sufficient Condition," *RealClimate*, 3:00 P.M., January 20, 2005, http://www.realclimate.org/index.php/archives/2005/01/peer-review-a-necessary-but-not-sufficient-condition/#comment-900.

103. Brian C, comment on "Peer Review: A Necessary But Not Sufficient Condition," *RealClimate*, 11:55 P.M., January 20, 2005, http://www.realclimate.org/index.php/archives/2005/01/peer-review-a-necessary-but-not-sufficient-condition/#comment-913.

104. Peter Wetzel, comment on "Peer Review: A Necessary But Not Sufficient Condition," *RealClimate*, 5:50 P.M., January 22, 2005, http://www.realclimate.org/index.php/archives/2005/01/peer-review-a-necessary-but-not-sufficient-condition/#comment-930.

105. John Hunter, comment on ""Peer Review: A Necessary But Not Sufficient Condition," *RealClimate*, 10:33 P.M., January 20, 2005, http://www.realclimate.org/index.php/archives/2005/01/peer-review-a-necessary-but-not-sufficient-condition/#comment-910.

106. "Communicating Climate," *RealClimate*, http://www.realclimate.org/index.php/archives/category/communicating-climate/reporting-on-climate/.

107. Gavin Schmidt, "How Not to Write a Press Release," *RealClimate*, April 21, 2006, http://www.realclimate.org/index.php/archives/2006/04/how-not-to-write-a-press-release/.

108. Schmidt, "How Not To Write," *RealClimate*.

109. Ibid.

110. Matthew Nisbet and Chris Mooney, "Framing Science," *Science*, April 6, 2007, 56.

111. Schmidt, "How Not To Write," *RealClimate*.

112. Myles Allen, comment on "How Not to Write a Press Release," 9:23 A.M., April 22, 2006, *RealClimate*, http://www.realclimate.org/index.php/archives/2006/04/how-not-to-write-a-press-release/#comment-12122.

113. Rasmus Benestad, "Communicating Science and Technology," *RealClimate*, June 23, 2006, http://www.realclimate.org/index.php/archives/2006/06/communicating-science-technology/.

114. Steve Corneliussen, comment on "Communicating Science and Technology," *RealClimate*, 9:39 A.M., June 23, 2006, http://www.realclimate.org/index.php/archives/2006/06/communicating-science-technology/#comment-14879.

115. Steve Corneliussen, comment on "Communicating Science and Technology," *RealClimate*, 8:44 A.M., June 24, 2006, http://www.realclimate.org/index.php/archives/2006/06/communicating-science-technology/#comment-14926.

116. Gavin Schmidt, "The Missing Repertoire," *RealClimate*, August 10, 2006, http://www.realclimate.org/index.php/archives/2006/08/the-missing-repertoire/. See also the IPPR report by Gil Ereaut and Nat Segnit, "Warm Words: How Are We Telling the Climate Story and Can We Tell it Better?," August 2006, http://www.ippr.org/publication/55/1529/warm-wordshow-are-we-telling-the-climate-story-and-can-we-tell-it-better.

117. Schmidt, "Missing Repertoire," *RealClimate*.

118. Ibid.

119. Ibid.

120. Henry Farrell, "The Blogosphere as a Carnival of Ideas," *Chronicle of Higher Education*, October 7, 2005, http://chronicle.com/free/v52/i07/07b01401.htm.

121. Bradford Plummer, "How High Will the Seas Go?," *The Vine* (blog), *New Republic*, April 16, 2008, http://web.archive.org/web/20081120194754/http://blogs.tnr.com/tnr/blogs/environmentandenergy/archive/2008/04/16/how-high-will-the-seas-go.aspx.

122. Andrew Leonard, "Climate Change, the North Pole, and an Imaginary Chinese Navy," *Salon*, February 7, 2007, http://www.salon.com/tech/htww/2007/02/07/imaginary_chinese_navy.

123. John Vidal et al., "50 People Who Could Save the Planet," *The Guardian*, January 5, 2008, http://www.guardian.co.uk/environment/2008/jan/05/activists.ethicalliving.

124. Alan Boyle, "Science Ran Headlong into Society in 2005," MSNBC, December 12, 2005, http://www.msnbc.msn.com/id/10372243/.

125. Stephen Luntz, "Comments, Corrections, Clarifications, and C*ckups," *Crikey*, July 16, 2008, http://www.crikey.com.au/Your-Say/20080716-Comments-corrections-clarifications-and-cckups.html. Note the additional layer of translation through concision.

126. Chris Turney, "We Must Acknowledge Global Warming, and Act," letter to the editor in *The Times*, December 21, 2007, http://www.timesonline.co.uk/tol/comment/letters/article3079805.ece.

127. Denis Bubay, "The Peril to Come," letter to the editor in *The News and Observer*, June 9, 2008, http://web.archive.org/web/20080906121917/http://www.newsobserver.com/opinion/letters/story/1101214.html.

128. Sharon Begley, "Resisting Change: Global Warming Deniers," *Newsweek*, August 8, 2008, http://www.newsweek.com/live-talk-climate-change-deniers-99079.

129. Habermas, *Between Facts and Norms*, 374.

130. Ibid., 373.

131. Nancy Fraser identifies bridging discourses as ways experts might translate the needs of oppositional social movements for the administrative state apparatus, in "Struggle Over Needs: Outline of a Socialist-Feminist Critical Theory of Late Capitalist Political Culture," in *Unruly Practices*, 161–90. The way that I conceptualize bridge discourses is slightly different: the process of needs interpretation is more dialogical, ordinary language instead of expert language is the default idiom of discussion, and the state is not necessarily the target of criticism. John Dryzek underlines how deliberation needs bridging rhetorics to link differently situated actors, institutions, and forums in "Rhetoric in Democracy: A Systemic Appreciation," *Political Theory* 38, no. 3 (2010): 319–39. Of course, Burke also discussed "bridging devices" in *Attitudes Toward History*, 224–25.

132. The power to bridge different discourse communities through translation is a new power in the sense that Manuel Castells identifies network societies as producing new modes of power. Castells identifies two new modes of power, the power to program and the power to switch networks on and off. See Castells, "Informationalism, Networks, and the Network Society," in *The Network Society*, 32.

133. Charles Willard, *Liberalism and the Problem of Knowledge: A New Rhetoric for Modern Democracy* (Chicago: University of Chicago Press, 1999), 201. Willard is focused on how academic fields can develop more satisfying interdisciplinary projects. My use of shallow quotation departs from Willard's to understand not interdisciplinarity but the interpenetration of scientific and public discourses—it is, if you will, a shallow quotation of shallow quotation.

134. Situating blogging as a mode of *knowledge management* implicitly acknowledges the necessity and benefits of shallow quotation. As information systems become more sophisticated, the need to manage dense information streams by selecting certain tidbits for broader public attention is accentuated. For connections between knowledge management and blogging, see Gabriela Avram, "At the Crossroads of Knowledge Management and Social Software," *Electronic Journal of Knowledge Management* 4, no. 2 (2006): 1–10, http://issuu.com/academic-conferences.org/docs/ejkm-volume4-issue1-article61?mode=a_p.

135. The flip side of shallow quotation in the production of discourse is shallow scanning in its reception. The protagonist in Gary Shteyngart's quasi-dystopian novel *Super Sad True Love Story* lives in a culture where reading books is passé. At one point in the novel, he notices that his girlfriend "caught me reading, not just text-scanning for data" (New York, Random House, 2010), 158. Shallow scanning for data—instead of, perhaps, meaning—is potentially an interpretive mode amplified by hypertext.

136. Willard, *Liberalism and the Problem of Knowledge*, 201.

137. C. P. Snow, *The Two Cultures* (1959; London: Cambridge University Press, 2001).

138. In Brockman, *The Third Culture: Beyond the Scientific Revolution* (New York: Simon & Schuster, 1995).

139. See Lyne, "Rhetoric and the Third Culture: Scientists and Arguers and Critics," in *Reengaging the Prospects of Rhetoric: Current Conversations and Contemporary Challenges*, ed. Mark Porrovecchio (New York: Routledge, 2010), 139.

140. Robyn Eckersley, *The Green State: Rethinking Democracy and Sovereignty* (Cambridge, Mass.: MIT Press, 2004), 140. Douglas Torgerson identifies the facilitation of debate

as the key enterprise of the green public sphere in *The Promise of Green Politics: Environmentalism and the Public Sphere* (Durham: Duke University Press, 1999), 161.

141. James Delingpole, "Climategate: The Final Nail in the Coffin of 'Anthropogenic Global Warming,'" *The Telegraph*, November 20, 2009, http://blogs.telegraph.co.uk/news/jamesdelingpole/100017393/climategate-the-final-nail-in-the-coffin-of-anthropogenic-global-warming/.

142. Sarah Palin, "Sarah Palin on the Politicization of the Copenhagen Climate Conference," *Washington Post*, December 9, 2009, http://www.washingtonpost.com/wp-dyn/content/article/2009/12/08/AR2009120803402.html.

143. James Inhofe, remarks at fifteenth United Nations climate change conference, Copenhagen, Denmark, December 17, 2009, http://www.epw.senate.gov/public/index.cfm?FuseAction=Minority.Speeches&ContentRecord_id=9cac1e35-802a-23ad-4540-3e4706eab1bd&Region_id=&Issue_id=.

144. "CRU Statement," from University of East Anglia website, November 24, 2009, http://www.uea.ac.uk/mac/comm/media/press/2009/nov/CRUupdate.

145. Group, "The CRU Hack," *RealClimate*, November 20, 2009, http://www.realclimate.org/index.php/archives/2009/11/the-cru-hack/.

146. "Climatologists Under Pressure," *Nature*, December 3, 2009, http://www.nature.com/nature/journal/v462/n7273/full/462545a.html.

147. "Statement from Phil Jones, Head of the Climactic Research Unit, University of East Anglia," from University of East Anglia website, November 24, 2009, http://www.uea.ac.uk/mac/comm/media/press/2009/nov/CRUupdate.

148. Leo Hickman, "Climate Scientist at Center of Leaked Email Row Dismisses Conspiracy Claim," *The Guardian*, November 24, 2009, http://www.theguardian.com/environment/2009/nov/24/climate-professor-leaked-emails-uea.

149. Group, "The CRU Hack."

150. Phil Jones, "Cherry-Picked Phrases Explained," from University of East Anglia website, November 23, 2011, http://www.uea.ac.uk/mac/comm/media/press/CRUstatements/rebuttalsandcorrections/phrasesexplained.

151. Juliet Eilperin, "Hackers Steal Electronic Data from Top Climate Research Center," *Washington Post*, November 21, 2009, http://www.washingtonpost.com/wp-dyn/content/article/2009/11/20/AR2009112004093.html.

152. David Stringer, "Scientist: Leak of Climate E-mails Appalling," Associated Press, November 23, 2009, http://phys.org/news178199129.html.

153. Kevin Trenberth, "Statement: Kevin Trenberth on Hacking of Climate Files," from National Center for Atmospheric Research website, n.d., http://www.cgd.ucar.edu/staff/trenbert/emails/.

154. "Climactic Research Unit Email Controversy," *Wikipedia*, http://en.wikipedia.org/wiki/Climatic_Research_Unit_email_controversy, last retrieved June 13, 2012.

155. "EPA's Denial of the Petitions to Reconsider the Endangerment and Cause or Contribute Findings for Greenhouse Gases Under Section 202(a) of the Clean Air Act," *Federal Register*, August 13, 2010, 75 (156), p. 49580–1, http://web.archive.org/web/20120531075651/http://epa.gov/climatechange/endangerment/downloads/response-decision.pdf.

156. Anthony Leiserowitz, Edward W. Maibach, Connie Roser-Renouf, Nicholas Smith, and Erica Dawson, "Climategate, Public Opinion, and the Loss of Trust," *Social Science Research Network* 57, no. 6 (2010): 818–37, doi:10.2139/ssrn.1633932.

Chapter 6

1. Catherine Helen Palczewski, "Argument in an Off Key: Playing with the Productive Limits of Argument," in *Critical Problems in Argumentation: Selected Papers from the 13th Biennial Conference on Argumentation*, ed. Charles Arthur Willard (Washington, D.C.: National Communication Association Convention, 2005), 2. Also see Christopher J. Gilbert,

"Playing With Hitler: Downfall and Its Ludic Uptake," *Critical Studies in Media Communication* 30, no. 5 (2013): 407–24, on the historical connection between play and rhetoric.

2. Barlow, *Rise of the Blogosphere*, 162.

3. Martin Dodge and Rob Kitchin, "The Ethics of Forgetting in an Age of Pervasive Computing," *CASA Working Papers*, 2005, http://eprints.ucl.ac.uk/1292/1/paper92.pdf.

4. Ibid., 7.

5. Although the notion of wearable computing at one time seemed fantastical, Microsoft's early experimentation with Sensecam (at http://research.microsoft.com/en-us/um/cambridge/projects/sensecam/) paved the way for an explosion of devices at the 2014 Consumer Electronics Show.

6. And, indeed, the idea behind the lifelog animates many science fiction films, like *Minority Report*, dir. Steven Spielberg (Universal City, Calif.: Dreamworks, 2002); *The Final Cut*, dir. Omar Naim (Santa Monica, Calif.: Lionsgate Entertainment, 2004), and *The Truman Show*, dir. Peter Weir (Hollywood: Paramount Pictures, 1998).

7. Dodge and Kitchin, "Ethics of Forgetting," 14–16.

8. Wilde, *The Picture of Dorian Gray* (London: Urban Romantics, 2011), 101.

9. Thanks to Jessy Ohl for observing that the intensification of publicity that I am calling hyperpublicity is reminiscent of Burke's commentary on neo-Malthusian limits. When principles are pushed to their limits, they return as irony; thus, when the principle of publicity is pushed to its limit in recording and circulating all information, what begins as a stimulant for democratic deliberation potentially returns as an impediment to public conversation. See Burke, *Attitudes Toward History*, 298–306.

10. Mayhill Fowler, "Obama: No Surprise that Hard-Pressed Pennsylvanians Turn Bitter," *The Huffington Post*, April 11, 2008, http://www.huffingtonpost.com/mayhill-fowler/obama-no-surprise-that-ha_b_96188.html.

11. Articulated in Thomas Frank's *What's the Matter with Kansas?: How Conservatives Won the Heart of America* (New York: Metropolitan Books, 2004).

12. Marc Cooper, "Inside the Obama-Guns-God-Bitterness Storm," *MarcCooper.com* (blog), April 11, 2008, http://marccooper.com/inside-the-obama-guns-god-bitterness-storm/.

13. Katherine Q. Seelye, "Blogger Is Surprised by Uproar over Obama Story, but Not Bitter," *New York Times*, April 14, 2004, http://www.nytimes.com/2008/04/14/us/politics/14web-seelye.html?scp=3&sq=bitter&st=nyt.

14. Cooper, "Inside the Obama."

15. Ibid.

16. Jay Rosen, "The Uncharted: From Off the Bus to *Meet the Press*," *The Huffington Post*, April 14, 2008, http://www.huffingtonpost.com/jay-rosen/the-uncharted-from-off-th_b_96575.html.

17. David Coleman, "I Was There: What Obama Really Said About Pennsylvania," *The Huffington Post*, April 14, 2008, http://www.huffingtonpost.com/david-coleman/i-was-there-what-obama-re_b_96553.html.

18. Seelye, "Blogger Is Surprised."

19. Will Bunch, "Obama Says He 'Misspoke But Didn't Lie' About Smalltown Pa.," *Attytood* (blog), *Philly.com*, April 14, 2008, http://www.philly.com/philly/blogs/attytood/Exclusive_Obama_says_he_misspoke_but_didnt_lie_about_smalltown_Pa.html.

20. Michael Barbaro and Ashley Parker, "With Rich Donors, a More Candid Romney Emerges," *New York Times*, September 22, 2011, http://www.nytimes.com/2012/09/23/us/politics/with-donors-a-more-candid-romney-emerges.html.

21. Tom Zeller Jr., "In Politics, the Camera Never Blinks (or Nods)," *New York Times*, January 29, 2007, http://www.nytimes.com/2007/01/29/technology/29link.html?fta=y.

22. Ryan Lizza, "The YouTube Election," *New York Times*, August 20, 2006, http://www.nytimes.com/2006/08/20/weekinreview/20lizza.html.

23. Qtd. in ibid.

24. Brockriede, "Arguers as Lovers," 7. Brockriede draws on Maurice Natanson's assessment of rhetoric, argumentation, and risk in "The Claims of Immediacy," in *Philosophy,*

Rhetoric, and Argumentation, ed. Maurice Natanson and Henry Johnstone Jr. (University Park: Pennsylvania State University Press, 1965), 10–19. Natanson claims that for argument to succeed as a philosophical or rhetorical proposition, it necessarily requires the arguer to take risks.

25. The rise of "Joe the Plumber" on the political scene is another topical example of hyperpublicity emerging from the 2008 presidential campaign. Joe Wurzelbacher, a plumber from Ohio, approached Barack Obama while Obama was campaigning in his neighborhood in Toledo. Wurzelbacher asked whether Obama's tax policy would increase his own taxes; Obama gave an extended answer that was caught on tape and posted to YouTube. In the final presidential debate between Obama and John McCain, McCain mentioned this exchange between Obama and Wurzelbacher twenty-one times! McCain picked up on a line Obama used in his discussion Wurzelbacher—that the United States should "spread the wealth"—in subsequent attacks on Obama's economic policy. See Larry Rohter, "Plumber from Ohio Is Thrust into Spotlight," *New York Times*, October 15, 2008, http://www.nytimes.com/2008/10/16/us/politics/16plumber.html.

26. See Rosa Eberly, *Citizen Critics: Literary Public Spheres* (Urbana: University of Illinois Press, 2000), and Gordon R. Mitchell, "Simulated Public Argument as a Pedagogical Play on Worlds," *Argumentation and Advocacy* 36 (Winter 2000): 134–50. Eberly argues that the classroom can function as a proto-public space where students generate *topoi* from texts that can then inform other public practices (170). Mitchell's work suggests that the insulated academic tournament debate competition provides a similarly safe space for students to experiment with ideas and thus facilitate their opinion formation before they are thrust into public deliberations with more at stake than tournament victory.

27. Although these results appear to be "objective," James G. Webster has identified the deeply social production of what he calls "user information regimes." See Webster, "The Duality of Media: A Structurational Theory of Public Attention," *Communication Theory* 21, no. 1 (2011): 50.

28. See Striphas, "How to Have Culture in an Algorithmic Age," *The Late Age of Print* (blog), June 14, 2010, http://www.thelateageofprint.org/2010/06/14/how-to-have-culture-in-an-algorithmic-age/.

29. As Chris Anderson posits in "Deliberative, Agonistic, and Algorithmic Audiences: Journalism's Vision of Its Public in an Age of Audience Transparency," *International Journal of Communication* 5 (2011): 542. In a more sinister vein, John Cheney-Lippold finds that the construction of new algorithmic identities creates new modes to manage and control populations. See "A New Algorithmic Identity: Soft Biopolitics and the Modulation of Control," *Theory, Culture, and Society* 28, no. 6 (2011): 164–81.

30. I have discussed the implications of many-to-many communication at more length in "Networked Expertise in the Era of Many-to-Many Communication: On *Wikipedia* and Invention," *Social Epistemology* 25, no. 3 (2011): 217–31.

31. Robert Burnett and P. David Marshall, *Web Theory: An Introduction* (New York: Routledge, 2003), 48.

32. Christian Fuchs, *Internet and Society: Social Theory in the Information Age* (New York: Routledge, 2008), 118.

33. David Bell, Brian Loader, Nicholas Pleace, and Douglas Schuler, *Cyberculture: The Key Concepts* (New York: Routledge, 2003), 117.

34. James Bohman, *Democracy Across Borders: From Demos to Demoi* (Cambridge, Mass.: MIT Press, 2007), 74.

35. See Jodi Dean's critique of communicative capitalism, "Communicative Capitalism: Circulation and the Foreclosure of Politics," *Cultural Politics* 1, no. 1 (2005): 55.

36. Collin Gifford Brooke's *Lingua Fracta: Towards a Rhetoric of New Media* (Cresskill, N.J.: Hampton Press, 2009) is a bold revisioning of the canons for networked media, but the project of adapting the canons is one that admits of many efforts.

37. See Gurak and Antonijević, "Digital Rhetoric and Public Discourse," in *The SAGE Handbook of Rhetorical Studies*, ed. Andrea Lunsford, Kirt Wilson, and Rosa Eberly (Thousand Oaks, Calif.: SAGE, 2009), 499.

38. Porter, "Recovering Delivery," 208. Also see Ridolfo and DeVoss, "Composing for Recomposition."

39. McCorkle, *Rhetorical Delivery*, 143.

40. Brooke, *Lingua Fracta*, 170.

41. Barbara Warnick, *Rhetoric Online: Persuasion and Politics on the World Wide Web* (New York: Peter Lang, 2007), especially chapter 5, "Intertextuality and Web-Based Public Discourse." For an example of how rhetoric and remix can be mutually informative, see Scott H. Church, "All Living Things Are DJ's': Rhetoric, Aesthetics, and Remix Culture" (Ph.D. diss., University of Nebraska–Lincoln, 2013).

42. Robert Asen, "A Discourse Theory of Citizenship," *Quarterly Journal of Speech* 90, no. 2 (2004): 189–211.

43. Gilles Deleuze, "Postscript on Control Societies," in *Negotiations*, trans. Martin Joughin (1990; repr., New York: Columbia University Press, 1995), 178–79. Deleuze describes a key modulation in the economic realm: the bonus. Rather than the disciplinary function of wages, bonuses serve to incentivize work, and of course there is always more one could do in order to warrant an ever-larger bonus.

44. Deleuze, "On Philosophy," in *Negotiations*, 140.

45. Clough, "Introduction."

46. Raymie McKerrow, "Critical Rhetoric: Theory and Praxis," *Communication Monographs* 56, no. 2 (1989): 91–111.

47. Gilles Deleuze, "Mediators," in *Incorporations*, ed. Jonathan Crary and Sanford Kwinter, Zone 6 (New York: Zone Books, 1992), 287–88.

BIBLIOGRAPHY

Abel, Marco. "Intensifying Affect." *Electronic Book Review*. October 24, 2008. http://www.electronicbookreview.com/thread/fictionspresent/immersed.
Adamic, L. A., and N. Glance. "The Political Blogosphere and the 2004 U.S. Election: Divided They Blog." Annual Workshop on the Weblogging Ecosystem, WWW2005, Japan, www.blogpulse.com/papers/2005/AdamicGlanceBlogWWW.pdf.
Adorno, Theodor, and Max Horkheimer. *Dialectic of Enlightenment: Philosophical Fragments*. Edited by Gunzelin Schmid Noerr. Translated by Edmund Jephcott. Stanford: Stanford University Press, 2002.
Alexanian, Janet. "Publicly Intimate Online: Iranian Web Logs in Southern California." *Comparative Studies of South Asia, Africa, and the Middle East* 26, no. 1 (2006): 134–45.
Alexiou, Margaret. *The Ritual Lament in Greek Tradition*. Cambridge: Cambridge University Press, 1974.
Anderson, Benedict. *Imagined Communities: Reflections on the Origin and Spread of Nationalism*. New ed. London: Verso, 2006.
Anderson, Chris W. "Deliberative, Agonistic, and Algorithmic Audiences: Journalism's Vision of Its Public in an Age of Audience Transparency." *International Journal of Communication* 5 (2011): 529–47.
Appadurai, Arjun. *Modernity at Large: Cultural Dimensions of Globalization*. Minneapolis: University of Minnesota Press, 1996.
Arendt, Hannah. *The Human Condition*. Chicago: University of Chicago Press, 1958.
Aristotle. *Nicomachean Ethics*. In *Aristotle in 23 Volumes*, vol. 19. Translated by H. Rackham. Cambridge, Mass.: Harvard University Press, 1934.
———. *On Rhetoric: A Theory of Civic Rhetoric*. Translated by George Kennedy. Oxford: Oxford University Press, 1991.
———. *Topics*. Translated by W. A. Pickard-Cambridge. Stilwell, Kans.: Digireads.com Publishing, 2006.
Asen, Robert. "A Discourse Theory of Citizenship." *Quarterly Journal of Speech* 90, no. 2 (2004): 189–211.
———. "Imagining the Public Sphere." *Philosophy & Rhetoric* 35, no. 4 (2002): 345–67.
Augustine. *On Christian Doctrine*. Translated by J. F. Shaw. Mineola, N.Y.: Dover, 2009.
Austin, Linda. "The Lament and the Rhetoric of the Sublime." *Nineteenth Century Literature* 53, no. 3 (1998): 279–306.
Avram, Gabriela. "At the Crossroads of Knowledge Management and Social Software." *Electronic Journal of Knowledge Management* 4, no. 2 (2006): 1–10.
Bagdikian, Ben. *The Media Monopoly*. 1983. Boston: Beacon Press, 1997.
Barber, Benjamin. *Strong Democracy: Participatory Politics for a New Age*. Berkeley: University of California Press, 1984.
Barlow, Aaron. *The Rise of the Blogosphere*. Westport, Conn.: Praeger, 2007.
Bauman, Zygmunt. *Liquid Modernity*. Cambridge: Polity Press, 2000.
Beck, Ulrich. *The Cosmopolitan Vision*. Cambridge: Polity Press, 2006.
———. *Risk Society: Towards a New Modernity*. Thousand Oaks, Calif.: SAGE, 1992.
Becker, Barbara, and Josef Wehner. "Electronic Networks and Civil Society: Reflections on Structural Changes in the Public Sphere." In *Culture, Technology, and Communication:*

Towards an Intercultural Global Village, edited by Charles Ess and Fay Sudweeks, 67–86. Albany: SUNY Press, 2001.
Bell, David, Brian Loader, Nicholas Pleace, and Douglas Schuler. *Cyberculture: The Key Concepts.* New York: Routledge, 2003.
Beller, Jonathan. *The Cinematic Mode of Production: Attention Economy and the Society of the Spectacle.* Lebanon, N.H.: University Press of New England, 2006.
Benhabib, Seyla. "Democratic Iterations: The Local, the National, and the Global." In *Another Cosmopolitanism*, edited by Robert Post, 45–82. Oxford: Oxford University Press, 2006.
Benkler, Yochai. *The Wealth of Networks: How Social Production Transforms Markets and Freedom.* New Haven: Yale University Press, 2006.
Benson, Rodney. "Bringing the Sociology of Media Back In." *Political Communication* 21, no. 3 (2004): 275–92.
———. "News Media as a 'Journalistic Field': What Bourdieu Adds to New Institutionalism and Vice Versa." *Political Communication* 23, no. 2 (2006): 187–202.
Berlant, Lauren. "Affect, Noise, Silence, Protest: Ambient Citizenship." *Transformations of the Public Sphere*, November 20, 2009, http://publicsphere.ssrc.org/berlant-affect-noise-silence-protest-ambient-citizenship/.
———. "Introduction." In *Intimacy*, edited by Lauren Berlant, 1–8. Chicago: University of Chicago Press, 2000.
Bickford, Susan. "Beyond Friendship: Aristotle on Conflict, Deliberation, and Attention." *Journal of Politics* 58 (May 1996): 398–421.
Biesecker, Barbara. "Coming to Terms with Recent Attempts to Write Women into the History of Rhetoric." *Philosophy & Rhetoric* 25, no. 2 (1992): 140–61.
———. "No Time for Mourning: The Rhetorical Production of the Melancholic Citizen-Subject in the War on Terror." *Rhetoric and Public Affairs* 40, no. 1 (2007): 147–69.
Billig, Michael. *Arguing and Thinking: A Rhetorical Approach to Social Psychology.* 1987. Reprint, New York: Cambridge University Press, 1996.
Bimber, Bruce. *Information and American Democracy: Technology in the Evolution of Political Power.* Cambridge: Cambridge University Press, 2003.
Bitzer, Lloyd. "Rhetorical Public Communication." *Critical Studies in Mass Communication* 4 (1987): 425–28.
———. "The Rhetorical Situation." *Philosophy & Rhetoric* 1, no. 1 (1968): 1–14.
Black, Edwin. "A Note on Theory and Practice in Rhetorical Criticism." *Western Journal of Speech Communication* 44, no. 4 (1980): 331–36.
Blair, Ann M. *Too Much to Know: Managing Scholarly Information Before the Modern Age.* New Haven: Yale University Press, 2010.
Bohman, James. *Democracy Across Borders: From Demos to Demoi.* Cambridge, Mass.: MIT Press, 2007.
———. "The Globalization of the Public Sphere: Cosmopolitan Publicity and the Problem of Cultural Pluralism." *Philosophy and Social Criticism* 24, nos. 2–3 (1998): 199–216.
———. *Public Deliberation: Pluralism, Complexity, and Democracy.* Cambridge, Mass.: MIT Press, 1996.
Boler, Megan. *Feeling Power: Emotions and Education.* New York: Routledge, 1999.
Bolter, Jay David, and Richard Grusin. *Remediation: Understanding New Media.* Cambridge, Mass.: MIT Press, 2000.
Booth, Wayne. *The Rhetoric of Rhetoric: The Quest for Effective Communication.* Oxford: Blackwell, 2004.
Bourdieu, Pierre. *The Rules of Art.* Stanford: Stanford University Press, 1996.
Bovard, James. *Attention-Deficit Democracy.* New York: Palgrave Macmillan, 2005.
boyd, danah, and Kate Crawford. "Critical Questions for Big Data: Provocations for a Cultural, Technological, and Scholarly Phenomenon." *Information, Communication & Society* 15, no. 5 (2012): 662–79.

Brady, Emily, and Arto Haapala. "Melancholy as an Aesthetic Emotion." *Contemporary Aesthetics* 1 (December 2003). http://www.contempaesthetics.org/newvolume/pages/article.php?articleID=214.
Branham, Robert. "'I Was Gone on Debating': Malcolm X's Prison Debates and Public Confrontations." *Argumentation and Advocacy* 31, no. 3 (1995): 117–37.
Brockman, John. *The Third Culture: Beyond the Scientific Revolution*. New York: Simon & Schuster, 1995.
Brockriede, Wayne. "Arguers as Lovers." *Philosophy & Rhetoric* 5, no. 1 (1972): 1–11.
Broda-Bahm, Ken, Daniela Kempf, and William Driscoll. *Argument and Audience: Presenting Debates in Public Settings*. New York: International Debate Education Association, 2004.
Brooke, Collin Gifford. *Lingua Fracta: Towards a Rhetoric of New Media*. Cresskill, N.J.: Hampton Press, 2009.
Brooks, Kevin, Cindy Nichols, and Sybil Priebe. "Remediation, Genre, and Motivation: Key Concepts for Teaching with Weblogs." In Gurak et al., *Into the Blogosphere*. http://blog.lib.umn.edu/blogosphere/remediation_genre.html.
Brouwer, Daniel C., and Robert Asen, eds. *Public Modalities: Rhetoric, Culture, Media, and the Shape of Public Life*. Tuscaloosa: University of Alabama Press, 2010.
Brown, James J., Jr. "Louis C. K.'s 'Weird Ethic': *Kairos* and Rhetoric in the Network." *Present Tense: A Journal of Rhetoric in Society* 3, no. 1 (2013). http://www.presenttensejournal.org/volume-3/louie-c-k-s-weird-ethic-kairos-and-rhetoric-in-the-network/.
Brummett, Barry. "Burke's Representative Anecdote as a Method in Media Criticism." *Critical Studies in Media Communication* 1, no. 2 (1984): 161–76.
Bruns, Axel. *Gatewatching: Collaborative Online News Production*. New York: Peter Lang, 2005.
Bruns, Axel, and Joanne Jacobs. "Introduction." In *The Uses of Blogs*, edited by Axel Bruns and Joanne Jacobs, 1–8. New York: Peter Lang, 2006.
Bryant, Donald. "Rhetoric: Its Functions and Its Scope." *Quarterly Journal of Speech* 39, no. 4 (1953): 401–24.
Burke, Kenneth. *Attitudes Toward History: An Anatomy of Purpose*. 1937. Berkeley: University of California Press, 1959.
———. *Counter-Statement*. 1931. Reprint, Berkeley: University of California Press, 1968.
———. *A Grammar of Motives*. 1945. Reprint, Berkeley: University of California Press, 1969.
———. *Language as Symbolic Action: Essays on Life, Literature, and Method*. Berkeley: University of California Press, 1966.
———. *Permanence and Change*. 1935. Reprint, Berkeley: University of California Press, 1984.
———. *A Rhetoric of Motives*. 1950. Reprint, Berkeley: University of California Press, 1969.
Burke, Peter. *The Fabrication of Louis XIV*. 1992. Reprint, Bath, U.K.: The Bath Press, 1999.
Burnett, Robert, and P. David Marshall. *Web Theory: An Introduction*. New York: Routledge, 2003.
Calhoun, Craig. "Imagining Solidarity: Cosmopolitanism, Constitutional Patriotism, and the Public Sphere." *Public Culture* 14, no. 1 (2002): 147–71.
———. "Introduction: Habermas and the Public Sphere." In *Habermas and the Public Sphere*, edited by Craig Calhoun, 1–48. Cambridge, Mass.: MIT Press, 1992.
Campbell, Karlyn Kohrs. *The Rhetorical Act*. Belmont, Calif.: Wadsworth, 1982.
Carey, James. *Communication as Culture: Essays on Media and Society*. 1989. Reprint, New York: Routledge, 2009.
———. "Historical Pragmatism and the Internet." *New Media & Society* 7, no. 4 (2005): 443–55.
Carr, Nicholas. *The Shallows: What the Internet Is Doing to Our Brains*. New York: W. W. Norton, 2010.
Castells, Manuel. *Communication Power*. Oxford: Oxford University Press, 2009.

———. *The Information Age: Economy, Society, and Culture*. 3rd ed. Volumes 1–3. Oxford: Blackwell, 2003.
———. *Internet Galaxy: Reflections on the Internet, Business, and Society*. Oxford: Oxford University Press, 2001.
———, ed. *The Network Society: A Cross-Cultural Perspective*. Northampton, Mass.: Edward Elgar, 2004.
———. *The Rise of the Network Society*. Oxford: Blackwell, 1996.
Castells, Manuel, and Gustavo Cardoso, eds. *The Network Society: From Knowledge to Policy*. Washington, D.C.: Johns Hopkins Center for Transatlantic Relations, 2006.
Cheney-Lippold, John. "A New Algorithmic Identity: Soft Biopolitics and the Modulation of Control." *Theory, Culture, and Society* 28, no. 6 (2011): 164–81.
Church, Scott H. "All Living Things Are DJ's: Rhetoric, Aesthetics, and Remix Culture." Ph.D. diss., University of Nebraska–Lincoln, 2013.
Cicero. *Cicero on the Emotions: Tusculan Disputations 3 & 4*. Translated, with commentary, by Margaret Graver. Chicago: University of Chicago Press, 2002.
———. *De Oratore, Books I–II*. Translated by Edward W. Sutton and Harris Rackham. Cambridge, Mass.: Harvard University Press, 1942.
Clagett, Marshall. *Greek Science in Antiquity*. 1955. Reprint, Mineola, N.Y.: Dover, 2001.
Clark, Torie. *Lipstick on a Pig: Winning in the No-Spin Era by Someone Who Knows the Game*. New York: Free Press, 2006.
Clough, Patricia Ticineto. "Introduction." In *The Affective Turn: Theorizing the Social*, edited by Patricia Ticineto Clough and Jean Halley, 1–33. Durham: Duke University Press, 2007.
Cohen, Jean, and Andrew Arato. *Civil Society and Political Theory*. Cambridge, Mass.: MIT Press, 1992.
Cohen, Kris. "A Welcome for Blogs." *Continuum: Journal of Media and Culture Studies* 20, no. 2 (2006): 161–73.
Cohen, Lizabeth. *A Consumers' Republic: The Politics of Mass Consumption in Postwar America*. New York: Alfred A. Knopf, 2003.
Comay, Rebecca. "Perverse History: Fetishism and Dialectic in Walter Benjamin." *Research in Phenomenology* 29, no. 1 (1999): 51–62.
Connolly, William E. *The Terms of Political Discourse*. Lexington, Mass.: D. C. Heath, 1974.
Connor, W. Robert. *The New Politicians of Fifth Century Athens*. Indianapolis: Hackett, 1992.
Cook, Timothy. "The Future of the Institutional Media." In *Mediated Politics: Communication in the Future of Democracy*, edited by W. Lance Bennett and Robert Entman, 182–202. Cambridge: Cambridge University Press, 2000.
Couldry, Nick, Sonia Livingstone, and Tim Markham. *Media Consumption and Public Engagement: Beyond the Presumption of Attention*. New York: Palgrave Macmillan, 2007.
Cowhey, Peter F., and Jonathan D. Aronson. *Transforming Global Information and Communication Markets: The Political Economy of Innovation*. Cambridge, Mass.: MIT Press, 2009.
Craig, David A. "Wal-Mart Public Relations in the Blogosphere." *Journal of Mass Media Ethics* 22, nos. 2–3 (2007): 215–28.
Crawford, Alice. "The Myth of the Unmarked Net Speaker." In *Critical Perspectives on the Internet*, edited by Greg Elmer, 89–104. Lanham, Md.: Rowman & Littlefield, 2002.
Crick, Nathan. *Democracy and Rhetoric: John Dewey on the Arts of Becoming*. Columbia: University of South Carolina Press, 2010.
———. "The Search for a Purveyor of News: The Dewey/Lippmann Debate in an Internet Age." *Critical Studies in Media Communication* 26, no. 5 (2009): 480–97.
Crick, Nathan, and Joseph Gabriel. "The Conduit Between Lifeworld and System: Habermas and the Rhetoric of Scientific Controversies." *Rhetoric Society Quarterly* 40, no. 3 (2010): 201–23.

Crossley, Nick. "Emotion and Communicative Action: Habermas, Linguistic Philosophy, and Existentialism." In *Emotions in Social Life: Critical Themes and Contemporary Issues*, edited by Gillian Bendelow and Simon Williams, 16–38. New York: Routledge, 2004.

Crosswhite, James. "Awakening the Topoi: Sources of Invention in *The New Rhetoric*'s Argument Model." *Argumentation and Advocacy* 44, no. 4 (2008): 169–84.

Dahlberg, Lincoln. "Rethinking the Fragmentation of the Cyberpublic: From Consensus to Contestation." *New Media & Society* 9, no. 5 (2007): 827–47.

Dean, Jodi. *Blog Theory: Feedback and Capture in the Circuits of Drive*. Malden, Mass.: Polity Press, 2010.

———. "Communicative Capitalism: Circulation and the Foreclosure of Politics." *Cultural Politics* 1, no. 1 (2005): 51–74.

Deleuze, Gilles. "Mediators." In *Incorporations*, edited by Jonathan Crary and Sanford Kwinter, 280–95. Zone 6. New York: Zone Books, 1992.

———. *Negotiations*. Translated by Martin Joughin. 1990. Reprint, New York: Columbia University Press, 1995.

DeLuca, Kevin, and Jennifer Peeples. "From Public Sphere to Public Screen: Democracy, Activism, and the 'Violence' of Seattle." *Critical Studies in Media Communication* 19, no. 2 (2002): 125–51.

Dewey, John. *Human Nature and Conduct: An Introduction to Social Psychology*. New York: Henry Holt, 1922.

———. "On Common Sense and Science." In *John Dewey: The Later Works, 1925–1953*, edited by Jo Ann Boydston, vol. 12. Carbondale: Southern Illinois University Press, 1990.

———. *The Public and Its Problems*. 1927. Reprint, Athens: Ohio University Press, 1954.

Dixon, Thomas. *From Passions to Emotions*. Cambridge: Cambridge University Press, 2003.

Dodge, Martin, and Rob Kitchin. "The Ethics of Forgetting in an Age of Pervasive Computing." *CASA Working Papers*, 2005. http://eprints.ucl.ac.uk/1292/1/paper92.pdf.

Domingo, David, and Ari Heinonen. "Weblogs and Journalism: A Typology to Explore the Blurring Boundaries." *Nordicom Review* 29, no. 1 (2008): 3–15.

Dryzek, John. "Rhetoric in Democracy: A Systemic Appreciation." *Political Theory* 38, no. 3 (2010): 319–39.

Eamon, William. *Science and the Secrets of Nature: Books of Secrets in Medieval and Early Modern Culture*. Princeton: Princeton University Press, 1994.

Eberly, Rosa. *Citizen Critics: Literary Public Spheres*. Urbana: University of Illinois Press, 2000.

Eckersley, Robyn. *The Green State: Rethinking Democracy and Sovereignty*. Cambridge, Mass.: MIT Press, 2004.

Edsall, Thomas. *The New Politics of Inequality*. New York: W. W. Norton, 1989.

Edsall, Thomas, and Mary Edsall. *Chain Reaction: The Impact of Race, Rights, and Taxes on American Politics*. New York: W. W. Norton, 1992.

Ehninger, Douglas. "Argument as Method: Its Nature, Its Limitations, and Its Uses." *Speech Monographs* 37, no. 2 (1970): 101–10.

———. "On Systems of Rhetoric." *Philosophy & Rhetoric* 1, no. 3 (1968): 131–44.

Eisenstein, Elizabeth. *The Printing Press as an Agent of Change*. Cambridge: Cambridge University Press, 1979.

Ezell, Margaret. *Social Authorship and the Advent of Print*. Baltimore: Johns Hopkins University Press, 1999.

Farrell, Thomas. *Norms of Rhetorical Culture*. New Haven: Yale University Press, 1993.

Fischer, Frank. *Citizens, Experts, and the Environment: The Politics of Local Knowledge*. Durham: Duke University Press, 2000.

Fisher, Walter. *Human Communication as Narration: Toward a Philosophy of Reason, Value, and Action*. Columbia: University of South Carolina Press, 1987.

Fiske, John. *Television Culture*. London: Methuen, 1987.

Fitzpatrick, Kathleen. "CommentPress: New (Social) Structures for New (Networked) Texts." *Journal of Electronic Publishing* 10, no. 3 (2007). doi:10.3998/3336451.0010.305.
Fleming, Marie. "Women and the 'Public Use of Reason.'" *Social Theory and Practice* 19, no. 1 (1993): 27–50.
Flichy, Patrice. *The Internet Imaginaire.* Translated by Liz Carey-Libbrecht. 2001. Reprint, Cambridge, Mass.: MIT Press, 2007.
Fortenbaugh, W. W. *Aristotle on Emotion.* 1975. London: Duckworth, 2002.
Frank, Thomas. *What's the Matter with Kansas?: How Conservatives Won the Heart of America.* New York: Metropolitan Books, 2004.
Fraser, Nancy. *Unruly Practices: Power, Discourse, and Gender in Contemporary Social Theory.* Minneapolis: University of Minnesota Press, 1989.
Freud, Sigmund. "Mourning and Melancholia." In *Collected Papers,* translated by Joan Riviere, 152–70. London: Hogarth Press, 1971.
———. "Mourning and Melancholia." In *The Standard Edition of the Complete Psychological Works of Sigmund Freud,* vol. 14, *1914–1916,* edited and translated by James Strachey, 243–58. London: Hogarth Press, 1957.
Friedland, Lewis, Thomas Hove, and Hernando Rojas. "The Networked Public Sphere." *Javnost—The Public* 13 (2006): 5–26.
Froomkin, Michael A. "Habermas@Discourse.net: Toward a Critical Theory of Cyberspace." *Harvard Law Review* 116, no. 3 (2003): 749–871.
Fuchs, Christian. *Internet and Society: Social Theory in the Information Age.* New York: Routledge, 2008.
Fuller, Steve. "The Constitutively Social Character of Expertise." In *The Philosophy of Expertise,* edited by Evan Selinger and Robert P. Crease, 342–57. New York: Columbia University Press, 2006.
Gadamer, Hans-Georg. *Truth and Method.* 1975. Reprint, New York: Continuum Books, 2004.
Gallagher, Winifred. *Rapt: Attention and the Focused Life.* New York: Penguin, 2009.
Gaonkar, Dilip. *Alternative Modernities.* Durham: Duke University Press, 2001.
Gastil, John, and Laura Black. "Public Deliberation as the Organizing Principle of Political Communication Research." *Journal of Public Deliberation* 4, no. 1 (2008): 1–47.
Gaukroger, Stephen, ed. *The Soft Underbelly of Reason: The Passions in the Seventeenth Century.* New York: Routledge, 1998.
Geiger, R. Stuart. "Does Habermas Understand the Internet? The Algorithmic Construction of the Blogo/Public Sphere." *Gnovis* 10, no. 1 (2009): 1–29. http://gnovisjournal.org/2009/12/22/does-habermas-understand-internet-algorithmic-construction-blogopublic-sphere/.
Gelbspan, Ross. *Boiling Point: How Politicians, Big Oil and Coal, Journalists, and Activists Are Fueling the Climate Crisis—and What We Can Do to Avert Disaster.* New York: Basic Books, 2004.
Gieryn, Thomas. "Boundary-Work and the Demarcation of Science from Non-science: Strains and Interests in Professional Ideologies of Scientists." *American Sociological Review* 48, no. 6 (1983): 781–95.
Gilbert, Christopher J. "Playing With Hitler: Downfall and Its Ludic Uptake." *Critical Studies in Media Communication* 30, no. 5 (2013): 407–28.
Ginzburg, Carlo. *Clues, Myths, and the Historical Method.* Translated by John and Anne C. Tedeschi. Baltimore: Johns Hopkins University Press, 1989.
Gitelman, Lisa. *Always Already New: Media, History, and the Culture of Data.* Cambridge, Mass: MIT Press, 2006.
Gleick, James. *The Information: A History, a Theory, a Flood.* New York: Pantheon Books, 2011.
Goggin, Gerard. "Blogging Said." In *Edward Said: The Legacy of a Public Intellectual,* edited by Ned Curthoys and Debjani Ganguly, 57–74. Carlton, Vic.: Melbourne University Press, 2007.

Golden, James L., and Edward P. J. Corbett, eds. *The Rhetoric of Blair, Campbell, and Whately.* 1968. Reprint, Carbondale: Southern Illinois University Press, 1990.
Goodnight, G. Thomas. "Opening up 'The Spaces of Dissension.'" *Communication Monographs* 64, no. 3 (1997): 271–75.
Gould, Deborah. *Moving Politics: Emotion and ACT UP's Fight Against AIDS.* Chicago: University of Chicago Press, 2009.
Graves, Lucas. "The Affordances of Blogging: A Case Study in Culture and Technological Effects." *Journal of Communication Inquiry* 31, no. 4 (2007): 331–46.
Greene, Ronald. "Rhetorical Pedagogy as a Postal System: Circulating Subjects Through Michael Warner's 'Publics and Counterpublics.'" *Quarterly Journal of Speech* 88, no. 4 (2002): 434–43.
Gregg, Melissa. "Posting with Passion: Blogs and the Politics of Gender." In *The Uses of Blogs*, edited by Axel Bruns and Joanne Jacobs, 151–60. New York: Peter Lang, 2006.
Gross, Daniel. *The Secret History of Emotion: From Aristotle's "Rhetoric" to Modern Brain Science.* Chicago: University of Chicago Press, 2006.
Gumpert, Gary, and Susan Drucker. "From the Agora to the Electronic Shopping Mall." *Critical Studies in Media Communication* 9, no. 2 (1992): 186–200.
Gunn, Joshua. "On Speech and Public Release." *Rhetoric and Public Affairs* 13, no. 2 (2010): 175–216.
Gurak, Laura, and Smiljana Antonijević. "Digital Rhetoric and Public Discourse." In *The SAGE Handbook of Rhetorical Studies*, edited by Andrea Lunsford, Kirt Wilson, and Rosa Eberly, 497–509. Thousand Oaks, Calif.: SAGE, 2009.
Gurak, Laura J., Smiljana Antonijević, Laurie Johnson, Clancy Ratliff, and Jessica Reyman, eds. *Into the Blogosphere: Rhetoric, Community, and the Culture of Weblogs.* June 2004. http://blog.lib.umn.edu/blogosphere/.
Habermas, Jürgen. *Between Facts and Norms: Contributions to a Discourse Theory of Law and Democracy.* Translated by William Rehg. Cambridge, Mass.: MIT Press, 1996.
———. "Further Reflections on the Public Sphere." In *Habermas and the Public Sphere*, edited by Craig Calhoun, 421–61. Cambridge, Mass.: MIT Press, 1992.
———. "New Social Movements." *Telos* 49 (Fall 1981): 33–37.
———. *Philosophical Discourses of Modernity: Twelve Lectures.* Translated by Frederick G. Lawrence. Cambridge, Mass.: MIT Press, 1990.
———. "Political Communication in Media Society: Does Democracy Still Enjoy an Epistemic Dimension? The Impact of Normative Theory on Empirical Research." *Communication Theory* 16, no. 4 (2006): 411–26.
———. *The Structural Transformation of the Bourgeois Public Sphere: An Inquiry into a Category of Bourgeois Society.* Translated by Thomas Burger. Cambridge, Mass.: MIT Press, 1989.
———. *Towards a Rational Society.* Translated by Jeremy Shapiro. 1968. Reprint, Boston: Beacon Press, 1970.
Hager, Carol. *Technological Democracy: Bureaucracy and Citizenry in the German Energy Debate.* Ann Arbor: University of Michigan Press, 1995.
Halavais, Alexander. "Scholarly Blogging: Moving Towards the Visible College." In *The Uses of Blogs*, edited by Axel Bruns and Joanne Jacobs, 117–26. New York: Peter Lang, 2006.
Hall, Jim. "The First Web War: 'Bad Things Happen in Unimportant Places.'" *Journalism Studies* 1, no. 3 (2000): 387–404.
Hall, Stuart. *Encoding and Decoding in the Television Discourse.* Birmingham, U.K.: Center for Contemporary Culture, 1974.
Hamilton, John Maxwell, and Eric Jenner. "New Foreign Correspondence." *Foreign Affairs* 82, no. 5 (2003): 131–38.
Hanisch, Carol. "The Personal Is Political." In *Notes from the Second Year: Women's Liberation*, edited by Shulamith Firestone and Ann Koedt, 76–78. New York: Notes from the Second Year Press, 1970.

Hansen, Mogens H. *The Athenian Democracy in the Age of Demosthenes: Structure, Principles, and Ideology.* Translated by J. A. Crook. 1991. Reprint, Norman: University of Oklahoma Press, 1999.

Hapke, Thomas. "Roots of Mediating Information: Aspects of the German Information Movement." In *European Modernism and the Information Society: Informing the Present, Understanding the Past,* edited by W. Boyd Raymond, 307–29. Surrey: Ashgate, 2008.

Harding, Jennifer, and E. Deirdre Pribram. "The Power of Feeling: Locating Emotions in Culture." *European Journal of Cultural Studies* 5, no. 4 (2002): 407–26.

Hariman, Robert. *Political Style: The Artistry of Power.* Chicago: University of Chicago Press, 1995.

Hariman, Robert, and John Lucaites. "Dissent and Emotional Management in a Liberal-Democratic Society: The Kent State Iconic Photograph." *Rhetoric Society Quarterly* 31, no. 3 (2001): 5–21.

———. *No Caption Needed: Iconic Photographs, Public Culture, and Liberal Democracy.* Chicago: University of Chicago Press, 2007.

Harris, Randy Allen, ed. *Rhetoric and Incommensurability.* West Lafayette, Ind.: Parlor Press, 2005.

Hart, Douglas, and Steven Simon. "Thinking Straight and Talking Straight: Problems of Intelligence Analysis." *Survival* 48, no.1 (2006): 35–60.

Hart, Roderick, Jay Childers, and Colene Lind. *Political Tone: How Leaders Talk and Why.* Chicago: University of Chicago Press, 2013.

Hartelius, E. Johanna. *The Rhetoric of Expertise.* Lanham, Md.: Lexington Books, 2011.

Harvey, David. *The Condition of Postmodernity: An Enquiry into the Origins of Cultural Change.* Oxford: Blackwell, 1989.

Havelock, Eric. *The Muse Learns to Write: Reflections on Orality and Literacy from Antiquity to the Present.* New Haven: Yale University Press, 1986.

Hawhee, Debra. "Kairotic Encounters." In *Perspectives on Rhetorical Invention,* edited by Janice Lauer and Janet M. Atwill. Knoxville: University of Tennessee Press, 2002.

Hawhee, Debra, and Christa J. Olson. "Pan-historiography: The Challenges of Writing History Across Time and Space." In *Theorizing Histories of Rhetoric,* edited by Michelle Ballif, 90–106. Carbondale: Southern Illinois University Press, 2013.

Hayes, Arthur S. *Press Critics Are the Fifth Estate: Media Watchdogs in America.* Westport, Conn.: Praeger, 2008.

Herring, Susan, Inna Kouper, Lois Ann Scheidt, and Elijah Wright. "Women and Children Last: The Discursive Construction of Weblogs." In Gurak et al., *Into the Blogosphere.* http://blog.lib.umn.edu/blogosphere/women_and_children.html.

Herring, Susan, Lois Ann Scheidt, Sabrina Bonus, and Elijah Wright. "Weblogs as a Bridging Genre." *Information Technology and People* 18, no. 2 (2005): 142–71.

Himmer, Steven. "The Labyrinth Unbound: Weblogs as Literature." In Gurak et al., *Into the Blogosphere.* http://blog.lib.umn.edu/blogosphere/labyrinth_unbound.html.

Hindman, Matthew. *The Myth of Digital Democracy.* Princeton: Princeton University Press, 2009.

Hirschmann, Albert. *The Passions and the Interests: Political Arguments for Capitalism Before Its Triumph.* 1977. Reprint, Princeton: Princeton University Press, 1997.

Hove, Thomas. "The Filter, the Alarm System, and the Sounding Board: Critical and Warning Functions of the Public Sphere." *Communication and Critical/Cultural Studies* 6, no. 1 (2009): 19–38.

Howard, Robert Glenn. "The Vernacular Web of Participatory Media." *Critical Studies in Media Communication* 25, no. 5 (2008): 490–513.

Hoyningen-Huene, Paul. "Context of Discovery and Context of Justification." *Studies in the History and Philosophy of Science* 18, no. 4 (1986): 501–15.

Hutchby, Ian. "Technologies, Texts, and Affordances." *Sociology: The Journal of the British Sociological Association* 35, no. 2 (2001): 441–56.

Isocrates. *Antidosis.* In *Isocrates.* Vol. 2. Translated by George Norlin. Cambridge, Mass.: Harvard University Press, 1929.
———. *Busiris.* In *Isocrates.* Vol. 3. Translated by La Rue Van Hook. Cambridge, Mass.: Harvard University Press, 1945.
Ivie, Robert. "Cold War Motives and the Rhetorical Metaphor: A Framework of Criticism." In *Cold War Rhetoric: Strategy, Metaphor, Ideology,* edited by Martin Medhurst, Robert Ivie, Philip Wander, and Robert Scott, 71–80. East Lansing: Michigan State University Press, 1997.
———. "The Metaphor of Force in Prowar Discourse: The Case of 1812." In *Critical Questions: Invention, Creativity, and the Criticism of Discourse and Media,* edited by William Northstine, Carole Blair, and Gary Copeland, 264–80. New York: St. Martin's Press, 1994.
Jackson, Michele H. "The Mash-Up: A New Archetype for Communication." *Journal of Computer-Mediated Communication* 14, no. 3 (2009): 730–34.
James, Susan. *Passion and Action: The Emotions in Seventeenth Century Philosophy.* Oxford: Oxford University Press, 1997.
Jamieson, Kathleen M. "Antecedent Genre as Rhetorical Constraint." *Quarterly Journal of Speech* 61, no. 4 (1975): 406–15.
Jarvis, Brian. *Postmodern Cartographies: The Geographical Imagination in Contemporary American Culture.* New York: St. Martin's Press, 1998.
Jenkins, Henry. *Convergence Culture: Where Old and New Media Collide.* New York: New York University Press, 2006.
———. *Fans, Bloggers, and Gamers: Inside Participatory Culture.* New York: New York University Press, 2006.
Jenkins, Henry, and David Thorburn. *Democracy and New Media.* Cambridge, Mass.: MIT Press, 2003.
Jordan, John. "Disciplining the Virtual Home Front: Mainstream News and the Web During the War in Iraq." *Communication and Critical/Cultural Studies* 4, no. 3 (2007): 287–93.
Kane, Carolyn L., and John Durham Peters. "Speaking into the iPhone: An Interview with John Durham Peters, or, Ghostly Cessation for the Digital Age." *Journal of Communication Inquiry* 34, no. 2 (2010): 119–33.
Karpowitz, Christopher, and Jane Mansbridge. "Disagreement and Consensus: The Importance of Dynamic Updating in Public Deliberation." In *The Deliberative Democracy Handbook: Strategies for Effective Civic Engagement in the Twenty-First Century,* edited by John Gastil and Peter Levine, 237–53. San Francisco, Calif.: John Wiley & Sons, 2005.
Kastely, James. "Rhetoric and Emotion." In *A Companion to Rhetoric and Rhetorical Criticism,* edited by Walter Jost and Wendy Olmsted, 221–37. Malden, Mass.: Blackwell, 2004.
Kaye, Barbara. "Blog Use Motivations: An Exploratory Study." In *Blogging, Citizenship, and the Future of Media,* edited by Mark Tremayne, 127–47. New York: Routledge, 2007.
Keane, John. "Structural Transformations of the Public Sphere." *Communication Review* 1, no. 1 (1995): 10.
Kelleher, Tom, and Barbara M. Miller. "Organizational Blogs and the Human Voice: Relational Strategies and Relational Outcomes." *Journal of Computer-Mediated Communication* 11, no. 2 (2006): 395–414.
Kellow, Aynsley. *Science and Public Policy: The Virtuous Corruption of Virtual Environmental Science.* Northampton, Mass.: Edward Elgar, 2007.
Kelly, John. "Pride of Place: Mainstream Media and the Networked Public Sphere." In *Media Re:Public.* Cambridge, Mass.: Berkman Center for Internet and Society at Harvard University, 2008. http://cyber.law.harvard.edu/sites/cyber.law.harvard.edu/files/Pride%20of%20Place_MR.pdf.

Kennedy, George A. *Classical Rhetoric and Its Christian and Secular Tradition from Ancient to Modern Times*. 2nd ed. Chapel Hill: University of North Carolina Press, 1999.

Keren, Michael. *Blogosphere: The New Political Arena*. New York: Rowman & Littlefield, 2006.

Kinniburgh, James, and Dorothy Denning. "Blogs and Military Information Strategy." *JSOU Report*, June 2006. http://www.au.af.mil/info-ops/iosphere/iosphere_summer06 _kinniburgh.pdf.

Kline, David. "I Blog, Therefore I Am." In *Blog! How the Newest Media Revolution Is Changing Politics, Business, and Culture*, edited by David Kline and Dan Burstein, 237–52. New York: CDS Books, 2005.

Kochan, Donald J. "The Blogosphere and the New Pamphleteers." *Nexus Law Journal* 11 (2006). Chapman University Law Research Paper 08-02. http://ssrn.com/abstract =908631.

Kovach, Bill, and Tom Rosenstiel. *Warp Speed: America in the Age of Mixed Media Culture*. New York: Century Foundation Press, 1999.

Kramer, Peter. "The Valorization of Sadness: Alienation and the Melancholic Temperament." *Hastings Center Report* 30, no. 2 (2000): 13–18.

Kulikova, Svetlana V., and David Perlmutter. "Blogging Down the Dictator? The Kyrgyz Revolution and *Samizdat* Websites." *International Communication Gazette* 69, no. 1 (2007): 29–50.

Lakoff, George, and Mark Johnson. *Metaphors We Live By*. Chicago: University of Chicago Press, 1980.

Landels, John G. *Music in Ancient Greece*. New York: Routledge, 1999.

Lanham, Richard. *The Economics of Attention: Style and Substance in the Information Age*. Chicago: University of Chicago Press, 2006.

———. *The Electronic Word: Democracy, Technology, and the Arts*. Chicago: University of Chicago Press, 1993.

Lauer, Claire. "Contending with Terms: 'Multimodal' and 'Multimedia' in the Academic and Public Spheres." *Computers and Composition* 26, no. 4 (2009): 225–39.

Lawrence, Eric, John Sides, and Henry Farrell. "Self-Segregation or Deliberation? Blog Readership, Participation, and Polarization in American Politics." *Perspectives on Politics* 8, no. 1 (2010): 141–57.

Lazarsfeld, Paul, and Robert Merton. "Mass Communication, Popular Taste, and Organized Social Action." In *The Communication of Ideas*, edited by Lyman Bryson. New York: Institute for Religious and Social Studies, 1948. Republished in *Mass Communication and American Social Thought: Key Texts, 1919–1968*, edited by John Durham Peters and Peter Simonson, 230–42. Lanham, Md.: Rowman & Littlefield, 2004.

LeFevre, Karen. *Invention as a Social Act*. Carbondale: Southern Illinois University Press, 1987.

Leff, Michael. "The Idea of Rhetoric as Interpretive Practice: A Humanist's Response to Gaonkar." In *Rhetorical Hermeneutics: Invention and Interpretation in the Age of Science*, edited by Alan G. Gross and William M. Keith, 89–100. Albany: SUNY Press, 1997.

Leiserowitz, Anthony, Edward W. Maibach, Connie Roser-Renouf, Nicholas Smith, and Erica Dawson. "Climategate, Public Opinion, and the Loss of Trust." *Social Science Research Network* 57, no. 6 (2010): 818–37. doi:10.2139/ssrn.1633932.

Lessig, Lawrence. *Free Culture: The Nature and Future of Creativity*. New York: Penguin, 2005.

Lessl, Thomas M. "The Priestly Voice." *Quarterly Journal of Speech* 75, no. 2 (1989): 183–97.

Lev-On, Azi, and Bernard Manin. "Happy Accidents: Deliberation and Online Exposure to Opposing Views." In *Online Deliberation: Design, Research, and Practice*, edited by Todd Davies and Seeta Peña Gangadharan, 105–22. Palo Alto, Calif.: Center for

the Study of Language and Information, 2009. http://odbook.stanford.edu/viewing/filedocument/46.
Levy, Pierre. *Collective Intelligence: Mankind's Emerging World in Cyberspace*. Translated by Robert Bononno. 1994. Reprint, New York: Basic Books, 1997.
Lewiński, Marcin. "Collective Argumentative Criticism in Informal Online Discussion Forums." *Argumentation and Advocacy* 47, no. 2 (2010): 86–107.
Lewis, Sian. *News and Society in the Greek Polis*. Chapel Hill: University of North Carolina Press, 1996.
Lim, Merlyna, and Mark E. Kann. "Politics: Deliberation, Mobilization, and Networked Practices of Agitation." In *Networked Publics*, edited by Kazys Varnelis, 77–108. Cambridge, Mass.: MIT Press, 2008.
Lippmann, Walter. *Public Opinion*. New York: Macmillan, 1922.
Lott, Trent. *Herding Cats: A Life in Politics*. New York: HarperCollins, 2005.
Lovink, Geert. *Zero Comments: Blogging and Critical Internet Culture*. New York: Routledge, 2007.
Lowrey, Wilson. "Mapping the Journalism-Blogging Relationship." *Journalism* 7, no. 4 (2006): 477–500.
Lupia, Arthur. "Can Online Deliberation Improve Politics? Scientific Foundations for Success." In *Online Deliberation: Design, Research, and Practice*, edited by Todd Davies and Seeta Peña Gangadharan, 59–70. Stanford, Calif.: Center for the Study of Language and Information, 2009. http://odbook.stanford.edu/static/filedocument/2009/11/10/ODBook.full.11.3.09.pdf.
Lyne, John. "Bio-rhetorics: Moralizing the Life Sciences." In *The Rhetorical Turn: Invention and Persuasion in the Conduct of Inquiry*, edited by Herbert W. Simons, 35–57. Chicago: University of Chicago Press, 1990.
———. "Rhetoric and the Third Culture: Scientists and Arguers and Critics." In *Reengaging the Prospects of Rhetoric: Current Conversations and Contemporary Challenges*, edited by Mark Porrovecchio, 139–53. New York: Routledge, 2010.
Lyotard, Jean-François. *The Postmodern Condition: A Report on Knowledge*. 1979. Reprint, Manchester: Manchester University Press, 1984.
MacNamara, James. "'Emerging' Media and Public Communication: Understanding the Changing Mediascape." *Public Communication Review* 1, no. 2 (2010): 3–17.
Madsen, Arnie. "Burke's Representative Anecdote as Critical Method." In *Extensions of the Burkeian System*, edited by James W. Chesebro, 208–29. Tuscaloosa: University of Alabama Press, 1993.
Maffesoli, Michael. *The Contemplation of the World: Figures of Community Style*. Translated by Susan Emanuel. Minneapolis: University of Minnesota Press, 1996.
Mailloux, Stephen. "Rhetorical Hermeneutics Still Again: or, On the Track of *Phronesis*." In *A Companion to Rhetoric and Rhetorical Criticism*, edited by Walter Jost and Wendy Olmsted, 457–72. Malden, Mass.: Blackwell, 2004.
Majone, Giandomenico. *Evidence, Argument, and Persuasion in the Policy Process*. New Haven: Yale University Press, 1989.
Malin, Brent. "Communication with Feeling: Emotion, Publicness, and Embodiment." *Quarterly Journal of Speech* 87, no. 2 (2001): 216–35.
Manovich, Lev. *The Language of New Media*. Cambridge, Mass.: MIT Press, 2001.
Mansbridge, Jane J. *Beyond Adversary Democracy*. Chicago: University of Chicago Press, 1980.
Marcus, George. *The Sentimental Citizen: Emotion in Democratic Politics*. University Park: Pennsylvania State University Press, 2002.
Matheson, Donald. "Weblogs and the Epistemology of the News: Some Trends in Online Journalism." *New Media & Society* 6, no. 4 (2004): 443–67.
Mathews, David. *Politics for People: Finding a Responsible Public Voice*. Urbana: University of Illinois Press, 1994.

Mattelart, Armand. *Networking the World, 1794–2000.* Translated by Liz Carey-Libbrecht and James Cohen. Minneapolis: University of Minnesota Press, 2000.

McCauliff, Kristen. "Blogging in Baghdad: The Practice of Collective Citizenship on the Blog *Baghdad Burning.*" *Communication Studies* 62, no. 1 (2011): 58–73.

McChesney, Robert. *The Problem of the Media: U.S. Communication Politics in the Twenty-First Century.* New York: Monthly Review Press, 2004.

———. *Rich Media, Poor Democracy: Communication Politics in Dubious Times.* Urbana: University of Illinois Press, 1999.

McCorkle, Ben. *Rhetorical Delivery as Technological Discourse: A Cross-Historical Study.* Carbondale: Southern Illinois University Press, 2012.

McGee, Michael Calvin. "Choosing a *Poros*: Reflections on How to Implicate Isocrates in Liberal Theory." *(F)ragments.* 1998. http://mcgeefragments.net/OLD/Choosing_Poros.html.

———. "Text, Context, and the Fragmentation of Contemporary Culture." *Western Journal of Speech Communication* 54, no. 3 (1990): 274–89.

McKeon, Richard. *Rhetoric: Essays on Invention and Discovery.* Edited by Mark Backmann. Woodbridge, Conn.: Ox Bow Press, 1987.

McKerrow, Raymie. "Critical Rhetoric: Theory and Praxis." *Communication Monographs* 56, no. 2 (1989): 91–111.

McLeod, Kembrew. *Freedom of Expression: Resistance and Repression in the Age of Intellectual Property.* Minneapolis: University of Minnesota Press, 2007.

———. *Owning Culture: Authorship, Ownership, and Intellectual Property.* New York: Peter Lang, 2001.

McLuhan, Marshall. *Understanding Media: The Extensions of Man.* Critical ed. Edited by Terence Gordon. 1964. Reprint, Corte Madera, Calif.: Gingko Press, 2003.

Merton, Robert. *On Social Structure and Science.* Edited by Piotr Sztompka. Chicago: University of Chicago Press, 1996.

Miller, Carolyn. "The Aristotelian *Topos*: Hunting for Novelty." In *Rereading Aristotle's Rhetoric,* edited by Alan G. Gross and Arthur E. Walzer, 130–46. Carbondale,: Southern Illinois University Press, 2000.

Miller, Carolyn, and Dawn Shepherd. "Blogging as Social Action: A Genre Analysis of the Weblog." In Gurak et al., *Into the Blogosphere.* http://blog.lib.umn.edu/blogosphere/blogging_as_social_action_a_genre_analysis_of_the_weblog.html.

Miller, Clark, and Paul Edwards. "Introduction." In *Changing the Atmosphere: Expert Knowledge and Environmental Governance,* edited by Clark Miller and Paul Edwards, 1–30. Cambridge, Mass.: MIT Press, 2001.

Minahan, Stella, and Julie Wolfram Cox. "Stitch'nBitch: Cyberfeminism, a Third Place, and the New Materiality." *Journal of Material Culture* 12, no. 1 (2007): 5–21.

Mitchell, Gordon R. "Higher-Order Strategic Maneuvering in Argumentation." *Argumentation* 24, no. 3 (2010): 319–35.

———. "Simulated Public Argument as a Pedagogical Play on Worlds." *Argumentation and Advocacy* 36 (Winter 2000): 134–50.

Mitchell, Gordon R., and Takeshi Suzuki. "Beyond the '*Daily Me*': Argumentation in an Age of Enclave Deliberation." In *Argumentation and Social Cognition,* edited by Takeshi Suzuki, Yoshiro Yano, and Takayuki Kato, 163–64. Tokyo: Japan Debate Association, 2004.

Mitra, Ananda. "Using Blogs to Create Cybernetic Space: Examples from People of Indian Origin." *Convergence: The International Journal of Research into New Media Technologies* 14, no. 4 (2008): 457–72.

Mitra, Ananda, and Eric King Watts. "Theorizing Cyberspace: The Idea of Voice Applied to the Internet Discourse." *New Media & Society* 4, no. 4 (2002): 479–98.

Morozov, Evgeny. *The Net Delusion: The Dark Side of Internet Freedom.* London: Penguin, 2011.

Muckelbauer, John. *The Future of Invention: Rhetoric, Postmodernism, and the Problem of Change*. Albany: SUNY Press, 2008.

Muhlberger, Peter. "Testing Cyber-realism." In *Democracy Online: The Prospects for Political Renewal Through the Internet*, edited by Peter Shane, 225–38. New York: Routledge, 2004.

Muñoz, José. "Photographies of Mourning: Melancholia and Ambivalence in Van Der Zee, Mapplethorpe, and *Looking for Langston*." In *Race and the Subject of Masculinities*, edited by Harry Stecopoulos and Michael Uebel, 337–60. Durham: Duke University Press, 1997.

Murphy, Dennis, and James White. "Propaganda: Can a Word Decide a War?" *Parameters* 37, no. 3 (2007): 15–27.

Mutz, Diane. *Hearing the Other Side: Deliberative Versus Participatory Democracy*. Cambridge: Cambridge University Press, 2006.

Nagle, Brendan. *The Household as the Foundation of Aristotle's Polis*. Cambridge: Cambridge University Press, 2006.

Natanson, Maurice. "The Claims of Immediacy." In *Philosophy, Rhetoric, and Argumentation*, edited by Maurice Natanson and Henry Johnston Jr., 10–19. University Park: Pennsylvania State University Press, 1965.

Neuman, W. Russell. *The Future of the Mass Audience*. Cambridge: Cambridge University Press, 1992.

Nichols, Marie Hochmuth. "Kenneth Burke and the 'New Rhetoric.'" *Quarterly Journal of Speech* 38, no. 2 (1952): 133–44.

Nietzsche, Friedrich. *The Portable Nietzsche*. Edited and translated by Walter Kaufmann. New York: Viking Press, 1977.

Nowotny, Stefan. "The Condition of Becoming Public." *Transversal*, December 2003, http://www.eipcp.net/transversal/1203/nowotny/en.

Oakley, Todd. *From Attention to Meaning: Explorations in Semiotics, Linguistics, and Rhetoric*. New York: Peter Lang, 2009.

Ó Baioll, Andrew. "Weblogs and the Public Sphere." In Gurak et al., *Into the Blogosphere*. http://blog.lib.umn.edu/blogosphere/weblogs_and_the_public_sphere.html.

Ober, Josiah. *Athenian Legacies: Essays on the Politics of Going On Together*. Princeton: Princeton University Press, 2005.

O'Keefe, Daniel. "Two Concepts of Argument." *Journal of the American Forensic Association* 13, no. 3 (1977): 121–28.

Ong, Walter. *Orality and Literacy: The Technologizing of the Word*. New York: Methuen, 1982.

———. *Ramus, Method, and the Decay of Dialogue*. London: Oxford University Press, 1958.

Outhwaite, William. *Habermas: A Critical Introduction*. Cambridge: Polity Press, 2009.

Palczewski, Catherine Helen. "Argument in an Off Key: Playing with the Productive Limits of Argument." In *Critical Problems in Argumentation: Selected Papers from the 13th Biennial Conference on Argumentation*, edited by Charles Arthur Willard, 1–23. Washington, D.C.: National Communication Association Convention, 2005.

Patterson, Robert, and Ronald Lee. "The Environmental Rhetoric of 'Balance': A Case Study of Regulatory Discourse and the Colonization of the Public." *Technical Communication Quarterly* 6, no. 1 (1997): 25–40.

Pax, Salam. *Salam Pax: The Clandestine Diary of an Ordinary Iraqi*. New York: Grove Press, 2003.

Pelias, Ronald. "The Critical Life." *Communication Education* 49, no. 3 (2000): 220–28.

Pensky, Max. *Melancholy Dialectics: Walter Benjamin and the Play of Mourning*. Amherst: University of Massachusetts Press, 1993.

Perelman, Chaim, and Lucie Olbrechts-Tyteca. *The New Rhetoric: A Treatise on Argumentation*. Translated by J. Wilkinson and P. Weaver. Notre Dame: University of Notre Dame Press, 1969.

Perlmutter, David. *Blogwars*. Oxford: Oxford University Press, 2008.

Persons, Georgia. "Defining the Public Interest: Citizen Participation in Metropolitan and State Policy Making." *National Civic Review* 79, no. 2 (2007): 118–31.

Peters, John Durham. "Broadcasting and Schizophrenia." *Media, Culture, and Society* 32, no. 1 (2010): 123–40.

———. *Courting the Abyss: Free Speech and the Liberal Tradition.* Chicago: University of Chicago Press, 2005.

———. "Distrust of Representation: Habermas on the Public Sphere." *Media, Culture, and Society* 15, no. 4 (1993): 541–71.

———. *Speaking into the Air: A History of the Idea of Communication.* Chicago: University of Chicago Press, 2001.

Peters, John Durham, and Peter Simonson, eds. *Mass Communication and American Social Thought: Key Texts, 1919–1968.* Lanham, Md.: Rowman & Littlefield, 2004.

Peterson, Valerie. "Beyond Dichotomy: The Sophists' Understanding of Antithetical Thought." *Advances in the History of Rhetoric* 1, no. 1 (1998): 1–8.

Pettitt, Tom. "Before the Gutenberg Parenthesis: Elizabethan-American Compatibilities." Paper presented at MIT5: Creativity, Ownership, and Collaboration in the Digital Age. Cambridge, Mass., April 27–29, 2007. web.mit.edu/comm.forum/mit5/papers/pettitt_plenary_gutenberg.pdf.

———. "Bracketing the Gutenberg Parenthesis." *Explorations in Media Ecology* 11, no. 2 (2012): 95–114.

Pfister, Damien Smith. "Networked Expertise in the Era of Many-to-Many Communication: On *Wikipedia* and Invention." *Social Epistemology* 25, no. 3 (2011): 217–31.

———. "'A Short Burst of Inconsequential Information': Networked Rhetorics, Avian Consciousness, and Bioegalitarianism." *Environmental Communication: A Journal of Nature and Culture,* forthcoming (2014).

Plato. *The Dialogues of Plato.* Vol. 2. Translated by Benjamin Jowett. New York: Scribner, Armstrong, 1873.

———. *Phaedrus.* Translated by W. C. Helmbold and W. G. Rabinowitz. New York: Macmillan, 1956.

———. *Plato in Twelve Volumes.* Translated by Harold N. Fowler. Cambridge, Mass.: Harvard University Press, 1925.

———. *The Republic.* Vol. 2. Translated by Paul Shorey. Cambridge, Mass.: Harvard University Press, 1935.

Porter, James. "Recovering Delivery for Digital Rhetoric and Human-Computer Interaction." *Computers and Composition* 26, no. 4 (2009): 207–24.

Postman, Neil. *Amusing Ourselves to Death: Public Discourse in an Age of Show Business.* New York: Penguin, 1985.

Poulakos, John. *Sophistical Rhetoric in Ancient Greece.* Columbia: University of South Carolina Press, 1995.

———. "Toward a Sophistic Definition of Rhetoric." *Philosophy & Rhetoric* 16, no. 1 (1983): 35–48.

Prelli, Lawrence. *A Rhetoric of Science: Inventing Scientific Discourse.* Columbia: University of South Carolina Press, 1989.

Putnam, Robert. *Bowling Alone: The Collapse and Revival of American Community.* New York: Simon & Schuster, 2000.

Qvortrup, Lars. *The Hypercomplex Society.* New York: Peter Lang, 2003.

Radden, Jennifer, ed. *The Nature of Melancholy: From Aristotle to Kristeva.* Oxford: Oxford University Press, 2000.

Radway, Janice. *Reading the Romance: Women, Patriarchy, and Popular Literature.* Chapel Hill: University of North Carolina Press, 1991.

Ramus, Peter. *Arguments in Rhetoric Against Quintilian: Translation and Text of Peter Ramus's "Rhetoricae Distinctiones in Quintilianum" (1549).* Edited by James Murphy. Translated by Carole Newlands. 1986. Reprint, Carbondale: Southern Illinois University Press, 2010.

Rettberg, Jill. *Blogging.* Cambridge: Polity Press, 2008.
Rice, Jeffrey. *The Rhetoric of Cool: Composition Studies and New Media.* Carbondale, IL: Southern Illinois University Press, 2007.
Rice, Jenny Edbauer. "The New 'New': Making a Case for Critical Affect Studies." *Quarterly Journal of Speech* 94, no. 2 (2008): 200–212.
Richards, I. A. *The Philosophy of Rhetoric.* New York: Oxford University Press, 1936.
Ridolfo, Jim, and Dànielle Nicole DeVoss. "Composing for Recomposition: Rhetorical Velocity and Delivery." *Kairos: A Journal of Rhetoric, Technology, and Pedagogy* 13, no. 2 (2009). http://kairos.technorhetoric.net/13.2/topoi/ridolfo_devoss/intro.html.
Roberts-Miller, Trish. "Parody Blogging and the Call of the Real." In Gurak et al., *Into the Blogosphere.* http://blog.lib.umn.edu/ blogosphere/parody_blogging.html.
Rosa, Hartmut. "Social Acceleration: Ethical and Political Consequences of a Desynchronized High-Speed Society." *Constellations* 10, no. 1 (2003): 3–33.
Rowland, Robert. "In Defense of Rational Argument: A Pragmatic Justification of Argumentation Theory and Response to the Postmodern Critique." *Philosophy & Rhetoric* 28, no. 4 (1995): 350–64.
Russell, Adrienne. "Digital Communication Networks and the Journalistic Field: The 2005 French Riots." *Critical Studies in Media Communication* 24, no. 4 (2007): 285–302.
Scannell, Paddy. "Benjamin Contextualized: On 'The Work of Art in an Age of Mechanical Reproduction.'" In *Canonic Texts in Media Research: Are There Any? Should There Be? How About These?*, edited by Elihu Katz, John Durham Peters, Tamar Liebes, and Avril Orloff, 74–89. Cambridge: Polity Press, 2003.
Scheuerman, William E. "Liberal Democracy and the Empire of Speed." *Polity* 34, no. 1 (2001): 41–67.
Schiappa, Edward. *Defining Reality: Definitions and the Politics of Meaning.* Carbondale: Southern Illinois Press, 2003.
Schiffer, Adam. "Blogswarms and Press Norms: News Coverage of the Downing Street Memo Controversy." *Journalism and Mass Communication Quarterly* 83, no. 3 (2006): 494–510.
Schiller, Dan. *How to Think About Information.* Urbana: University of Illinois Press, 2007.
Schmidt, Jan. "Blogging Practices in the German-Speaking Blogosphere: Findings from the 'Wie Ich Blogge?!' Survey." New Communication Media Research Centre Working Paper 07–02 (June 2007), https://www.uni-bamberg.de/fileadmin/uni/fakultaeten/split_professuren/journalistik/Fonk/pdfs-Veroeffentlichungen/Blogging_practices.pdf.
Schneider, Stephen. "Is the 'Citizen-Scientist' an Oxymoron?" In *Science, Technology, and Democracy*, edited by Daniel Lee Kleinman, 103–20. Albany: SUNY Press, 2000.
Schudson, Michael. *Discovering the News: A Social History of American Newspapers.* New York: Basic Books, 1978.
Schultze, Quentin J. *Habits of the High-Tech Heart: Living Virtuously in the Internet Age.* Grand Rapids, Mich.: Baker Academic, 2004.
Scoble, Robert, and Shel Israel. *Naked Conversations: How Blogs Are Changing the Way Businesses Are Talking to Customers.* Hoboken, N.J.: John Wiley & Sons, 2006.
Scott, D. Travers. "Tempests of the Blogosphere: Presidential Campaign Stories that Failed to Ignite Mainstream Media." In *Digital Media and Democracy: Tactics in Hard Times*, edited by Megan Boler, 271–300. Cambridge, Mass.: MIT Press, 2008.
Scott, Esther. "'Big Media' Meets the 'Bloggers': Coverage of Trent Lott's Remarks at Strom Thurmond's Birthday Party." *Kennedy School of Government Case Program*, 2004. http://www.ksg.harvard.edu/presspol/Research_Publications/Case_Studies/1731_0.pdf.
Scott, Robert L., James R. Andrews, Howard H. Martin, J. Richard McNally, William F. Nelson, Michael M. Osborn, Arthur L. Smith, and Harold Zyskind. "Report of the Committee on the Nature of Rhetorical Invention." In *The Prospects of Rhetoric*, edited by Lloyd Bitzer and Edwin Black, 228–36. Englewood Cliffs, N.J.: Prentice Hall, 1971.

Senecah, Susan. "The Trinity of Voice: The Role of Practical Theory in Planning and Evaluating the Effectiveness of Environmental Participatory Processes." In *Communication and Public Participation in Environmental Decision-Making*, edited by Stephen P. Depoe, John W. Delicath, and Marie-France Aepli Elsenbeer, 13–34. Albany: SUNY Press, 2004.

Sennett, Richard. *The Fall of Public Man*. New York: Alfred A. Knopf, 1974.

Serfaty, Vivian. *The Mirror and the Veil: An Overview of American Online Diaries and Blogs*. Amsterdam: Rodopi, 2004.

Shannon, Claude, and Warren Weaver. *The Mathematical Theory of Communication*. Urbana: University of Illinois Press, 1963.

Sheller, Mimi, and John Urry. "Mobile Transformations of 'Public' and 'Private' Life." *Theory, Culture & Society* 20, no. 3 (2003): 107–25.

Shteyngart, Gary. *Super Sad True Love Story*. New York: Random House, 2010.

Shirky, Clay. *Here Comes Everybody: The Power of Organizing Without Organizations*. New York: Penguin, 2008.

Shouse, Eric. "Feeling, Emotion, Affect." *Media/Culture* 8, no. 6 (2005): 26. http://journal.media-culture.org.au/0512/03-shouse.php.

Simmons, W. Michele, and Jeffrey T. Grabill. "Toward a Civic Rhetoric for Technologically and Scientifically Complex Places: Invention, Performance, and Participation." *College Composition and Communication* 58, no. 3 (2007): 419–48.

Simon, Herbert. "Designing Organizations for an Information-Rich World." In *Computers, Communication, and the Public Interest*, edited by Martin Greenberger, 37–72. Baltimore: Johns Hopkins University Press, 1971.

Simonson, Peter. *Refiguring Mass Communication: A History*. Urbana: University of Illinois Press, 2010.

Sloane, Thomas O. *On the Contrary: The Protocol of Traditional Rhetoric*. Washington, D.C.: Catholic University Press, 1997.

Sloterdijk, Peter. *Critique of Cynical Reason*. Translated by Michael Eldred. Minneapolis: University of Minnesota Press, 1987.

Smith, Christina M., and Kelly MacDonald. "The Arizona 9/11 Memorial: A Case Study in Public Dissent and Argumentation through Blogs." *Argumentation and Advocacy* 47, no. 2 (2010): 123–39.

Snow, C. P. *The Two Cultures*. 1959. London: Cambridge University Press, 2001.

Sokolon, Marlene K. *Political Emotions: Aristotle and the Symphony of Reason and Emotion*. DeKalb: Northern Illinois University Press, 2006.

Spencer, Herbert. *The Philosophy of Style*. 2nd edition. Edited by Fred N. Scott. Boston: Allyn and Bacon, 1892.

Sprague, Rosamund Kent. *The Older Sophists: A Complete Translation by Several Hands of the Fragments in "Die Fragmente der Vorsokratiker."* 1972. Reprint, Indianapolis: Hackett, 2001.

Stalder, Felix. *Manuel Castells: The Theory of the Network Society*. Cambridge: Polity Press, 2006.

Stearns, Peter N. *Global Outrage: The Impact of World Opinion on Contemporary History*. Oxford: Oneworld Publications, 2005.

St. John, Jeffrey. "Communication as Failure." In *Communication As . . . : Perspectives on Theory*, edited by Gregory Shepherd, Jeffrey St. John, and Ted Striphas, 249–56. Thousand Oaks, Calif.: SAGE, 2006.

Steele, Meili. "Hiding from History: Habermas' Elision of Public Imagination." *Constellations*, September 2005, 409–36.

Sterne, Jonathan. "What if Interactivity Is the New Passivity?" *Flow* 15, no. 10 (April 9, 2012). http://flowtv.org/2012/04/the-new-passivity.

Striphas, Ted. "Communication as Translation." In *Communication As . . . : Perspectives on Theory*, edited by Gregory Sheperd, Jeffrey St. John, and Ted Striphas, 232–41. Thousand Oaks, Calif.: SAGE, 2006.

Sunstein, Cass. *Infotopia: How Many Minds Produce Knowledge.* Oxford: Oxford University Press, 2006.

———. *Republic.com.* Chicago: University of Chicago Press, 2001.

Suter, Ann. "Introduction." In *Lament: Studies in the Ancient Mediterranean and Beyond,* edited by Ann Suter, 3–17. Oxford: Oxford University Press, 2008.

Tannen, Deborah. *The Argument Culture: Moving from Debate to Dialogue.* New York: Random House, 1998.

Taylor, Charles. *Modern Social Imaginaries.* Durham: Duke University Press, 2003.

———. "To Follow a Rule. . . ." In *Bourdieu: Critical Perspectives,* edited by Craig Calhoun, Edward LiPuma, and Moishe Postone, 45–61. Chicago: University of Chicago Press, 1993.

Thompson, John. *The Media and Modernity: A Social Theory of Media.* Cambridge: Polity Press, 1995.

Thrift, Nigel. "Intensities of Feeling: Towards a Spatial Politics of Affect." *Geografiska Annaler* 86 B (2004): 57–78.

Torgerson, Douglas. *The Promise of Green Politics: Environmentalism and the Public Sphere.* Durham: Duke University Press, 1999.

Toulmin, Stephen. *The Uses of Argument.* Cambridge: Cambridge University Press, 1958.

Touraine, Alain. *A New Paradigm for Understanding the World.* Cambridge: Polity Press, 2007.

Trammell, Kaye, and Ana Keshelashvili. "Examining the New Influencers: A Self-Presentation Study of A-List Blogs." *Journalism and Mass Communication Quarterly* 82, no. 4 (2005): 968–92.

Turkle, Sherry. "Always-On/Always-On-You: The Tethered Self." In *Handbook of Mobile Communication Studies,* edited by James Katz, 121–38. Cambridge, Mass.: MIT Press, 2008.

Turner, Fred. *From Counterculture to Cyberculture: Stewart Brand, the Whole Earth Network, and the Rise of Digital Utopianism.* Chicago: University of Chicago Press, 2008.

Turner, Stephen. *Liberal Democracy 3.0: Civil Society in an Age of Experts.* Thousand Oaks, Calif.: SAGE, 2003.

Van Dyk, Krista K. Betts. "From the Plaint to the Comic: Kenneth Burke's *Towards a Better Life.*" *Rhetoric Society Quarterly* 36, no. 1 (2006): 31–53.

Varnelis, Kazys, ed. *Networked Publics.* Cambridge, Mass.: MIT Press, 2008.

Vatz, Richard. "The Myth of the Rhetorical Situation." *Philosophy & Rhetoric* 6, no. 3 (1973): 154–61.

Vico, Giambattista. *On the Most Ancient Wisdom of the Italians.* 1710. Translated by L. M. Palmer. London: Cornell University Press, 1988.

Vlahos, Michael. "The Politics of a Network World: A Speculation." In *The Civic Web: Online Politics and Democratic Values,* edited by David Anderson and Michael Cornfeld, 185–202. Lanham, Md.: Rowman & Littlefield, 2003.

Wallace, Karl R. "The Substance of Rhetoric: Good Reasons." *Quarterly Journal of Speech* 49, no. 3 (1963): 239–49.

Walsh, Peter. "That Withered Paradigm: The Web, the Expert, and the Information Hegemony." In *Democracy and New Media,* edited by Henry Jenkins and David Thorburn, 365–72. Cambridge, Mass.: MIT Press, 2003.

Warner, Michael. *Publics and Counterpublics.* New York: Zone Books, 2005.

Warnick, Barbara. *Rhetoric Online: Persuasion and Politics on the World Wide Web.* New York: Peter Lang, 2007.

Weaver, Richard. *The Ethics of Rhetoric.* 1953. Reprint, Davis, Calif.: Hermagoras Press, 1985.

Webster, James G. "The Duality of Media: A Structurational Theory of Public Attention." *Communication Theory* 21, no. 1 (2011): 43–66.

———. "Structuring a Marketplace of Attention." In *The Hyperlinked Society: Questioning Connections in the Digital Age,* edited by Joseph Turow and Lokman Tsui, 23–38. Ann Arbor: University of Michigan Press, 2008.

Weger, Harry, and Mark Aakhus. "Arguing in Internet Chat Rooms: Argumentative Adaptations to Chat Room Design and Some Consequences for Public Deliberation at a Distance." *Argumentation and Advocacy* 40, no. 1 (2003): 23–38.
Welch, Matt. "Blogworld and Its Gravity: The New Amateur Journalists Weigh In." *Columbia Journalism Review* 42, no. 3 (2003): 21–26.
———. "The New Age of Alternative Media." *Columbia Journalism Review* 42, no. 5 (2003): 20.
Wells, Susan. "Logos." In *The Encyclopedia of Rhetoric*, edited by Thomas Sloane, 456–68. Oxford: Oxford University Press, 2001.
Wess, Robert. "Representative Anecdotes in General, with Notes Toward a Representative Anecdote for Burkean Ecocriticism in Particular." *K. B. Journal* 1, no. 1 (2004). http://www.kbjournal.org/node/54.
Willard, Charles. *Liberalism and the Problem of Knowledge: A New Rhetoric for Modern Democracy.* Chicago: University of Chicago Press, 1999.
Williams, Raymond. *The Long Revolution.* 1961. Reprint, Peterborough, Ont.: Broadview Press, 2001.
Winans, James Albert. *Public Speaking.* New York: The Century Company, 1915.
Windt, Theodore. "The Diatribe: Last Resort for Protest." *Quarterly Journal of Speech* 58, no. 1 (1972): 1–14.
———. *Presidents and Protesters: Political Rhetoric in the 1960s.* Tuscaloosa: University of Alabama Press, 1990.
Wissinger, Elizabeth. "Always on Display: Affective Production in the Modeling Industry." In *The Affective Turn: Theorizing the Social*, edited by Patricia Ticineto Clough and Jean Halley, 231–60. Durham: Duke University Press, 2007.
Xenos, Michael. "New Mediated Deliberation: Blog and Press Coverage of the Alito Nomination." *Journal of Computer-Mediated Communication* 13, no. 2 (2008): 485–503.
Young, Iris Marion. *Justice and the Politics of Difference.* Princeton: Princeton University Press, 1990.
Young, Richard, and Yameng Liu. "Introduction." In *Landmark Essays on Rhetorical Invention*, edited by Richard Young and Yameng Liu. Mahwah, N.J.: Lawrence Erlbaum, 1994.
Zappen, James P. "Digital Rhetoric: Towards an Integrated Theory." *Technical Communication Quarterly* 14, no. 3 (2005): 319–25.
Ziman, John. "Are Debatable Scientific Questions Debatable?" *Social Epistemology* 14, nos. 2–3 (2000): 187–99.
Zulick, Margaret, and Anne Laffoon. "Enclaved Publics as Inventional Resources: An Essay in Generative Rhetoric." In *Argument in Controversy: Proceedings of the Seventh SCA/AFA Conference on Argumentation*, edited by Donn Parson, 249–55. Annandale, Va.: Speech Communication Association, 1991.

INDEX

affect, 91–92, 100–104, 110, 115–16, 124–30, 193, 233 n. 182. *See also* emotion, *pathos*
affordances, 13–15, 75–76, 100, 150–51, 172, 191. *See also* technology
agenda-setting, 14, 33–34, 61–68, 76–77, 84, 180. *See also* gatekeeping, gatewatching, journalism
agonism, 53, 82–83
agora
    as analogy, 29, 33, 38–40
    Athenian version of, 8, 20–22, 25, 47–49, 99, 137
Alexiou, Margaret, 120
algorithms, 141, 174, 186–87, 194
alphabet, 41, 138–39. *See also* manuscript culture
ambient intimacy, 11, 15–17, 128–29, 131–33, 166, 175. *See also* emotion, tone
Anderson, Benedict, 127–28
anonymity, 44, 188
Antonijević, Smiljana, 188–89
Appadurai, Arjun, 59
Arab Spring, 44, 78, 193
archives, 62–63, 176–77
Arendt, Hannah, 21–22, 38
Aristotle
    in historical context, 18, 30, 50, 112
    on *logos*, 50–51, 54–55, 63, 189
    on *pathos*, 93–94, 138, 189
argumentation. *See also* democratic iterations, public sphere, rational-critical debate, *topoi*
    and blogs, 8, 32, 65–68, 79, 155, 206 n. 54
    and the internet, 23–24, 28–29, 39–40, 43, 48–49, 163–64
    and refutation, 155–57, 166
    as a social act, 51–52, 58–60, 72–73, 175–76
    in democratic cultures, 1–5, 14, 20–21, 36, 82–85, 183

argument pools, 59–60, 66–67, 71–72. *See also* enclave deliberation, group polarization, public sphere
articulation, 174, 178, 188, 190
Asen, Robert, 12, 192–93
astroturfing, 85–87
attention. *See also* information abundance, networked public sphere
    and barking of lonely poodles, 31
    and deliberation, 35–37, 43, 48–49, 74–77, 85, 92
    and media, 28–29, 43, 61, 66, 70, 130
    as constitutive, 31
    bloggers as orchestrators of, 31–32, 67–69, 73, 76–79
    economics of, 29–30, 59, 127
    moral dramaturgy and, 105, 110
    rhetoric as art of, 24, 30–31, 51–53, 80–81, 94, 185–87
    routines, 16, 61, 74–76, 94, 126–27, 186
    thin version of, 30, 61, 91, 100–101, 115, 146
augmented reality, 194
Augustine, 55–56
aura, 102–3, 227 n. 65
Austin, Linda, 118–20

Barber, Benjamin, 126, 199 n. 24
Barlow, Aaron, 177, 205 n. 54
Bauman, Zygmunt, 59
Beck, Ulrich, 59
Benhabib, Seyla, 198 n. 9
Benkler, Yochai, 48–49, 79
Berlant, Lauren, 95, 232 n. 166
Berlin, Leslie, 5
Big Data, 22–23, 174. *See also* information abundance
Bimber, Bruce, 41
binaries, 29, 39, 201 n. 31
Bittergate, 179–82
Blair, Hugh, 57, 95

blogosphere. *See also* intercast, networks, networked public sphere, public sphere
  and network theory, 43–45
  comments and, 147–50
  etymology of, 7, 48
  history of, 4–7
blogswarm, 67–8
Bohman, James, 35, 188, 233 n. 185
boundary work, 70–72
Bourdieu, Pierre, 62
Brady, Emily, 113
Branham, Robert, 59–60
bread and circus, 127, 193–94
Brockman, John, 167
Brooke, Collin, 190
Brown, Jim, 108
Bruns, Axel, 79. *See also* gatewatching, intercast
Bryant, Donald, 199 n. 23
Burke, Kenneth
  and affect, 201 n. 35, 231 n. 154
  and attention, 30, 185, 229 n. 107
  on banishing terms, 48
  and circumferential analysis, 13–14
  and representative anecdote, 15
  and media, 200 n. 26
  and metaphor, 16
  and rhetoric, 25, 30–31, 48, 143, 185
  and transcendence, 212 n. 22
  and translation, 143
  definition of rhetoric, 25, 31
buzz, 86, 102. *See* blogswarm

Calhoun, Craig, 35, 232 n. 166
Campbell, Karlyn Kohrs, 30
Carey, James, 201 n. 32, 203 n. 15
Carr, Nicholas, 28
Castells, Manuel, *See also* networks
  and power, 241 n. 132
  and scandal, 217 n. 100
  space of flows, 59
  theory of network society, 40–46, 208 n. 84
censorship, 44, 78
Crichton, Michael, 152–55
Crick, Nathan, 211 n. 14, 218 n. 112, 221 n. 153
chat rooms, 78, 190, 220 n. 144
Churchill, Winston, 37
Cicero, 41, 55, 94
circulation. *See also* argument pools, hyperpublicity, legitimacy
  of affect, 92, 127
  of blog posts, 63, 69, 104, 123
  of communication, 8, 21–23, 30, 41, 133, 138
citizen journalism. *See* blogosphere, journalism
CIVIC, 123
civil society. *See also* public sphere
  historical account of, 32, 75, 116, 166–68
  signaling problems of, 75–76, 87
Climategate, 169–73
Cobain, Kurt, 38
Cohen, Kris, 98
Cohen, Lizabeth, 38
communicative capitalism, 233 n. 181, 244 n. 35
complexity. *See also* information abundance
  and culture, 2, 15, 26, 43–44, 128, 166
  and technical issues, 126, 140, 145, 166
  hyper-, 42–44, 79, 103

control societies, 44, 46, 78, 127, 193–94. *See also* disciplinary power
convergence, media, 5, 10, 45, 191
copiousness, 59, 66, 79, 83–84
copyright, 56
cosmopolitanism, 6, 131, 192–93
Council of 500, 138
Crawford, Kate, 23
Crossfire, 61. *See also* group polarization, argumentation, disciplinary power
Crosswhite, James, 84
cultural pluralism, 7, 19, 41–43, 131, 191. *See also* identity
cyberutopianism, 45, 48. *See also* pragmatism
cynicism. *See also* affect, snark, tone
  ancient history of Cynics, 99
  blogging and, 100–103
  diatribe, 105, 110
  and hypocrisy, 107
  toward institutions, 108–9
Daily Show, The, 61
DARPA, 44
Dean, Jodi, 130. *See also* communicative capitalism
Deleuze, Gilles, 193–94
deliberation trap, related to
  invention, 57, 73
  emotion, 124–25
  expertise, 136, 146
demes, 138
democratic iterations, 3, 7, 25, 74, 82, 137. *See also* argumentation
Descartes, René, 95
Dewey, John, 53, 85, 139–40

dialectic, 22, 56–57, 104. *See also* melancholy, Plato
digital divide, 26, 46
digital rhetoric, 10. *See also* networked rhetorics
Diogenes, 99, 101, 107, 178
disciplinary power, 132, 176, 181, 193–94. *See also* control societies
discourse communities, 5, 7, 134, 164–66, 208 n. 90. *See also* language game, shallow quotation, translation
dissipation of speech, 184
dissoi logoi, 53, 83, 176. *See also* Sophists
Dodge, Martin, 177
dooced, being, 131–33. *See also* ambient intimacy, oversharing
doxa, 93–94. *See also* public opinion

Eamon, William, 55
Eberly, Rosa, 184
eloquence, 31, 53, 194. *See also* attention, invention, style
embodiment, 92, 99, 128, 138, 177, 186, 193
emo, 121–22, 191
emotion. *See also* affect, emo, *pathos*
 coded as voice, 90, 124
 competitive vs. complementary models of, 92, 95, 175
 as a democratic challenge, 1–3, 8, 48
emotional-intimate communication, 124–25, 128
enclaved deliberation, 59–60, 67, 78–79. *See also* argument pools, group polarization, public sphere
enlightenment, 33, 42, 114–15, 139, 206 n. 59, 208 n. 90, 219 n. 139. *See also* postmodernism, public sphere
Erasmus, 83
ethics of forgetting, 177, 184
ethos, 9, 50, 63, 144. *See also* expertise
experimentation, 4, 17, 175–78, 181–85, 189
expertise. *See also* complexity, ordinary language, technocracy, third culture
 advisory model of, 136
 autism metaphor and, 144, 165–66
 broadcast model of, 136
 and common sense, 140, 143, 236 n. 46
 counselor model of, 136
 as a democratic challenge, 1–3, 8, 48, 139–40
 history of, 137–39
 and journalistic balance, 145–46
 and metaphor, 151–52

 pedagogical vs. participatory models of, 136–37, 162–63, 168, 175
 and peer review, 147, 158–61, 173
 rituals of participation, 144–45
 technocracy, 140–41

face-to-face, 3, 36, 39, 49, 137, 144, 146. *See also* oral culture
Facebook, 4, 27, 128, 132, 184, 187
Farrell, Thomas, 25, 35
fifth estate, 64. *See also* gatewatching
Fight Club, 105
filtering. *See also* attention, public sphere
 as function of rhetoric, 31
 and networked media, 43, 65, 77, 90, 186, 220 n. 141
 as press function, 4, 34
flooding the zone, 6, 60, 65–68, 79, 82, 85–87. *See also* copiousness, invention
Foucault, Michel, 176, 193, 229 n. 114. *See also* disciplinary power
fragmentation, 59–60, 78–79, 83, 208 n. 87
framing, 54, 64, 69–70, 131, 161–62, 176. *See also* attention
Fraser, Nancy, 225 n. 45, 241 n. 131
Freud, Sigmund, 113–15, 132
Friedland, Lewis, 84

Gadamer, Hans-Georg, 212 n. 22
Gaonkar, Dilip, 45
Gates, Bill, 22
gatekeeping, 3, 64, 186, 188. *See also* agenda-setting
gatewatching, 64, 77
Gelbspan, Ross, 145–46
genre, 4–5, 9–10, 102, 107, 114, 130
Gibson, William, 46
Google, 27, 122, 172, 187, 194, 220 n. 140
Gorgias, 18
Greene, Ron, 83
group polarization, 13, 59–61, 135, 145–46, 176. *See also* argument pools, enclaved deliberation
Gurak, Laura, 188–89
Gutenberg parenthesis, 19–20, 31, 49–50, 187. *See also* oral culture, manuscript culture, print culture

Haapala, Arto, 113
Habermas, Jürgen. *See also* legitimacy, public opinion, public sphere, technocracy
 critique of mass media, 37–39

Habermas, Jürgen (*continued*)
  critique of networked media, 78–82
  Foucault's criticism of, 176
  hermeneutic bridges, 166
  mature theory of democracy, 74–76
  and technical reason, 140–44
hacking, 61, 168–73
Halavais, Alex, 63
Hall, Jim, 118
Hariman, Robert, 98, 224 n. 25, 224 n. 26, 226 n. 54
Havelock, Eric, 224 n. 22
Hawhee, Debra, 13, 211 n. 7
Hegel, G. W. F., 53, 206 n. 59
hetaireia, 21, 33
Himmer, Steve, 121
hockey stick controversy, 135, 147–49, 171–72
Hove, Thomas, 84, 221 n. 155
Huffington, Arianna, 73, 178
Huffington Post, 73, 178–81
Hume, David, 95
hyperlink, 4, 19, 28–32, 70, 75–76, 155–57, 172, 205 n. 42
hyperpublicity, 17, 175–85, 188, 194. *See also* publicity

identity, 7, 33–34, 43, 74, 96, 122, 137, 222 n. 178. *See also* cultural pluralism, digital divide
ideology, 24, 33, 35, 58, 157, 217 n. 101
imaginaries
  classical, 14, 20–21
  modern, 14, 33–35, 42, 49, 55–58, 91–92
  networked, 11, 40, 46, 72–74, 87, 174
  rhetorical, 11–14, 45, 114, 124–28, 157, 174
  social, 11–12, 47, 96–97, 103
information abundance. *See also* attention, complexity, copiousness, Big Data
  and deliberation, 45, 59, 84, 142
  and media, 4, 16, 26–27, 67, 83
  and rhetoric, 28–32, 100, 126, 175, 185–86, 194
  signal-to-noise metaphor, 8, 23, 75–76
informationism. *See also* Big Data
  account of, 22–24, 30, 174–75, 190
  and emotion, 99, 103–4, 115, 125
  and expertise, 143, 168
  and invention, 51–52, 56–57, 72, 80–82
interactivity, 9, 39, 44, 152, 163, 188–90, 192
intercast, 4, 7, 40, 65, 73, 178

interruption science, 28
intimacy, 91, 95–96, 98, 124, 127–29, 178, 188. *See also* ambient intimacy, public sphere, emotion, stranger sociability
invention. *See also* eloquence, copiousness, copyright, *topoi*
  and commonplaces, 26, 54–55, 93, 105, 163, 230 n. 130
  as a democratic challenge, 1–3, 8, 48, 74–75
  discovery vs. generative models of, 51–52, 57–58, 69–72, 79–81, 175
  and novelty, 68, 73, 75, 194
  and interactivity, 83, 192
Isocrates, 18, 20, 53, 138, 205 n. 47

Jenkins, Henry, 90. *See also* convergence, media
Johnson, Mark, 16
Jordan, John, 71
journalism. *See also* agenda-setting, boundary work, political economy
  norms, 57–58, 118, 145–46, 164, 179–80
  and objectivity, 58, 89, 97–98, 115, 125, 145
juggler's brain, 28

kairos, 82, 186, 188
Kant, Immanuel, 95, 206 n. 59, 221 n. 151
Keats, John, 113
Keren, Michael, 91–92, 114–16, 121–26, 219 n. 127
Kitchin, Rob, 177

Lakoff, George, 16
language games, 142, 166, 208 n. 90
Lanham, Richard, 24–26, 29–32, 35, 83, 185, 201 n. 31
Lazarsfeld, Paul, 27–28
Lefevre, Karen, 53–54
Leff, Michael, 198 n. 11
legitimacy. *See also* boundary work, public sphere, technocracy
  as cultural phenomenon, 11, 21, 100, 168, 174, 184
  and democratic governance, 3, 33, 36, 76, 84, 97
  and scientific decision-making, 141–42
Lessl, Thomas, 138
Liebling, A. J., 26
lifelogs, 177. *See also* pervasive computing
lifeworld, 43, 75, 80–81, 92, 113, 140, 177
Lippmann, Walter, 95, 126, 140
logic, 36, 56–57, 80, 95, 137. *See also* logos

logos, 9, 36, 51–52, 56, 63, 93–94. *See also* argumentation, invention
Lovink, Geert, 91–92, 100–104, 107–8, 110–11, 124–26
Lucaites, John, 98, 224 n. 26, 226 n. 54
Lupia, Arthur, 35
Lyne, John, 80, 167–68
Lyotard, Jean-Francois, 208 n. 90, 229 n. 114

"Macacagate," 86–87, 182
Madison, James, 95
Malin, Brent, 129
Manovich, Lev, 28–29, 204 n. 41
manuscript culture, 8, 18, 20, 26, 138, 178. *See also* alphabet, Gutenberg Parenthesis
many-to-many communication, 12, 85, 137, 150–52, 168, 187–88. *See also* networked public sphere, networks
Marcus, George, 126–27
mass media. *See* agenda-setting, attention, journalism, political economy, public sphere
McCorkle, Ben, 190
McGee, Michael Calvin, 41–42, 202 n. 6, 208 n. 87
McKerrow, Raymie, 194
McLuhan, Marshall, 12
media of invention, 83
melancholy. *See also* affect, emo, tone
  blogging and, 114–16
  dialectics of, 113, 115, 123
  Freud's pathologization of, 113–14
  history of, 112–13
  and ineffability, 118–19
  laments, 117–18, 123
  and music, 121–22
  ubi sunt, 119–20
meme, 190–91
Merton, Robert, 27–28, 63
Miller, Carolyn, 197 n. 2, 212 n. 24
Mitchell, Gordon, 239 n. 86, 244 n. 26
metarhetorical analysis, 16–17, 51–52, 82, 92, 139
mobile devices, 16, 28, 37, 44, 129, 132, 176, 182, 193
Morozov, Evgeny, 209 n. 99
Muckelbauer, John, 52
Mutz, Diane, 226 n. 55

narcotizing dysfunction, 28
narrative
  counter-, 111, 118, 120, 123
  journalistic, 57, 73, 208 n. 87
  meta-, 42, 103, 208 n. 90
  novelistic, 128, 152
nation-state, 18–19, 32, 46–47, 107, 127. *See also* political economy, public sphere
networked media, 9–10
networked public sphere. *See also* blogosphere, networks, public sphere
  Benkler's theory of, 48–49
  definition of, 10, 15, 19–20, 40, 47–48
  functions of, 77–79, 82–84, 91, 127–28, 136, 166–68
  maturing, 4–5, 178, 193
networked rhetorics, 10–11, 174–75, 185–94
networks. *See also* Castells, many-to-many communication, networked public sphere
  architecture of, 5, 9, 48, 77, 88, 104
  and audiences, 177–78, 244 n. 29
  and flexibility, 44–45
  vs. fundamentalism, 46–47
  and scalability, 44
  and survivability, 44
  as hybridizing, 9–10, 47, 49, 165
  as master trope of rhetoric, 174
Neumann, W. Russell, 28
new rhetoric, 9–10, 15, 28, 124, 187–88. *See also* networked rhetorics
New York Times, 66, 72, 102, 118, 160, 164, 179–80
Nietzsche, Friedrich, 57, 102

Oakley, Todd, 30
Ober, Josiah, 138
Olson, Christa, 13
Ong, Walter, 54, 224 n. 22
oral culture, 3, 9–10, 19–20, 137–38, 177–78, 189–91. *See also* Gutenberg Parenthesis, voice
ordinary language, 136, 142–43, 145, 148–49. *See also* shallow quotation, translation
"Organization Man," 42
organized intelligence, 140. *See also* Lippmann, Walter
ornamentation, 29–30, 51, 57, 204 n. 41
Orwell, George, 107
Outhwaite, William, 79–80
oversharing, 14, 131–33. *See also* ambient intimacy

Palczewski, Cate, 176
pamphlets, 34, 74
parasites, 71, 78

pathos, 9, 51, 91–94. *See also* emotion, affect
Pensky, Max, 113
pervasive computing, 176–77, 183, 194
Peters, John Durham, 144, 210 n. 106, 227 n. 66, 228 n. 82
Pettitt, Thomas, 19–20, 31, 49–50, 201 n. 31
pharmakon, 22
philosopher-king, 3, 138. *See also* dialectic, Plato
Plato, 18, 22, 53–54, 93, 138, 178
polis, 20–21, 32, 54, 95, 138
political economy
  and globalization, 40–41
  of mass media, 4, 60–62, 74, 160
  of networked media, 41, 88, 101, 172, 178
political tones. *See* tone
Porter, James, 190
Postman, Neil, 38
postmodernism, 42, 101, 103. *See also* narrative
Poulakos, John, 211 n. 11
power law, 77
power relations, 62, 116, 193. *See also* identity, political economy, public sphere
pragmatism, 14, 31, 48, 53, 58, 213 n. 41
press. *See* journalism
priestly voice, 138
print culture. *See also* Gutenberg Parenthesis
  pamphleteering, 34, 74
  printing press, 18, 41, 55–57
  and science, 139
propaganda, 22, 85, 122, 125, 222 n. 169
proprioception, 128. *See also* ambient intimacy, circulation
pseudonymity, 62, 74, 90, 131
publicity. *See also* attention, hyperpublicity, public sphere
  Arendtian conception of, 21
  blurring with privacy, 3, 98, 100, 128–29, 132, 226 n. 49, 231 n. 153
  critical, 33–34, 48, 180, 184
  cultural technologies of, 20, 32, 39
  public relations sense, 86–87, 145, 161–62
  representative, 33, 140
public opinion, 11, 33–35, 61, 87, 93. *See also* public sphere
public sphere. *See also* argumentation, identity, networked public sphere, public opinion, publicity, rational-critical debate, technocracy
  bourgeois version of, 7, 32–34, 74, 77–79, 95–98, 114
  criticism of, 47–48
  declinist narrative of, 37–39, 114–16
  definition of, 37, 47–48
  gendered communication in, 96–97, 150
  global dimensions of, 105, 110–11, 127–28, 131–33, 192–93, 232 n. 172
  greening of, 168
  relation to intimate sphere, 95–97
Putnam, Robert, 37–9

Quintilian, 55

rant. *See* cynicism
rational-critical debate, 8, 33–34, 81, 95–97, 100, 145. *See also* argumentation, emotion, public sphere
Reddit, 27, 178
reflexivity, 34–36, 64, 67, 74–76, 84, 161–68, 186, 235 n. 9
Ramus, Peter, 55–57, 224 n. 25
remediation, 19, 40–41, 49, 71, 76–77, 200 n. 26
remix, 12, 19–20, 31, 191–92
Renegar, Val, 10
representative anecdote, 14–16, 38
Rettberg, Jill, 197 n. 3
rhetorical canons, 10, 21, 188–92
rhetorical criticism, 16, 32, 34, 53, 69, 83–84, 115. *See also* fifth estate
rhetorical pedagogy, 176, 184–85, 193
Richards, I. A., 24, 231 n. 154
Riesman, David, 38
Roberts-Miller, Patricia, 90
Rojas, Hernando, 84

scandal, 67, 69, 86, 109, 136, 169–73
Scott, D. T., 68
shallow quotation, 7, 136, 155, 166–73, 175, 241 n. 135. *See also* expertise, translation
Say Anything, 26
Sennett, Richard, 37
Shannon, Claude, 22–23
Shirky, Clay, 77, 79, 197 n. 3, 233 n. 182
Shouse, Eric, 125–6
Simonson, Peter, 83
Sloane, Thomas, 83
Sloterdijk, Peter, 99, 110, 225 n. 43
snark, 107–8, 191. *See also* cynicism, political tones, style
Snow, C. P., 167
social bookmarking, 67–68

social movements, 35, 39, 42, 98–100
Socrates, 53, 104, 136, 212 n. 22
software, 44, 100, 104, 168, 188, 194
solidarity, 42, 175. *See also* ambient intimacy, stranger sociability, public sphere
Sophists, 53, 82–83, 138
Sokolon, Marlene, 94
specified ignorance, 63, 84
spectacle, 61, 146, 161–64, 168, 173. *See also* political economy
speed, 44, 82–83, 124, 160, 188–90, 215 n. 69
Spencer, Herbert, 24
spontaneous communication, 60, 75–77, 85–87, 181–84
stranger sociability, 92, 127, 130, 133
Striphas, Ted, 186
structure of feeling, 91–92, 99, 130, 224 n. 26
stuff and fluff, 25–26, 29, 40–41, 115, 190. *See also* attention
style, 25, 56–57, 149, 163–64, 188, 191–93. *See also* boundary work, emo, identity, snark, tone
subjectivity, 91, 96, 98, 129, 225 n. 43
Sunstein, Cass, 59–60, 67, 73, 78–79
symposia, 21
Szylak, Moe, 208 n. 90

Tannen, Deborah, 145
Taylor, Charles, 11–12, 200 n. 28, 202 n. 39
technê, 9
technocracy, 136, 139 140–41, 144–45. *See also* legitimacy, public sphere
technological determinism, 40. *See also* affordances
technology, 5, 9–10, 26–27, 41–43, 177, 191. *See also* affordances
Theory of the Forms, 22, 56
third culture, 167–68, 175. *See also* expertise

Thrift, Nigel, 130–32
Thompson, Clive, 128, 204 n. 37
Thorburn, David, 90
tone. *See also* affect, cynicism, emo, melancholy, snark, style
 literal, 57, 125
 metaphorical, 1, 98, 104, 111
 political tones, 92, 104–5, 125–26
topoi, 54, 60–61, 82–84, 118. *See also* argumentation, invention
translation, 136, 143, 147, 149–50, 157, 164, 166. *See also* ordinary language, shallow quotation, expertise
transmission model, 22, 25, 81–82, 125, 190, 203 n. 15. *See also* informationism
trolling, 101, 108, 151, 191
Twitter, 4, 27, 44, 128–29, 137, 193

Vico, Giambattista, 57
voice, 61, 75, 90, 111, 167, 189. *See also* oral culture
vulgar details, 177

warblogging, 90, 111
Warner, Michael, 206 n. 65
wearable computing, 194, 243 n. 5. *See also* pervasive computing
Weaver, Richard, 208 n. 88, 213 n. 39
Weaver, Warren, 22–3
Wegman Report, 135
Willard, Charles, 16, 166–67
Winans, James, 30
WikiLeaks, 217 n. 94
Wikipedia, 43, 137, 172, 187–88
Windt, Ted, 99, 104, 110
Wingspread Conference, 57, 213 n. 36
wisdom, 31, 135

Young, Iris Marion, 226 n. 48
YouTube, 4, 27, 86–87, 132, 182

Zúniga, Markos Moulitsas, 32, 71, 86

RHETORICAND**DEMOCRATIC**DELIBERATION

EDITED BY CHERYL GLENN AND J. MICHAEL HOGAN
THE PENNSYLVANIA STATE UNIVERSITY

Books in the series:

Karen Tracy *Challenges of Ordinary Democracy: A Case Study in Deliberation and Dissent* / VOLUME 1

Samuel McCormick, *Letters to Power: Public Advocacy Without Public Intellectuals* / VOLUME 2

Christian Kock and Lisa S. Villadsen, eds., *Rhetorical Citizenship and Public Deliberation* / VOLUME 3

Jay P. Childers, *The Evolving Citizen: American Youth and the Changing Norms of Democratic Engagement* / VOLUME 4

Dave Tell, *Confessional Crises: Confession and Cultural Politics in Twentieth-Century America* / VOLUME 5

David Boromisza-Habashi, *Speaking Hatefully: Culture, Public Communication, and Political Action in Hungary* / VOLUME 6

Arabella Lyon, *Deliberative Acts: Democracy, Rhetoric, and Rights* / VOLUME 7

Lyn Carson, John Gastil, Janette Hartz-Karp, and Ron Lubensky, eds., *The Australian Citizens' Parliament and the Future of Deliberative Democracy* / VOLUME 8

Christa Olson, *Constitutive Visions: Indigeneity and Commonplaces of National Identity in Republican Ecuador* / VOLUME 9